MERCHANT BANKING AND FINANCIAL SERVICES

Dr. Ravichandran Krishnamurthy

B.Sc. (Maths), MBA (Finance),
M.Phil. (Management),
Ph.D., PDF (Malaysia).

Himalaya Publishing House

ISO 9001:2015 CERTIFIED

FIRST EDITION : 2008
SECOND REVISED EDITION : 2016
REPRINT : 2019
REPRINT : 2023

Published by : Mrs. Meena Pandey
for **HIMALAYA PUBLISHING HOUSE PVT. LTD.,**
"Ramdoot", Dr. Bhalerao Marg, Girgaon, Mumbai - 400 004.
Phone: 022-23860170, 23863863; **Fax:** 022-23877178
E-mail: himpub@bharatmail.co.in; **Website:** www.himpub.com

Branch Offices :

New Delhi : "Pooja Apartments", 4-B, Murari Lal Street, Ansari Road, Darya Ganj, New Delhi - 110 002. Phone: 011-23270392, 23278631; Fax: 011-23256286

Nagpur : Kundanlal Chandak Industrial Estate, Ghat Road, Nagpur - 440 018. Phone: 0712-2721215, 2721216

Bengaluru : Plot No. 91-33, 2nd Main Road, Seshadripuram, Behind Nataraja Theatre, Bengaluru - 560 020. Phone: 080-41138821; Mobile: 09379847017, 09379847005

Hyderabad : No. 3-4-184, Lingampally, Besides Raghavendra Swamy Matham, Kachiguda, Hyderabad - 500 027. Phone: 040-27560041, 27550139

Chennai : No. 34/44, Motilal Street, T. Nagar, Chennai - 600 017. Mobile: 09380460419

Pune : "Laksha" Apartment, First Floor, No. 527, Mehunpura, Shaniwarpeth (Near Prabhat Theatre), Pune - 411 030. Phone: 020-24496323, 24496333; Mobile: 09370579333

Cuttack : Plot No 5F-755/4, Sector-9, CDA Market Nagar, Cuttack - 753 014, Odisha. Mobile: 09338746007

Kolkata : 3, S.M. Bose Road, Near Gate No. 5, Agarpara Railway Station, North 24 Parganas, West Bengal - 700109. Mobile: 09674536325

DTP by : Sudhakar Shetty

Printed at : M/s. Aditya Offset Process (I) Pvt. Ltd., Hyderabad. On behalf of HPH.

PREFACE TO THE SECOND REVISED EDITION

Merchant Banking and Financial Services is a complete book which covers both merchant banking and emerging trends in financial services. This book would be widely useful by a wide section of readers, particularly teachers, advance students of Commerce, Business Management and Practicing Managers and Equity Market investors.

The subject matter of this edition covers a wide range of applications in financial services which will be helpful for the students to get a wide range of knowledge about the subject matter. In the first edition, I covered 15 chapters and now I will be adding Derivatives as the 16th chapter. Also I have changed all the Merchant banking data which was related to 2006 to 2014. A short note on various topics covered in this book is given below:

Chapter I covers the overview of financial services and it explains the evolution of financial services and about its regulatory authorities.

Chapter II tells about the entire working of merchant banking activities, its functions and it clearly explains all the important functions in detail. This chapter will be very important for students who are undertaking a course of this subject.

Chapter III gives a brief historical account of Mutual Funds, its evolution, regulatory aspects and points out the future of mutual fund industry in India.

Chapter IV deals with Lease Finance, and it gives an account of its total operation and explains the current condition of lease finance. Chapter V section deals with Hire Purchase, its evolution, various laws concerning, tax implications and also it clearly explains about the differences between Hire purchase and Lease.

Chapter VI covers Factoring Services rendered in India, its evolution, growth, functions and the various recommendations of the committees concerns to factoring.

Chapter VII gives a brief outline about the capital market and explains the role of stock market and its operations.

Chapter VIII outlines the operating mechanisms of Venture Capital. It gives a brief note about the various venture capital firms available in India and also it tells us about the way to manage these firms.

Chapter IX explains the role of Insurance industry in India. It tells us the history of this industry with regulations and discusses about the future of this industry in India.

Chapter X presents the role of housing finance, its institutional framework, policies and tells us the importance of housing finance in India.

Chapter XI introduces the concept of securitisation, its pros and cons and the growth of this service in India.

Chapter XII dwells on the role of Credit Rating services in India and it gives a brief account of various agencies available in India.

Chapter XIII deals with consumer finance, which is the evergreen market in India. This chapter will be very useful to know the regulations of this service

Chapter XIV gives a clear picture about working mechanism of Credit Card services and gives a brief note about the various types of credit cards available in India.

Chapter XV tells us about the emerging service in finance industry which is Micro Finance. This chapter clearly explains about the concept and about its various implications.

Chapter XVI briefly explains about Derivatives, the emerging product of today's market.

In the preparation of this book, I got various help from my fellow colleagues of Bharthidasan Institute of Management. I am very much thankful to them towards their contribution in completing this book successfully.

Also I would be failing in my duty if I don't put on record, my deep sense of obligation towards my family members who provided an environment conductive to hard work.

Dr. K. Ravichandran

CONTENTS

CHAPTER 1

Financial Services

Objectives

The student, after studying the chapter, should be able to:

- State the meaning and significance of Financial Services.
- Describe the history of Financial Services.
- List out the functions of Financial Services.
- Familiarise with the Regulating authorities and features of Financial Services.
- Explain the problems in Financial Services.

Structure:

1.1 INTRODUCTION

Financial system of a country refers to a set of closely linked complex network of institutions, agents, practices, markets, transactions, claims and liabilities in the economy. Finance is the study of the nature, creation, behaviour, regulation and administration of money. Therefore, financial system includes all those activities dealing in finance, organised into a system. The financial system consists of financial institutions, financial markets, financial instruments and the services provided by the financial institutions. Chart 1.1 gives a clear picture of the financial system of our economy.

Any Financial System Comprises of Four Major Parts:

1. **Financial Institutions:** They mobilise the savings and transfer it to deficit units. The Financial Institutions are divided into regulatory, intermediaries, non-intermediaries and others. They deal only in financial assets like deposits, securities, loans etc. They collect funds from those units having savings and send to those who need funds.
2. **Financial Markets:** This is the place from where savings are transferred from surplus units to deficit units. There are two segments of financial market. They are money market and capital market. Money market is concerned with short-term funds or claims. Capital market deals with those financial assets, which have maturity period of more than a year. Another classification could be primary and secondary markets. Primary market deals with new issues. The secondary market deals with outstanding securities. Primary markets mobilise savings directly by issuing New Securities and the secondary markets provide liquidity to the Financial Market."
3. **Financial Instruments:** The products, which are traded in a financial market, are financial assets or financial instruments. The requirement of lenders and borrowers are varied. Therefore, there is a variety of securities in the financial markets. Financial assets represent a claim on the repayment of principal at a future date.
4. **Financial Services:** Financial services include the services offered by both types of companies – Asset Management Companies and Liability Management Companies.

1.2 MEANING AND SIGNIFICANCE

Financial services are an important component of the financial system. Financial services cater to the needs of financial institutions, in turn, are geared to serve individual and institutional investors. Financial institutions and financial markets help the financial system through financial instruments. They require a number of services of financial nature in order to fulfill the tasks assigned. Financial services are considered as the fourth element of the financial system. The functioning of the system very much depends on the range of financial services provided by the providers, and their efficiency.

Two types of companies provide financial services. They are Asset Management Companies (AMC) and Liability Management Companies (LMC). AMCs include leasing companies, mutual funds, merchant bankers, and portfolio managers. LMCs consist of bill discounting houses and acceptance houses.

1.3 EVOLUTION OF FINANCIAL SERVICES IN INDIA

- The Merchant Banking Services were introduced in 1960.
- The General Insurance business was nationalised in the early 1970.
- Leasing made its mark in the closing years of the 1970s. The number of leasing firms has gone up by 400 in 2000.
- Over-the-counter services, share transfers, pledging of shares, mutual funds, factoring, discounting, venture capital and credit rating have found their origin from 1980.

Chart 1.1

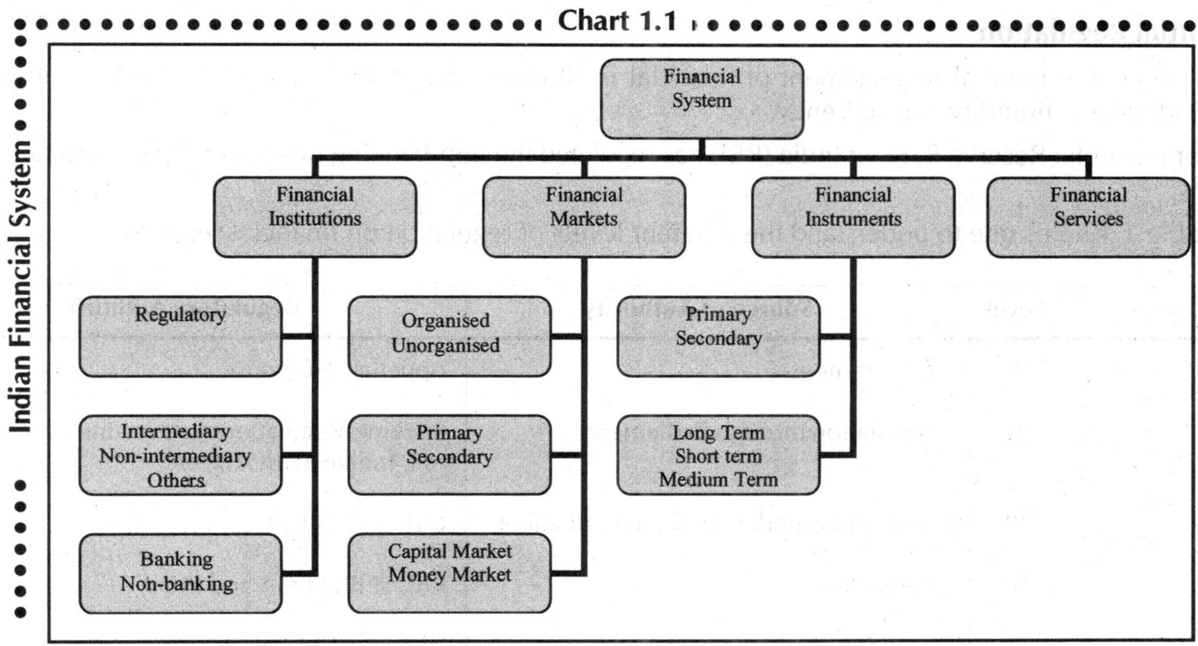

1.4 FUNCTIONS OF FINANCIAL SERVICE INSTITUTIONS

The following are some functions carried out by Financial Service Institutions:

1. Financial services firms not only help to raise the required funds but also assure the efficient deployment of funds.
2. They assist in deciding the financing mix.
3. They extend their services up to the stage of servicing of lenders.
4. They provide services like bill discounting, factoring of debtors, parking of short-term funds in the money market, e-commerce, securitisation of debts, etc. in order to ensure an efficient management of funds.
5. Financial services firms provide some specialised services like credit rating, venture capital financing, lease financing, factoring, mutual funds, merchant banking, stock lending, depository, credit cards, housing finance, book building, etc. These services are generally provided by banking companies, insurance companies, stock exchanges, and non-banking finance companies.

1.5 REGULATING AUTHORITIES OF FINANCIAL SERVICES

The regulatory framework relating to financial services can be broadly grouped into three main types. They are:

1. The Structural Regulation,
2. The Prudential Regulation, and
3. The Investor Protection Regulation.

Structural Regulation

It determines the types of activities that various forms of institutions are permitted to engage in. For example, Securities Exchange Board of India (SEBI) insists that merchant bankers and stock broking institutions to separate all their fund-based activities.

Prudential Regulation

It covers the internal management of financial institutions and other financial service firms in relation to capital adequacy, liquidity and solvency.

For example: Reserve Bank of India (RBI) has regulated the non-banking finance companies in raising public deposits.

Table 1.1 helps one to understand the different levels of regulation on financial services.

Table 1.1

Level	Source of Authority	Regulatory Authority
I	Government	Appellate Authority
II	Legislation through Parliament	Banking Regulation Act, Insurance Act, MRTP Act, Indian Trust Act, etc.
III	Institutions under an Act of Parliament	UTI, LIC, GIC, etc.
IV	Regulators	RBI, SEBI, FEMA and IRDA
V	Regulation of Regulators	RBI Directives to Commercial Banks, NBFCs, SEBI Regulations, Guidelines, Notifications, etc.
VI	Self-regulations	Bye-laws, Rules and Regulations and Code of Conduct issued by the various Financial Service Industry, Associations, like AMFI.

Investor Protection Regulation

It is generally known that investors are the weakest participants of the financial markets. Therefore, they need protection from malpractice, fraud and collapse. For example, SEBI has stipulated that all AMCs should publish the half-yearly NAVs for the perusal of investors.

1.6 FEATURES OF FINANCIAL SERVICES

Financial services are totally different from other services. Their features are as follows:

1. It is a customer-intensive industry. Identification of needs and wants of customer is the first step. It will help the financial service firms to design the financial strategy, which gives due respect to costs, liquidity and maturity considerations.
2. Financial services are intangible in nature. The institutions providing the services should have a good image and confidence among the clients. They have to focus on quality and innovation of their services. This will build credibility and gain the trust of clients.
3. Production and supply of financial services must be performed simultaneously. This demands a clear-cut perception between the financial service organisations and their clients. Demand and supply must be properly balanced. This is because of the perishable nature of financial services.
4. Marketing of financial service is people intensive. It is subject to variability of performance and quality of service. The personnel in financial services firms need to be selected, based on their suitability. They must be trained to fulfill the twin objectives of performance and quality.

5. Financial services firms should always be proactive in visualising in advance what the market wants, or reactive to the needs and wants of customers. They must always be adoptive to the tune of the market.

1.7 CONSTITUENTS OF FINANCIAL SERVICES

There are four major constituents of financial services:

(a) **Instruments:** They are equity instruments, debt instruments, hybrid and exotic instruments

(b) **Market Players:** They are banks, financing institutions, mutual funds, merchant bankers, stock brokers, consultants, underwriters, market makers, etc.

(c) **Specialised Institutions:** They are acceptance houses, discount houses, factors, depositories, credit rating agencies, venture capital institutions, etc.

(d) **Regulatory Bodies:** These include Department of Banking and Insurance of the Central Government, Reserve Bank of India, Securities Exchange Board of India, Board of Industrial and Financial Reconstruction, etc.

1.8 PROBLEMS

Financial services firms face many problems in India. Important problems faced by these firms are as follows:

(a) Indian financial industry hardly finds suitable personnel to deal with financial services. Right personnel are not found. Public sector firms face financial constraint to pay higher salary to right people. Private sectors do not match the offers made by the multinationals.

(b) Expensive physical infrastructure is another problem being faced by the financial services firms.

(c) The financial services firms lack core competence.

(d) They cannot review their performance without a benchmarking. This prevents them to implement cost-control measures and cost-review techniques.

(e) They fully depend on fee-based businesses. It hits the firms severely. It should be fund-based.

(f) Lack of proper appreciation of the advantages that could be derived by using the advances in computer and telecommunication technology has constrained the growth of the industry.

1.9 FINANCIAL SERVICES IN INDIA

1. Financial system in India has made commendable progress in extending its geographical spread and functional reach.

2. Nationalisation of commercial banks in 1969 gave a new direction and adequate credit support for viable productive endeavour especially in agriculture and small sector.

3. Along with the quantitative expansion and functional diversification of the banking system that lasted few decades, the Indian financial system had witnessed a significant expansion of the activities of development of financial institutions for investments, especially in private sector. A significant fact in the operations of the institutions is that they were based on assured sources of funds, also provided credit at relatively stable lending rates. It inculcated debt culture in the corporate sector thus increasing dependence on these institutions. They also invested in equity of the private corporate sector through either conversion clause or underwriting commitments.

4. Specialised financial institutions emerged in the Indian financial system to cater to the financial needs of sick industrial units, export finance, rural development, etc. These institutions include IDBI, IFCI, ICICI and IRBI. Insurance companies also played a prominent role in resource mobilisation and directing

investments in productive area. Non-bank private financial organisations also have been in operation but their role in Indian financial system have not been very significant. These organisations operate as hire-purchase, leasing, investment and finance companies.

5. In the changing economic scenario, with increase in financial deregulation and industrial liberalisation, the role of the financial sector is increasing manifold. The financial service sector has thus emerged as the fastest growing sunrise industry.
6. With the onset of liberalisation process, several new institutions, both public and private, have appeared on the financial scene. These institutions like merchant banks, leasing companies, venture capital companies, factoring companies and mutual funds, etc., have expanded the range of financial services available.

1.10 REVIEW QUESTIONS

Short Answer Questions

1. What do you mean by Financial Market?
2. List out the various financial functions of a financial market.
3. Identify the various sub-markets in the financial market.
4. Differentiate money market from capital market.
5. Distinguish between primary market and secondary market.
6. List out various methods of floating fresh issues.
7. What is call or notice money?
8. Define Certificate of Deposits (COD).
9. What are the features of Commercial Paper?
10. Differentiate Reverse Repo from Repo?
11. List the participants in the money market.
12. Explain the term money market.
13. What are Asset Management Companies?
14. What are Liability Management Companies?
15. What are the various constituents of financial services?
16. List the names of agencies regulating financial services in India.

Essay Type Questions

1. What do you mean by 'Financial System'? Explain the various components of financial system.
2. What is a financial market? Explain its role and functions.
3. Define financial services. Bring out the importance of such services.
4. Discuss the functions of modern financial services firms in India.
5. Discuss the problems of financial services firms in India. Suggest suitable measures to overcome such problems.
6. What is the future scenario for financial services sector in India?

❋ ❋ ❋

CHAPTER 2

Merchant Banking

Objectives

The student, after studying the chapter, should be able to:

- State the basics of merchant banking.
- Discuss the history of merchant banking.
- List out the requirements for the registration of a merchant banker.
- Describe with the various functions of a merchant banker.
- Understand the regulations involved in the issue management.
- Evaluate the performance of merchant banker in India.

Structure:

2.1 Basics of Merchant Banking
2.2 Meaning
2.3 Origin of Merchant Banking
2.4 Registration of Merchant Banker
2.5 Scope of Merchant Banking Activities
2.6 Functions of a Merchant Banker
2.7 Issue Management
2.8 Issue Manager
2.9 Primary Market Issue Management
2.10 Cost of Public Issue
2.11 Pricing of Public Issue
2.12 Code of Conduct for Merchant Bankers

2.1 BASICS OF MERCHANT BANKING

Merchant banking is a relatively new concept in the area of financial services in India. It caters to the needs of trade and industry by acting as intermediary, consultant, financial and liaison agency. If a business has the capital (money) to purchase all that is needed to operate the business, there is no need for financing, whether debt or equity. Many businesses neither have adequate funds for this, nor have enough time. The expectation that the business will generate money at some time in the future to repay the amount lent or invested, plus a return to the owner of the funds, is the basis of banking.

Those with the ideas or the skills to operate the business may not have the money, and those with the money may not have the skills, time or desire to operate the business successfully. Historically, if the bank lends the money, it is commercial banking. If the bank is the agent, then it brings those with money together with those who need it. It is Known as investment banking, sometimes called as merchant banking because merchants were the first who need this type of funding.

2.2 MEANING

The dictionary meaning of "Merchant Bank" is:

"An organisation that underwrites corporate securities and advises clients on issues like corporate mergers, etc. involved in the ownership of commercial ventures."

A standard definition to the word "Merchant Banking" is given under:

"Merchant banking means any person who is engaged in the business of issue management either by making arrangements regarding selling, buying, underwriting or subscribing to the securities as underwriter, manager, consultant, advisor or rendering corporate advisory services in relation to such issue management."

Observe the following points, which will enable you to understand the meaning of merchant bank in a clear way:

1. Merchant bank is simply an organisation. Individuals are not called merchant banker rather he is called a broker. There is a subtle difference between these two terms, which is beyond the scope of our study.
2. The merchant banker generally is engaged in a business of issue management. You may ask what an issue management is. Every company depends on intermediary to get money from the potential investors. The company cannot go and catch hold of potential investors. Here comes the role of merchant banker. The merchant banker sells the shares of a company to the public, or it may buy the shares from such companies for resale, or it may subscribe to the securities. Whatever be the mode of getting money from the public, the intention of merchant banker is to help companies.
3. Therefore, the merchant banker plays the role of the manager, consultant, and advisor. Sometimes the merchant banker extends only advice with respect to the issue management.

   Is it that simple to do the merchant banking business? It is a good question at this point. Merchant bankers in India have diversified their activities beyond issue management and loan syndication. They also stretch their activities beyond these two major functions. They have diversified into portfolio management, corporate counseling, project counseling, consultancy to ailing sick units, providing and procuring venture capital to new entrepreneurs, lease financing, debenture trusteeship, arranging finances, etc. You will know each function in detail elsewhere in the chapter.

The possible services of merchant banks are listed in the following table:

Table 2.1 Services Rendered by Merchant Banker

Sr. No.	Possible Services
1	Corporate Counseling
2	Project Counseling and Pre-investment Studies
3	Capital Restructuring
4	Credit Syndication and Project Finance
5	Issue Management and Underwriting
6	Portfolio Management
7	Non-resident Investment
8	Working Capital Finance
9	Acceptance Credit and Bill Discounting
10	Mergers, Amalgamations and Takeovers
11	Venture Capital Financing
12	Lease Financing
13	Foreign Currency Finance
14	Fixed Deposit Broking
15	Mutual Funds Floatation and Management
16	Arrange for Rehabilitation of Sick Projects

2.3 ORIGIN OF MERCHANT BANKING

Is the concept of merchant banking borrowed from others? Alternatively, were they evolved in India itself? If so, when was it evolved? What kind of activities did they carry out in those days? Let us try to find answers to these questions.

The concept of merchant banking originated in Italy during the 3th century. The first known firms which have been involved in merchant banking were Riccadi of Luca, Medici, Fuggier, and so on.

Functional Nature of Merchant Banking of Old Era

In olden times, merchant banks were also known as "accepting and issuing houses" in the UK and "investment banks" (IB) in the USA. Except for this distinction in nomenclature, there is no essential functional difference between them. Usually, they handled coastal trade and master's goods on a commission basis and financed risky venture projects, for which they charged heavy interest. They often incurred heavy losses. They accepted bills for payment. These were in addition to their Merchant Banking functions of commercial banking.

In fact, there was no distinction between the functions of merchant banking and commercial banks until 1932. Later, the Glass Steagall Act, 1933, distinguished the functions of merchant banking or investment banking from commercial banking. However, in 2000, the Clinton Administration allowed investment banks to run the functions of commercial banks in addition to their usual functions of investment banking. This was effected through an amendment in the Glass Steagall Act.

Origin of Merchant Banking in India

Prior to the enactment of the Indian Companies Act, 1956, managing agencies acted as an issue house for securities. They evaluated the projects before promoting them. They designed the capital structures. They provided the venture capital in a small way. Few share broking firms functioned as merchant bankers with small capital base.

National Grindlays Bank in India initiated merchant banking services in 1969. The Citibank followed it in 1970. The State Bank of India was the first Indian commercial bank to set up a separate Merchant Banking Division in 1973. ICICI followed it in 1974. Both these Indian merchant bankers emerged as leaders in merchant banking having done significant business during the period 1974-85 in comparison to foreign banks. A number of commercial banks, financial institutions and other organisations are now engaged in providing merchant banking services. The merchant banks in India operate as issue houses rather than full-fledged merchant banks.

Somewhere above, you have read that there is no difference between the functions of merchant banking and commercial banking. What makes the difference between these two terms? A few differences are given for clarity purpose.

Difference between Merchant Banks and Commercial Banks

Merchant banking is the forerunner of modern commercial banking. Its foundational value is being increasingly recognised and its resurrection seriously considered. The proof is that this ancient form of merchant banking has begun to make a comeback in the UK and the USA. Particularly when the limitations of contemporary commercial banks are gradually showing through in the face of certain practical problems of present-day commercial banking.

1. The basic difference between merchant banking and commercial banking is that the merchant bank offers mainly financial advice and services for a fee. It also collects deposits through the non-cash mode of finance, i.e., security papers. Commercial banks accept deposits and lend money in the mode of cash.
2. The merchant bank offers portfolio services to its customers (individuals and corporate). The commercial bank provides retail trade banking services to its customers.
3. The regulatory body for commercial banks in India is Ministry of Finance/Reserve Bank of India. The Banking Regulation Act has also guided those banks. On the other hand, the regulatory body for merchant banks in India is the Securities Exchange Board of India (SEBI). They define merchant banking as follows:

   "Merchant banks mostly provide advisory services, issue management, portfolio management and underwriting, which require less capital but generate more income (non-interest income)."

   Since these services require less funds, commercial banks could opt to provide these services side by side with their traditional services/functions. Merchant banking services reduce the pressure of supervision/monitoring activities that reduce the related cost.
4. Merchant banks invest their funds mostly in project-oriented and security papers. These security papers are encashable in the stock market. This will solve the liquidity crisis of merchant banker. The liquidity problems of commercial banks cannot easily be solved as they lend their funds to the trading or commercial houses in the form of Term Loan, Working Capital, etc.

   How should the liquidity problem of commercial bank be solved?

   The commercial banks in India should think of entering in the field of merchant banking. Considering the practical problems of cost and liquidity issues, commercial banks should go for merchant banking operation.

2.4 REGISTRATION OF MERCHANT BANKER

Registration with SEBI is mandatory to carry out the business of merchant banking in India. An applicant should comply with the following norms:

1. The applicant should be a body corporate.
2. The applicant should not carry on any business other than those connected with the securities market.
3. The applicant should have necessary infrastructure like office space, equipment, manpower, etc.
4. The applicant must have at least two employees with prior experience in merchant banking.
5. Any associate company, group company, subsidiary or interconnected company of the applicant should not have been a registered merchant banker.
6. The applicant should not have been involved in any securities scam or proved guilty for any offence.
7. The applicant should have a minimum net worth of ₹ 5 crores

2.5 SCOPE OF MERCHANT BANKING ACTIVITIES

Merchant banking activity helps:

(a) In channelising the financial surplus of the general public into productive investment avenues.

(b) To co-ordinate the activities of various intermediaries to the share issue such as the registrar, bankers, advertising agency, printers, underwriters, brokers, etc.

(c) To ensure the compliance with rules and regulations governing the securities market.

2.6 FUNCTIONS OF A MERCHANT BANKER

The following comprise the main functions of a merchant banker:

1. **Management of debt and equity offerings**

   This forms the main function of the merchant banker. He assists the companies in raising funds from the market. The main areas of work in this regard include: instrument designing, pricing the issue, registration of the offer document, underwriting support, marketing of the issue, allotment and refund, listing on stock exchanges, etc.

2. **Promotional activities**

   A merchant bank functions as a promoter of industrial enterprises in India. He helps the entrepreneur in conceiving an idea, identification of projects, preparing feasibility reports, obtaining Government approvals, and incentives, etc. Some of the merchant banks also provide for technical and financial collaborations, not joint ventures.

3. **Placement and distribution**

   The merchant banker helps in distributing various securities like equity shares, debt instruments, mutual fund products, fixed deposits, insurance products, commercial papers to name a few. The distribution network of the merchant banker can be classified as institutional and retail in nature. The institutional network consists of mutual funds, foreign institutional investors, private equity funds, pension funds, financial institutions, etc. The size of such a network represents the wholesale reach of the merchant banker. The retail network depends on networking with investors.

4. Corporate advisory services

Merchant bankers offer customised solutions to their clients' financial problems. The following are the main areas in which their advice is sought:

Financial structuring includes determining the right debt-equity ratio and gearing ratio for the client. The appropriate capital structure theory is also framed. Merchant bankers also explore the refinancing alternatives of the client, and evaluate cheaper sources of funds.

Rehabilitation and turnaround management is yet another area of merchant banking. In case of sick units, merchant bankers may design a revival package in coordination with banks and financial institutions.

Risk management is another area where advice from a merchant banker is sought. He advises the client on different hedging strategies and suggests the appropriate strategy.

5. Project advisory services

Merchant bankers help their clients in various stages of the project undertaken by the clients. They assist them in conceptualising the project idea in the initial stage. Once the idea is formed, they conduct feasibility studies to examine the viability of the proposed project. They also assist the client in preparing different documents like the detailed project report.

6. Loan syndication

Merchant bankers arrange to tie up loans for their clients. This takes place in a series of steps. First, they analyse the pattern of the client's cash flows, based on which the terms of borrowings can be defined. Then the merchant banker prepares a detailed loan memorandum, which is circulated to various banks and financial institutions and they are invited to participate in the syndicate. The banks then negotiate the terms of lending based on which the final allocation is done.

7. Providing venture capital and mezzanine financing

Merchant bankers help companies in obtaining venture capital financing for financing their new and innovative strategies.

8. Leasing Finance

Merchant bankers provide leasing finance facilities to their clients.

9. Bought-out deals

It involves a deal where the entire securities are bought in lots. It is done with an intention of offloading them later in the market. The deal is done in two stages — first, the client issues shares to the retail investors at a higher price. The merchant banker is required to appraise the project, invest in the client and offer the shares to the public for subscription. The merchant banker has the lucrative possibility of picking up the difference between the price at which they bought the shares from the client and the public offer price. The client, on the other hand, need not wait for months together to use the issue proceeds and gets an attractive price for his shares. In addition, it allows companies to raise capital without facing the uncertainties of the marketplace.

10. Non-resident Investment

The merchant bankers provide investment advisory services in terms of identification of investment opportunities, selection of securities, portfolio management, etc. to attract NRI investment in the primary and secondary markets. They also take care of the operational details like purchase and sale of securities securing the necessary clearances from RBI under FEMA for repatriation of interest and dividends, etc.

11. Advisory services relating to mergers and acquisitions

Mergers and takeovers are very popular in these days. There may be several reasons for mergers and acquisitions. They vary from elimination of competition, expansion of capital through tie-ups and to go global. Merchant bankers play very important role in the field of mergers and takeovers.

12. Portfolio management

Merchant bankers offer services not only to the clients issuing the securities but also to the investors. They advise their clients, mostly institutional investors, regarding investment decisions. Merchant bankers even undertake the function of purchase and sale of securities for their clients and provide them assistance to:

(a) identify the potential targets of takeovers,

(b) appraise the merger/takeover proposals with respect to financial viability and technical feasibility,

(c) negotiate with interested parties,

(d) determine the purchase consideration and the appropriate exchange ratio,

(e) assist in matters related to procedural and legal aspects, and

(f) obtain necessary approvals.

To help clients achieve the objectives of these restructuring strategies, the merchant banker participates in different activities at various stages. They include understanding the objectives behind the strategy (objectives could be either to obtain financial, marketing, or production benefits), and help in searching for the right partner in the strategic decision and financial valuation of the proposal.

2.7 ISSUE MANAGEMENT

As already stated, it is good to study about issue management now. Issue management refers to management of securities offering of clients to the general public and existing shareholders on right basis. Issue managers are known as Merchant Banker or Lead Managers. Merchant banker has many more tasks to be carried out. Of which, issue management is the most important and sizable function within. The terms 'Merchant Banking' and Issue Management' are generally used interchangeably. Public Issue and Rights Issue of more than ₹ 50 lakhs is required to be managed by a category I Merchant Banker under SEBI Guidelines. Industry at present is badly in need of funds. Issue management has tremendous scope and potential in supplying such funds to the industry.

Merchant bankers provide their skills and experience to clients in managing the capital issues. It essentially aims at converting the savings of household into viable investment of clients. The investment covers investment on new projects, expansion, modernisation and diversification of existing units and augmenting the long-term sources for working capital purpose.

Type of Issues

Issues are of three types. They are as follows:

(a) Public Issue,

(b) Right Issue, and

(c) Private Placements.

2.7.1. Public Issue

By issuing Prospectus, companies raise fund from the public. This is a most common method of raising fund. Companies issue prospectus to issue shares. Shares issued through prospectus are in a fixed number. Shares may be issued either at premium, or on discount or at par. SEBI lays down guidelines for raising funds through this mode for which, SEBI approves a Merchant Banker. The first public offer of securities by a company after its inception is known as an Initial Public Offering (IPO). IPO dilutes the ownership stake and diffuses corporate control as it provides ownership to investors in the form of equity shares. It can be used as both an exit strategy and a financing strategy. As a financing strategy, its main purpose is to raise funds for the company. When used as an exit strategy, existing investors can offload their equity holdings to the public.

Reasons for Going Public

1. To raise funds for financing capital expenditure needs like expansion, diversification, etc.
2. To finance increased working capital requirement.
3. As an exit route for existing investors.
4. For debt financing.

Advantages

1. The IPO provides avenues for funding future needs of the company.
2. It provides liquidity for the existing shares.
3. The reputation and visibility of the company increases.
4. Additional incentive for employees in the form of the company's stocks. This also helps to attract potential employees.
5. It commands better valuation for the company.

Disadvantages

1. The profit earned by the company should be shared with its investors in the form of dividends.
2. An IPO is a costly affair. Around 15-20% of the fund realised is spent on raising the same.
3. In an IPO, the company has to disclose results of operations and financial position to the public and the Securities and Exchange Board of India (SEBI).
4. The company's management has to invest substantial time and effort.

Eligibility Norms

I. For Unlisted Companies

1. It should have a pre-issue net worth of a minimum amount of ₹ 1 crore in 3 out of the preceding 5 financial years. In addition, the company should compulsorily meet the minimum net worth level during the two immediately preceding years.
2. It should have a track record of distributable profits as given in Section 205 of the Companies Act, 1956, for at least 3 years in the preceding 5-year period.
3. The issue size (*i.e.,* offer + firm allotment + promoters' contribution through the offer document) should not exceed an amount equal to five times its pre-issue net worth.

II. For Listed Companies

1. It must have a track record of distributable profits in compliance with Section 205 of the Companies Act, 1956 for at least 3 of the 5 immediately preceding years.
2. It must have a pre-issue net worth of not less than ₹ 1 crore in 3 out of the 5 preceding years, with the minimum net worth to be met during the immediately preceding 2 years.

The IPO Process in India

The IPO process in India consists of the following steps:

1. Appointment of merchant banker and other intermediaries,
2. Registration of offer document,
3. Marketing of the issue, and
4. Post-issue activities.

Appointment of Merchant Banker and Other Intermediaries

One of the crucial steps for successful implementation of the IPO is the appointment of a merchant banker. A merchant banker should have a valid SEBI registration to be eligible for appointment. A merchant banker can be any of the following: lead manager, co-manager, underwriter or advisor to the issue. Certain guidelines are laid down in Section 30 of the SEBI Act, 1992 on the maximum limits of intermediaries associated with the issue.

The number of co-managers should not exceed the number of lead managers. There can only be one advisor/ consultant to the issue. There is no limit on the number of underwriters. The limit for the Lead Managers is given in Table 2.2.

Table 2.2 **Limit of Lead Managers**

Size of the Issue (in ₹)	No. of Lead Managers
50 crore	2
50-100 crore	3
100-200 crore	4
200-400 crore	5
Above 400 crore	5 or more as agreed by the board

Source: **SEBI**

Other Intermediaries

Registrar to the Issue: Registration with SEBI is mandatory to take on responsibilities as a registrar and share transfer agent. The registrar provides administrative support to the issue process. The registrar of the issue assists in everything. He helps the lead manager in the selection of bankers. He helps the Issue and the Collection Centres in preparing the allotment and application forms, collection of applications and allotment money, reconciliation of bank accounts with application money, listing of issues and grievance handling.

Bankers to the Issue: Any scheduled bank registered with SEBI can be appointed as the banker to the issue. There are no restrictions on the number of bankers to the issue. The main functions of the banker involve collection of application forms with money. It maintains a daily report. The banker transfers the proceeds to the share application money account maintained by the controlling branch. He also forwards the money collected with the application forms to the registrar.

Underwriters to the Issue: Underwriting involves a commitment from the underwriter to subscribe to the shares of a particular company to the extent it is undersubscribed by the public or existing shareholders of the corporate. An underwriter should have a minimum net worth of ₹ 20 lakhs. His total obligation at any time should not exceed 20 times the underwriter's net-worth. A commission is paid to the underwriters on the issue price for undertaking the risk of undersubscription.

The maximum rate of underwriting commission paid is given in Table 2.3.

Table 2.3 **Maximum Rate of Underwriting Commission**

Nature of Issue	On amounts devolving on underwriters	On amounts subscribed by public
Equity shares, preference shares and debentures	2.5%	2.5%
Issue amount upto ₹ 5 lakhs	2.5%	1.5%
Issue amount exceeding ₹ 5 lakhs	2.0%	1.0%

Source: **SEBI**

Broker to the Issue: Any member of a recognised stock exchange can become a broker to the issue. A broker offers marketing support, underwriting support, disseminates information to investors about the issue and distributes issue stationery at retail investor level.

Registration of the Offer Document

For registration, 10 copies of the draft prospectus should be filed .with SEBI. The draft prospectus filed is treated as a public document. The lead manager also files the document with all listed stock exchanges. Similarly, SEBI uploads the document on its website www.sebi.com. Any amendments to be made in the prospectus should be done within 21 days of filing the offer document. Thereafter the offer document is deemed to have been cleared by SEBI.

Promoters' Contribution

In the public issue of an unlisted company, the promoters shall contribute not less than 20% of the post-issue capital as given in Chapter IV of the SEBI Act, 1992. The entire contribution should have been made before the opening of the issue.

Lock-in Requirement

The minimum promoter's contribution will be locked in for a period of 3 years. The lock-in period commences from the date of allotment or from the date of commencement of commercial production, whichever is earlier.

Marketing of the Issue

1. Timing of the Issue
2. Retail Distribution
3. Reservation of the Issue
4. Advertising Campaign

Timing of the Issue: An appropriate decision regarding the timing of the IPO should be made, keeping in mind the general sentiments prevailing in the investor market. For example, if recession is prevailing in the economy, then the firm will not be able to get a good pricing for its IPO, as investors may not be willing to put their money in stocks.

Retail Distribution: Retail distribution is the process through which an attempt is made to increase the subscription. Normally, a network of brokers undertakes retail distribution. The Issuer Company organises road shows in which conferences are held, which are attended by high net worth investors, brokers and sub-brokers. The company makes presentations and solves queries raised by participants. This is one of the best ways to raise subscription.

Reservation of the Issue: Sometimes reservations are tailored to a specific class of investors. This reduces the amount to be issued to the public. The following are the classes of investors for whom reservations are made:

1. Mutual Funds.
2. Banks and Financial Institutions, Non-Resident Indians (NRI) and Overseas Corporate Bodies (OCBs). The total reservation for NRI/OCB should not exceed 10% of the post-issue capital, and individually it should not exceed 5% of the post-issue capital.
3. Foreign Institutional Investors (FII). The total reservation for FII cannot exceed 10% of the post-issue capital, and individually it should not exceed 5% of the post-issue capital.
4. Employees. Reservation under this category should not exceed 10% of the post-issue capital.
5. Group Shareholders. Reservation in this category should not exceed 10% of the post-issue capital.

At any point of time, the net offer made to the public should not be less than 25% of the total issue.

Post-issue Activities

1. **Principles of Allotment:** After the closure of the subscription list, the merchant banker should inform, within 3 days of the closure, whether 90% of the amount has been subscribed or not. If it is not subscribed up to 90%, then the underwriters should bring the shortfall amount within 60 days. In case of over-subscription, the shares should be allotted on a pro-rata basis, and the excess amount should be refunded with interest to the shareholders within 30 days from the date of closure.
2. **Formalities associated with Listing:** The SEBI lists certain rules and regulations to be followed by the issuing company. These rules and regulations are laid down to protect the interests of investors. The issuing company should disclose to the public its profit and loss account, balance sheet, information relating to bonus and rights issue and any other relevant information.

2.7.2. Rights Issue

Existing shareholders have pre-emptive right in taking part in the right issue. In right issue, shares are offered to existing shareholders according to the proportion of their shareholding. The shareholders, who are offered shares, do not have any legal obligation to accept the offer. On the other hand, they have right to renounce the offer in favour of any person.

2.7.3. Private Placement

The direct sale of shares by a company to investors is called private placement. No prospectus is issued in private placement. Private placement covers equity shares, preference shares and debentures. It is presumed that the investors have sufficient knowledge and experience to be capable of evaluating the merits and risks of the investment. Merchant banker or any other intermediary plays an important role in preparing an offer memorandum and negotiating with potential investors. Private placement has an advantage of speed and confidentiality. Private placement offers access to capital more quickly than public issue. It is possible to tap resources within two or three months through private placement, which is impossible in the public issue or right issue.

2.8 ISSUE MANAGER

Issue managers generally do issue management. To be an issue manager, they register themselves with SEBI.

SEBI has abolished three out of four categories of merchant bankers. SEBI initiated it to be stringent in implementing the regulations. The objective of the move is to facilitate only high net worth companies to operate as merchant bankers to provide quality service and to have screening effect. Sole proprietorship and partnership forms of organisations are not allowed to be merchant banker. Body corporate alone will be registered with SEBI as merchant banker. This aims at enhancing the corporate discipline and professionalism in issue management.

Roles of Issue Manager

The roles played by the issue manager are multidimensional. They are as follows:

(a) Merchant banker floats the shares for and on behalf of issuing company. It may be either right or public issue. It is the stipulation of SEBI.

(b) One of the important areas of issue management relates to capital structuring, capital gearing and financial planning for the company. Merchant banker acts as a master designer in performing these activities.

(c) Merchant banker underwrites and invests in the issue managed by them.

(d) They invest, continue to hold and offer buy and sell quotes for the scrips of the company after listing. His association with the company is not merely restricted to the management of the issue but continues throughout.

(e) Every merchant banker is expected to perform due diligence while managing a capital issue.

(f) A merchant banker is required to coordinate with a large number of institutions and agencies.

(g) They are expected to interact and file offer documents with SEBI while managing issues. They file number of reports related to issues. They have to revolve around SEBI.

(h) Marketing of an issue is an essential component of issue management. Merchant banker makes number of promises to the potential investors. He puts him in the shoes of a dream merchant.

PROJECT APPRAISAL

A project is a proposal for capital investment to develop facilities to provide goods and services. JARGONS such as project evaluation, appraisal and assessment are used interchangeably. Project evaluation is used to analyse the soundness of an investment project. Project analysis is done to implement it. The possible net cash flows of the investment are the bases for project analysis. Merchant bankers usually carry out the project analysis for every proposal. The investment proposal may be for setting up a new unit. It may be an expansion of an existing unit. It may aim at improving the existing facilities.

Why should project evaluation be done? Project evaluation is indispensable because resources are scarce. The same resources may have high-yielding alternative opportunities. Project evaluation helps an entrepreneur or a firm to select the best proposal for investment. Project selection can only be rational if it is superior to others in terms of commercial viability.

The various appraisals, initiated by the merchant banker as a part of project appraisal, are depicted in Chart 2.1.

Chart 2.1

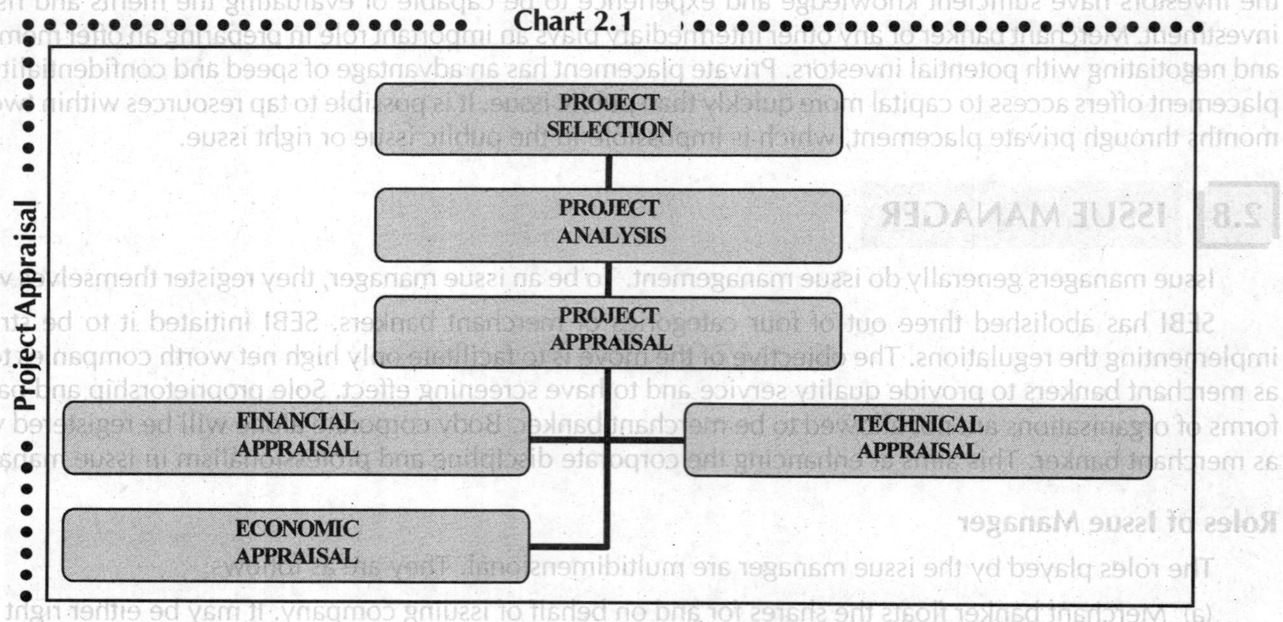

Financial Appraisal: It is concerned with assessing the feasibility of a new proposal for investment. The project's costs and benefits are estimated at the prevailing market prices. This analysis is used to appraise the viability of a project. It helps one to match projects based on their profitability. The financial appraisal is concerned with the measurement of profitability of resources invested in the project without reference to their source.

Financial analysis is the integral part of financial appraisal. Financial analysis takes into account the financial features of a project, including sources of financing. It helps to determine smooth operation of the project over its entire life cycle. Liquidity analysis and capital structure analysis are two aspects of financial analysis. Liquidity ratios measure a project's viability to meet its short-term obligations. Capital structure analysis measures the long-term solvency. It means the project's viability to meet the company's long-term commitments to creditors.

Technical Appraisal: Technical appraisal is concerned primarily with materials and inputs, production technology, plant capacity, location and site, machinery and equipment, structure and civil works, project charts and layouts and work schedule. The project should be able to deliver marketable product from the resources deployed. The cost of resources deployed should leave a margin sufficient to service the investment. It should also plough back a reasonable amount to enable the firm to consolidate its position.

Economic Appraisal: Economic appraisal is also called social cost benefit analysis. It is concerned with judging from the larger social point of view. The focus is on the economic costs and benefits of a project, which may often be different from the monetary cost and benefit (financial appraisal) to the firm. The questions sought to be answered in social cost benefit analysis are:

(a) What are the direct economic benefits and costs of the project which is measured in terms of shadow (efficiency) prices and not in terms of market prices?

(b) What would be the impact of the project on the distribution of income in the society?

(c) What would be the impact of the project on the level of savings and investment in society?

(d) What would be the contribution of the project toward the fulfillment of certain wants like self-sufficiency, employment, and social order?

There are categories of economic aggregates. The first deals with the effect of the project on employment and foreign exchange and the second deals with the impact of the project on net social benefit or welfare. Table 2.4 presents an idea of various costs of a project and the means of financing it.

Table 2.4 Costs and Means of Financing a Project

Cost	Means of Financing
Land and Site development Buildings	Equity
Plant and Machinery	Leasing
Working Capital Debt Miscellaneous Fixed Technical Know-how	Assets
Preliminary and Pre-operative Expenses Contingencies	Incentives Subsidies

Capital Structure

Financial structure is different from capital structure. Capital structure is financed by long-term sources. Long-term sources consist of debt and equity. On the other hand, financial structure, which includes all forms of debt and equity, covers all financial resources. These include short-term as well as long-term sources. Merchant banker restricts his activities to two major long-term sources like debt and equity, when he deals with capital structure of a firm.

Financing Capital Structure: Promoters' contributions, issue of shares and issue of debentures are the various sources of capital structure. Net worth represents owned capital. It consists of equity shares and retained profit. Equity share capital is the core of capital structure. It represents risk capital. Equity shareholders are the owners of the company. They have voting rights. They take part in the management of a company and possess residuary interest in the company. Equity shares do not have any right to dividend.

Debt-equity Ratio: Debt-equity ratio, which is normally prescribed by the Government or a financial institution or stock exchanges, determines the proportion of equity in the capital structure. The standard debt-equity ratio is

2 : 1. In practice, debt-equity ratio is administered with considerable degree of flexibility. Therefore, the debt-equity ratio in capital-intensive projects in the range of 3 : 1 to 6 : 1 is permitted.

Financing Decisions and Cost of Capital: Traditional theories advocate that the firm can lower its cost of capital and increase the market value per share. This is done through a tool called 'leverage'. If a firm raises debt fund to use the leverage, the financial lenders will begin to charge higher interest rate on debt. The investors penalise the price earning ratio increasingly all other things remaining constant. Beyond a level, the cost of capital begins to escalate. This has to be kept in mind while deciding capital structure of a company.

2.9 PRIMARY MARKET ISSUE MANAGEMENT

Merchant banker is the intermediary appointed by companies in the primary market issue. It has to look at the entire issue management and work as the Manager to the public issue.

Principal steps in a public issue are as follows:

1. **Vetting of Prospectus:** The prospectus is a document to communicate information about the company and the proposed security issue to the investing public. The draft prospectus containing the disclosures has to be vetted by SEBI before a public issue is made.
2. **Appointment of Underwriters:** An underwriter agrees to subscribe to a given number of shares when the public does not subscribe to them. The underwriter, in essence, gives guarantee for public subscription in consideration for the underwriting commission.
3. **Appointment of bankers**: The bankers to the issue collect money on behalf of the company from the applicants.
4. **Appointment of Registrar**: The registrars to issue perform a series of tasks from the time the subscription is closed to the time the allotment is made.
5. **Appointment of Brokers and Principal Brokers:** The brokers to the issue facilitate its subscription.
6. **Filing of the Prospectus with the Registrar of Companies.**
7. **Printing and Despatch of Prospectus and Application Form:** After the prospectus is filed with the Registrar of Companies, the company should print the prospectus and the application form.
8. **Filing of Initial Listing Application:** Within ten days of filing the prospectus, the initial listing application must be made to the concerned stock exchange, along with the initial listing fees.
9. **Promotion of the Issue:** The promotional campaign typically commences with the filing of the prospectus with the Registrar of Companies. It ends with the release of the statutory announcement of the issue.
10. **Statutory Announcement:** The statutory announcement of the issue must be made after seeking the approval of the lead stock exchange. This must be published at least ten days before the opening of the subscription list.
11. **Collection of Application:** The statutory announcement (as well as the prospectus) specifies when the subscription would open. It also states when it would close. It should mention usually the name of the bank, the applications can be made.
12. **Processing of Applications:** The application forms received by the bankers are transmitted to the registrars to the issue for processing.
13. **Establishing the Liability of Underwriters:** If the issue is undersubscribed, the liability of the underwriters has to be established.
14. **Allotment of Shares**: If the issue is undersubscribed or just fully subscribed, the company may allot shares applied for by the applicants after securing the formal approval of the concerned stock exchange(s).
15. **Listing of the Issue:** The detailed listing application should be submitted to the concerned stock exchange along with the listing agreement and the listing fee.

2.10 COST OF PUBLIC ISSUE

The cost of public issue is normally between 8% and 12% depending on the size of the issue and the level of marketing effort. The important expenses incurred for a public issue are Underwriting Expenses, Brokerage, Fees to the Managers to the Issue, Fees for Registrars to the Issue, Printing Expenses, Postage Expenses, Advertising and Publicity Expenses, Listing Fees, Stamp Duty, etc.

In addition to the above procedural matter, the most important aspect relates to the pricing of the issue. The merchant banker has to see that the issue is priced properly.

2.11 PRICING OF PUBLIC ISSUE

The salient features of SEBI guidelines with respect to pricing of public issues are as below:

1. A new company set up by entrepreneurs without a track record will be permitted to issue shares to the public only at par.
2. A new company set up by existing companies with a five-year track record of consistent profitability will be free to price its issue provided the participation of the promoting companies is not less than 50% of the equity of the new company and the issue price is made applicable to all new investors uniformly.
3. An existing private/closely held company with a three-year track record of consistent profitability shall be permitted to freely price the issue.
4. An existing listed company can raise fresh capital by freely pricing further issue.

2.12 CODE OF CONDUCT OF MERCHANT BANKERS

There is a legislation to prescribe the code of conduct, if there is a profession. SEBI prescribes code of conduct for merchant bankers. They are as follows:

1. A merchant banker in the conduct of his business shall observe high standards of integrity and fairness in all his dealings with his clients and other merchant bankers.
2. A merchant banker shall render at all times high standards of service, exercise due diligence, ensure proper care and exercise independent professional judgement. He shall, wherever necessary, disclose to the clients, possible sources of conflict of duties and interests, while providing unbiased services.
3. A merchant banker shall not make any statement or become privy to any act, practice or unfair competition, which is likely to be harmful to the interests of other merchant bankers or is likely to place such other merchant bankers in a disadvantageous position in relation to the merchant banker, while competing for or executing any assignment.
4. A merchant banker shall not make any exaggerated statement, whether oral or written, to the client either about the qualification or the capability to render certain services or his achievements in regard to services rendered to other clients.
5. A merchant banker shall always endeavour to:
   (a) render the best possible advice to the clients having regard to the clients' needs and the environments and his own professional skill; and
   (b) ensure that all professional dealings are effected in a prompt, efficient and cost-effective manner.
6. A merchant banker shall not —
   (a) divulge to other clients, press or any other party any confidential information about his client, which has come to his knowledge; and

(b) deal in securities of any client company without making disclosure to the Board as required under the regulations and also to the Board of Directors of the client company.

7. A merchant banker shall endeavour to ensure that—

(a) the investors are provided with true and adequate information without making any misguiding or exaggerated claims and are made aware of attendant risks before any investment decision is taken by them;

(b) copies of prospectus, memorandum and related literature are made available to the investors;

(c) adequate steps are taken for fair allotment of securities and refund of application money without delay; and complaints from investors are adequately dealt with.

8. The merchant bankers shall not generally and particularly in respect of issue of any securities be party to—

(a) creation of false market;

(b) price rigging or manipulation;

(c) passing of price-sensitive information to brokers, members of the stock exchanges and other players in the capital market or take any other action which is unethical or unfair to the investors.

9. A merchant banker shall abide by the provisions of the Act, rules and regulations which may be applicable and relevant to the activities carried on by the merchant banker.

2.13 REGISTRATION AND RENEWAL FEES

According to SEBI, the charges payable by the merchant bankers are as under:

(a) Category I Merchant Banker

A sum of ₹ 2.5 lakhs to be paid annually for the first two years commencing from the date of initial registration and thereafter a sum of ₹ 1 lakh to keep the registration in force.

(b) Category II Merchant Banker

A sum of ₹ 1.5 lakhs to be paid annually for the first two years commencing from the date of initial registration and thereafter a sum of ₹ 50,000 to keep the registration in force.

(c) Category III Merchant Banker

A sum of ₹ 1 lakh to be paid annually for the first two years commencing from the date of initial registration and thereafter a sum of ₹ 25,000 to keep the registration in force.

(d) Category IV Merchant Bankers

A sum of ₹ 5,000 to be paid annually for the first two years commencing from the date of initial registration and thereafter a sum of ₹ 1,000 to keep the registration in force.

2.14 SUMMARY OF THE SEBI GUIDELINES ON MERCHANT BANKING

1. Objectives of Merchant Banking Regulations

The following are the objectives of Merchant Banking Regulations :

1. It regulates the raising of funds in Primary Market.
2. It assures the issuer a market for raising resources at low cost, effectively and easily.
3. It ensures a high degree of protection to the interests of the investors.

4. It provides for the merchant bankers a dynamic and competitive market with high standard of professional competence, honesty, integrity and solvency.
5. It ensures a fair, efficient and flexible primary market to all involved in the process of primary issue.

2. Authorised Activities

The legislation authorises some activities to facilitate merchant banking.

They are:

(a) Issue management:

It consists of preparation of prospectus and other information relating to the:

- Issue of shares and securities.
- Determining financing structure.
- Tie-up of finances.
- Final allotment.
- Refund of subscriptions.

(b) Corporate advice:

It consists of advising the company on the issue.

(c) Managing, consultation and advising:

It covers all the three aspects related to issue and underwriting.

(d) The other authorised activities will be portfolio management services.

3. Method of Authorisation

The criteria for authorisation considers:

(a) Professional qualification in finance, law or business management.

(b) Adequate office space, equipment and manpower.

(c) At least two persons to be employed with experience to carry on the business of merchant banking.

(d) Capital adequacy.

(e) Previous track record, experience, general reputation and fairness in all their transactions.

4. Terms of Authorisation

The following terms and guidelines are laid down by SEBI regarding authorisation:

(a) There are four categories of Merchant banks. The first three levels are determined according to the net worth expressed in rupee value. They are ₹ 5 crores (with effect from 7 February 1995), ₹ 50 lakhs and ₹ 20 lakhs respectively. There is no prescription of rupee limit for fourth category.

(b) The authorisation is valid for an initial period of 3 years.

(c) SEBI collects the initial authorisation fees, an annual fee and renewal fee.

(d) At least one authorised merchant banker, as a sole manager or lead manager, should manage all issues. The number of lead merchant bankers for issues upto ₹ 50 crores is restricted to two. If the issue goes upto ₹ 400 crores and beyond, the numbers may go upto five. If the issue is below ₹ 50 lakhs, companies need not appoint merchant bankers.

(e) The specific responsibilities of each lead manager must be submitted to SEBI prior to the issue.

(f) Merchant bankers should exercise due diligence independently. They should verify the contents of the prospectus and reasonableness of the views expressed therein. SEBI expects a certificate from him regarding it.

(g) The Merchant Bank Regulations link issue management with underwriting. This is with a view to ensuring a stake of merchant bankers in the issue managed by them. Lead managers to issue are required to accept a minimum of 5% underwriting obligation or ₹ 25 lakhs in the issue subject to a ceiling. Other intermediaries generally handle post-issue services. However, Merchant Banking regulations ensure involvement of merchant bankers in post-issue services too. Merchant bankers would be responsible for ensuring timely refunds and allotment of securities to the investors and listing of the instrument on the stock exchange.

(h) Merchant bankers should submit to SEBI whatever information, returns and reports as may be prescribed and called for.

(i) Merchant bankers should adhere to a code of conduct prescribed by SEBI now and then.

(j) SEBI suspends or cancels authorisation in case of violation of the guidelines. Merchant Banker has also a chance to make an appeal to Government of India against the orders of SEBI.

5. Prospectus

The Registrar of Companies (Companies Act, 1956) is advised that the merchant banker, who is authorised by SEBI, only can file the prospectus, for which, each merchant banker is assigned a code number by SEBI. If the prospectus is in contravention of the provisions of any law or statutory rules and regulations, SEBI can instruct the Registrar of Companies not to register such prospectus.

6. Categories of Merchant Banking

The Category classification of MB was applicable between 1991-1996. All categories below level one were abolished by SEBI on 5 September 1997. One could see only one category in the list published by SEBI every year. This is due to the amendments made in this regard. As a student, one should know about all these categories originally evolved by the Board. The range of activities and their Responsibilities are mentioned below:

Category	**Activities and Responsibilities**
First	1. Issue Management. 2. Preparation of prospectus. 3. Determining the financial structure. 4. Tie-up of financiers 5. Final allotment and refund of the subscription amount. 6. Manager, advisor, or consultant to an issuer. 7. Portfolio manager, and 8. Underwriter.
Second	1. Co-manager. 2. Advisor. 3. Consultant. 4. Underwriter. 5. Portfolio Manager.

All these capacities are concerned with an issue.

Third
1. Underwriter.
2. Advisor
3. Consultant.

All these capacities are concerned with an issue.

Fourth
1. Advisor.
2. Consultant.

Two capacities are concerned with an Issue.

7. Minimum net worth requirement

Category	Minimum net worth requirement
I	1 Crore
II	50 Lakhs
III	20 Lakhs
IV	Nil

8. Renewal Fees (Refer Section 2.13):

(i) Category I, ₹ 1 lakh is to be paid annually in first two years and thereafter ₹ 20,000.

(ii) Category II, ₹ 75,000 for first two years and ₹ 10,000 from third year onwards will be collected by SEBI.

(iii) Category III, ₹ 50,000 for first two years and ₹ 5,000 from third year onwards will be collected by SEBI.

(iv) Category IV, ₹ 5,000 for first two years and ₹ 2,500 from third year normally will be collected by SEBI.

9. Lead Managers

The number of lead managers to be appointed depends on the size of the public issue. The guidelines stipulate that for an issue upto ₹ 50 crores, the number of lead managers should not exceed two. For issues between ₹ 50 and ₹ 100 crores, it is three. For issues between ₹ 100 and ₹ 200 crores, the prescribed limits is four. If the issue is above ₹ 200 crores but less than ₹ 400 crores, the limit is five. And above ₹ 400 crores, five or as may be agreed by SEBI will be the limit.

10. Code of Conduct

About code of conduct, refer to Section 2.12 of this chapter.

11. Obligation and Responsibilities of Merchant Banker

The following are the general obligations and responsibilities of merchant bankers.

1. He should keep and maintain a copy of the balance sheet, a copy of the auditor's report and a statement of financial position. Merchant bankers should inform SEBI where the accounts, records and documents are maintained.
2. He should furnish final statements and such other documents to SEBI.
3. He should submit half-yearly working results to SEBI with a view to monitor their capital adequacy.

12. Responsibilities of Lead Manager

Lead managers should not agree to manage any issue. He may be allowed to do so if he fulfills the conditions laid down by SEBI. They are as below:

(a) Lead merchant banker in Category I should accept a minimum underwriting obligation of five per cent of the total underwriting commitment or ₹ 25 lakhs.

(b) The lead merchant banker should submit a due diligence certificate about verification of prospectus to SEBI at least two weeks before opening of an issue.

(c) The lead merchant banker should submit the following documents:

(i) Particulars of issue and draft prospectus.

(ii) Any other literature intended to be circulated to the investors including the shareholders, and

(iii) Such other documents relating to prospectus or letter of offer as the case may be.

These documents should be furnished at least two weeks before filing the draft prospectus with the Registrar of Companies.

13. Acquisition of Shares

Merchant banker should submit particulars of any transaction of acquisition of shares of a company whose issue is managed by them within 15 days from the date of entering in to such transaction.

Lead managers are permitted by SEBI from September 1995 onwards to take a stake of upto 5% of the company's post-issue equity offerings. This stake would be from the reserved category of shares for institutional investors and other corporate bodies.

14. Procedure for Inspection

(a) Inspection

SEBI may inspect books of accounts, records and documents of merchant bankers to ensure that the books of accounts are maintained in the required manner. SEBI may investigate complaint against the merchant banker. It may investigate *suo moto* in the interest of securities business or investors interest into the affairs of the merchant banker. SEBI may either give reasonable notice or undertake inspection without notice in the interest of investors. The findings of inspection report are communicated to merchant banker. SEBI may appoint a qualified auditor to investigate into the books and affairs of merchant banker.

Penalties of non-compliance of conditions for registration and contravention of the provision of the merchant banking regulations include suspension or cancellation of registration. SEBI has classified defaults and the penalty points they attract.

(b) Default of Merchant Bankers and Penalty Points

S. No.	Defaults	Penalty Points
1.	General	1
2.	Minor	2
3.	Major	3
4.	Serious	4

(c) General Defaults

The following are the general defaults. It attracts one penalty point.

(a) Non-receipt of draft prospectus from the lead manager by SEBI before filing it.

(b) Non-receipts of *inter-se* allocation of responsibilities of lead manager in an issue by SEBI, before opening the issue.

(c) Non-receipt of due diligence certificate before opening the issue.

(d) Failure to ensure submission of certificate of minimum 90% subscription to the issue required.

(e) Failure to ensure publicising of dispatch of refund orders, securities certificates and filing of listing application by the issuer.

(d) Minor Defaults

The following are the minor defaults which attract two penalty points.

(a) Promotional materials not being in conformity with contents of the prospectus.

(b) Exaggerated information being given in the prospectus.

(c) Failure to substantiate matters contained in highlights to the issue in the prospectus.

(d) Failure to exercise due diligence in verifying contents of the prospectus.

(e) Failure to give adequate and fair disclosure to investors and objective information about risk factors in the prospectus.

(f) Delay in refund of securities.

(g) Non-handling of investors grievances promptly.

(f) Major Defaults

The following are the major defaults fetching three penalty points.

1. Mandatory underwriting not taken up by the lead manager.
2. Excess number of lead managers.

(g) Serious Defaults

The following activities are classified under serious default. It fetches four penalty points:

1. Unethical practice by merchant banker or violation of code of conduct.
2. Not cooperating with SEBI in furnishing desired information, documents, and evidence as may be called for.

A merchant banker on reaching the cumulative penalty points of eight attracts action from SEBI in terms of suspension or cancellation of authorisation.

15. Enquiry

An enquiry officer is appointed by SEBI to inquire into the defaults of a merchant banker. He issues notice in this regard to the merchant banker. Merchant banker may furnish a reply with evidences sought by Board within thirty days. The enquiry officer gives reasonable opportunity to the banker to explain. The merchant banker can appear personally or through others. Based on the enquiry, the officer submits a report to the board.

16. Action by SEBI

On receipt of report from enquiry officer, the board initiates action as below:

(a) It issues a show-cause notice. The merchant banker has to respond to the notice within twenty-one days. The board acts on the response not later than thirty days. It issues an order with reasons for levying penalty.

(b) The merchant banker ceases to carry business on and from the date of the suspension.

(c) The order of suspension shall be published in atleast two daily newspapers by the board.

(d) Aggrieved person may apply to the Central Government against the order.

2.15 INDIAN EXPERIENCE

Deficit units of one country depend on surplus units for funds. Surplus units save money and direct the saved money as investment. Entrepreneurs convert such surplus money in the form of products and services. Such surplus money is generally converted into securities. Someone has to do the job of directing the surplus money from surplus units to deficit units through an investment vehicle. The investment vehicle is nothing but the primary market. It provides a link between live savings and investment across the entities. The issuers of securities, Government as well as corporate, raise resources to meet their requirements by issuing or creating fresh securities in exchange of funds either through public issues and/or as private placement. When equity shares are exclusively offered to the existing shareholders, it is called rights issue and when it is issued to selected mature and sophisticated institutional investors as opposed to general public, it is called Private Placement. Issuers may issue the securities at face value, or at a discount or premium and these securities may take a variety of forms such as equity, debt or some hybrid instruments. The issuers may issue the securities in domestic market.

2.15.1. Capital Raised During 2002-03 — During 2006-07

During 2006-07, 124 companies accessed the primary market and raised ₹ 33,508 crores through public and rights issues compared to 139 companies which had raised ₹ 27,382 crores in 2005-06. Even though the number of companies accessing the primary market was lower, the amount mobilised was higher in 2006-07 as compared to the previous year. Of the 85 public issues, 77 were Initial Public Offerings (IPOs) and eight were Follow on Public Offerings (FPOs). Resources raised through IPOs and FPOs were ₹ 28,504 crores and ₹ 226 crores in 2005-06 to ₹ 351 crores in 2006-07. The average size of IPOs increased from ₹ 138 crores to ₹ 370 crores during the same period. The share of IPOs in the total resource mobilisation was 85.1% in 2006-07 as compared to 40.0% in 2005-06. The amount mobilised through rights issues declined form ₹ 4,088 crores in 2005-06 to ₹ 3,711 crores in 2006-07. Due to introduction of QIP in 2006-07, the resources raised through FPO route declined from 45.1% in 2005-06 to 3.9% in 2006-07. As per the data made available by NSE and BSE, four companies only at BSE and 21 companies both at NSE and BSE raised ₹ 4,963 crores at BSE and ₹ 4,530 crores at NSE through the QIP route. The private sector companies dominated the resource mobilisation from the primary market in 2006-07. There were 122 issues from the private sector companies and only two issues from the public sector. The private sector and the public sector raised ₹ 31,728 crore and ₹ 1,779 crore respectively. The public sector issues were from Power Finance Corporation Ltd. (a financial company) and Indian Bank Ltd.

Table 2.5 **Resource Mobilisation through Public and Rights Issues** *(₹ Crore)*

Particulars	2005-06		2006-07		Percentage Share in Total Amount	
	No.	Amount	No.	Amount	2005-06	2006-07
1	2	3	4	5	6	7
Public Issues	103	23,294	85	29,797	85.07	88.93
of which						
IPOs	79	10,936	77	28,504	39.94	85.07
FPOs	24	12,358	8	1,293	45.13	3.86
Rights Issues	36	4,088	39	3,711	14.93	11.07
Total	139	27,382	124	33,508	100.00	100.00
Memo Item:						
Offer for Sale	3	296	6	587	1.08	1.75

Source: SEBI.

Table 2.5a **Resource Mobilisation through Public and Rights Issues**

Items	Jan. 15		Dec. 14		2014-15$		2013-14$	
	No. of issues	Amount (₹ crores)	No. of issues	Amount (₹ crores)	No. of issues	Amount (₹ crores)	No. of issues	Amount (₹ crores)
1	2	3	4	5	6	7	8	9
(a) Public Issues (i) + (ii)	3	749	3	754	54	9,481	50	30,853
(i) Public issue (Equity) of which	2	7	2	354	34	1,427	27	1,176
IPOs	2	7	2	354	34	1,427	27	1,176
FPOs	0	0	0	0	0	0	0	0
(ii) Public Issue (Debt)	1	743	1	400	20	8,055	23	29,677
(b) Rights Issues	1	1,539	1	8	13	4,352	12	9,190
Total Equity Issues (i + b)	3	1,545	3	361	47	5,778	39	10,366
Total (a + b)	4	2,288	4	761	67	13,833	62	40,043

Notes: 1. IPOs — Initial Public Offers, FPOs — Follow on Public Offers.
2. $ indicates as of last day of January of respective year.
Source: SEBI.

During 2013-14, 90 companies accessed the primary market and raised ₹ 55,652 crores through public (75) and rights issues (15) as against 69 companies which raised ₹ 32,455 crores in 2012-13 through public (53) and rights issues (16) (Table 2.1). Primary market activities in 2013-14 were on a resurgent mode as compared to 2012-13. The number of IPOs in 2013-14 stood at 38 as compared to 33 in the year 2012-13. Of the 38 IPOs, 37 have been listed at the SME platform. The amount raised through IPOs in 2013-14 was lower at ₹ 1,236 crores as compared to ₹ 6,528 crores during 2012-13. During the year, offer for sale by existing shareholders mobilised ₹ 3,096 crores through four IPOs and FPOs. There were two FPOs worth ₹ 7,457 crores in 2013-14 as compared to none in 2012-13. The share of public issues in the total resource mobilisation increased to 91.8% during 2013-14 from 72.4% during 2012-13 and the share of rights issues decreased from 27.6% in 2012-13 to 8.2% in 2013-14 (Chart 2.1). Of the public issues, the share of debt issues in the total resource mobilisation was the largest at 76.2% and that of equity issues was 23.8% in 2013-14.

Table 2.6 **Sector-wise Resource Mobilisation** *(₹Crore)*

Sector	2005-06		2006-07		Percentage Share in the Total Amount	
	No.	Amount	No.	Amount	2005-06	2006-07
1	2	3	4	5	6	7
Private	131	20,199	122	31,728	73.77	94.69
Public	8	7,183	2	1,799	26.23	5.31
Total	139	27,382	124	33,508	100.00	100.00

Table 2.7 **Size-wise Resource Mobilisation** *(₹ Crore)*

	2005-06		2006-07		Percentage Share in the Total Amount	
	No.	Amount (Cr.)	No.	Amount (Cr.)	2001-02	2002-03
1	2	3	4	5	6	7
< ₹ 5 crore	6	20	3	10	0.07	0.03
≥ ₹ 5 crore & < ₹10 crore	4	32	6	45	0.12	0.14
≥ ₹ 10 crore & < ₹ 50 crore	47	1,325	40	1,129	4.84	3.37
≥ ₹ 50 crore & < ₹ 100 crore	33	2,189	31	2,386	8.00	7.12
≥ ₹ 100 crore & < ₹ 500 crore	40	8,309	33	7,537	30.35	22.49
≥ ₹ 500 crore	9	15,506	11	22,400	56.63	66.85
Total	139	27,382	124	33,508	100.00	100.00

2.15.2. Trends on Total Resource Mobilisation

During 2006-07, 94.7% of total resource mobilisation (Table 2.6) was from private sector compared to 73.8% in previous year. The share of public sector has declined from 26.2% in 2005-06 to 5.3% in 2006-07. The average issue size was larger in 2006-07 as compared to 2005-06. The average size of the issues rose from ₹ 197 crores in 2005-06 to ₹ 270 crores in this financial year. In contrast to the trend in the previous financial year, substantial amount of fund mobilisation was through large issues. There were 11 issues in the above ₹ 500 crores category, which mobilised ₹ 22,400 crores and 33 issues were in ₹ 100 crore to ₹ 500 crores category, which mobilised ₹ 7,537 crores (Table 2.7).

Table 2.8 **Sector-wise Resource Mobilisation**

Sector	2012-13		2013-14		Percentage share in total amount	
	No. of issues	Amount (₹ crore)	No. of issues	Amount (₹ crore)	2012-13	2013-14
1	2	3	4	5	6	7
Private	55	17,690	70	11,681	54.5	21.0
Public	14	14,765	20	43,970	45.5	79.0
Total	**69**	**32,455**	**90**	**55,652**	**100.0**	**100.0**

Sector-wise classification of the resource mobilisation shows that 70 private sector issues and 20 public sector issues were mobilised through primary market in 2013-14 as compared to 55 private sector issues and 14 public sector issues in 2012-13. Private sector issues mobilised ₹ 11,681 crores compared to ₹ 43,970 crores mobilised by the public sector companies (Table 2.8). Private sector contributed 21.0% in the total resource mobilisation in 2013-14 as compared to 54.5% in 2012-13. The amount raised through public sector issues was 79.0% of the total resource mobilisation comparing with 45.5% during the year 2012-13.

2.15.3. State-wise Resource Mobilisation

Various measures were initiated by the Government, RBI and SEBI during the year to further refine the market design of the primary market and boost the market sentiments. Measures initiated during the April 2002 to June 2003 are detailed below.

The average size of an issue (including public and rights) which accessed the primary market in 2013-14 increased to ₹ 618 crores as compared to ₹ 470 crores in 2012-13. The average issue size of public issues increased in 2013-14. In 2013-14, the mean public issue size was ₹ 681 crores compared to ₹ 444 crore in 2012-13. However, the mean IPO size declined from ₹ 198 crores in 2012-13 to ₹ 33 crores in 2013-14.

Table 2.9 **State-wise Resource Mobilisation**

Issue Size	2012-13		2013-14		Percentage share in Total Amount	
	No. of issues	Amount (₹ crore)	No. of issues	Amount (₹ crore)	2012-13	2013-14
1	2	3	4	5	6	7
< ₹ 5 crore	2	7	14	41	0	0.1
≥ ₹ 5 crore & < ₹ 10 crore	12	79	17	122	0.2	0.2
≥ ₹ 10 crore & < ₹ 50 crore	16	297	10	174	0.9	0.3
≥ ₹ 50 crore & < ₹ 100 crore	6	440	3	221	1.4	0.4
≥ ₹ 100 crore & < ₹ 500 crore	18	4,416	19	4,261	13.6	7.7
≥ ₹ 500 crore	15	27,216	27	50,832	83.9	91.3
Total	**69**	**32,455**	**90**	**55,652**	**100.0**	**100.0**

2.15.4. Underwriting by Merchant Banking, Subsidiaries of Commercial Banks

In order to provide a level playing field to the merchant banking subsidiaries of banks, RBI decided to make that in partial modification on the earlier guidelines, according to which the existing ceiling on underwriting commitments prescribed therein would not be applicable for merchant banking subsidiaries of banks.

The merchant banking subsidiaries of banks regulated by SEBI would, consequently, be governed by the norms on the various aspects of the underwriting exercise taken up by them. The prudential exposure ceiling on underwriting and similar commitments of banks, however, remain unchanged and they-shall be continued to be reckoned within the norms prescribed by RBI earlier on overall single borrower/issue size limits from time to time. Banks should ensure continued viability of their merchant banking subsidiaries through periodic reviews of their performance. Other prudential norms on capital market exposure, asset-liability management, allocation of additional capital for risk weighted assets of the subsidiaries will also continue to apply.

2.15.5. Market Design

The market design for primary market is provided in the provision of the Companies Act, 1956, which deals with issues, listing and allotment of securities. In addition, DIP guidelines issued by issuer, promoter, management, project, risk factors and eligibility norms for accessing the market. However, in this section, the market design as provided in securities laws has been discussed.

2.15.6. DIP Guidelines, 2000

The issues of capital to public by Indian companies are governed by the Disclosure and Investor Protection (DIP) Guidelines of SEBI, which were issued in June 1992. SEBI has been issuing clarifications to these guidelines from time to time aiming at streamlining the public issue process. In order to provide a comprehensive coverage of all DIP guidelines, SEBI issued a compendium series in January 2000, known as SEBI (DIP) Guidelines, 2000. The guidelines provide norms relating to eligibility for companies issuing securities, pricing of issues, listing requirements, disclosure norms, lock-in period for promoter's contributions, contents of offer documents, pre- and post-issue obligation, etc. The guidelines apply to all public issues, offers for sale and rights issues by listed and unlisted companies.

2.15.7. Eligibility Norms

Any company issuing securities through the offer document has to satisfy the following conditions:

(a) A company making a public issue of securities has to file a draft prospectus with SEBI, through an eligible merchant banker, at least 21 days prior to the filing of prospectus with the Registrar of Companies (ROCs). The filing of offer document is mandatory for a listed company issuing security through a rights issue where the aggregate value of securities, including premium, if any, exceeds ₹ 50 lakhs. A company cannot make a public issue unless it has made application for listing of those securities with stock exchange(s). The company must also have entered into an agreement with the depository for dematerialisation of its securities and also the company should have given an option to subscribers/shareholders/investors to receive the security certificates or securities in dematerialised form with the depository. A company cannot make an issue if the company has been prohibited from accessing the capital market under any order or discretion passed by SEBI.

(b) An unlisted company can make public issue of equity shares or any other security convertible into equity shares, on fixed price basis or on book building basis, provided.

(c) It has a pre-issue net worth of not less than ₹ 1 crore in 3 out of the 5 preceding years and has minimum net worth in immediately preceding two years.

(d) It has a track record of distributable profits in terms of Section 205 of the Companies Act, 1956, for at least 3 out of the preceding 5 years, and

(e) The issue size (offer through offer document plus firm allotment plus promoters' contribution through the offer document) does not exceed five times its pre-issue net worth. An unlisted company can make a public issue of equity shares or any security convertible into equity shares only through the book-building process, if it fails to comply with the above criteria and its proposed issue size exceeds five times its pre-issue net worth (sixty per cent of the issue size shall be allotted to the Qualified Institutional Buyers (QIBs), failing which the full subscription monies will be refunded).

(f) In case of undersubscription of the issue, the lead merchant banker responsible for underwriting arrangements has to invoke underwriting obligations and ensure that the underwriters subscribe to the unsubscribed portion of the issue. It should ensure the minimum number of collection centres. It should also ensure that the issuer company has entered into an agreement with all the depositories for dematerialisation of securities.

(g) All the other formalities related to post-issue obligations like allotment, refund and despatch of certificates are also taken care of by the lead merchant banker.

(h) A compliance officer shall be appointed who will directly liaise between the Board and the issuer company with regard to compliance of various laws, rules, regulations and other directives issued by the Board.

(i) After a period of 21 days from the date the draft offer document was made public, the lead merchant banker shall file a statement with the Board giving a list of complaints received by it, a statement by it whether it is proposed to amend the draft offer document or not, and, highlight those amendments, if any.

(j) The lead manager should also ensure that the issuer company has entered into agreements with all the depositories for dematerialisation of securities. He should also ensure that an option has been given to the investors to receive allotment of securities in dematerialised form through any of the depositories.

2.15.8. Book-Building

Book-building is a process of offering securities in which bids are invited at various prices from investors and based on bids, demand for the security is assessed and its price is discovered. In case of normal public issue, the price is known in advance to investor and the demand is known at the close of the issue. In case of public issue through book-building, demand can be known at the end of everyday but price is known at the close of issue. TCS had come out with a Public Issue during August 2004 with a price bond of ₹ 750 to ₹ 900.

(a) An issuer company proposing to issue capital through book-building has two options; *viz.*, 75% book-building route and 100% book-building route.

(b) If 100% book-building route is adopted, not more than 60% of net offer to public can be allocated to QIBs, not less than 15% of the net offer to the public can be allocated to non-institutional investors applying for more than 1000 shares and not less than 25% of the net offer to public can be allocated to retail investors applying for upto 1000 shares.

(c) In case 75% of net public offer is made through book-building, not more than 60% of the net offer can be allocated to QIBs and not less than 15% of the net offer can be allocated to non-institutional investors. The balance 25% of the net offer to public, offered at a price determined through book-building, are available to retail investors who have either not participated in book-building or have not received any allocation in the book-built portion.

(d) Allotment to retail individual or non-institutional investors is made on the basis of proportional allotment system (Prorata basis).

(e) Allotment to institutional investors is made on a discretionary basis within 15 days of the closure of the issue failing which interest at the rate of 15% shall be paid to the investors.

(f) In case of undersubscription in any category, the unsubscribed portion is allocated to the bidders in other categories. The book-built portion, 100% or 75%, as the case may be, of the net offer to public, are compulsorily underwritten by the syndicate members or bookrunners.

Other requirements of book-building include:

(a) issuer to provide indicative floor price and no ceiling price,

(b) bids to remain open for at least 5 days,

(c) only electronic bidding is permitted,

(d) bids are submitted through syndicate members,

(e) investors can bid at any price,

(f) retail investors have option to bid at cut-off price,

(g) bidding demand is displayed at the end of everyday, and

(h) the lead manager analyses the demand generated and determines the issue price in consultation with the issuer.

2.15.9. e-IPOS

A company proposing to issue capital to public through online system of the stock exchange has to comply with Sections 55 to 68A of the Companies Act, 1956 and SEBI (DIP) Guidelines, 2000. The following steps are to be taken with respect to e-IPOs:

(a) The company is required to enter into an agreement with the stock exchange(s) which have the requisite system for online initial public offer of securities.

(b) The agreement should cover rights, duties, responsibilities and obligations of the- company and the stock exchanges *inter-se* with provision for a dispute resolution mechanism between the company and the stock exchange.

(c) The issuer company appoints a Registrar to the Issue having electronic connectivity with the stock exchanges.

(d) The issuer company can apply for listing of its securities at any exchange through which it offers its securities to public through online system, apart from the requirement of listing on the regional stock exchange. The stock exchange appoints brokers for the purpose of accepting applications and placing orders with the company.

(e) The lead manager would coordinate all the activities amongst various intermediaries connected in the system.

In addition to the above sections, the DIP guidelines also provide details of the contents of the offer document and advertisement, other requirements for issues of securities, like those under Rule 19(2)(b) of SC(R) Rules, 1957. The guidelines also lay down detailed norms for issue of debt instruments, OTCEI issues, issue of capital by designated financial institutions and preferential/bonus issues.

2.15.10. Credit Rating

Credit rating is governed by the SEBI (Credit Rating Agencies) Regulations, 1999. The Regulations cover rating of securities only and not rating of fixed deposits, foreign exchange, country ratings, real estates, etc. CRAs can be promoted by public financial institutions, scheduled commercial banks, foreign banks operating in India, foreign credit rating agencies recognised in the country of their incorporation, having at least five years' experience in rating, or any company or a body corporate having continuous net worth of minimum ₹ 100 crore for the previous five years. CRAs would be required to have a minimum net worth of ₹ 5 crores. No Chairman, Director or Employee of the promoters shall be Chairman, Director or Employee of CRA or its rating committee. A CRA cannot rate:

(a) A security issued by its promoter,

(b) Securities issued by any borrower, subsidiary, an associate promoter of CRA, if there are common Chairman, Directors and Employees between the CRA or its rating committee and these entities,

(c) A security issued by its associate or subsidiary if the CRA or its rating committee has a Chairman, Director or Employee who is also a Chairman, Director or Employee of any such entity.

For all public rights issues of debt securities of issue size greater than or equal to ₹ 100 crores, two ratings from different CRAs would be required. An obligation has been cast on the issuer to disclose in the offer documents all the ratings it has got during the previous 3 years for any of its listed securities, at the time of accessing market through a rated security. CRAs would have to carry out periodic reviews of the ratings given during the lifetime of the rated instrument.

2.15.11. Merchant Banking

The merchant banking activity in India is governed by SEBI (Merchant Bankers) Regulations, 1992. All merchant bankers have to be registered with SEBI. The person applying for certificate of registration as merchant banker has to be a body corporate other than a non-banking financial company, has necessary infrastructure, and has at least two persons in his employment with experience to conduct the business of the merchant banker. The applicant has to fulfill the capital adequacy requirements, with prescribed minimum net worth. The regulations specify the code of conduct to be followed by merchant bankers, responsibilities of lead managers, payments of fees and disclosures to SEBI. They are required to appoint a Compliance Officer, who monitors compliance requirements of the securities laws and is responsible for redressal of investor grievance.

2.15.12. Demat Issues

- As per SEBI mandate, all new IPOs are compulsorily traded in dematerialised form.
- The admission to a depository for dematerialisation of securities is a prerequisite for making a public or rights issue or an offer for sale.
- The investors would however, have the option of either subscribing to securities in physical form or dematerialised form.
- The Companies Act, 1956 requires that every public listed company making IPO of any security for ₹ 10 crores or more shall issue the same only in dematerialised form.

2.15.13. Private Placement

- The private placement involves issue of securities, debt or equity, to a limited number of subscribers, such as:
  - I. Banks,
  - II. Financial Institutions,
  - III. Mutual Funds, and
  - IV. High net worth individuals.

Table 2.10 **Mega Issues in 2006-07***

Name of the Entity	Type of Issue	Type of Instrument	Date of Opening of Issue	Offer size (₹ crore)	Percentage Share in the Total Amount
1	2	3	4	5	6
Sun TV Ltd.	IPO	Equity	03-Apr-06	603	2.31
Reliance Petroleum Ltd.	IPO	Equity	13-Apr-06	8,100	31.03
Patel Engineering Ltd.	FPO	Equity	03-May-06	423	1.62
Deccan Aviation Ltd.	IPO	Equity	18-May-06	363	1.39
GMR Infrastructure Ltd.	IPO	Equity	31-July-06	801	3.07
Tech Mahindra Ltd.	IPO	Equity	01-Aug-06	465	1.78
Parsvnath Developers Ltd.	IPO	Equity	06-Nov-06	997	3.82
Lanco Infratech Ltd.	IPO	Equity	06-Nov-06	1,067	4.09
Tata Teleservices (Maharaashtra) Ltd.	Rights	Equity	21-Nov-06	491	1.88
Sobha Developers Ltd.	IPO	Equity	23-Nov-06	569	2.18
Tanla Solution Ltd.	FPO	Equity	11-Dec-06	420	1.61
Cairn India Ltd.	IPO	Equity	11-Dec-06	5,261	20.15
Bajaj Auto Finance Ltd.	Rights	Equity	15-Dec-06	409	1.57
Aditya Birla Nuvo Ltd.	Rights	Equity	26-Dec-06	779	2.98
Akruti Nirman Ltd.	IPO	Equity	15-Jan-07	362	1.39
House of Pearl Fashions Ltd.	IPO	Equity	16-Jan-07	329	1.26
First Source Solutions Ltd.	IPO	Equity	29-Jan-07	444	1.70
Power Finance Corporation Ltd.	IPO	Equity	31-Jan-07	997	3.82
Indian Bank	IPO	Equity	05-Feb-07	782	
Idea Cellular Ltd.	IPO	Equity	12-Feb-07	2,444	3.00
					9.36
Total				26,107	100.00

* Mega issues relate to issue size of ₹ 300 crores and above.

- It is arranged through a merchant or investment banker, who acts as an agent of the issuer and brings together the issuer, and the investor(s).
- On the presumption that these securities are allotted to a few sophisticated and experienced investors and the public at large don't have much stake in it, the securities offered in a private placement are exempt from the public disclosure regulations and registration requirements of the regulatory body.
- What distinguishes private placement from public issues is while the latter invite application from as many subscribers, the subscriptions in the private placement are normally restricted to a limited number. In terms of the Companies Act, 1956, offer of securities to more than 50 persons is deemed to be public issue.

2.15.14. Market Outcome

Public Issues

- The resource mobilisation from the primary market by way of IPOs and new issues by listed companies saw a decline during the year 2002-03 as compared to the previous year with only ₹ 40,703 million as against ₹ 75,431 million according to SEBI data (Table 2.10).
- The total number of scheme in 2002-03 were only 26 as compared to 35 in year 2001-02. Public issues (by listed companies and IPOs) 86% and 89% of total resources raised during 2001-02 and 2002-03 respectively, while the rest was by way of rights issues. The mobilisation by rights issues was lower by approximately 59% compared to the previous year.
- Only twelve companies used the right route which was the lowest number ever in the last decade. According to a press statement released by of the Prime Database, the continuing fall in the number of companies tapping the rights route can be ascribed to the depressed secondary market prices of a vast majority of companies mainly due to poor fundamentals. Thus it is clearly seen that the companies opt for mobilising money through the general public rather than the existing shareholders.
- It is also observed from Table 2.10 that listed companies mobilised only ₹ 30,316 million through 20 issues during 2002-03, accounting for 74% of the resources, while there were 28 issues by listed companies for ₹ 63,413 million during 2001-02 with their share being 84%. A sharp fall of approximately 46% can be seen in the total resource mobilisation from the public issues.
- During 2002-03, there were 12 mega issues (₹ 100 crores and above) as against 15 such issues in the preceeding year. The average size of an issue was ₹ 4,094 million in 2002-03 as against ₹ 3,380 million in 2001-02. There was no issue below ₹ 3 crores during 2002-03.
- Most of the issues were made by private sector companies, which made 18 issues and mobilised 46.6% of total resources during 2002-03 whereas the public sector companies made issues of only 8 in number but mobilised resources more than that of private sector companies with a contribution of 53.4% to the total resource mobilisation (Table 2.9). The joint sector did not make any issue of capital for the past three years.

As per data available from Prime Database, the response to public issues has been worsening in the recent years.

- But as compared to 2001-02 where no issue was subscribed over ten times during 2002-03 (Table 2.12), 7% of the issues were subscribed over ten times during 2002-03. The most subscribed issue during 2002-03 was by Divis Laboratories Ltd., which was oversubscribed 15.06 times. Only 28% of the public issues failed to elicit adequate response (1.5 times) during 2002-03, as compared to 80% of issues being subscribed less than 1.5 times during 2001-02. Traditionally, debentures seem to dominate the public issues. But no clear trend is visible in the recent past.

There were 30 mega issues in 2013-14 as compared to 19 mega issues in 2012-13 (Table 2.11). The mega issues mobilised ₹ 52,112 crores which amounts to 93.6% of the ₹ 55,652 crores worth of total resource mobilisation during the year. The largest issue during 2013-14 was the equity FPO issue of M/s Power Grid Corporation of India Ltd. (₹ 6,959 crores) which was followed by the debt issues of M/s Indian Railways Finance Corporation Limited (₹ 4,083 crores), M/s Power Finance Corporation Limited (₹ 3,876 crores) and M/s National Highways Authority of India (₹ 3,698 crores).

Table 2.11 **Mega Issues 2013-2014**

No.	Name of the entity	Type of issue	Type of instrument	Date of opening of issue	Offer size (₹ crore)	Percentage share in total amount
1	2	3	4	5	6	7
1	Just Dial Ltd.	IPO	Equity	20-May-13	919	1.76
2	Kesoram Industries Ltd.	Rights	Equity	3-Jun-13	416	0.80
3	Reliance Mediaworks Ltd.	Rights	Equity	6-Aug-13	600	1.15
4	Godrej Properties Ltd.	Rights	Equity	28-Aug-13	700	1.34
5	Power Grid Corporation of India Ltd.	FPO	Equity	3-Dec-13	6,959	13.35
6	Engineers India Ltd.	FPO	Equity	6-Feb-14	498	0.96
7	The Tata Power Company Limited	Rights	Equity	31-Mar-14	1,993	3.83
8	Shriram Transport Finance Company Limited	Public	Bond	16-Jul-13	736	1.41
9	Rural Electrification Corporation Limited	Public	Bond	30-Aug-13	3,441	6.60
10	India Infoline Finance Limited	Public	Bond	17-Sep-13	1,050	2.01
11	Housing and Urban Development Corporation Limited	Public	Bond	17-Sep-13	2,370	4.55
12	India Infrastructure Finance Company Limited	Public	Bond	3-Oct-13	1,213	2.33
13	Shriram Transport Finance Company Limited	Public	Bond	7-Oct-13	500	0.96
14	Power Finance Corporation Limited	Public	Bond	14-Oct-13	3,876	7.44
15	NHPC Limited	Public	Bond	18-Oct-13	1,000	1.92
16	Housing and Urban Development Corporation Limited	Public	Bond	2-Dec-13	2,153	4.13
17	NTPC Limited	Public	Bond	3-Dec-13	1,750	3.36
18	India Infrastructure Finance Company Limited	Public	Bond	9-Dec-13	3,000	5.76
19	India Infoline Housing Finance Limited	Public	Bond	12-Dec-13	500	0.96
20	Muthoot Finance Limited	Public	Bond	27-Dec-13	500	0.96
21	National Housing Bank	Public	Bond	30-Dec-13	2,100	4.03
22	Indian Railways Finance Corporation Limited	Public	Bond	6-Jan-14	4,083	7.84
23	National Highways Authority of India	Public	Bond	15-Jan-14	3,698	7.10
24	ECL Finance Limited	Public	Bond	16-Jan-14	500	0.96
25	Indian Renewable Energy Development Agency Limited	Public	Bond	17-Feb-14	722	1.38
26	India Infrastructure Finance Company Limited	Public	Bond	17-Feb-14	2,665	5.11
27	Kamarajar Port Limited	Public	Bond	18-Feb-14	365	0.70
28	Indian Railway Finance Corporation Limited	Public	Bond	28-Feb-14	1,745	3.35
29	Rural Electrification Corporation Limited	Public	Bond	28-Feb-14	1,059	2.03
30	National Housing Bank	Public	Bond	7-Mar-14	1,000	1.92
	Total				**52,112**	100

Table 2.12 Industry-wise Resource Mobilisation

Industry	2005-06			2005-06		
	No.	Amount	Percentage share in the Total Amount	No.	Amount	Percentage share in the Total Amount
1	2	3	4	5	6	7
Banks/FIs	12	12,439	45.43	5	2,190	6.53
Cement & Construction	11	1,020	3.72	13	2,747	8.20
Chemical	2	128	0.47	5	147	0.44
Electronics	2	54	0.20	9	480	1.43
Engineering	6	1,124	4.11	2	465	1.39
Entertainment	7	710	2.59	8	1,219	3.64
Finance	7	824	3.01	9	2,765	8.25
Food Processing	9	427	1.56	9	634	1.89
Healthcare	10	651	2.38	2	208	0.62
Information Technology	15	902	3.30	12	2,077	6.20
Paper & Pulp	4	182	0.66	1	15	0.05
Plastic	0	0	0.00	3	106	0.32
Power	6	2,164	7.90	1	30	0.09
Printing	1	43	0.16	2	121	0.36
Telecommunication	0	0	0.00	3	2,994	8.94
Textile	13	771	2.81	15	1,064	3.17
Miscellaneous	34	5,944	21.71	25	16,246	48.49
Total	**139**	**27,382**	**100.00**	**124**	**33,508**	**100.00**

Table 2.12a Industry-wise Resource Mobilisation

Industry	2012-13		2013-14		Percentage share in total amount	
	No. of issues	Amount (₹ crore)	No. of issues	Amount (₹ crore)	2012-13	2013-14
1	2	3	4	5	6	7
Banks/FIs	7	2,475	14	29,700	7.6	53.3
Cement & Construction	1	9	4	731	0	1.3
Chemical	1	9	0	0	0	0
Electronics	0	0	0	0	0	0
Engineering	2	74	5	591	0.2	1.1
Entertainment	1	12	2	602	0	1.1
Finance	16	16,536	26	6,058	51	10.9
Food Processing	2	19	0	0	0.1	0
Healthcare	2	210	0	0	0.6	0
Information Technology	1	4	1	19	0	0
Paper & Pulp	0	0	1	28	0	0
Plastic	0	0	3	18	0	0
Power	0	0	4	11,702	0	21
Printing	0	0	0	0	0	0
Telecom	1	4,173	1	5	12.9	0
Textile	4	582	3	14	1.8	0
Miscellaneous	31	8,352	26	6,184	25.7	11.1
Total	**69**	**32,455**	**90**	**55,652**	**100.0**	**100.0**

Table 2.13 **Market Capitalisation at BSE** *(₹ in crore)*

Year/ Month	All Listed Companies	Percentage Variation	BSE Sensex	Percentage Variation	BSE-TECK	Percentage Variation	BANKEX Variation	Percentage PSU	BSE	Percentage Variation
1	2	3	4	5	6	7	8	9	10	11
2003-04	12,01,206	109.9	6,25,173	148.93	1,45,053	63.47	1,13,094	151.09	4,11,532	158.75
2004-05	16,98,428	41.39	7,25,553	16.06	2,82,425	94.70	1,54,048	36.21	5,16,365	25.47
2005-06	30,22,190	77.94	14,24,112	96.28	4,68,278	65.81	2,19,894	42.74	7,48,614	44.98
2006-07	35,45,041	17.30	17,11.241	20.16	7,17,127	53.14	2,57,026	16.89	7,22,517	–3.49
Apr-06	32,55,565	7.72	14,99,822	5.32	4,72,542	0.91	2,17,176	–1.24	7,52,585	0.53
May-06	28,42,049	–12.70	12,92,241	–13.84	4,18,267	–11.49	1,98,272	–8.70	6,41,069	–14.82
Jun-06	27,21,677	–4.24	13,38,055	3.55	4,26,028	1.86	1,78,697	–9.87	6,06,059	–5.46
Jul-06	27,12,143	–0.35	13,61,372	1.74	4,77,664	12.12	1,96,637	10.04	6,15,974	1.64
Aug-06	29,93,779	10.38	14,76,960	8.49	5,18,690	8.59	2,20,797	12.29	6,77,442	9.98
Sept-06	31,85,679	6.41	15,55,101	5.29	5,45,229	5.12	2,51,354	13.84	7,09,238	4.69
Oct-06	33,70,675	5.81	16,42,242	5.60	6,21,844	14.05	2,66,829	6.16	7,27,371	2.56
Nov-06	35,77,307	6.13	17,53,745	6.79	6,85,493	10.24	2,94,388	10.33	7,55,032	3.80
Dec-06	36,24,356	1.32	17,58,866	0.29	7,04,338	2.75	2,87,709	–.27	7,35,712	–2.56
Jan-07	37,79,741	4.29	18,06,201	2.69	7,48,214	6.23	2,85,708	–0.70	7,80,293	6.06
Feb-07	34,89,213	–7.69	16,70,852	–7.49	6,94,527	–7.18	2,52,376	–11.67	7,07,665	–9.31
Mar-07	35,45,041	1.60	17,11,241	2.42	7,17,127	3.25	2,57,026	1.84	7,22,517	2.10

Source: BSE.

During 2013-14, Banks/Financial Institutions raised the largest amount in the industry-wise classification of resource mobilisation. 14 issues from the industry contributed 53.3% to the total resource mobilisation (Table 2.6). Power sector with four issues mobilised 21% of the total resource mobilisation. Finance sector had relatively lesser share of 10.9% in 2013-14 as compared to the preceding years.

Market capitalisation figures are reflective of the expanding stock market activities. The market capitalisation of BSE has been higher than that of NSE in India reflecting large number of shares being listed in BSE. The market capitalisation of BSE rose by 16.1% to ₹ 74,15,296 crores in 2013-14 from ₹ 63,87,887 crores in 2012-13 (Table 2.13a). On the other hand, at NSE market capitalisation increased by 16.6% to ₹ 72,77,720 crores in 2013-14 from ₹ 62,39,035 crores in 2012-13. The growth at both BSE and NSE was strongest in March 2014. The year saw some months of decline while experiencing mostly an uptrend In BSE, the market capitalisation of the Sensex scrips appreciated by 21.7% in 2013-14. Market capitalisation of BSE Teck index rose highest by 31.7% followed by BSE Sensex in 2013-14 over the previous year.

Market capitalisation of the shares included in CNX Nifty index increased by 21.0% during the financial year. (Table 2.14). The market capitalisation increased for all the indices analysed for NSE in 2013-14 compared to the previous year. At NSE, among sectoral indices analysed, rise in market capitalisation was the highest for CNX Midcap (51.0%) followed by CNX IT (36.6%).

Table 2.13a **Market Capitalisation at BSE**

Year/ Month	All Listed Companies	Percentage Variation	BSE Sensex	Percentage Variation	BSE Teck	Percentage Variation	Bankex	Percentage Variation	BSE PSU	Percentage Variation
1	2	3	4	5	6	7	8	9	10	11
2008-09	30,86,075	−39.9	15,07,742	−32.2	4,10,923	−39.7	2,33,895	-38.0	9,49,211	−17.7
2009-10	61,65,619	99.8	26,17,900	73.6	7,40,817	80.3	5,54,127	136.9	17,33,662	82.6
2010-11	68,39,084	10.9	29,44,451	12.5	8,69,794	17.4	6,89,751	24.5	19,48,555	12.4
2011-12	62,14,941	-9.1	14,59,141	−50.4	3,45,958	−60.2	3,90,614	-43.4	16,03,085	−17.7
2012-13	63,87,887	2.8	16,07,224	10.1	3,91,259	13.1	4,40,395	12.7	14,38,155	−10.3
2013-14	74,15,296	16.1	19,55,490	21.7	5,15,301	31.7	5,07,014	15.1	14,27,356	−0.8
Apr-13	66,45,785	4.0	16,65,038	3.6	3,48,477	−10.9	4,85,969	10.3	15,27,857	6.2
May-13	66,78,737	0.5	16,85,820	1.2	3,61,616	3.8	4,92,193	1.3	14,88,047	-2.6
Jun-13	64,05,118	−4.1	16,55,225	−1.8	3,74,824	3.7	4,55,541	−7.4	13,77,860	−7.4
Jul-13	62,63,106	−2.2	16,55,287	0.0	4,43,120	18.2	3,93,474	−13.6	12,18,421	−11.6
Aug-13	60,30,078	−3.7	15,84,253	−4.3	4,62,977	4.5	3,52,227	−10.5	11,15,578	−8.4
Sep-13	63,86,134	5.9	16,66,323	5.2	4,60,356	−0.6	3,74,881	6.4	12,17,571	9.1
Oct-13	68,44,233	7.2	18,00,318	8.0	4,99,594	8.5	4,47,555	19.4	12,97,647	6.6
Nov-13	68,10,475	−0.5	17,75,253	−1.4	4,91,905	−1.5	4,35,437	−2.7	12,98,792	0.1
Dec-13	70,44,258	3.4	18,39,438	3.6	5,28,571	7.5	4,41,470	1.4	13,26,067	2.1
Jan-14	67,44,398	−4.3	17,80,806	−3.2	5,40,780	2.3	3,97,461	−10.0	12,36,069	−6.8
Feb-14	68,93,083	2.2	18,43,256	3.5	5,52,703	2.2	4,27,321	7.5	12,38,390	0.2
Mar-14	74,15,296	7.6	19,55,490	6.1	5,15,301	−6.8	5,07,014	18.6	14,27,356	15.3

The ratios such as market capitalisation to GDP (m-cap ratio), traded value to GDP (traded value ratio) and price to earnings per share (P/E ratio) are monitored to gauge the extent of development of stock market. After declining for three successive years the market capitalisation ratios have improved during 2013-14. The BSE market capitalisation to GDP ratio has increased from 63.2% in 2012-13 to 65.3% in 2013-14. Similarly, at NSE also the ratio has increased from 61.7% in 2012-13 to 64.1% in 2013-14 (Table 2.14). The all-India cash turnover to GDP ratio however declined further in 2013-14 to 29.5% from 32.2% in 2012-13. In the derivative segment, there was a substantial increase in the turnover-GDP ratio from 382.6% in 2012-13 to 417.7% in 2013-14.

Table 2.14 **Market Capitalisation at NSE** (₹ in crore)

Year/ Month	All Listed Companies	Percentage Variation	S&P CNX	Percen-tage Variation Nifty	CNX Mid	Percentage Variation Cap	CNX IT	Percentage Variation	CNX Bank	Percentage Variation	S&P CNX	Percentage Variation Pharma
1	2	3	4	5	6	7	8	9	10	11	12	13
2003-04	11,20,976	108.7	6,38,599	NA	81,280	–1.32	1,03,168	39.52	1,01,928	NA	68,831	83.69
2004-05	15,85,585	41.44	9,51,672	49.02	1,48,019	82.11	2,27,191	120.2	1,36,921	34.33	93,126	35.30
2005-06	28,13,201	77.42	15,90,155	67.09	3,38,927	128.98	3,48,096	53.22	2,00,503	46.44	1,47,124	57.98
2006-07	33,67,350	19.70	19,09,448	20.08	3,41,869	0.87	4,20,814	20.89	2,29,084	14.25	1,46,394	–0.50
Apr-06	29,90,200	6.29	16,63,860	4.64	3,64,694	7.60	3,47,575	-0.15	1,95,727	–2.38	1,51,322	2.85
May-06	26,12,639	–12.63	14,37,366	–13.61	3,14,442	–13.78	3,10,190	-10.76	1,77,466	–9.33	1,31,592	–13.04
Jun-06	25,24,659	–3.37	14,95,329	4.03	2,82,645	–10.11	3,18,189	2.58	1,59,729	–9.99	1,22,089	–7.22
Jul-06	25,14,261	–0.41	15,03,314	0.53	2,78,554	–1.45	3,30,893	3.99	1,75,612	9.94	1,24,553	2.02
Aug-06	27,77,401	10.47	16,33,200	8.64	3,10,540	11.48	3,57,695	8.10	1,97,881	12.68	1,37,424	10.33
Sept-06	29,94,132	7.80	17,81,134	9.06	3,26,474	5.13	3,65,885	2.29	2,27,284	14.86	1,42,097	3.40
Oct-06	31,38,319	4.82	18,60,568	4.46	3,36,475	3.06	3,94,852	7.92	2,40,812	5.95	1,41,375	–0.51
Nov-06	33,73,652	7.50	19,68,913	5.82	3,51,287	4.40	4,25,709	7.81	2,67,142	10.93	1,46,222	3.43
Dec-06	34,26,236	1.56	19,75,603	0.34	3,62,332	3.14	4,39,187	3.17	2,59,056	–3.03	1,49,994	2.58
Jan-07	35,71,487	4.24	20,36,797	3.10	3,68,357	1.66	4,48,204	2.05	2,56,750	–0.89	1,52,038	1.36
Feb-07	32,96,931	–7.69	18,69,473	–8.22	3,40,880	–7.46	4,15,479	–7.30	2,26,048	–11.96	1,40,071	–7.87
Mar-07	33,67,350	2.14	19,09,448	2.14	3,41,869	0.29	4,20,814	1.28	2,29,084	1.34	1,46,394	4.51

Table 2.14a Market Capitalisation at NSE

Year/ Month	All listed Companies	Percent-age Variation	CNX Nifty	Percent-age Variation	CNX Mid Cap	Percent-age Variation	CNX IT	Percent-age Variation	CNX Bank	Percent-age Variation
1	2	3	4	5	6	7	8	9	10	11
2008-09	28,96,194	–40.4	18,92,629	–33.6	2,73,627	–40.9	2,01,810	–37.5	2,24,132	–36.1
2009-10	60,09,173	107.5	33,00,069	74.4	6,95,714	154.3	5,17,626	156.5	5,20,665	132.3
2010-11	67,02,616	11.5	42,06,042	27.5	10,53,214	51.4	10,47,434	102.4	6,10,563	17.3
2011-12	60,96,518	-9	35,16,863	–16.4	8,58,665	–18.5	6,04,581	–42.3	5,84,359	–4.3
2012-13	62,39,035	2.3	37,46,177	6.5	7,84,403	–8.6	7,10,397	17.5	6,52,629	11.7
2013-14	72,77,720	16.6	45,34,597	21.0	11,84,322	51.0	9,70,460	36.6	7,29,345	11.8
Apr-13	64,90,373	4.0	38,46,019	2.7	9,84,691	25.5	5,22,279	–26.5	7,20,637	10.4
May-13	65,18,227	0.4	38,72,310	0.7	9,83,689	–0.1	5,59,973	7.2	7,12,778	–1.1
Jun-13	62,48,442	–4.1	37,84,042	–2.3	9,22,987	–6.2	5,70,606	1.9	6,63,248	–6.9
Jul-13	60,98,779	–2.4	37,49,870	–0.9	8,70,449	–5.7	6,83,401	19.8	5,72,719	–13.6
Aug-13	58,46,627	–4.1	35,99,664	–4.0	8,39,181	–3.6	7,45,348	9.1	5,13,848	–10.3
Sep-13	61,91,626	5.9	39,17,459	8.8	9,59,260	14.3	8,41,095	12.8	5,46,125	6.3
Oct-13	66,91,531	8.1	42,46,394	8.4	10,29,564	7.3	9,05,226	7.6	6,44,459	18.0
Nov-13	66,44,844	–0.7	41,46,727	–2.3	10,50,144	2.0	8,88,472	–1.9	6,31,548	–2.0
Dec-13	68,84,167	3.6	42,59,658	2.7	10,96,688	4.4	9,72,117	9.4	6,44,297	2.0
Jan-14	65,90,785	–4.3	41,10,730	–3.5	10,28,462	–6.2	10,12,901	4.2	5,75,455	–10.7
Feb-14	67,25,934	2.1	42,06,042	2.3	10,53,214	2.4	10,47,434	3.4	6,10,563	6.1
Mar-14	72,77,720	8.2	45,34,597	7.8	11,84,322	12.4	9,70,460	–7.3	7,29,345	19.5

Table 2.15 Average Daily Volatility of Benchmark Indices*

(Per cent)

2006-07	BSE Sensex	S&P CNX Nifty	BSE Mid-Cap	BSE Small-Cap	BSE 500
1	2	3	4	5	6
April	1.64	1.67	1.53	1.38	1.49
May	2.55	2.77	2.65	2.85	2.62
June	3.25	3.22	3.36	3.88	3.39
July	1.97	1.93	1.83	1.58	1.77
August	0.67	0.72	0.70	1.06	0.72
September	1.06	1.06	1.07	1.02	1.05
October	0.94	0.93	0.83	0.88	0.79
November	0.58	0.61	0.64	0.93	0.65
December	1.48	1.51	1.56	1.59	1.54
January	1.16	1.15	1.07	0.86	1.02
February	1.54	1.56	1.59	1.86	1.57
March	1.95	2.00	1.88	1.84	1.83

* Volatility is measured in terms of standard deviation and is computed from the returns based on closing values of indices as on the last date of the month.

Source: NSE, BSE.

The Indian Equity markets boomed back in 2013-14 to not only surpass the previous year benchmarks but also reach an all-time high in terms of benchmark indices and market capitalisation in secondary markets. A host of domestic and global factors have facilitated this revival that includes various politico-economic indicators as well. While lower trade deficit, lower CAD and lower inflation fuelled the buoyancy outlining the investor optimism. Mixed cues from overseas markets after consumer confidence slumped in September to a four-month low, further influenced the market sentiment. Expectations that the US government's partial shutdown and US political impasse could lead to the US Federal Reserve postponing tapering of monetary stimulus to the US economy also contributed to the volatility.

The annualised volatility of BSE Sensex, measured by standard deviation of log returns, increased to 17.5% in 2013-14 from 12.5% in 2012-13. Similar trend was also observed for CNX Nifty which moved to 18.1% from 12.9% during the same period. Month-wise analysis of the volatility of benchmark and other indices show that September 2013 has been the most volatile month in 2013-14 (Table 2.15a). The lowest volatility in the benchmark indices was seen in March 2014. BSE Small cap index and CNX Nifty Junior witnessed the highest volatility in August 2013. Compared to other indices, volatility in CNX Bank index was high throughout the year.

Table 2.15a **Average Daily Volatility of Benchmark Indices** *(in per cent)*

Month	BSE Sensex	CNX Nifty	BSE 100	BSE Small Cap	CNX 500	CNX Nifty Junior	CNX BANK	SX40
1	2	3	4	5	6	7	8	9
Apr-13	1.03	0.99	0.98	0.97	0.91	0.90	1.40	0.89
May-13	1.12	1.15	1.11	0.88	1.07	0.93	1.53	1.02
Jun-13	1.24	1.23	1.23	0.89	1.18	1.30	1.60	1.17
Jul-13	0.97	1.03	1.08	0.88	1.01	1.20	1.87	0.92
Aug-13	1.71	1.71	1.75	1.16	1.62	1.76	2.39	1.71
Sep-13	1.80	1.90	1.78	0.74	1.68	1.52	3.43	1.78
Oct-13	0.84	0.91	0.87	0.54	0.83	0.86	1.77	0.77
Nov-13	1.07	1.10	1.08	0.79	1.01	1.02	1.80	1.02
Dec-13	0.81	1.25	0.80	0.62	1.16	1.19	1.63	0.71
Jan-14	0.80	0.79	0.82	1.09	0.81	1.12	1.40	0.72
Feb-14	0.68	0.70	0.66	0.44	0.64	0.63	1.06	0.53
Mar-14	0.66	0.72	0.66	0.52	0.59	0.67	1.45	0.60
Annualised Volatility	**17.5**	**18.1**	**17.6**	**13.1**	**16.9**	**17.9**	**30.5**	**16.5**

Table 2.16 P/E Ratio, Return, and Volatility of Select International Indices During 2006-07

Per cent

Country	Index	Apr.	May.	Jun.	Jul.	Aug.	Sep.	Oct.	Nov.	Dec.	Jan.	Feb.	March	Annua Listed Volatility
1	2	3	4	5	6	7	8	9	10	11	12	13	14	15
DEVELOPED MARKETS														
USA	DJIA	0.57	0.80	0.92	0.93	0.48	0.48	0.39	0.50	0.40	0.44	0.85	0.75	10.25
USA	NASDAQ	0.72	0.94	1.36	1.24	0.81	0.85	0.77	0.79	0.61	0.79	1.06	0.99	14.66
UK	FTSE 100	0.58	1.53	1.11	0.92	0.66	0.73	0.48	0.58	0.43	0.68	0.86	1.02	13.38
France	CAC	0.74	1.54	1.40	1.09	0.88	0.76	0.54	0.77	0.75	0.78	0.91	1.10	15.46
Germany	DAX	0.83	1.55	1.39	1.30	0.91	0.72	0.47	0.75	0.70	0.73	0.92	1.18	15.87
Australia	AS 30	0.71	1.05	1.27	0.90	0.81	0.79	0.60	0.74	0.57	0.75	0.80	1.03	13.50
Japan	NKY	1.08	1.30	1.88	1.41	1.08	1.04	0.89	0.96	0.51	0.79	0.94	1.38	17.99
Hong Kong	HSI	0.89	1.32	1.32	0.85	0.84	0.73	0.59	0.95	1.00	1.27	1.17	1.43	16.54
Singapore	STI	0.44	1.40	1.40	0.97	0.59	0.61	0.80	0.84	0.88	0.97	1.51	1.46	16.49
EMERGING MARKETS														
Taiwan	TWSE	0.63	0.99	1.93	1.10	1.02	0.91	0.84	0.57	0.76	0.89	0.71	1.27	16.39
Russia	CRTX	1.57	4.22	4.23	2.02	1.68	2.14	1.54	1.15	0.85	1.87	1.79	1.76	35.85
Malaysia	KLCI	0.38	0.61	0.60	0.60	0.25	0.38	0.39	0.66	0.84	0.70	1.39	1.66	12.61
South Korea	KOSPI	1.05	1.47	1.82	1.26	0.88	0.80	0.87	0.60	0.86	0.91	1.03	1.07	17.04
Thailand	SET	1.04	1.32	1.52	1.20	0.82	0.86	0.72	0.68	4.57	1.49	0.88	0.54	24.98
China	SHCOMP	1.07	2.16	1.70	1.64	1.12	0.77	1.05	1.02	1.78	2.72	3.34	1.35	26.90
S.Africa	JALSH	0.79	1.75	2.86	1.41	1.10	1.12	0.64	0.87	0.75	0.95	1.10	1.21	20.92
Brazil	IBOV	1.28	2.09	2.39	1.74	1.11	1.42	1.20	1.15	1.04	1.59	2.02	2.05	25.54
Colombia	IGBC	1.04	3.95	5.99	2.42	1.09	1.57	0.79	1.21	0.89	1.74	1.32	1.28	37.93
Hungary	BUX	1.19	2.16	2.46	1.45	1.07	1.65	1.03	1.27	1.26	0.98	0.97	0.97	22.87
Egypt	HERMES	1.88	2.68	2.00	2.41	1.18	0.96	1.06	1.10	1.08	1.18	1.15	1.05	25.15
Indonesia	JCI	1.02	2.55	2.01	1.07	0.98	0.83	0.51	0.97	1.16	1.48	0.87	1.28	21.13
Argentina	IBG	1.38	2.48	2.00	1.51	0.98	1.05	0.83	1.12	0.90	1.08	1.73	1.51	23.05
Chile	IPSA	0.59	0.93	1.50	0.74	0.49	0.45	0.50	0.87	0.49	0.78	1.85	1.00	14.73
Mexico	MEXBOL	0.94	1.78	2.56	2.35	0.85	0.94	1.22	0.90	0.77	1.11	1.56	1.39	23.33
India	BSE SENSEX	1.64	2.55	3.25	1.97	0.67	1.06	0.94	0.58	1.48	1.16	1.54	1.95	27.57
India	S&P CNX NIFTY	1.67	2.77	3.22	1.93	0.72	1.06	0.93	0.61	1.51	1.15	1.56	2.00	28.03

* Annualised volatility is calculated by multiplying the standard deviation of the logarithmic returns with the square root of the number of trading days for the period.

Mathematically $\sigma = {}^{\sigma}\sqrt{t}$.

Source: Bloomberg Financial Services.

A comparison of volatility of indices across the developed and emerging market indices is shown in Table 2.16a. Among the emerging markets, Russia depicted the highest volatility (25.8%), followed by Argentina (25.5%) and Indonesia (21.8%). The volatility in Indian benchmark indices was a tad to bit higher than the comparative emerging markets. Among the developed markets, the annualised volatility was highest in Japan (26.9%) followed by Hong Kong (15.9%) and Euro region (15.9%).

Table 2.16a **Trends in Daily Volatility of International Stock Market Indices during 2013-14**

(in Per cent)

Country	Index	Apr.	May.	Jun.	Jul.	Aug.	Sep.	Oct.	Nov.	Dec.	Jan.	Feb.	Mar.	Annualised Volatility
1	2	3	4	5	6	7	8	9	10	11	12	13	14	15
DEVELOPED MARKETS														
USA	DJIA	0.7	0.6	1.1	0.4	0.5	0.6	0.8	0.5	0.7	0.7	0.8	0.7	10.8
USA	Nasdaq	1.1	0.7	1.0	0.5	0.8	0.5	0.9	0.8	0.6	1.0	0.9	0.9	13.1
UK	FTSE 100	0.8	0.9	1.2	0.9	0.8	0.5	0.6	0.5	0.7	0.6	0.6	0.8	12.2
Europe	DJ Stoxx	1.3	0.9	1.4	1.0	0.9	0.8	0.8	0.6	1.1	1.0	0.7	1.3	15.9
France	CAC	1.4	0.9	1.4	1.0	0.9	0.8	0.8	0.6	1.1	0.9	0.6	1.2	15.5
Germany	DAX	1.2	0.9	1.3	1.0	0.9	0.7	0.6	0.4	1.0	0.9	0.8	1.4	15.3
Australia	AS30	0.9	0.7	1.1	0.9	0.7	0.6	0.7	0.6	0.8	0.7	0.7	0.6	11.8
Japan	NKY	1.5	2.6	2.8	1.5	1.8	1.3	1.3	1.1	1.2	1.7	1.9	1.4	26.9
Hong Kong	HIS	1.1	1.0	1.4	1.2	1.0	0.9	0.8	1.0	0.6	0.9	1.1	1.0	15.9
Singapore	STI	0.4	0.7	1.0	0.7	0.7	0.9	0.4	0.4	0.6	0.6	0.6	0.6	10.5
EMERGING MARKETS														
Taiwan	TWSE	0.9	0.7	1.1	1.0	0.8	0.6	0.6	0.7	0.5	0.5	0.8	0.6	11.6
Russia	CRTX	1.3	1.6	1.6	1.4	1.1	1.4	0.9	1.2	0.8	1.2	1.3	3.9	25.8
Malaysia	KLCI	0.4	0.9	0.7	0.4	0.8	0.4	0.3	0.4	0.4	0.5	0.5	0.4	8.7
South Korea	KOSPI	0.8	0.7	1.2	0.9	0.9	0.5	0.6	0.8	0.6	0.8	0.7	0.7	12.5
Thailand	SET	1.1	0.9	1.7	1.6	1.3	1.8	1.0	1.2	0.8	1.6	0.8	0.6	21.1
China	SHCOMP	1.0	0.8	1.6	1.3	0.9	1.2	1.1	1.0	0.9	0.9	1.1	1.1	16.9
S. Africa	JALSH	1.1	1.1	1.6	1.1	0.9	0.8	0.6	0.8	1.0	0.7	0.7	0.8	14.9
Brazil	IBOV	1.5	1.0	1.7	1.6	1.5	1.5	1.1	1.2	1.1	1.1	1.5	1.3	21.4
Colombia	IGBC	1.0	0.6	1.2	1.0	0.6	0.4	0.4	1.1	0.8	0.6	1.0	0.9	13.4
Hungary	BUX	0.9	0.6	1.1	1.5	1.1	0.8	0.7	1.0	0.9	1.0	1.2	1.8	17.3
Egypt	HERMES	0.7	0.9	1.8	2.2	1.5	0.9	0.9	1.0	0.8	1.0	0.8	1.4	19.7
Indonesia	JCI	0.6	1.1	2.3	1.5	2.2	2.1	0.8	1.0	1.0	1.3	0.7	1.1	21.8
Argentina	IBG	1.2	2.0	1.1	1.3	1.1	1.6	2.0	2.2	1.4	1.7	1.8	1.1	25.5
Chile	IPSA	0.8	0.6	1.3	1.1	1.3	1.5	0.7	1.0	0.6	1.0	0.8	0.9	15.7
Mexico	MEXBOL	1.0	0.9	1.6	1.0	1.0	1.3	1.1	0.9	0.6	0.8	1.0	0.9	16.4
India	BSE Sensex	1.1	1.1	1.2	1.0	1.7	1.8	0.8	1.1	0.8	0.8	0.7	0.7	17.5
India	CNX Nifty	1.1	1.2	1.3	1.0	1.8	1.9	0.9	1.1	0.8	0.8	0.7	0.7	18.1

Price earnings ratio (P/E) is reflective of the valuation of shares (Table 2.17). At the end of March 2014, the P/E ratio of BSE Sensex and S&P CNX Nifty were 18.3 and 18.9 respectively as compared to 16.9 and 17.6 respectively as of end March 2013. Month-wise data indicate P/E ratios of BSE Sensex was lowest in September 2013 while that of CNX Nifty was lowest in August 2013. During 2013-14, except CNX Mid Cap and CNX PSE, there was an increase in the P/E ratios of all the indices analysed. P/E ratio of CNX IT was high as compared to other sectoral and mid-cap indices.

Table 2.17 **Price to Earnings Ratio**

Year/ Month	BSE Sensex	BSE 100	CNX Nifty	CNX Mid Cap	CNX IT	CNX Bank	CNX PSE	SX40
1	2	3	4	5	6	7	8	9
2008-09	13.7	15.3	14.3	9.8	11.5	7.7	18.1	Na
2009-10	21.3	21.1	22.3	15	23.5	17.7	15.3	Na
2010-11	21.2	20.7	22.1	17.7	26.6	18.5	15	Na
2011-12	17.8	18.8	18.7	18.1	20.9	15.3	15.4	Na
2012-13	16.9	16.0	17.6	16.7	19.3	13.6	9.9	Na
2013-14	18.3	17.8	18.9	14.3	21.3	14.3	9.6	20.3
Apr-13	17.5	18.6	17.9	17.3	15.8	14.8	10.5	19.2
May-13	17.6	16.7	18.0	17.8	16.9	14.6	10.1	19.6
Jun-13	17.2	16.2	17.8	16.3	17.6	13.7	9.3	19.2
Jul-13	17.2	15.9	17.1	15.8	20.3	11.6	8.4	18.8
Aug-13	17.0	14.4	15.8	12.7	21.6	10.3	6.4	17.2
Sep-13	16.8	15.9	16.8	12.9	21.7	11.0	6.9	18.2
Oct-13	18.3	17.3	18.2	13.8	22.4	12.9	7.3	19.1
Nov-13	17.6	16.9	18.4	14.0	21.9	12.9	8.4	19.4
Dec-13	18.2	17.3	18.7	14.8	23.7	13.2	8.7	20.5
Jan-14	17.1	16.3	17.7	14.0	23.2	11.7	8.2	19.3
Feb-14	17.2	16.4	17.7	14.1	23.6	12.0	8.6	19.3
Mar-14	18.3	17.8	18.9	14.3	21.3	14.3	9.6	20.3

2.16 GLOSSARY

Allotment

Allotment is the distribution of shares to the public during an offer. The normal rule of allocation is to allocate the shares in case of oversubscription on a proportionate basis. This, however, excludes the firm allotment portion.

Annual General Meeting (AGM)

The shareholder's meeting usually held at the end of each financial year to discuss the previous year performance and outlook.

Authorised Capital

The maximum equity capital a company can raise, which is mentioned in the Memorandum of Association and Articles of Association of the Company. However, share premium is excluded from the definition of authorised capital.

Book-building

In a book-building offer, the syndicate members decide the price range and the people decide the price of the issue based on a tender method.

Bankers to the Issue

Bankers to the issue are entities that are registered by SEBI and act as issue and collecting centres for IPO forms and cheques.

Brokers

Companies making public issues appoint brokers to obtain subscription. The managers to the issue distribute prospectuses and application forms to the brokers. These brokers form a very important link in the distribution value chain of financial products.

Brokerage

It is the commission paid to the brokers for the purchase and sale of Shares Bonus Issues. They are the shares issued to capitalise on the reserves and surplus of the company without charging the shareholders. From the accounting perspective, it involves a debit to the free reserves and a credit to the share capital.

Bridge Loan

A Bridge Loan is a loan that is used for a short duration of time until permanent financing is put in place. Companies that come out with an IPO issue access bridge finance for the interim period before the issue proceeds are actually realised.

Conditional Offer

An offer to purchase securities depending on the effectiveness of a registration statement and the pricing of an IPO.

Dematerialisation

Dematerialisation or "Demat" is a process of converting the physical securities into electronic form and storing in computers by a Depository. Securities present in the physical form are surrendered to the respective company which will then nullify them and credit the depository account.

Direct Public Offerings

Offering of securities to the public directly by an issuer without the assistance of any Investment Banking firm.

Draft Prospectus

A draft prospectus provides the information on the financials of the company, promoters, background, tentative issue price, etc. It is filed by the Lead Managers with SEBI to provide issue details. Overview of the draft prospectus can be seen on www.sebi.gov.in (SEBI's website). The final prospectus is printed after obtaining the clearance from SEBI and Registrar of Companies (ROC).

Bought-out Deals

A boughtout deal is a process by which an investor (usually the investment banker) buys out a significant portion of the equity of an unlisted company with a view to make it public within an agreed time frame.

Private Placement

A type of offering, exempted from registration that allows the issuing company to avoid registration requirements and save underwriting fees by offering company shares directly to institutional and accredited investors.

Rights Issues

If a company wants to increase its subscribed capital by allotment of further shares after 1 or 2 years of first allotment, it has to offer the shares to the existing shareholders first in proportion to the capital paid up on the shares held by them.

Global Depository Receipt (GDR)

They are negotiable certificates held by a bank of one country that represent a certain number of shares of a foreign stock traded on another exchange, usually a European exchange. The accounting requirements for GDRs are not as stringent as that for ADRs.

Firm Allotment

Out of the total amount the company proposes to raise in the market, some portion is fixed to the promoters in order to avoid diluting their stake in the company. This is called Firm Allotment.

Filing

A copy of prospectus having attached to the documents required to be submitted to the Registrar of Companies (ROC).

Flipping

The practice of subscribing to a new security offer and quickly selling it in the after market.

Secondary Offering

The sale of newly issued securities by an issuer which already has publicly traded securities.

Issued Capital

The capital proposed by the company to be raised from the market. Out of the issued capital the shares for which both application and allotment moneys are paid in full represents the paid-up capital.

Guest User

A person who is not a trading member (and hence cannot subscribe a new issue, but is eligible to view listings and prospectus of new issues.

IPO

Initial Public Offer (IPO) is a source of collecting money from the public for the first time in the market to fund for its projects. In return, the company gives the share to the investors in the company.

Investment Banking Firm

A financial entity acting as an underwriter or agent, and serves as an intermediary between an issuer of securities and the investing public. Investment bankers perform various services: financing, facilitating mergers, corporate restructuring activities, broking and trading on their own accounts, etc.

Issuer

An entity, like a company, municipality or government, that has the power to issue and distribute securities.

Joint Applications

Applications can be filled in single or in joint names (more than one person). In joint application, all payments will be made in favour of the first applicant.

Listing

The process of making the securities officially quoted on the notified stock exchange for the trade.

Multiple Applications

Two or more applications submitted on a single name are considered as multiple applications (An applicant is supposed to submit only one application irrespective of the number of shares applied for). The applications submitted for both electronic and physical equity shares are considered as multiple applications.

Minimum Subscription

The minimum shares the company needs to get from the public out of the total issue by the date of closure (presently/every company needs to raise 90% of the issued amount). Else, the company shall refund the whole amount received. This 90% has to be exclusive of the cheques that are not cleared.

Oversubscription

Any extra amount received by the company over the proposed capital.

Lead Manager

The lead manager is appointed by the company, which desires to raise capital from the market. The lead manager performs the following activities:

Designing the instrument

Pricing the issue

Timing the issue

Marketing

Preparing the offer document

Listing

Allotment/Refund.

Merchant Banker

Merchant banker facilitates the issue process.

Role of Merchant Banker

Directing and coordinating the activities with underwriters.

Registrars and bankers.

Assuring the investors of the soundness of the issue.

Promising companies/entrepreneurs/promoters to tap resources.

Complying with SEBI guidelines.

National Securities Depository Limited (NSDL)

This is an organisation, which is an intermediary between the Registrar and the company for dematerialisation of shares.

Net Offer

The rest of the issued capital after allotting to promoters, which would be raised from the public is called Net Offer.

Paid-up capital

The part of the issued capital of a company that has been paid up by the shareholders.

Preferential Shares

These are the shares issued at a fixed coupon rate to investors, which entails the foregoing of the right to participate in the management.

Price Earning (P/E) Ratio

P/E ratio is the ratio of a company's share price to earnings per share. It essentially shows the amount that an investor is willing to pay for every one rupee earned by the company.

Prospectus

The official offer document included in the registration statement filed with SEBI in conjunction with a public offer. The prospectus contains information about the offer of securities. It should be given to the original purchasers not later than the written confirmation of their purchase.

Road Show

The process by which underwriters acquaint potential institutional investors with the products, people and finances of a company planning to go public. Generally, this presentation is a face-to-face meeting. However, they are emerging on online and video presentations.

Registration Statement

A document that must be filed with SEBI before securities can be sold to the public. It contains information about the business of the issuer of the securities, how the proceeds of the offering will be used, audited financial statements, some background on the principal executives, and other pertinent data.

External Risk Factors

The external factors that influence the company's performance *vis-à-vis* share performance, which has to be spelt out by the company in the offer document. These are usually factors like changes in macroeconomic variables, which are outside the control of the company.

Internal Risk Factors

The internal factors that influence the company's performance *vis-à-vis* share performance, which has to be spelt out by the company in the offer document. These are usually factors pertaining to the company's internal operations and management, which are within the control of the company.

Management Perception of Risk Factors

The management's comment on the possible impact of the risk factors and a statement of how the company is prepared to tackle and overcome these risk factors.

Rights Issue

In order to avoid dilution of stake of existing shareholders, company issues "rights" shares in proportion to their current holding. This is done when the company plans to tap the market after their IPO.

Registrar

They play an administrative role in conducting a public issue. They are responsible for collecting information from the collecting banks, report to the companies, and lead managers about the issue collections. They advise the company regarding the closure or extension of closing date of the issue.

Underwriter

An investment banking firm, which enters a contract with the issuer of new securities to distribute them to the investing public.

Underwriting Commission

The commission paid to the underwriter for bearing the risk of an issue.

Venture Capital

An important source of financing used to fund start-up companies that do not have access to capital markets. Venture Capital typically entails significant investment risk but offers the potential for above-average future returns.

2.17 REVIEW QUESTIONS

Short Answer Questions

1. Define Merchant Banking.
2. Explain the term Public Issue.
3. What is right issue?
4. Define the term Private Placement.
5. Distinguish between financial appraisal and financial analysis.
6. What are the major components of project cost?
7. How can a project be financed?
8. Identify the various appraisals involved in the process of project appraisal.
9. How do you categorise the merchant bankers?

Essay Type Questions

1. Define Merchant Banking. Discuss the functions of merchant banking.
2. Comment on the development and trends in merchant banking in India.
3. Critically examine the regulatory framework for merchant bankers.
4. What is the code of conduct for merchant bankers in India? Comment on its appropriateness.
5. Discuss the nature and scope of merchant banking functions.
6. Discuss the various factors, which have to be kept in mind by a merchant banker while appraising a project.
7. Write a detailed note on public issue management.
8. Explain the factors, which have to be taken into account while pricing an issue.
9. Give an account about the growth of merchant banking services in India.

❋ ❋ ❋

CHAPTER 3

Mutual Funds

Objectives

The student, after studying the chapter, should be able to:

- State the meaning of the word 'Mutual Fund" and its reward.
- Give a brief historical account of Fund.
- Classify the Mutual Fund according to its nature.
- Apply different models to evaluate a Fund.
- Familiarise the regulatory aspects related to Mutual Fund.
- Explain the growth of Mutual Fund in India.

Structure:

3.1 Meaning
3.2 Evolution of Mutual Fund
3.3 Types of Mutual Fund Schemes
3.4 Financial Risk
3.5 Performance Measures of Mutual Funds
3.6 Mutual Fund Organisation
3.7 Advantages of Mutual Funds
3.8 Regulatory Aspects
3.9 Mutual Fund Taxation in India
3.10 Growth of Mutual Funds
3.11 Unit Trust of India

3.1 MEANING

Investment objectives vary from person to person. While somebody wants security, others might give more weightage to returns. Somebody else might want to plan for his child's education while yet somebody might be saving for the proverbial rainy day or even life after retirement. With objectives defying any range, it is obvious that the products required will vary as well. Though still at a nascent stage, Indian Mutual Fund industry offers a plethora of schemes and serves broadly all type of investors. The range of products includes equity funds, debt, liquid, gilt and balanced funds. There are also funds meant exclusively for young and old, small and large investors. Moreover, the set up of a legal structure ensures that the investors are not cheated out of their hard-earned money. It must have teeth to safeguard investors' interest. Benefits provided by them cut across the boundaries of investor category and thus create for them, a universal appeal.

Investors of all categories could choose to invest on their own in multiple options but opt for mutual funds for the sole reason that all benefits come in a package. A Mutual Fund is a trust that pools the savings of a number of investors who share a common financial goal.

Mutual funds represent pooled savings of numerous investors which are invested by professional fund managers as diversified portfolio to obtain optimum return on investments with least risk to the investors.

Mechanism of Mutual Fund Operation

The professional manager of a fund invests the collected money in different types of securities for and on behalf of the investors. (Refer Chart 3.1). The investment is based on the objectives for which the money is collected. The investment avenues could range from shares to debentures to money market instruments. The income earned through these investments and the capital appreciation realised by the scheme are shared by its unit holders in proportion to the number of units owned by them (pro rata). The received income again is invested

Chart 3.1

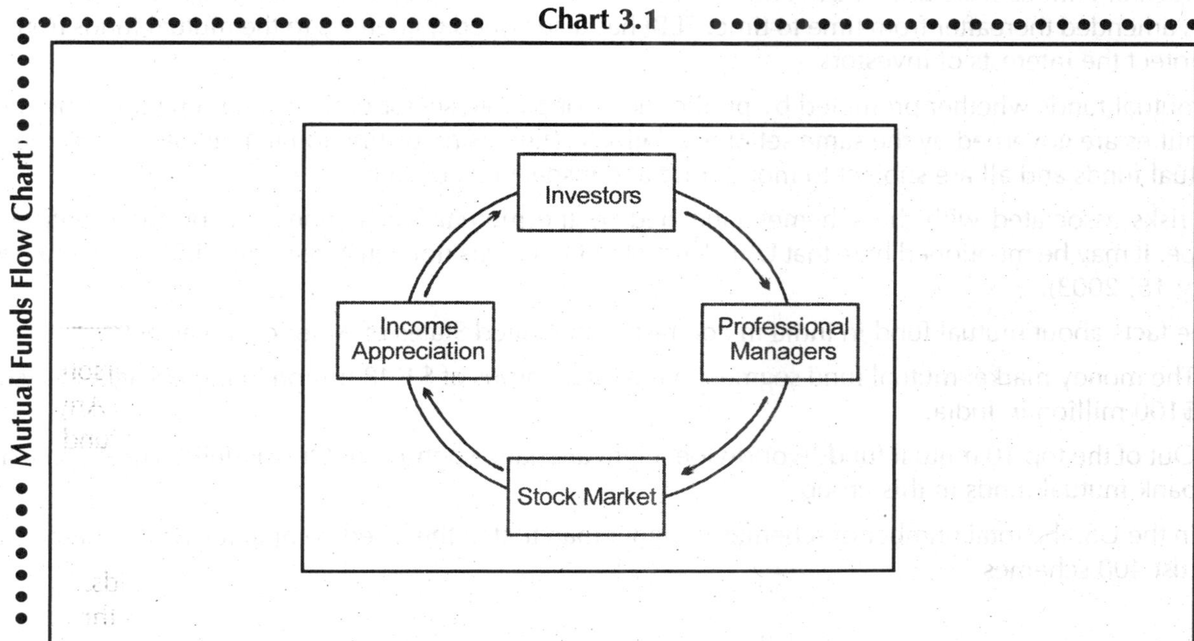

on funds by investors. Thus, a Mutual Fund is the most suitable investment for the common person as it offers an opportunity to invest in a diversified, professionally managed portfolio at a relatively low cost. Anybody with an investible surplus of as little as a few thousand rupees can invest in mutual funds. Each mutual fund scheme has a defined investment objective and strategy.

Reward for Investment

Mutual fund earns income by way of interest or dividend or both from the securities it holds. It deducts fees, operating expenses and management income and then passes the remainder to wealth holders through dividends on the mutual fund share. The dividend fluctuates with the income on mutual funds investments.

3.2 EVOLUTION OF MUTUAL FUND

Around the World

Mutual funds originated in Britain in the late 19th century. It developed in US in the late 19th century and early 20th century in principal money centres of North East. The funds originally evolved in both countries were primarily close ended. The crash of stock markets in 1929 led to the demise of these close-ended funds. The enactment of Securities Act of 1933, Investment Company Act of 1940 and Investment Advisors Act, 1940 led to the revival of mutual funds in the USA. In 1940, US had about 68 funds; in 1998, it exceeded 5,000. In 1965, in US, there were only 2% to 3% of US households who owned fund shares; whereas more than one-fourth of all US households invest in mutual fund today.

In India

Unit Trust of India (UTI) was the first mutual fund set up in India in the year 1963. In early 1990s, Government allowed public sector banks and institutions to set up mutual funds.

In the year 1992, Securities and Exchange Board of India (SEBI) Act was passed. The objectives of SEBI are to protect the interest of investors in securities, to promote the development of, and to regulate the securities market.

As far as mutual funds are concerned, SEBI formulates policies and regulates the mutual funds to protect the interest of the investors. SEBI notified regulations for the mutual funds in 1993. Thereafter, mutual funds sponsored by private sector entities were allowed to enter the capital market. The regulations were fully revised in 1996 and have been amended thereafter from time to time. SEBI has also issued guidelines to the mutual funds from time to time to protect the interests of investors.

All mutual funds whether promoted by public sector or private sector entities including those promoted by foreign entities are governed by the same set of regulations. There is no distinction in regulatory requirements for these mutual funds and all are subject to monitoring and inspections by SEBI.

The risks associated with the schemes launched by the mutual funds sponsored by these entities are of similar type. It may be mentioned here that Unit Trust of India (UTI) is not registered with SEBI as a mutual fund (as on January 15, 2003).

Some facts about mutual fund in India in contrast with United States of America are as below:

1. The money market mutual fund segment has a total corpus of $1.48 trillion in the US against a corpus of $100 million in India.
2. Out of the top 10 mutual funds worldwide, eight are bank-sponsored. Only Fidelity and Capital are non-bank mutual funds in this group.
3. In the US, the total number of schemes is higher than that of the listed companies while in India we have just 400 schemes.

4. Internationally, mutual funds are allowed to go short. In India, fund managers do not have such leeway.
5. In the US about 9.7 million households will manage their assets online by the year 2003, such a facility is not yet of avail in India.
6. Online trading is a great idea to reduce management expenses from the current 2% of total assets to about 0.75% of the total assets.
7. 72% of the care customer base of mutual funds in the top 50 broking firms in the US are expected to trade online by 2003.

3.3 TYPES OF MUTUAL FUND SCHEMES

Mutual fund can be classified according to its maturity period, and the investment objective of the investors (Refer Chart 3.2.)

Based on Maturity Period

A mutual fund scheme can be classified into open-ended scheme or close-ended scheme depending on its maturity period.

Open-ended Fund or Scheme: An open-ended fund is available for subscription and repurchase on a continuous basis. Repurchases are generally allowed at specified rates. The sale and repurchase prices are fixed by the mutual fund concerned from time to time. These do not have a fixed maturity. Investors can conveniently buy and sell units at Net Asset Value (NAV) related prices. The NAV prices are declared on a daily basis.

For example, UTI's Unit Scheme-64 (US-64) has no prescribed time limit when it would be redeemed. The essential feature of open-end schemes is liquidity.

Close-ended Schemes: Schemes that have a stipulated maturity period (e.g., 5-7 years) are called close-ended schemes. One can invest directly in the scheme at the time of the initial issue. Thereafter he can buy or sell the units of the scheme on the stock exchanges where they are listed. The market price at the stock exchange could vary from the scheme's NAV because of demand and supply situation, unit holders' expectations and other market factors.

One of the characteristics of the close-ended schemes is that they are generally traded at a discount to NAV. If maturity approaches, the discount rate narrows. Some close-ended schemes give an additional option of selling one's units directly to the Mutual Fund through periodic repurchase at NAV-related prices. SEBI Regulations ensure that at least one of the two exit routes is provided to the investor. These mutual funds schemes disclose NAV generally on weekly basis.

Based on Investment Objective

A scheme can also be classified as growth scheme, income scheme, or balanced scheme considering its investment objective. Such schemes may be open-ended or close-ended schemes as described earlier. Such schemes may be classified mainly as follows:

Growth or Equity-oriented Scheme: The aim of growth funds is to provide capital appreciation over the medium to long term. The investment is made in equity stock, which have above average growth potential. Such funds have comparatively high risks. These schemes provide different options to the investors like dividend option, capital appreciation, etc. and the investors may choose an option depending on their preferences. The investors must indicate the option in the application form. The mutual funds also allow the investors to change the options later. Growth schemes are good for investors having a long-term outlook seeking appreciation over a period of time. These schemes are not for investors seeking regular income or need their money back in the short-term.

This scheme is ideal for:

- Investors in their prime earning years.
- Investors seeking growth over the long-term.

Income or Debt-oriented Scheme: Income fund is established to maximise the current income (i.e., interest and dividend) of investors. Such schemes generally invest in fixed income securities such as bonds, corporate debentures, Government securities and money market instruments. Such funds are less risky compared to equity schemes. These funds are not affected because of fluctuations in equity markets. However, opportunities of capital appreciation are also limited in such funds. The NAVs of such funds are affected because of change in interest rates in the country. If the interest rates fall, NAVs of such funds are likely to increase in the short run and *vice versa*. However, long-term investors may not bother about these fluctuations.

Chart 3.2

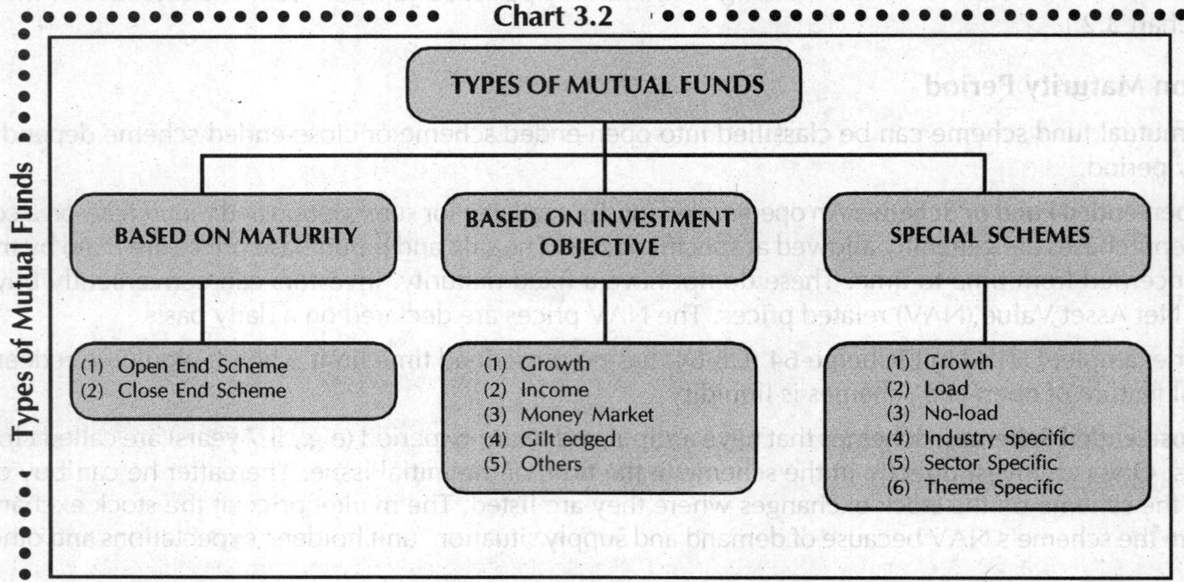

This scheme is ideal for:

- Retired people and others with a need for capital stability and regular income.
- Investors who need some income to supplement their earnings.

Balanced Fund: Some mutual funds are called as 'Balanced Funds' where assets are a mixture of equity shares and debentures. The aim of balanced funds is to provide both growth and regular income, as such schemes invest both in equities and fixed income securities in the proportion indicated in their offer documents. These are appropriate for investors looking for moderate growth. They generally invest 40-60% in equity and debt instruments. These funds are also affected because of fluctuations in share prices in the stock markets. However, NAVs of such funds are likely to be less volatile compared to pure equity funds.

This fund is ideal for:

- Investors looking for a combination of income and moderate growth.

Money Market or Liquid Fund: The aim of this money market fund is to provide easy liquidity, preservation of capital and moderate income. These funds are also income funds. These schemes invest exclusively in safer short-term instruments such as treasury bills, certificates of deposit, commercial paper, inter-bank call money, government securities, etc. Returns on these schemes fluctuate much less compared to other funds. These funds are appropriate for corporate and individual investors as a means to park their surplus funds for short periods.

Liquid fund is ideal for:

- Corporates and individual investors as a means to park their surplus funds for short periods or awaiting a more favourable investment alternative.

Gilt Fund: These funds invest exclusively in government securities. Government securities have no default risk. NAVs of these schemes also fluctuate due to change in interest rates and other economic factors as is the case with income or debt-oriented schemes.

Index Funds: Index Funds simply follow the pattern of the portfolio of a particular index such as the BSE Sensitive Index, S&P NSE 50 Index (Nifty), etc. These schemes invest in the securities in the same weightage comprising of an index. NAVs of such schemes would rise or fall in accordance with the rise or fall in the index, though not exactly by the same percentage due to some factors known as "tracking error" in technical terms. Necessary disclosures in this regard are made in the offer document of the mutual fund scheme. There are also exchange traded index funds launched by the mutual funds, which are traded on the stock exchanges.

Other Schemes

Tax Saving Schemes: These schemes offer tax rebates to the investors under tax laws as prescribed from time to time. This is made possible because the Government offers tax incentives for investment in specified avenues. For example, investments made in Equity Linked Savings Schemes (ELSS) and Pension Schemes are allowed as deduction under Section 88 of the Income Tax Act, 1961. The Act also provides opportunities to investors to save capital gains under Section 54EA and 54EB by investing in Mutual Funds, provided the capital asset has been sold prior to April 1, 2000 and the amount is invested before September 30, 2000. The details of such tax savings are provided in the relevant offer documents.

This scheme is ideal for:

- Investors seeking tax rebates.

Special Schemes

This category includes index schemes as already seen, that attempt to replicate the performance of a particular index such as the BSE Sensex or the NSE 50, or industry specific schemes (which invest in specific industries) or sectoral schemes (which invest exclusively in segments such as 'A' Group shares or initial public offerings). Index fund schemes are ideal for investors who are satisfied with a return approximately equal to that of an index. Sectoral fund schemes are ideal for investors who have already decided to invest in a particular sector or segment. Keep in mind that any one scheme may not meet all your requirements for all time. You need to place your money judiciously in different schemes to be able to get the combination of growth, income and stability that is right for you. Higher the return one seeks, higher the risk one should be prepared to take. A few frequently used terms are explained below:

Load Funds: A Load Fund is one that charges a commission for entry or exit. That is, each time you buy or sell units in the fund, a commission will be payable. Typically, entry and exit loads range from 1% to 2%. It could be worth paying the load, if the fund has a good performance history.

No-load Funds: A No-load Fund is one that does not charge a commission for entry or exit. That is, no commission is payable on purchase or sale of units in the fund. The advantage of a no-load fund is that the entire corpus is put to work.

Industry Specific Schemes: Industry Specific Schemes invest only in the industries specified in the offer document. The investment of these funds is limited to specific industries like InfoTech, FMCG, Pharmaceuticals, etc.

Sectoral Schemes: These are the funds, which invest in the securities of only those sectors, or industries as specified in the offer documents, *e.g.*, Pharmaceuticals, Software, Fast Moving Consumer Goods (FMCG), Petroleum stocks, etc. The returns in these funds are dependent on the performance of the respective sectors or industries.

While these funds may give higher returns, they are more risky compared to diversified funds. Investors need to keep a watch on the performance of those sectors or industries and must exit at an appropriate time. They may also seek advice of an expert on a continuous basis.

3.4 FINANCIAL RISK

Understanding Risks: Every investment entails risk. Mutual funds too are not risk-free investments. Even funds invested in government bonds (sovereign papers) are susceptible to some kinds of risk.

Risk: Risk is a measure of the possibility that the investor will not receive an expected return on his investment. Risk and reward move hand in hand. The greater the risk that an investment may lose money, the greater its potential for providing a substantial return. The following are some risks associated with investment in mutual funds.

Market Risk: Market risk exposes one to a potential loss of principal. In all likelihood, the market value of a stock will fluctuate based on factors such as developments affecting the company's financial status, earnings of the company or impact of economic slowdown on the company. Likewise, debt funds too are subject to market risk. Prices of bonds and government securities fluctuate with change in interest rates.

One could minimise the market risk by diversifying among a variety of instruments rather than investing his money in one or two stocks. Diversification helps minimise risks. Thus, when one asset class is adversely affected by market or other conditions, another class may be less affected. Because mutual funds invest in many companies, they offer the best opportunity to diversify.

Interest Rate Risk: The value of a fixed income security will drop as interest rates rise. It is called interest rate risk. Government security prices are inversely related to interest rates. If interest rates decline, then the prices of securities increase and *vice versa*. This risk cannot be avoided.

Example: Suppose a person buys a bond for ₹ 100 with a coupon rate of 10%. In other terms, the person should get ₹ 110 at the end of the year. If the RBI announces a hike in the bank rate, then the market yield for the duration of the bond increased, say to 11%. The prices of the bond will fall around to ₹ 90.91 in order to adjust to the market yield. This is termed as interest rate risk in financial jargon. It is precisely what happened in 2000 when RBI had hiked the interest rates.

An investor stands to benefit in the opposite scenario, when the interest rates are cut, as then the prices of bonds go up, leading to better returns from the fund. For example, the interest rate in the above example, falls to 9%. A person still gets ₹ 10 as interest. In order to align the amount received to the prevailing market yield, the price of the bond adjusts to ₹ 111.11. In this case, the investor is better of by selling it at ₹ 111.11 than holding it to its maturity, as then he will only get ₹ 110.

Inflation Risk: The return on investments will not increase with rising consumer prices. It is called inflation risk. Conservative instruments like debt funds provide less return over time. They are more prone to the inflation risk.

Though this risk cannot be avoided, one can manage it by investing a small portion in equity mutual funds. Equity funds always provide higher returns over a period. In comparison, debt funds give less return.

Business Risk: A company issuing a security may not be financially sound due to factors like poor management, low product demand, or huge operating expenses. It is known as business risk. Such situations can result in a decline in the security's value. Since mutual funds invest in a variety of companies, the effect of such a risk spreads out.

Credit Risk: An issuer will default on a fixed income security by failing to pay interest or principal when due. It is called as the credit risk. Most of the bond instruments are rated by rating agencies. The higher the rating given to the bond, the higher is the credit quality implying low credit risk and *vice versa*.

This risk can be limited by investing in mutual funds having a high exposure to quality paper with rating of AA/AAA which denotes high credit quality.

Political Risk: Political events may unfavourably influence the value of a security. It is known as political risk. Other political risks could include wars, change in government, etc. Political risks cannot be avoided. However, no two companies will be affected in a similar manner when any change in law or a new legislation takes place.

Liquidity Risk: A mutual fund's underlying securities, *i.e.*, low profile securities cannot be sold at a fair price when the need arises. It affects the liquidity of a security. It is known as liquidity risk. Hence, marketability of a security is a very important consideration.

One can minimise liquidity risk by investing in securities of the actively traded companies. In an open-ended scheme, one can enter and exit at his convenience. Close-ended funds do not give an investor an option to exit at his convenience.

Timing Risk: Buying or selling a security at the wrong time is leading to this risk. For example, there is the chance that a few days after an investor sells a fund it will go up in value or there is decline in value of a fund after he buys it. The best way to counter market timing is to invest systematically. He can actually take advantage of short-term market volatility by investing a fixed amount on a regular basis to build a portfolio over a period. This approach, called rupee-cost averaging, lets one buy more mutual fund units when NAVs are low and fewer units when NAVs are high.

Some of the risks stated above can be avoided through strategic planning. If investors were conservative, it would make sense if they invest in schemes, which are not affected by the swings of the stock market.

3.5 PERFORMANCE MEASURES OF MUTUAL FUNDS

Past performance alone cannot be indicative of future performance. It is, frankly the only quantitative way to judge how good a fund is at present. Therefore, there is a need to assess the past performance of different mutual funds correctly.

The performance of a mutual fund, in general, can be evaluated by using the beginning and the end period net asset values (NAVs) as follows:

$$R_p = ((NAV_t - NAV_{T-1}) + D_1 + C_1) / NAV_{T-1}$$

The one period rate of return for a mutual fund (R_p) is defined as the change in net asset value (NAV) plus its cash disbursements (D) and capital gains disbursements (C). Net asset values of the fund are adjusted for bonus and rights.

Net Asset Value (NAV)

The net asset value of the fund is the cumulative market value of the assets of the fund net of its liabilities. In other words, if the fund is dissolved or liquidated, by selling off all the assets in the fund, this is the amount that the shareholders would collectively own. This gives rise to the concept of net asset value per unit, which is the value, represented by the ownership of one unit in the fund. It is calculated simply by dividing the net asset value of the fund by the number of units. However, most people refer loosely to the NAV per unit as NAV, ignoring the "per unit". We also abide by the same convention.

Calculation of NAV

The most important part of the calculation is the valuation of the assets owned by the fund. Once it is calculated, the NAV is simply the net value of assets divided by the number of units outstanding. The detailed methodology for the calculation of the asset value is given below.

Asset value is equal to = Sum of market value of shares or debentures

+ Liquid assets or cash held, if any

+ Dividends or interest accrued

– Amount due on unpaid assets

– Expenses accrued but not paid

Details on the above items:

For liquid shares or debentures, valuation is done on the basis of the last or closing market price on the principal exchange where the security is traded.

For liquid and unlisted and/or thinly traded shares or debentures, the value has to be estimated. For shares, this could be the book value per share or an estimated market price if suitable benchmarks are available. For debentures and bonds, value is estimated on the basis of yields of comparable liquid securities after adjusting for illiquidity. The value of fixed interest-bearing securities moves in a direction opposite to interest rate changes. Valuation of debentures and bonds is a big problem since most of them are unlisted and thinly traded. This gives considerable leeway to the AMCs on valuation and some of the AMCs are believed to take advantage of this and adopt flexible valuation policies depending on the situation.

Interest is payable on debentures or bonds on a periodic basis say every 6 months. But, with every passing day, interest is said to be accrued, at the daily interest rate, which is calculated by dividing the periodic interest payment with the number of days in each period. Thus, accrued interest on a particular day is equal to the daily interest rate multiplied by the number of days since the last interest payment date.

Usually, dividends are proposed at the time of the Annual General Meeting and become due on the record date. There is a gap between the dates on which it becomes due and the actual payment date. In the intermediate period, it is deemed to be "accrued".

Expenses including management fees, custody charges, etc. are calculated on a daily basis.

Return alone should not be considered as the basis of measurement of the performance of a mutual fund scheme. It should also include the risk taken by the fund manager because different funds will have different levels of risk attached to them. Risk associated with a fund, in a general, can be defined as variability in the returns generated by it. The higher the fluctuations in the returns of a fund during a given period, higher will be the risk associated with it. These fluctuations in the returns generated by a fund are resultant of two guiding forces.

First, general market fluctuations, which affect all the securities, present in the market, called market risk or systematic risk and second, fluctuations due to specific securities present in the portfolio of the fund, called unsystematic risk. The total risk of a given fund is the sum of these two and is measured in terms of standard deviation of returns of the fund.

Systematic risk, on the other hand, is measured in terms of Beta. It represents fluctuations in the NAV of the fund *vis-à-vis* market. The more responsive the NAV of a mutual fund is to the changes in the market; higher will be its beta. Beta is calculated by relating the returns on a mutual fund with the returns in the market. Unsystematic risk can be diversified through investments in a number of instruments. Systematic risk cannot be diversified. By using the risk-return relationship, we try to assess the competitive strength of the mutual funds *vis-à-vis* one another in a better way.

In order to determine the risk-adjusted returns of investment portfolios, several eminent authors have worked since 1960s to develop composite performance indices to evaluate a portfolio by comparing alternative portfolios within a particular risk class. The most important and widely used measures of performance are:

1. The Treynor Measure
2. The Sharpe Measure

3. Jenson Model
4. Eugene Fama Model

3.5.1. The Treynor Measure

Jack Treynor developed this model. The model evaluates funds based on Treynor's Index. This index is a ratio of return generated by the fund over and above risk-free rate of return (generally taken to be the return on securities backed by the government, as there is no credit risk associated), during a given period and systematic risk associated with it (beta). Symbolically, it can be represented as:

$$\text{Treynor's Index } (T_i) = (R_i - R_f)/B_i$$

where, R_i represents return on fund, R_f is risk-free rate of return and B_i is beta of the fund.

All risk-averse investors would like to maximise this value. While a high and positive Treynor's Index shows a superior risk-adjusted performance of a fund, a low and negative Treynor's Index is an indication of unfavourable performance.

3.5.2. The Sharpe Measure

William Sharpe developed this model. The model is named after his name, Sharpe Ratio. It is a ratio of returns generated by the fund over and above risk-free rate of return and the total risk associated with it. According to Sharpe, it is the total risk of the fund that the investors are concerned about. So, the model evaluates funds on the basis of reward per unit of total risk. Symbolically, it can be written as:

$$\text{Sharpe Index } (S_i) = (R_i - R_f)/S_i$$

where, S_i is standard deviation of the fund.

While a high and positive Sharpe Ratio shows a superior risk-adjusted performance of a fund, a low and negative Sharpe Ratio is an indication of unfavourable performance.

Comparison of Sharpe and Treynor

Sharpe and Treynor measures are similar in one aspect. They both divide the risk premium by a numerical risk measure. The total risk is appropriate when we are evaluating the risk-return relationship for well-diversified portfolios. On the other hand, the systematic risk is the relevant measure of risk when we are evaluating less than fully diversified portfolios or individual stocks. For a well-diversified portfolio, the total risk is equal to systematic risk. Rankings based on total risk (Sharpe Measure) and systematic risk (Treynor Measure) should be identical for a well-diversified portfolio, as the total risk is reduced to systematic risk. Therefore, a poorly diversified fund that ranks higher on Treynor Measure, compared with another fund that is highly diversified, will rank lower on Sharpe Measure.

3.5.3. Jenson Model

Michael Jenson developed this model. Jenson's model proposes another risk-adjusted performance measure. It is also referred to as the Differential Return Method. It involves evaluation of the returns that the fund has generated over the returns actually expected out of the fund given the level of its systematic risk. The surplus between the two returns is called Alpha. It measures the performance of a fund compared with the actual returns over the period. Required return of a fund at a given level of risk (B_i) can be calculated as:

$$R_i = R_f + B_i (R_m - R_f)$$

where, R_m is average market return during the given period.

After calculating it, alpha can be obtained by subtracting required return from the actual return of the fund.

Higher alpha represents superior performance of the fund and *vice versa*. Limitation of this model is that it considers only systematic risk, not the entire risk associated with the fund and an ordinary investor cannot mitigate unsystematic risk, as his knowledge of market is primitive.

3.5.4. Eugene Fama Model

The Eugene Fama model is an extension of Jenson model. This model compares the performance, measured in terms of returns, of a fund with the required return commensurate with the total risk associated with it. The difference between these two is taken as a measure of the performance of the fund and is called net selectivity.

The net selectivity represents the stock selection skill of the fund manager, as it is the excess returns over and above the return required to compensate for the total risk taken by the fund manager. Higher value of which indicates that fund manager has earned returns well above the return commensurate with the level of risk taken by him.

Required return can be calculated as: $R_i = R_f + S_i/S_m (R_m - R_f)$

where, S_m is standard deviation of market returns.

The net selectivity is then calculated by subtracting this required return from the actual return of the fund.

Suitability of Models

Among the above performance measures, two models namely, Treynor measure and Jenson model use systematic risk based on the premise that the unsystematic risk is diversifiable. These models are suitable for large investors like institutional investors with high risk taking capacities as they do not face paucity of funds and can invest in a number of options to dilute some risks. For them, a portfolio can be spread across a number of stocks and sectors. However, Sharpe measure and Fama model that consider the entire risk associated with fund are suitable for small investors, as the ordinary investor lacks the necessary skill and resources for diversification. Moreover, the selection of the fund based on superior stock selection ability of the fund manager will also help in safeguarding the money invested largely. The investment in funds that have generated big returns at higher levels of risks leaves the money all the more prone to risks of all kinds that may exceed the individual investors' risk appetite.

3.6 MUTUAL FUND ORGANISATION

A Mutual Fund can be constituted either as a corporate entity or a trust. Indian banks when permitted to operate mutual funds were asked to create trusts to run these funds. The basic difference between a corporation and a trust is that in the case of the company, the liability is limited whereas in case of the trust it is unlimited. In addition, a corporation enjoys the status of a separate legal entity who can act on its behalf. A trust has to work on behalf of its trustees. Indian banks operating mutual funds had made a convincing plea before the government to allow their mutual funds to constitute them as 'Asset Management Companies'. The Department of Company Affairs, Ministry of Law, Justice and Company Affairs have issued guidelines in respect of registration of Asset Management Companies (AMCs), in consultation with Securities and Exchange Board of India (SEBI), as follows:

(a) Mutual Funds are to be established in the forms of trusts under the Indian Trusts Act and are to be operated by separate Asset Management Companies (AMCs) or it can be initiated as a company under the Indian Companies Act, 1956. Accordingly, no company can register an AMC under the Companies Act, 1956 without the Memorandum and Articles of Association being approved by SEBI.

(b) AMCs shall have a minimum net worth of ₹ 5 crores.

(c) AMCs and trustees of mutual funds are to be two separate legal entities and that an AMC cannot act as a manager for any other fund.

(d) Mutual funds dealing exclusively with money market instruments are to be regulated by the Reserve Bank of India.

(e) Mutual funds dealing primarily in the capital market instruments and partly in money market instruments are to be regulated by the SEBI.

(f) All schemes floated by mutual funds are to be registered with SEBI.

Major Players Helping in Running Mutual Fund

Major Players who help in running a Mutual Fund are as follows:

(a) Registrars and Transfer Agents

1. He receives and processes the application form of investors.
2. He issues unit certificate.
3. He maintains detailed records of unit holders.
4. He purchases, sells, transfers and redeems the unit certificate.
5. He issues income warrants, broker cheques, etc.
6. He creates security interest on units for allowing loans against them.

(b) Advertiser

1. He helps funds to prepare a media plan for marketing the fund.
2. He issues or buys the space in newspapers and other e-media for advertising.
3. He arranges for hoarding at public places.

(c) Advisor/Manager

It is generally a corporate entity who does the following jobs:

1. It extends professional advice on the fund's investments.
2. It advises on Asset Management Services.

(d) Trustees

Trustees provide the overall management services and charge management fee.

(e) Custodian

A custodian is a corporate body. It does the following functions:

1. It holds securities.
2. It receives and delivers securities.
3. It collects income on the securities.
4. It holds and processes cash.

Besides the above, other players are as follows:

(f) Fund Administrator

(g) Fund Accounting Services

(h) Legal Advisors

(i) Fund Officers

(j) Underwriters/Distributors

(k) Legal Advisors

In India, the mutual funds have taken the services of the following outside agencies:

(a) Registrars and Transfer Agents,

(b) Advertisers,

(c) Legal Advisors, and

(d) Custodians.

3.7 ADVANTAGES OF MUTUAL FUNDS

Mutual funds represent pooled savings of numerous investors invested by professional fund managers as diversified portfolio to obtain optimum return on investments with least risk to the investors. The dividend fluctuates with the income on mutual funds investments. Mutual Funds are advantageous to individual investors in relation to their direct involvement in investment portfolio activity covering the following aspects.

Reduced risk: Mutual funds provide small investors access to reduced investment risk resulting from diversification, economies of scale in transaction cost and professional finance management.

Diversified investment: Small investors participate in larger basket of securities and share the benefits of efficiently managed portfolio by experts, and are freed of keeping any records of share certificates, etc. of various companies, tax rules, etc.

Stress free investment: Investors get freedom from emotional stress involved in buying or selling securities. Mutual funds relieve them from such stress as it is managed by professional experts who act scientifically with right timings in buying and selling for their clients.

Revolving type of investment: Automatic reinvestment of dividends and capital gains provides relief to the members of mutual funds.

Selection and timings of investment: Expertise in stock selection and timing is made available to investors so that invested fund generates higher returns to them.

Wide investment opportunities: Availment of wider investment opportunities that create an increased level of liquidity for the fund holders become possible because of package of more liquid securities in the portfolio of mutual funds. These securities could be converted into cash without any loss of time.

Investment care: Care for a security is available through mutual fund to the investors relieving them from various rules and regulations.

Low investment and easy liquidity: Initial investment in units is as low as ₹ 1,000 (100 units of ₹ 10 each) prompting investors to have saving habits which they encash as per the term of the issue either through direct repurchase by mutual fund or through secondary market of listed securities.

Tax benefits: Investors are offered tax exemptions on investments made in mutual funds with a view to motivate them to invest in mutual funds and provide finance to industry.

Advantages from Investment in Money Market Mutual Funds

1. Individual with short-term investible funds park their funds temporarily in money market instruments until some long-term avenues open.
2. Individual investors share through MMMFs the economic advantages of bulk purchases, expertise of professional fund managers and high yield on short-term investments.
3. Individual investors are benefited in terms of high safety and liquidity of their investments, which MMMFs provide because of their early redemption features and reduced risk resulting from diversified investments.
4. Individual saving habits get stimulated with readily available investment avenue for the short-term.
5. Individual savers cannot invest huge sums required for money market instruments, as the minimum investment requirements for each of the money market instruments are very high because MMMFs are the vehicles of raising huge funds for short-term requirements.

3.8 REGULATORY ASPECTS

Schemes of a Mutual Fund

1. The asset management company shall launch no scheme unless the trustees approve such scheme and a copy of the offer document has been filed with the Board.
2. Every mutual fund shall along with the offer document of each scheme pay filing fees.
3. The offer document shall contain disclosures which are adequate in order to enable the investors to make informed investment decision including the disclosure on maximum investments proposed to be made by the scheme in the listed securities of the group companies of the sponsor. A close-ended scheme shall be fully redeemed at the end of the maturity period. "Unless a majority of the unit holders otherwise decide for its rollover by passing a resolution."
4. The mutual fund and asset management company shall be liable to refund the application money to the applicants —
   (I) If the mutual fund fails to receive, the minimum subscription amount referred to in clause (a) of sub-regulation (1);
   (II) If the moneys received from the applicants for units are in excess of subscription as referred to in clause (b) of sub-regulation (1).
5. The asset management company shall issue to the applicant, whose application has been accepted, unit certificates or a statement of accounts specifying the number of units allotted to the applicant as soon as possible but not later than six weeks from the date of closure of the initial subscription list and/or from the date of receipt of the request from the unit holders in any open-ended scheme.

Rules Regarding Advertisement

The offer document and advertisement materials shall not be misleading or contain any statement or opinion, which are incorrect or false.

Investment Objectives and Valuation Policies

The price at which the units may be subscribed or sold and the price at which such units may at any time be repurchased by the mutual fund shall be made available to the investors.

General Obligations

(a) Every asset management company for each scheme shall keep and maintain proper books of accounts, records and documents, for each scheme so as to explain its transactions and to disclose at any point of time the financial position of each scheme and in particular give a true and fair view of the state of affairs of the fund and intimate to the Board the place where such books of accounts, records and documents are maintained.

(b) The financial year for all the schemes shall end as of March 31 of each year. Every mutual fund or the asset management company shall prepare in respect of each financial year an annual report and annual statement of accounts of the schemes and the fund as specified in Eleventh Schedule.

(c) Every mutual fund shall have the annual statement of accounts audited by an auditor who is not in any way associated with the auditor of the asset management company.

Procedure for Action in Case of Default

On and from the date of the suspension of the certificate or the approval, as the case may be, the mutual fund, trustees or asset management company, shall cease to carry on any activity as a mutual fund, trustee or asset management company, during the period of suspension, and shall be subject to the directions of the Board with regard to any records, documents, or securities that may be in its custody or control, relating to its activities as mutual fund, trustees or asset management company.

Restrictions on Investments

1. A mutual fund scheme shall not invest more than 15% of its NAV in debt instruments issued by a single issuer, which are rated not below investment grade by a credit rating agency authorised to carry out such activity under the Act. Such investment limit may be extended to 20% of the NAV of the scheme with the prior approval of the Board of trustees and the Board of asset management company.
2. A mutual fund scheme shall not invest more than 10% of its NAV in unrated debt instruments issued by a single issuer and the total investment in such instruments shall not exceed 25% of the NAV of the scheme. All such investments shall be made with the prior approval of the Board of trustees and the Board of asset management company.
3. No mutual fund under all its schemes should own more than 10% of any company's paid-up capital carrying voting rights.
4. Such transfers are done at the prevailing market price for quoted instruments on spot basis. The securities so transferred shall be in conformity with the investment objective of the scheme to which such transfer has been made.
5. A scheme may invest in another scheme under the same asset management company or any other mutual fund without charging any fees, provided that aggregate inter-scheme investment made by all schemes under the same management or in schemes under the management of any other asset management company shall not exceed 5% of the net asset value of the mutual fund.
6. The initial issue expenses in respect of any scheme may not exceed 6% of the funds raised under that scheme.
7. Every mutual fund shall buy and sell securities on the basis of deliveries and shall in all cases of purchases, take delivery of relative securities and in all cases of sale, deliver the securities and shall in no case put itself in a position whereby it has to make short sale or carry forward transaction or engage in badla finance.
8. Every mutual fund shall get the securities purchased or transferred in the name of the mutual fund on account of the concerned scheme, wherever investments are intended to be of long-term nature.
9. Pending deployment of funds of a scheme in securities in terms of investment objectives of the scheme a mutual fund can invest the funds of the scheme in short-term deposits of scheduled commercial banks.
10. No mutual fund scheme shall make any investment in:
    (I) Any unlisted security of an associate or group company of the sponsor; or
    (II) Any security issued by way of private placement by an associate or group company of the sponsor; or

    The listed securities of group companies of the sponsor which is in excess of 30% of the net assets [of all the schemes of a mutual fund].
11. No mutual fund scheme shall invest more than 10% of its NAV in the equity shares or equity-related instruments of any company. But, the limit of 10% shall not be applicable for investments in index fund, sector, or industry specific scheme.
12. A mutual fund scheme shall not invest more than 5% of its NAV in the equity shares or equity-related investments in case of open-ended scheme and 10% of its NAV in case of close-ended scheme.

Rights of Mutual Fund Unit Holder

An investor, in a mutual fund scheme is governed by the SEBI (Mutual Funds) Regulations, accordingly he is entitled to:

- Receive unit certificates or statements of accounts confirming the title within 6 weeks from the date of closure of the subscription or within 6 weeks from the date of request for a unit certificate is received by the Mutual Fund.
- Receive information about the investment policies, investment objectives, financial position and general affairs of the scheme.
- Receive dividend within 42 days of their declaration and receive the redemption or repurchase proceeds within 10 days from the date of redemption or repurchase.
- Vote in accordance with the Regulations to:
  - (a) Approve or disapprove any change in the fundamental investment policies of the scheme, which are likely to modify the scheme or affect the interest of the unitholder. The dissenting unitholder has a right to redeem the investment.
  - (b) Change the Asset Management Company.
  - (c) Wind up the schemes.

Inspect the documents of the mutual funds specified in the scheme's offer document.

3.9 MUTUAL FUND TAXATION IN INDIA

Taxation policies in India with respect to mutual funds have varied over the years. The purpose, over all these years, in part, has been to encourage the growth of the industry. Currently, a variety of tax laws applies to mutual funds. Tax provisions applying to fund investments and funds themselves in respect of various matters are listed below:

(1) Capital Gains

Units of mutual fund schemes are treated as long-term capital assets if they are held for a period more than 12 months. In this case, the unit holder has the option to pay capital gains tax at either 20% (with indexation) or 10% without indexation.

(2) Tax Deducted at Source (TDS)

For any income credited or paid by a fund, no tax is deducted or withheld at source. The relevant Sections in the Income Tax Act governing this provision are Section 194K and 196A.

(3) Wealth Tax

Mutual fund units are not currently treated as assets under Section 2 of the Wealth Tax Act and are therefore not liable to tax.

(4) Income from Units

Any income received from units of the schemes of a mutual fund specified under Section 23(D) is exempt under Section 10(33) of the Act. While Section 10(23D) exempts income of specified mutual funds from tax (which currently includes all mutual funds operating in India), Section 10(33) exempts income from funds in the hands of the unitholders. However, this does not mean that there is no tax at all on income distributions by mutual funds.

(5) Income Distribution Tax

As per prevailing tax laws income distributed by schemes other than open-end equity schemes is subject to tax at 10% (plus surcharge of 2%). For this purpose, equity schemes have been defined to be those schemes that have more than 50% of their assets in the form of equity. Open-end equity schemes have been left out of the purview of this distribution tax for a period of three years beginning from April 1999.

(6) Section 88

The investment in mutual funds designated as Equity-Linked Saving Scheme (ELSS) qualifies for rebate under Section 88. The maximum amount that can be invested in these schemes is ₹ 10,000, therefore the maximum tax benefit available works out to ₹ 2,000. Apart from ELSS schemes, the benefit of Section 88 is also available in select schemes of some funds such as UTI, ULIP, KP Pension Plan, etc. Now, an investor can invest a maximum of ₹ 1,00,000 in MF for claiming tax exemption.

3.10 GROWTH OF MUTUAL FUNDS

During 04-07, the fundamentals are strong and macroeconomic indicators are strong, one would expect most sectors to perform well and are expecting a Bull Run in the market. The market is expected to gain around 20-25% and mutual funds will be able to provide those kind of returns enabling one to take advantage of the markets. If a fund is smartly managed, it can even beat the market and provide superior returns to the market.

- The economy slowly picked up after September 11 issues in year 2002. However, poor monsoon affected the stock markets.
- Disinvestment stories, Securitisation Bill, Security Interest Bill, entrance of IT players in IT segment and other positive news boosted the stock market and that helped the equity funds to post the good returns.
- Fixed income markets witnessed a steep decline in interest rates of around 300 basis points in 2001.

How does one know whether the fund sector in a country has grown or not?

There are several yardsticks available to measure the performance of a fund sector. They are:

(a) Asset Under Management (AUM),

(b) Number of Unit Schemes in Operation,

(c) Net Asset Value,

(d) Return, and

(e) Volume of Investment expressed in Rupee Value.

3.10.1. Asset Under Management (AUM)

What is meant by the term 'asset under management'? Before understanding the term 'Asset Under Management', it is required to know about Asset Management Companies. A mutual fund is a collection of investments. It is a pool of money, the combined contributions of a number of individuals. While the mutual fund is a collection of moneys, it requires some person or body to mobilise and manage these assets. This entity is usually an organisation, aptly known as an asset management company. The AMC is thus the physical entity, the organisation, the company, which generates the collective investment from the public with a view to invest in securities and generate returns.

By virtue of its mobilisation function, the AMC has offices or branches in a number of cities. These branches collect money from investors and are one of the visible faces of the mutual fund company. As this money has to be invested and managed, the AMC has an investment team. The collected fund is to be managed in order to bring the expected return from the stock and money market. The fund is generally known as Asset Under Management (AUM). This has become a yardstick to measure the performance of mutual fund at a particular point of time.

As at the end of January 2003, there were 33 mutual funds with total assets of ₹ 1,21,805 crores. The Unit Trust of India with ₹ 44,541 crores of assets under management was way ahead of other mutual funds. In February 2003, following the repeal of the Unit Trust of India Act, 1963 UTI was bifurcated into two separate entities. One is the Specified Undertaking of the Unit Trust of India with assets under management of ₹ 29,835 crores as at the end of January 2003, representing broadly, the assets of US-64 scheme, assured return and certain other schemes. The Specified Undertaking of Unit Trust of India, functioning under an administrator and under the rules framed by Government of India and does not come under the purview of the Mutual Fund Regulations. The second is the UTI Mutual Fund Ltd. sponsored by SBI, PNB, BOB and LIC. It is registered with SEBI and functions under the Mutual Fund Regulations. With the bifurcation of the erstwhile UTI which had in March 2000 more than ₹ 76,000 crores of assets under management and with the setting up of a UTI Mutual Fund, conforming to the SEBI Mutual Fund Regulations, and with recent mergers taking place among different private sector funds, the mutual fund industry has entered its current phase of consolidation and growth. As at the end of September, 2004, there were 29 funds, which manage assets of ₹ 1,53,108 crores under 421 schemes. The Graph 3.3 indicates the growth of assets over the years.

AUM of balanced schemes is down by 23% in 2002. The growth scheme is up by 16.25% in 2002. It is likely to go up further. Many mutual funds have lined up a slew of equity schemes in 2002 and are waiting for SEBI's approval for the same.

The assets under management (AUM) of income schemes jumped up by 40.57% from ₹ 54,194 crores to ₹ 76,182 crores in November 2002. Debt schemes have mobilised around 76.26% (₹ 92,575 crores) of the total assets under management as against ₹ 28,818 crores garnered by equity funds. (Refer Table 3.1)

Table 3.1 Scheme-wise Resource Mobilisation and Assets under Management of Mutual Funds During 2006-07

Schemes	No. of Schemes	Gross Funds Mobilised (₹ crore)	Repurchased Redemption (₹ crore)	Net Inflow/ Outflow of Funds (₹ crore)	Cumulative Asset under Management as on March 31, 2007 (₹ crore)	Percentage Variation over March 31, 2006
1	2	3	4	5	6	7
A.: Income/Debt-oriented Schemes *of which*	**450 (325)**	**18,39,668 (10,08,129)**	**17,75,601 (9,91,508)**	**64,067 (16,622)**	**1,93,585 (1,24,913)**	**54.98 (17.57)**
(i) Liquid/Money Market	55	16,26,790	16,21,805	4,985	72,006	17.08
(ii) Gilt	28	1,853	2,816	-964	2,257	-28.01
(iii) Debt	367	2,11,026	1,50,980	60,046	1,19,322	97.95
B.: Growth/Equity Oriented Schemes of which	**267 (231)**	**94,351 (86,014)**	**66,145 (50,783)**	**28,206 (35,231)**	**1,23,597 (99,456)**	**24.27 (158.43)**
(i) Equity Linked Saving Scheme	40	4,669	216	4,453	10,212	54.99
(ii) Others	227	89,683	65,929	23,753	1,13,386	22.10
C.: Balanced Schemes	**38 (36)**	**4,473 (4,006)**	**2,762 (3,079)**	**1,711 (927)**	**9,110 (7,493)**	**21.58 (53.96)**
TOTAL (A+B+C)	**755 (592)**	**19,38,493 (10,98,149)**	**18,44,508 (10,45,370)**	**93,985 (52,779)**	**3,26,292 (2,31,862)**	**40.93 (54.99)**

Note: Figures in parentheses relate to 2005-06.

The assets under management (AUM) increased by 17.6% to ₹ 8,25,240 crores at the end of March 2014 from ₹ 7,01,443 crores a year ago. The AUM was the highest for income/debt-oriented schemes at ₹ 6,00,945 crores while the AUM under growth/equity oriented schemes was ₹ 1,91,107 crores. In terms of growth in AUM, Other ETF schemes (206%) achieved the highest increase followed by FOF schemes (55.3%) and liquid/money market schemes (42.7%) during the year. The highest decline in AUM was registered for the Gold ETF schemes at 25.5%. As on March 31, 2014, there were 1,638 mutual fund schemes of which, 1,178 were income/debt-oriented schemes, 363 were growth/equity oriented schemes and 30 were balanced schemes (Table 3.1a). In addition, there were 40 Exchange Traded Funds, of which 14 were Gold ETFs and 26 other ETFs. Also, there were 27 schemes operating as Fund of Funds which invested in overseas securities. Maturity-wise there were 777 open-ended schemes and 796 close-ended schemes as on March 31, 2014. For the income/debt-oriented schemes category, the number of close-ended schemes exceeded open-ended schemes.

Table 3.1a Scheme-wise Resource Mobilisation and Assets under Management by Mutual Fund as on March 31, 2014

Schemes	No. of Schemes	Gross Funds Mobilised ('crore)	Repurchase/ Redemption (₹ crore)	Net Inflow/ Outflow of Funds (₹ crore)	Assets under Management as on Mar 31, 2014 (₹ crore)	Percentage Variation over March 31, 2013
1	2	3	4	5	6	7
A. Income/Debt-oriented Schemes						
(i) Liquid/Money Market	53	90,98,547	90,74,448	24,098	1,33,280	42.7
(ii) Gilt	44	9,917	11,785	–1,868	6,114	–24.2
(iii) Debt (other than assured returns)	1,077	6,00,736	5,60,189	40,547	4,60,672	16.3
(iv) Infrastructure Debt Fund (IDF)	4	562	0	562	879	Na
Subtotal (i to iv)	1,178	97,09,762	96,46,422	63,339	6,00,945	20.8
B. Growth/Equity Oriented Schemes						
(i) ELSS	52	2,661	4,303	–1,642	25,547	12.3
(ii) Others	311	43,432	51,059	–7,626	1,65,560	10.5
Subtotal (i+ii)	363	46,093	55,362	–9,268	1,91,107	9.7
C. Balanced Schemes						
Balanced schemes	30	3,435	5,421	–1,986	16,793	3.0
D. Exchange Traded Funds						
(i) Gold ETF	14	403	2,697	–2,293	8,676	–25.5
(ii) Other ETFs	26	6,466	3,576	2889	4,528	206.0
Subtotal (i + ii)	40	6,869	6,273	596	13,204	0.6
E. Fund of Funds Investing Overseas						
Fund of Funds investing overseas	27	1,941	840	1,101	3,191	55.3
TOTAL (A + B + C + D + E)	1,638	97,68,100	97,14,318	53,782	8,25,240	17.6

The growth potential of mutual funds in India is very high. This could be understood by comparing the mutual funds with deposits of commercial banks. The banking industry has deposits worth ₹ 14,00,000 crores, almost 14 times the assets under management (AUM) of mutual funds. The wide gap is attributed to many factors.

Graph 3.3: GROWTH IN ASSETS UNDER MANAGEMENT

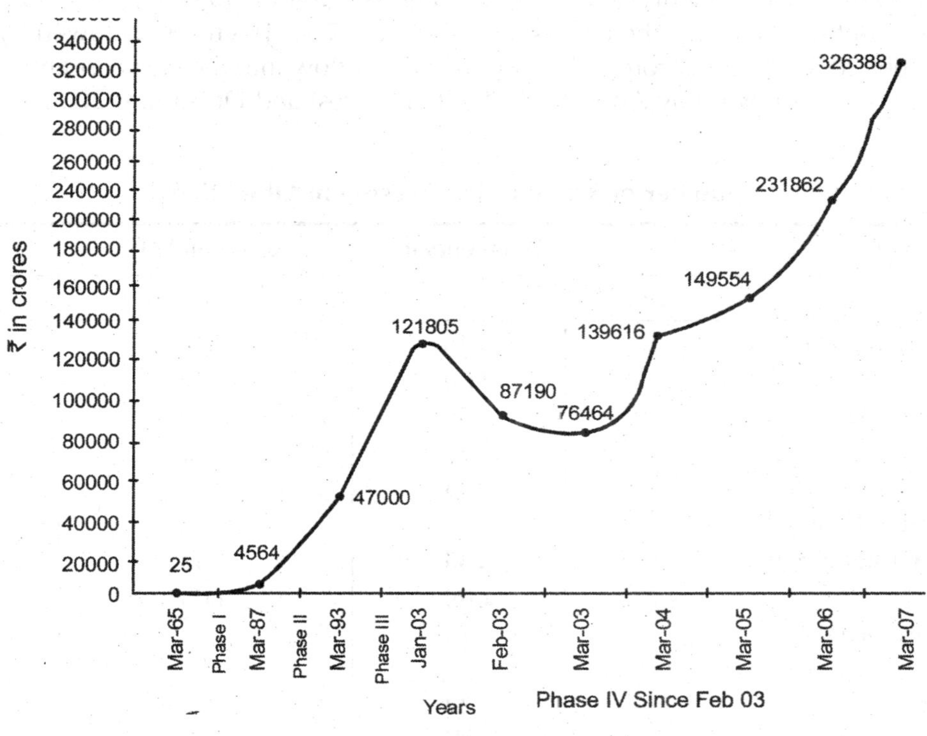

Lack of awareness about mutual funds among potential investors and limited reach of private sector players within metros are the two reasons behind the numbers.

3.10.2. Number of Unit Schemes in Operation

Many mutual funds launched innovative products. Few are exchange traded fund, dynamic plan, floating rate fund, P/E ratio fund and international plan.

Some innovative products like real estate mutual fund, pension fund, and derivative fund are on the cards in 2003. These funds, newly introduced, would give the benefit of diversification or professional fund management or liquidity to investors. Capital guaranteed plan is also an interesting scheme.

As on March 31, 2007, there were 755 mutual fund schemes, of which, 450 were income/debt-oriented schemes, 267 equity/ growth-oriented schemes and 38 balanced schemes. During the financial year 2006-2007, 163 schemes were added, of which 125 were income/debt-oriented schemes. As on March 31, 2007, there were 485 open-ended schemes and 270 close-ended schemes (Table 3.2). The number of close-ended schemes rose substantially from 47 in 2004-05 to 129 in 2005-06, and further to 270 in 2006-07. There were 234 close-ended debt-oriented schemes in 2006-07 as against 112 in 2005-06. The number of equity oriented schemes which were open-ended and close-ended was 235 and 32 respectively. The total assets under management (AUM) of all mutual funds rose by 40.7% to ₹ 3,26,292 crores as on March 31, 2007 from ₹ 2,31,862 crores a year ago. The net assets of all categories of mutual fund schemes witnessed a rise in 2006-07 over the previous year. The rise in AUM was the highest for debt-oriented schemes at 55.0%. This was commensurate with the spurt in resource mobilisation by the debt-oriented schemes. A rise of 24.3% was seen in the AUM of equity oriented schemes. A negative growth of 28.1% was recorded for AUM of gilt schemes. The mutual funds have traditionally been the active participants in the debt segment of Indian stock market. The heightened activity of mutual funds in the equity segment in 2005-06 did not continue at the same pace in 2006-07 except a few months of the financial year. In the first two months of the financial year, however, their inflow into the equity segment was higher, after which it declined. During 2006-07, the combined investment in debt and equity was ₹ 61,606 crores compared to

₹ 51,103 crores in 2005-06, indicating a rise of 20.6% (Table 3.5). Bulk of this investment was in the debt segment. Their total inflow into the debt segment was ₹ 52,543 crores as against ₹ 36,801 crores in 2005-06. Month-wise, their inflow into the debt segment was the highest for July 2006 (₹ 7,716 crores) followed by May 2006 (₹ 7,612 crores) and November 2006 (₹ 6,335 crores). The mutual fund inflow into the equity segment was the highest for May 2006 (₹ 7,893 crores) followed by April 2006 (₹ 3,121 crores) and December 2006 (₹ 1,627 crores) (Table 3.2).

Table 3.2 **Number of Schemes by Investment Objectives***

Schemes	Open-ended	Close-ended	Total
1	2	3	4
A.: Income/Debt-oriented Schemes	**216** **(213)**	**234** **(112)**	**450** **(325)**
(i) Liquid/Money Market	55	0	55
(ii) Gilt	28	0	28
(iii) Debt (other than assured return)	133	234	367
(iv) Debt (assured return)	0	0	0
B. Growth/Equity Oriented Schemes	**235** **(216)**	**32** **(15)**	**267** **(231)**
(i) Equity Linked Saving Scheme	29	11	40
(ii) Others			
C. Balanced Schemes	**34** **(34)**	**4** **(2)**	**38** **(36)**
TOTAL (A + B + C)	**485** **(463)**	**270** **(129)**	**755** **(592)**

As on March 31 of respective year.
Note: Figures in parentheses relate to 2005-06.

Table 3.2a **Number of Schemes by Investment Objective as on March 31, 2014**

Schemes	Open-ended	Close-ended	Interval	Total
1	2	3	4	5
A. Income/Debt Oriented Schemes				
(i) Liquid/Money Market	53(55)	0(0)	0(0)	53(55)
(ii) Gilt	44(42)	0(0)	0(0)	44(42)
(iii) Debt (other than assured returns)	259(237)	753(481)	65(42)	1,077(760)
(iv) Debt (assured returns)	0(0)	0(0)	0(0)	0(0)
(v) Infrastructure Debt Fund (IDF)	0	4	0	4
Subtotal (i to v)	**356(334)**	**757(481)**	**65(42)**	**1,178(857)**
B. Growth/Equity Oriented Schemes				
(i) ELSS	38(36)	14(14)	0(0)	52(50)
(ii) Others	287(292)	24(5)	0(0)	311(297)
Subtotal (i+ii)	**325(328)**	**38(19)**	**0(0)**	**363(347)**

C. Balanced Schemes				
Balanced schemes	29(31)	1(1)	0(0)	30(32)
D. Exchange Traded Funds				
(i) Gold ETF (ii) Other ETFs **Subtotal (i + ii)**	14(14) 26(23) **40(37)**	0(0) 0(0) **0(0)**	0(0) 0(0) **0(0)**	14(14) 26(23) **40(37)**
E. Fund of Funds Investing Overseas				
Fund of Funds investing overseas	**27(21)**	**0(0)**	**0(0)**	**27(21)**
TOTAL (A + B + C + D + E)	**777(751)**	**796(501)**	**65(42)**	**1,638(1,294)**

Notes: (1) 40 schemes in the nature of fund of funds (domestic) as on March 31, 2014 is not included in the above data
(2) Figures in parentheses indicate corresponding figures for 2012-13.

3.10.3. Net Asset Value (NAV)

The total net assets of all domestic schemes of mutual funds were ₹ 1,00,594 crores as on March 31, 2002. The details are given in Table 3.3.

Table 3.3 **Sector-wise Resource Mobilisation by Mutual Funds during 2006-07** *(₹ crore)*

Particular	Private Sector MFs			Public Sector MFs			UTI MF*			Grand Total
	Open-ended	Closed-ended	Total	Open-ended	Closed-ended	Total	Open-ended	Closed-ended	Total	
1	2	3	4	5	6	7	8	9	10	11
Mobilisation of Funds	14,82,588 (8,75,917)	1,17,286 (38,786)	15,99,874 (9,14,703)	1,85,500 (1,10,142)	10,840 (176)	1,96,340 (1,10,319)	1,32,070 (71,058)	10210 (2,069)	142280 (73127)	1938493 (1098149)
Repurchase/ Redemption Amount	14,62,528 (8,59,367)	58,308 (12,360)	1,52,0836 (8,71,727)	18,2981 (10,3580)	5,738 (360)	1,88,719 (1,03,940)	1,30,749 (68,387)	4204 (1316)	134954 (69704)	1844508 (1045370)
Net Inflow/ Outflow of Funds	20,060 (16,550)	58,978 (26,426)	79,038 (42,977)	2,519 (6,562)	5,102 (–183)	7,621 (6,379)	1,321 (2,671)	6005 (753)	7326 (3424)	93985 (52779)

Notes: Figures in parentheses relate to 2005-06.
*Net Assets of ₹ 2,214.67 crores pertaining to fund of funds schemes are not included in the above data.

Simple comparison of the net assets as on March 31, 2002 with that of March 31, 2001 will help one to understand the status of debt fund. The share of net assets of UTI has declined substantially from 64.0% to 51.1% whereas net assets of mutual funds of private sector have risen substantially from 28.6% to 41.2%. Assets of other public sector mutual funds have marginally increased from 7.3% to 7.6%.

Mutual fund industry continued to exhibit positive growth in assets under management in 2013-14. The gross mobilisation of resources by all mutual funds during 2013-14 was at ₹ 97,68,100 crores compared to ₹ 72,67,885 crores during the previous year indicating an increase of 34.4% over the previous year (Table 3.3a). Correspondingly, redemption also increased by 35.1% to ₹ 97,14,318 crores in 2013-14 from ₹ 71,91,346 crores in 2012-13. The net resources mobilised by all the mutual funds aggregated to ₹ 53,782 crores in 2013-14 compared to net inflow of ₹ 76,539 crores in 2012-13.

As of at the end of March 2014, the cumulative net assets managed by all the mutual funds totaled to ₹ 8,25,240 crores as against ₹ 7,01,443 crores at the end of March 2013, representing a rise 17.6%.

Table 3.3a **Growth in Assets under Management** *(₹ crore)*

Year	Gross Mobilisation	Redemption	Net Inflow	Assets at the end of period
1	2	3	4	5
2007-08	44,64,376	43,10,575	1,53,802	5,05,152
2008-09	54,26,353	54,54,650	–28,296	4,17,300
2009-10	1,00,19,022	99,35,942	83,080	6,13,979
2010-11	88,59,515	89,08,921	–49,406	5,92,250
2011-12	68,19,678	68,41,702	–22,024	5,87,217
2012-13	72,67,885	71,91,346	76,539	7,01,443
2013-14	97,68,100	97,14,318	53,782	8,25,240

The private sector mutual funds retained the dominant place in the mutual fund industry with 82.4% share in the gross resource mobilisation and 90.8% in the net resource mobilisation. The corresponding shares of UTI mutual fund and other public sector mutual funds was 8.2% and 9.4% in the gross resource mobilisation and 0.7% and 8.4% in the net resource mobilisation.

In absolute terms, the gross resource mobilisation by private sector mutual funds rose by 35.8% to ₹ 80,49,397 crores in 2013-14 from ₹ 59,27,947 crores in 2012-13 (Table 3.3b). Due to the heavy redemptions in the last three quarters of 2013-14, the net resource mobilisation by private sector mutual funds declined by 25.0 percent to ₹ 48,838 crores in 2013-14 compared to ₹ 65,102 crores in 2012-13. The net resources raised by UTI mutual fund and other public sector mutual funds was much lesser at ₹ 401 crores and ₹ 4,542 crores respectively in 2013-14 and represented a decline of 91.3 percent and 33.3 percent respectively over the previous financial year.

3.10.4. Foreign Institutional Investment

Foreign Institutional Investment (FII) is one of the main channels of foreign investment in India. Foreign Institutional Investors (FIIs) were permitted to invest in Indian securities market in 1993. Since then, their investments into Indian equity market have grown by leaps and bounds. In fact, FIIs, as a class of institutional investors, have assumed a major role in mature and emerging market economies, in recent years. The FII in the Indian equity markets has risen steadily since 2003. The gross purchases of debt and equity together by FIIs increased by 50.0% to ₹ 5,20,508 crores in 2006-07 from ₹ 3,46,978 crores in 2005-06. The gross sales by FIIs also rose by 60.3% to ₹ 4,89,667 crores from ₹ 3,05,512 crores during the same period. However, the net investment by FIIs in 2006-07 declined by 25.6% to ₹ 30,840 crores in 2006-07 from ₹ 41,467 crores in 2005-06 mainly due to large net outflows from the equity segment. But the cumulative net investment by FIIs in Indian stock market (since 1993) crossed USD 50 billion at the end of March 2007. As on March 31, 2007, the cumulative net investment by FIIs was USD 52 billion. The cumulative net investment by FIIs at acquisition cost, which was USD 15.8 billion at the end of March 2003, had risen to USD 45.3 billion at the end of March 2006 The FII in equity, which was high in the previous years, declined in 2006-07. During 2006-07, FIIs reduced their investment, in both equities as well as debt securities. The net FII investment in equity during 2006-07 was ₹ 25,236 crores, at its lowest in past three years. This was mainly due to large net sales in some months of 2006-07. Month-wise, FII was negative in the months of May 2006, December 2006 and March 2007. However, during the remaining months of the financial year, there was positive net equity investment by FIIs, particularly in middle of 2006-07, which drove the benchmark indices to historic highs. The net FII in November 2006 was the highest for 2006-07, followed by October 2006,

Table 3.3b Sector-wise Resource Mobilisation by Mutual Funds during 2013-14

(₹ crore)

Month/ Year	Private Sector MFs				Public Sector MFs				UTI MF				
	Open-ended	Close-ended	Interval	Total	Open-ended	Close-ended	Interval	Total	Open-ended	Close-ended	Interval	Total	Grand Total
1	2	3	4	5	6	7	8	9	10	11	12	13	14
Mobilisation of Funds													
2012-13	58,62,749	58,175	7,022	59,27,947	6,98,358	8,230	NA	7,06,589	6,26,821	5,641	888	6,33,350	72,67,885
2013-14	79,12,853	1,21,634	14,909	80,49,397	9,01,807	14,377	166	9,16,351	7,92,865	8,356	1,130	8,02,352	97,68,100
Repurchases/Redemption													
2012-13	57,76,161	80,387	6,297	58,62,845	6,86,483	13,131	166	6,99,781	6,21,562	5,067	2,092	6,28,720	71,91,346
2013-14	79,19,832	70,564	10,161	80,00,559	9,02,818	8,925	64	9,11,808	7,95,328	5,136	1,486	8,01,950	97,14,318
Net Inflow/Outflow of Funds													
2012-13	86,588	–22,212	725	65,102	11,875	-4,901	-166	6,808	5,259	574	–1,204	4,629	76,539
2013-14	-6,979	51,069	4,748	48,838	-1,011	5,452	101	4,542	-2,463	3,220	-355	401	53,782

and February 2007. Unlike last year when FII in debt segment was negative for all the months, in 2006-07 the same was positive for all months except for January 2007. Their total net investment in the debt segment in 2006-07 was ₹ 5,605 crores. Reflecting the congenial investment climate, total number of FIIs registered with SEBI rose to 997 as on March 31, 2007 compared to 882 a year ago. A distinctive feature of the profile of the newly registered FIIs was the rise in registration from the unconventional countries like Slovenia, Brussels, Guernsey, Cyprus, Oman, Sweden, Japan etc. other than the traditional investors from USA, United Kingdom, Singapore, Malaysia, Hong Kong, Luxembourg and others.

Indian Wholesale Debt Market

Table 3.4 **Investment by Foreign Institutional Investors**

Year	Gross Purchase (₹ crore)	Gross Sales (₹ crore)	Net Investment (₹ crore)	Net Investment (US $ mn)	Cumulative Net Investment (US $ mn)
1	2	3	4	5	6
1992-93	17	4	13	4	4
1993-94	5,593	466	5,126	1,634	1,638
1994-95	7,631	2,835	4,796	1,528	3,167
1995-96	9,694	2,752	6,942	2,036	5,202
1996-97	15,554	6,979	8,574	2,432	7,634
1997-98	18,695	12,737	5,957	1,650	9,284
1998-99	16,115	17,699	-1,584	-386	8,898
1999-00	56,856	46,734	10,122	2,339	11,237
2000-01	74,051	64,116	9,934	2,159	13,396
2001-02	49,920	41,165	8,755	1,846	15,242
2002-03	47,061	44,373	2,689	562	15,805
2003-04	1,44,858	99,094	45,765	9,950	25,755
2004-05	2,16,953	1,71,072	45,881	10,172	35,927
2005-06	3,46,978	3,05,512	41,467	9,332	45,259
2006-07	5,20,508	4,89,667	30,840	6,708	51,967

The Wholesale debt market (WDM) analysed in this section pertains to NSE. The net traded value declined by 53.9% to ₹ 2,19,106 crores in 2006-07 from ₹ 75,523 crores in 2005-06. The net traded value was the highest in November 2006 at ₹ 29,339 crores. Compared to 2005-06, the net traded value was lower for every month in 2006-07 except November 2006. It was at the lowest in June 2006 at ₹ 11,790 crores. Average daily traded value in the WDM segment of NSE declined from ₹ 1,755 crores in 2005-06 to ₹ 899 crores in 2006-07. The total number of trades in the WDM segment also declined from 61,891 in 2005-06 to 19,575 in 2006-07. Instrument-wise share of securities traded in the WDM segment of NSE shows that government securities continued to dominate the WDM segment in 2006-07, followed by Treasury Bills (Table 3.6). The share of G-Sec in the total traded value declined from 72.7% in 2005-06 to 70.0% in 2006-07. However, there was a rise in the share of T-bills from 22.1% in 2005-06 to 23.7% in 2006-07. Trading members had a share of 30.9% in the turnover . The share of Indian banks and foreign banks in the turnover of WDM segment constituted 26.0% and 20.6% respectively, in 2006-07. In fact the foreign banks increased their share from 14.1% in 2005-06 to 20.57% in 2006-07 while the share of Indian banks declined from 28.1% in 2005-06 to 26.0% in 2006-07.

Capital flows into emerging markets are influenced more by global than domestic forces. The global cues with the likes of the US Fed tapering maneuver the capital flows to a large extent. While the domestic macroeconomic policy actions have ensured resumption of capital flows into the country, specific measures undertaken by SEBI to smoothen the process of investment have been instrumental in encouraging the flows. With the economy on its road to recovery and investor optimism at a new high acting as enablers, the conditions seem encouraging for the flow of foreign capital. FII investments into India have grown remarkably since 2009-10. India received a total FII net investments per cent. In US dollar terms, the net investments amounted to USD 8,876 million in 2013-14. The combined gross purchases of debt and equity by FIIs increased by 12.8% to ₹ 10,21,010 crores in 2013-14 from ₹ 9,04,845 crores in 2012-13 (Table 3.4a). The combined gross sales by FIIs increased by 31.6% to ₹ 9,69,361 crores from ₹ 7,36,481 crores during the same period in previous year. The cumulative net investment of FIIs in Indian markets amounted to USD 180,405 million as at the end of March 2014 compared to USD 171,529 million in 2012-13, registering an increase of 5.2%.

Table 3.4a **Investment by Foreign Institutional Investors**

Year	Gross Purchase (₹ crore)	Gross Sales (₹ crore)	Net Investment (₹ crore)	Net Investment (USD mn.)	Cumulative Investment (USD mn.)
1	2	3	4	5	6
1992-93	18	4	13	4	4
1993-94	5,593	467	5,127	1,634	1,638
1994-95	7,631	2,835	4,796	1,528	3,167
1995-96	9,694	2,752	6,942	2,036	5,202
1996-97	15,554	6,980	8,575	2,432	7,635
1997-98	18,695	12,737	5,958	1,650	9,285
1998-99	16,116	17,699	−1,584	−386	8,899
1999-00	56,857	46,735	10,122	2,474	11,373
2000-01	74,051	64,118	9,933	2,160	13,532
2001-02	50,071	41,308	8,763	1,839	15,372
2002-03	47,062	44,372	2,689	566	15,937
2003-04	1,44,855	99,091	45,764	10,005	25,943
2004-05	2,16,951	1,71,071	45,880	10,352	36,294
2005-06	3,46,976	3,05,509	41,467	9,363	45,657
2006-07	5,20,506	4,89,665	30,841	6,820	52,477
2007-08	9,48,018	8,81,839	66,179	16,442	68,919
2008-09	6,14,576	6,60,386	−45,811	−9,837	59,081
2009-10	8,46,438	7,03,780	1,42,658	30,251	89,333
2010-11	9,92,599	8,46,161	1,46,438	32,226	121,559
2011-12	9,21,285	8,27,562	93,725	18,923	140,482
2012-13	9,04,845	7,36,481	1,68,367	31,047	171,529
2013-14	10,21,010	9,69,361	51,649	8,876	180,405

Mutual Funds have historically been investing more in debt than equity. During 2013-14, the combined net investments by the mutual funds in debt and equity was ₹ 5,22,023 crores compared to ₹ 4,50,711 crores in 2012-13, accounting an increase of 15.8% (Table 3.5a). Mutual Funds were net sellers in equity segment to the tune of ₹ 21,224 crores, whereas, their net investments in the debt segment rose to ₹ 5,43,247 crores during the same period. Since 2009-10, on an yearly basis there has been offloading of investments by mutual funds from the equity market. Investments in the debt segment was the highest in March 2014 (₹ 99,457 crores) followed by September 2013 (₹ 81,970 crores). While the net investments of mutual funds in the debt segment were positive for all the months during the year, that in the equity segment were negative for all months except August 2013.

Table 3.5 Trends in Transactions on Stock Exchanges by Mutual Funds (*₹ in crore*)

Year/ Month	Equity			Debts			Total		
	Gross Purchase	Gross Sales	Net Purchase/ Sales	Gross Purchase	Gross Sales	Net Purchase/ Sales	Gross Purchase	Gross Sales	Net Purchase/ Sales
1	2	3	4	5	6	7	8	9	10
2004-05	45,045	44,597	448	62,186	45,199	16,987	1,07,232	89,796	17,435
2005-06	1,00,436	86,134	14,302	1,09,805	73,004	36,801	2,10,241	1,59,137	51,103
2006-07	1,35,948	1,26,886	9,062	1,53,733	1,01,190	52,543	2,89,681	2,28,075	61,606
Apr-06	12,752	9,632	3,121	11,228	6,800	4,428	23,980	16,432	7,548
May-06	18,345	10,452	7,893	15,386	7,774	7,612	33,732	18,226	15,506
Jun-06	7,844	9,820	–1,977	14,236	8,907	5,329	22,079	18,727	3,352
Jul-06	7,552	7,634	-82	15,983	8,266	7,716	23,535	15,900	7,635
Aug-06	8,852	8,425	426	16,169	11,853	4,316	25,021	20,278	4,743
Sep-06	10,345	9,006	1,340	12,879	9,591	3,287	23,224	18,597	4,627
Oct-06	9,944	9,948	–4	10,314	7,930	2,385	20,259	17,877	2,381
Nov-06	12,675	12,700	–25	13,297	6,962	6,335	25,972	19,662	6,310
Dec-06	13,181	11,554	1,627	7,585	6,256	1,329	20,766	17,811	2,956
Jan-07	11,644	12,986	–1,342	10,831	8,427	2,403	22,474	21,413	1,061
Feb-07	12,697	12,971	–274	10,352	7,683	2,669	23,049	20,654	2,395
Mar-07	10,116	11,757	–1,641	15,474	10,740	4,734	25,590	22,497	3,093

An analysis of the FII net investments reveal that the majority is invested in equity. This has been the trend over the years except 2011-12. In 2013-14, the FII net investments into equity segment declined by 43.1% to ₹ 79,708 crores from ₹ 1,40,033 crores in 2012-13 (Table 3.5b). In the debt segment, the FII net investments was ₹ 28,061 crores in 2013-14 as compared to ₹ 28,334 crores in 2012-13.

Table 3.5a Trends in Transactions on Stock Exchanges by Mutual Funds (*₹ crore*)

Year/ Month	Equity			Debt			Total		
	Gross Purchase	Gross Sales	Net Purchase/ Sales	Gross Purchase	Gross Sales	Net Purchase/ Sales	Gross Purchase	Gross Sales	Net Purchase/ Sales
1	2	3	4	5	6	7	8	9	10
2008-09	1,44,069	1,37,085	6,985	3,27,744	2,45,942	81,803	4,71,814	3,83,026	88,787
2009-10	1,95,662	2,06,173	–10,512	6,24,314	4,43,728	1,80,588	8,19,976	6,49,901	1,70,076
2010-11	1,54,217	1,74,018	–19,802	7,62,644	5,13,493	2,49,153	9,16,861	6,87,511	2,29,352
2011-12	1,32,137	1,33,494	–1,358	11,16,760	7,81,940	3,34,820	12,48,897	9,15,434	3,33,463
2012-13	1,13,758	1,36,507	–22,749	15,23,393	10,49,934	4,73,460	1,637,150	11,86,440	4,50,711
2013-14	1,12,131	1,33,356	–21,224	15,38,087	9,94,842	5,43,247	16,50,219	11,28,197	5,22,023
Apr-13	6,321	7,744	–1,423	1,51,371	99,516	51,855	1,57,692	1,07,260	50,432
May-13	9,067	12,575	–3,508	1,38,989	1,12,149	26,840	1,48,056	1,24,725	23,332
Jun-13	9,582	9,851	–269	1,57,883	92,936	64,948	1,67,466	1,02,787	64,679
Jul-13	10,485	12,654	–2,169	1,12,008	1,35,748	–23,740	1,22,493	1,48,401	–25,909
Aug-13	13,109	11,502	1,607	65,168	61,417	3,752	78,277	72,919	5,359
Sep-13	8,173	10,974	–2,801	1,22,606	40,636	81,970	1,30,779	51,610	79,169
Oct-13	7,157	11,175	–4,018	91,637	54,466	37,171	98,794	65,641	33,153
Nov-13	8,067	8,549	–482	97,156	55,533	41,624	1,05,223	64,082	41,141
Dec-13	10,051	10,462	–411	1,25,320	73,378	51,942	1,35,371	83,840	51,531
Jan-14	9,349	11,864	–2,515	1,43,614	98,198	45,415	1,52,963	1,10,063	42,900
Feb-14	8,469	9,814	–1,345	1,18,153	56,138	62,015	1,26,622	65,952	60,669
Mar-14	12,301	16,191	–3,890	2,14,183	1,14,727	99,457	2,26,485	1,30,918	95,567

Table 3.5b **Investments by Foreign Institutional Investors (Equity and Debt)** *(₹ crore)*

Year/	Net Investment by FIIs		
Month	Equity	Debt	Total
1	2	3	4
2008-09	–47,706	1,895	–45,811
2009-10	1,10,220	32,438	1,42,658
2010-11	1,10,121	36,317	1,46,438
2011-12	43,738	49,988	93,725
2012-13	1,40,033	28,334	1,68,367
2013-14	79,708	–28,061	51,649
Apr-13	5,414	5,334	10,748
May-13	22,169	5,969	28,138
Jun-13	–11,027	–33,135	–44,162
Jul-13	–6,086	–12,038	–18,124
Aug-13	–5,923	–9,773	–15,695
Sep-13	13,058	–5,678	7,380
Oct-13	15,706	–13,578	2,128
Nov-13	8,116	–5,984	2,133
Dec-13	16,086	5,290	21,376
Jan-14	714	12,609	13,323
Feb-14	1,404	11,337	12,741
Mar-14	20,077	11,586	31,663

3.10.5. Volume of Investment Expressed in Rupee Value

During April-December 2001, mutual funds were net sellers of equity shares while they were net buyers of debt. The gross purchase of equity amounted to ₹ 7,489 crores, while sales amounted to ₹ 8,762 crores, resulting in a net negative investment in equity. In the case of debt, gross purchase amounted to ₹ 19,578 crores against the sale of ₹ 12,385 crores, resulting in net investment in debt amounting to ₹ 7,193 crores during this period. Table 3.5. presents data on purchase and sale transactions of mutual funds on stock exchanges.

During the year 2001-02, mutual funds were net sellers in the equity segment to the tune of ₹ 3,795.9 crores and net buyers in the debt segment to the tune of ₹ 10,959.2 crores. The month-wise details of purchases and sales in the market during the year are given in Table 3.6.

The trend in the instrument-wise share of securities traded in the WDM segment at NSE shows that share of G-Secs has declined prominently over the years. The share of G-Sec has declined from 69.7% in 2008-09 to 40.3% in 2013-14 (Table 3.6a). On the other hand, the share of Treasury bills increased from 16.9% in 2008-09 to 34.2% in 2013-14. While there has been a significant rise in the share of PSU/institutional bonds to 18.0% in 2013-14 from 8.9% in 2008-09 and 'others' which include mainly corporate debt securities, rose to 7.5% in 2013- 14 from 4.4% in 2008-09. At BSE, the instrument-wise share of securities traded reveal that PSU/Institutional Bonds contributed the maximum at 81.0% while Treasury Bills accounted for a share of 11.2% followed by G-Secs at 7.8%.

Table 3.6 Instrument-wise Share of Securities Traded in the Wholesale Debt Market Segment of NSE

	2006-07			
Month	Govt. Dated Securities	Treasury Bills	PSU/Institutional Bonds	Others
1	2	3	4	5
April	66.87 (56.02)	29.03 (39.82)	2.21 (1.87)	1.89 (2.29)
May	71.43 (73.20)	19.25 (22.71)	2.79 (1.42)	6.53 (2.67)
June	54.41 (90.06)	36.45 (6.46)	4.26 (1.86)	4.88 (1.62)
July	55.05 (86.73)	35.69 (8.54)	2.78 (2.32)	6.48 (2.41)
August	63.67 (60.06)	32.00 (32.95)	0.85 (3.40)	3.48 (3.59)
September	74.75 (69.49)	20.65 (21.66)	1.55 (4.52)	3.05 (4.33)
October	72.37 (59.85)	23.29 (33.38)	1.44 (4.21)	2.89 (2.56)
November	78.27 (68.08)	18.11 (28.10)	1.35 (2.32)	2.27 (1.50)
December	75.40 (64.38)	19.37 (28.88)	1.16 (3.31)	4.07 (3.43)
January	73.69 (65.68)	18.56 (26.88)	2.63 (3.38)	5.12 (4.06)
February	71.48 (75.51)	20.1 (19.79)	2.04 (1.13)	6.38 (3.56)
March	70.72 (63.65)	17.41 (28.27)	3.02 (5.57)	8.85 (2.51)
Average	70.00 (72.67)	23.71 (22.13)	2.02 (2.56)	4.27 (2.64)

Table 3.6a **Instrument-wise Share of Securities Traded in the Wholesale Debt Market Segment of NSE and BSE**

(Per cent)

Month/ Year	Govt. Dated Securities	Treasury Bills	PSU/ Institutional Bonds	Others	Govt. Dated Securities	Treasury Bills	PSU/ Institutional Bonds	Others
	NSE				BSE			
1	2	3	4	5	6	7	8	9
2008-09	69.7	16.9	8.9	4.4	Na	Na	Na	Na
2009-10	58.2	16.5	15.4	10.0	Na	Na	Na	Na
2010-11	54.5	17.6	19.6	8.3	Na	Na	Na	Na
2011-12	50.4	22.0	19.6	8.0	Na	Na	Na	Na
2012-13	51.6	23.7	16.3	8.3	Na	Na	Na	Na
2013-14	40.3	34.2	18.0	7.5	7.8	11.2	81.0	0.0
Apr-13	50.7	23.5	18.0	7.8	3.7	1.1	95.3	0.0
May-13	57.8	10.4	22.3	9.4	0.6	0.8	98.5	0.0
Jun-13	48.2	21.4	21.8	8.7	9.5	0.0	90.5	0.0
Jul-13	28.5	29.6	31.0	10.9	3.2	2.2	94.6	0.0
Aug-13	21.9	53.0	18.1	6.9	1.6	1.2	97.2	0.0
Sep-13	39.9	41.1	13.8	5.1	1.1	0.0	98.9	0.0
Oct-13	43.4	32.6	17.6	6.5	0.6	0.0	99.4	0.0
Nov-13	43.6	28.6	17.9	9.9	8.7	3.0	88.2	0.0
Dec-13	36.7	49.4	10.3	3.6	0.9	1.2	97.9	0.0
Jan-14	36.1	39.8	15.2	9.0	22.4	36.9	40.7	0.0
Feb-14	42.1	43.6	9.5	4.8	17.8	45.7	36.4	0.0
Mar-14	35.2	37.0	20.2	7.7	23.1	42.1	34.7	0.0

Challenges

The mutual fund industry very much depends on the investors' trust. It is important to win them rather than their wallet. The Indian mutual fund industry does not perform up to the mark in gaining investor confidence. The AUM has stagnated at around ₹ 1,00,000 crores over last five years. This stagnation is partly attributed to industry's inability to instill confidence in the minds of potential investors in India. Possible areas which need to be checked are given below:

(a) Most of the products introduced in the mutual fund market do not suit to the needs of the potential investors. Principle Protected Funds, Floating Interest Rate Funds, High Yield Bond or Equity Funds and Real Estate Mutual Funds are some of the products gaining momentum among investors. SEBI and RBI can also introduce the international products under the newly permitted guidelines. Indian investor is very much worried about the safety of his investment.

(b) The fund must be managed professionally. Investor believes that the fund managers are simply momentum chasers.

(c) Poor service is another bottleneck for the growth of mutual fund industry in India. Though they manage large sums of money, they do not reach the retail investors. The facilities for collecting money from B and C categories are not in existence. The technology alone can bring these two ends together.

(d) Investor education is must at this point of time. Many have learnt lessons from the deeds of UTI. Investors generally feel that the mutual fund managers are experts and they are professionally trained. In fact, most of the fund managers do not know the difference between relative return and absolute return. The well-managed fund is generally defensive to the vicious fluctuations of the stock market. This is the basic investment strategy of a genuine fund manager. On the other hand, investor predicts that such fund performs poorly. This demands indoctrination through investor education.

(e) Undue importance should not be given to any particular asset in the asset allocation exercise.

(f) Liquidity is the ability of an investor to convert investments into cash readily. The investor can sell the units at the prevailing net asset value to the Mutual Fund itself. Therefore, Mutual funds are considered liquid investments.

(g) Mutual funds allow investors to invest small amounts of money on a regular basis. Instead of having large amounts of capital to diversify a portfolio, investors can gradually add to their investment through automatic investment plans.

(h) A mutual fund must offer several products, such as a growth fund, a balanced fund, a bond fund, a money market fund, etc. An investor can usually switch his investment from one fund to another, within the same family at little or no charge. This gives the investor the option to switch funds if their objectives change.

(i) Investor must get regular information about the value of his investment in addition to disclosure on the specific investments made by his scheme, the proportion invested in each class of assets and the fund manager's investment strategy and future outlook.

3.11 UNIT TRUST OF INDIA

Introduction

Unit Trust of India (UTI) is India's largest mutual fund organisation. UTI manages funds over ₹ 58,221 crores as on 30/6/2001 and over 41.80 million investors account under 85 schemes.

UTI is a trust without ownership capital and independent Board of Trustees. The first scheme was Unit Scheme 1964 (US-64). The contributors of initial capital of ₹ 5 crores for US-64 scheme were RBI, LIC, SBI and some foreign banks. Under the provision of the Act, the Government of India would appoint Chairman of the board. Today, it has 54 branch offices, 266 chief representatives and about 67,000 agents. It provides complete range of services to its investors.

UTI has set up associate companies in the field of banking, securities, trading, investor servicing, investment advice and training, meeting investor's varying needs under a common umbrella.

Aims of UTI

UTI was set up in 1964 by an Act of Parliament. It commenced its operation from July 1964, with a view to encouraging saving and investment and participation in the income, profit and gain accruing to corporation from the acquisition, holding, management and disposal of securities.

Performance

1. UTI was a lonely player with just one scheme in 1964. Now, it competes with as many as 400 odd products and 34 players in the market. In spite of the stiff competition and losing market share, UTI remains a formidable force to reckon with.
2. UTI has shown a large outflow of funds of ₹ 7,284 crores during the financial year 2001-02 as against net inflow of ₹ 323 crores during 2000-01 and net inflow of ₹ 4,548 crores during the year 1999-2000.
3. When we compare the net assets as on March 31, 2002 with that of March 31, 2001, the share of net assets of UTI has declined substantially from 64.0% to 51.1%. On the other hand, net assets of private sector mutual funds have risen substantially from 28.6% to 41.2%.

4. Out of 3.08 crores investors in the mutual funds industry, 2.44 crores or 79.15% of the total investors are in UTI. The percentage of total investors in private sector mutual funds is 13.50% (0.41 crores) and public sector mutual funds is 7.35% (0.23 crores).
5. Comparison of the performance of UTI with other mutual fund institutions is given in Table 3.4. Of total value of AUM ₹ 1,22,600 crores as on Dec. 2002, the share of UTI constitutes ₹ 45,899 crores. When the number of schemes introduced by UTI is compared with number of schemes introduced by foreign players, it is a dismal performance on the part of UTI. Of total 30,868 schemes, UTI has only 460 schemes whereas the foreign players have 12,514 schemes. That shows to what extent the foreign institutions are able to understand the sentiments of the potential investors of Indian market.
6. Out of 3.02 crores investors under the category of 'individuals', the total number of individual investors is the largest in UTI with 79.43%. It is followed by private sector mutual funds with 13.23% and public sector mutual funds with 7.34%. Thus, it is observed that UTI has the largest number of small individual investors who contribute 72.61% to UTI's total net assets.
7. However, in case of private and public sector mutual funds, the corporates and institutions are the largest contributors to the net assets to the tune of 61.80% and 57.59% respectively.
8. In July 2001, the Trust suspended the US-64 scheme amidst a blaze of negative publicity dragging its problems to Centre stage.
9. Analysis of the trends in market share of mutual funds revealed that UTI suffered significant loss in market share from around 85% in 1996 to 50% in 2001. The cumulative net asset position of mutual funds at the end of December 2001 is given in Table 3.7.

Table 3.7 Cumulative Net Assets of Mutual Funds (As on December 31, 2001)

Sector	Amount (₹ crores)
Private	42,582
Public	8,059
UTI	51,181
Total	1,01,822

***Source*: SEBI.**

10. Product innovation is now passed with the game shifting to performance delivery in fund management as well as service. Those directly associated with the fund management industry like distributors, registrars and transfer agents, and even the regulators have become more mature and responsible.
11. While UTI has always been a dominant player on the bourses as well as the debt markets, the new generation of private funds which have gained substantial mass are now seen flexing their muscles.
12. The private sector, especially those in which foreign AMCs are involved, will together start matching UTI for market share.
13. The reasons for UTI's problems are varied and have been well documented. First was the US-64 mess and now it is the turn of the assured returns schemes.
14. Even if UTI is able to survive these adverse developments, it is unlikely that its fortunes will substantially improve, especially under the present system of management. Privatisation is being discussed loudly. However, by the time, a final decision is taken a great deal of goodwill will be lost.

Financial Intervention

In order to arrest the poor performance and to instil confidence in the investing public and unitholders, UTI with the help of the Government of India, resorted to the following measures:

The Government hopes to address not only UTI's problems but also the concerns of the investing community and the capital market at large. Now, that the UTI has been assured of full support from government irrespective of the size of the fund required, a financial restructuring package is indeed being worked out helping the once-venerated institution regain investor confidence.

Period	Type of Intervention
1. June 29, 1999	(a) Government of India did a buy back. It bought from UTI PSU shares at book Value. It was higher than the then prevailing market value. This effectively constituted a transfer of ₹ 1,528 crores to the investors in US-64.
2. August, 2001	(a) Investors were given an assurance that up to 3000 units (per investor) could be sold back to UTI at an administratively determined price. It started from ₹10 in August 2001. It would go by ₹0.10 per month until it will reach ₹ 12 in May 2003. (b) UTI has to repurchase the units at a price above NAV due to the promises made. Government of India makes up the difference to UTI. The programme covered roughly 40% of the assets of US-64.
3. Dec, 2001	(a) The limit of 3000 units was raised to 5000 units. In addition, investors holding above 5000 units were given an assurance that if they exited in May 2003, they would get the higher of NAV or ₹ 10. Again, Government would make up the gap between the repurchase price and NAV experienced by UTI, if any.
4. March 2002	(a) Government of India paid ₹ 1,000 crores for the US-64 scheme in two sections of ₹ 500 crores each, as part of its batch of supplementary demand for grants for ₹ 8,007.16 crores for 2002. Ministry of Finance promised to meet the UTI liabilities arising out of the assured return schemes. The commitment costs ₹ 11,000 crores according to a conservative estimate. The cabinet committee on economic reforms did it. (b) UTI received the permission for sale of its portfolio of blue chips to mitigate the burden said above. (c) The agreed sale includes its 13.49% in tobacco major ITC. The government has decided to split the Unit Trust of India into UTI-I and UTI-II. It extended tax sops to US-64 investors and to provide support to US-64 and assured return schemes (ARS). UTI after bifurcation will thus consist of two parts — sick and the healthy. UTI-I will comprise US-64 and ARSs. Government-appointed administrator and a team of advisers nominated by the government will manage it.
5. 31st August 2002	The current shortfall in case of US-64 scheme has been estimated at ₹ 6,000 crores. In respect of ARS, the current shortfall is likely to be ₹ 8,561 crores. The government would take on all the liabilities arising out of UTI-I. The government will provide necessary monetary support to the US-64 scheme and plan to provide certain tax concessions to US-64 investors with a view to prompting them to remain invested with the scheme. The tax sops will include exemption from dividend tax and capital gains tax. On the assured return schemes, the Cabinet has also approved interest reset on the assured return scheme. It has also authorised the government to consider foreclosure where possible. Both these measures would be considered in consultation with SEBI. UTI-II, which will manage other net asset value (NAV) based schemes, will ultimately be privatised. UTI-II would be a "pure mutual fund" with a professional team running it. Privatisation of UTI-II would take place after its valuation had improved under professional fund managers. LIC, PNB and BoB jointly own UTI-II. The fund has 47 schemes right now. It has also ₹ 15,179 crores corpuses.

3.12 EXCHANGE TRADED FUND (ETF)

3.12.1. Introduction

Mr. A.P. Kurian, Chairman, Association of Mutual Fund in India (AMFI) said, "Unlike 2002, when equity inflows were lackluster, 2003 will be the year of revival of equity schemes. Inflows will start picking up if the markets give sustained rally". The Chairman of AMFI has a positive attitude towards the funds, which have been performing poor over last two years. Of the 80 equity fund schemes, 57 have underperformed on the BSE Sensex. The situation forces the investor to rethink the benefits associated with mutual funds.

Supposing, an investor likes to invest on an index fund. If it is so, it would have been better for him or her to have a portfolio of 30 shares of the BSE sensex having weightage of each share exactly equal to its respective weightage in the index. Why should it be thirty shares? The Index basket of BSE sensex has thirty popularly traded shares. Therefore, the investor has to match it with his investment. Generally, an investor cannot do so. Owning 30 shares today (at the sensex level of around 4000) would require a minimum investment of ₹ 1,00,000. This may not be possible for a small investor. Secondly, purchasing 30 different shares involves a substantial cost of transaction in the form of brokerage. Finally, not all the investors would be comfortable doing this. The viable alternative is, at present, investment on Exchange Traded Fund (ETF).

3.12.2. Exchange Traded Fund

An exchange traded fund is a mutual fund. However, it is traded like a share. Just like an index fund such as the S&P 500, an ETF represents a basket of stocks that reflect an index. An ETF, however, is not a mutual fund. Unlike a mutual fund, that has its net asset value (NAV) calculated at the end of each trading day, an ETF's price changes throughout the day. It is important to remember that while ETFs attempt to replicate perfectly the return on indices, there is no guarantee that they will do so. It is common to see a 1% or more difference between the actual indices year-end return and that of an ETF.

ETF is a generic phrase coined around the year 2000 for any type of stock exchange traded index type instrument. In USA, SPDRs, QQQs and Diamonds can all be classified as ETFs since they are traded on stock exchanges.

Exchange-traded funds are hybrids of the open- and closed-end mutual fund. Shares can be bought and sold in the stock market at prices that are almost always very close to net asset value. This is because the fund sponsors stand ready to create and redeem shares, but only in very large increments that institutional traders would use to capture any discount or premium that happens to momentarily arise.

3.12.3. ETF in Other Countries

QUBEs (QQQs)

This is the ETF that represents the NASDAQ-100. The symbol "QQQ" represents it on the American Stock Exchange (AMEX). This security offers broad exposure of the tech sector by tracking the NASDAQ-100 Index. It consists of the 100 largest and most actively traded non-financial stocks on the NASDAQ. The QQQ is a great way to invest into the long-term prospects of the technology industry because it does not impose the risk that comes with investing in individual stocks. This can be a huge advantage when there is volatility in the markets. If companies miss earnings, these companies get hit hard.

SPDRs

It is usually referred to as Spiders. This is an investment that bundles the benchmark S&P 500 and gives one ownership in the index. One could perceive the trouble of trying to buy all 500 stocks in the S&P 500. SPDRs allow individual investors to do this in a cost-effective manner. Another feature of SPDRs is that they divide various sectors of the S&P 500 stocks and sell them as separate ETFs. The "Technology Select Sector Index" for example, contains over 85 stocks covering products developed by defense manufacturers, telecommunications equipment, microcomputer components, integrated computer circuits, etc. It trades under the symbol XLK on the AMEX.

i-Shares

i-shares is Barclay's brand of ETFs. Barclay has recently put out a number of technology oriented i-shares that follow Goldman Sachs's technology indices. All these trade on the AMEX.

Diamonds

These ETF shares match the Dow Jones Industrial Average. The fund is structured as a unit investment trust. The ticker symbol of the Dow Diamonds is "DIA", and it trades on the American Stock Exchange.

3.12.4. Performance of ETF in the World

(a) Despite the global bear market, the ETF business outside the US had a banner year in 2001, and assets under management continued to surge in the first quarter of 2002. In that 15-month period, US ETFs grew by 35%, and there were 22 new ETFs listed in the US Comparing that with non-US listed ETFs, funds invested into them nearly tripled, from $9 billion to $24 billion, and 119 new ETFs were launched in the same period. From a share of 12% of the global market at the start of 2001, non-US. ETFs today represent 21% of all money invested in ETFs.

(b) There is about $85 billion currently invested in Exchange Traded Funds in North America (2002). This is forecast to grow to $400 billion in the next 3 years. Exchange traded Funds will have a huge important role to play in the portfolios of Canadians over the next few years.

(c) In Europe, ETFs are a more recent trend but are growing quickly. In the 15 months to April 1, 2001, ETFs listed in Europe went from 6, with $675 million in assets, to 92, with $6.9 billion. To date, all ETF portfolios are based on market indices. In other words, they are designed to mimic a basket of stocks, such as the S&P 500 or the Nikkei 225.

3.12.5. Performance of ETF in India

ETFs are passively managed mutual funds that track a particular index, like BSE Sensex and S&P CNX Nifty. They are tradable on the stock exchange. ETFs are basically mutual fund units representing fixed basket of securities that can be traded just like an equity share.

1. The Sensex UTI Notional Depository Receipts Scheme (SUNDERS) is the first exchange-traded fund managed by Unit Trust of India which will be traded on the Bombay Stock Exchange. Hence, SUNDERS will track the price and yield performance of the underlying sensex as accurately as possible.
2. India's first Exchange Traded Fund (ETF) from Benchmark Asset Management Company has been listed on the capital market segment of the National Stock Exchange (NSE) on January 8, 2003. ETF raised ₹ 21 crores from investors in December. The fund's corpus will be invested in the entire 50 scrips, constituting Standard and Poor's (S&P) CNX Nifty index in proportion to the weightage for each stock, Benchmark AMC Chairman, S.A. Dave told. With this listing, India becomes the first emerging economy in Asia to have launched an ETF. Benchmark has appointed seven leading NSE brokers as authorised participants who, as practised internationally, will perform the role of market makers.
3. Prudential ICICI Mutual Fund launched SPIcE (Sensex Prudential ICICI Exchange Traded Fund) in India. It is India's first exchange-traded fund (ETF) to track the Sensex. SPIcE combines the features of both an open-ended scheme and an exchange-listed security. It will be listed at the Bombay Stock Exchange (BSE) and Delhi Stock Exchange (DSE). SPIcE can be bought and sold on the BSE/DSE (Delhi Stock Exchange) terminal through a stock broker. The minimum lot size is one unit of SPIcE. The price of one

unit will be equal to l/100th of the Sensex value. The scheme will be managed by Prudential ICICI Mutual Fund.

3.12.6. Evolution

Advantages of ETFs

Proponents of ETFs say they are better than conventional mutual funds because:

(a) ETF is cheaper than any other similar instrument in the market. The transaction cost is initially lower, if not in the long run. One can buy or sell them at current market prices whenever the markets are open, rather than waiting for the day's closing price as is typical with open-ended funds. Though NAV can be compared, it is not a sole deciding criterion to evaluate ETF. Therefore, market prices play very important role in ETF trading.

(b) One can use them for short sales and other hedging transactions. It is not possible for short sales and hedging transactions in fund market.

(c) One can trade them as often as he or she likes without incurring short-term redemption fees or other expressions of the fund manager's wrath.

Disadvantages of ETFs

Unfortunately, exchange traded funds do have some negatives:

1. As stated elsewhere in the chapter, ETF is traded like a share in the share market. Like stocks, the investor has to bear with the transaction cost similar to shares. The cost may be in the form of brokerage, commission and charges.
2. ETF is generally suitable for extremely rich and institutional buyers. They only can deal with brokers. Retail trade of ETF is unthinkable and impractical. Volume of business of ETF may be huge. However, the involvement of large investing public shall be very small.
3. Net Asset Value (NAV) is the base on which the mutual fund is built and evaluated. The fund has to publish its NAV now and then, because Securities and Exchange Board of India prescribes so. Though NAV helps one to evaluate the ETF, ETFs do not necessarily trade at the net asset value of their underlying holdings. It means an ETF could potentially trade above or below the value of the underlying portfolio.
4. The sponsors of ETFs and the exchanges on which they are listed sometimes squabble about who is supposed to pick up the marketing tab to sell them to investors.
5. Regulators are sometimes unsure how to go about regulating them. ETFs can only track a benchmark, on which it is built. If the market as a whole is not doing well, the ETF will not have good returns.
6. Sometimes too many product features and differentiation can also confuse investors. Increased complexity also makes things difficult to manage and it becomes quite susceptible to event risks.
7. Another aspect is the cost. Many products include futures, which add costs to the investor. For example, in the case of umbrella funds or fund of funds, which are very popular today, the costs go up to four% per annum.
8. The tax advantage may be felt in the beginning. As volume of trade on ETF increases, the fund may attract more taxes, as is the case of any other product in the fund market.

Still, it is evident that the benefits of ETFs clearly outweigh the drawbacks. Experts in the capital market predict that the global fund industry will be dominated by ETFs in ten years. Will ETF be a special scheme, as it is predicted, or will it be another fund in the market? This will be seen as time passes.

3.13 PERFORMANCE OF MUTUAL FUNDS

Mutual fund is a most preferred investment vehicle nowadays in India. Does mutual fund deserve it? One cannot come to a conclusion without evaluating it. Mutual fund is preferred because it is said to be a less risky investment avenue. There are different yardsticks which help one to know the performance of the mutual fund over years. The mutual fund performance is evaluated with resource mobilised by mutual funds over a period, net inflow or outflow of funds, trading of mutual fund units in the market and so on.

3.13.1. Flow of Funds

- 182 new schemes were launched in the quarter and a sum of ₹ 55,095 crores was mobilised – ₹ 34,675 crores under Income Schemes, ₹ 18,831 crores under Equity Schemes, ₹ 793 crores under Liquid Schemes, ₹ 33 crores under Gilt Schemes, ₹ 760 crores under the Equity Linked Savings Schemes and ₹ 3 crores under Gold Exchange Traded Funds.
- Total funds mobilised for the quarter stood at ₹ 14,81,106 crores as against ₹ 6,12,328 crores for the corresponding quarter last year representing an increase of 142%.
- Redemptions at ₹ 14,51,298 crores were 143% higher than the redemptions of ₹ 5,97,956 crores in the corresponding quarter last year.
- On a net basis, there was an inflow of ₹ 29,808 crores during the quarter as against an inflow of ₹ 14,372 crores in the corresponding quarter last year.
- Data on Fund of Funds is given in Table 3.1a.
- 612 new schemes were launched during the year as against 414 in the previous year. The amount mobilised was ₹ 1,60,773 crores as against ₹ 1,40,298 crores in the previous year.
- Total Funds mobilised during the year stood at ₹ 44,64,376 crores as against ₹ 19,38,592 crores in the last year representing an increase of 130%.
- Redemptions at ₹ 43,10,575 crores were 134% higher than the redemptions of ₹ 18,44,512 crores in the previous year.
- On a net basis, there was an inflow of ₹ 1,53,801 crores as compared to ₹ 94,080 crores in the last year registering an increase of 63%.
- The Assets Under Management as on March 31, 2008 stood at ₹ 5,05,152 crores as against ₹ 3,26,388 crores as at the end of the previous year, registering an increase of 55% over the year.
- Data on Fund of Funds.
- Table 3.7 gives the Type and Category wise composition of the Assets Under Management.

Table 3.8 **Mutual Fund Data for the Quarter January-March 2008**

Category	Sales All Schemes					Redemptions All Schemes		Total Assets under Management As on 31.03.08
	From New Schemes#		From Existing Schemes	Total for the Quarter	Total for the year ended 31.03.08	Total for the Quarter	Total for the year ended 31.03.08	
	No.	Amount	Amount					
A. Bank Sponsored								
I. Joint Ventures Predominantly Indian (2)	4 1	940 1,843	50,645 18,319	51,585 20,162	143,324 52,512	48,554 17,161	135,645 48,942	28,669 16,807
II. Others (2)	2 4	3,196 921	135,661 50,601	138,857 51,522	346,270 161,501	139,315 53,163	335,629 154,351	48,478 37,763
Total (I+II)	6 5	4,136 2,764	186,306 68,920	190,442 71,684	489,594 214,013	187,869 70,324	471,274 203,293	77,147 54,570
B Institutions (1)	4 7	749 664	66,461 31,270	67,210 31,934	194,030 124,607	67,409 33,913	191,851 120,381	12,384 9,643
C Private Sector								
I. Indian (11)	49 66	22,467 22,983	461,552 1,36,678	484,019 1,59,661	13,69,180 4,79,754	4,68,767 1,52,564	13,11,006 4,50,447	1,52,795 80,157
II. Foreign (3)@	9 —	3,399 —	53,764 —	57,163 —	1,82,305 —	54,717 —	1,75,937 —	30,294 —
III. Joint Ventures Predominantly Indian (5)	60 55	16,860 19,412	4,17,568 1,90,382	4,34,428 2,09,794	13,92,729 6,21,899	4,21,731 2,01,229	13,41,120 5,91,457	1,61,273 1,04,779
IV. Joint Ventures Predominantly	54 68	7,484 15,658	2,40,360 1,23,597	2,47,844 1,39,255	8,36,538 4,98,319	2,50,805 1,39,926	8,19,387 4,78,934	71,259 77,239
Total (I+II+III+IV)	172 189	50,210 58,053	11,73,244 4,50,657	12,23,454 5,08,710	37,80,752 15,99,972	11,96,020 4,93,719	36,47,450 15,20,838	4,15,621 2,62,175
Grand Total (A+B+C)	182 201	55,095 61,481	14,26,011 5,50,847	14,81,106 6,12,328	44,64,376 19,38,592	14,51,298 5,97,956	43,10,575 18,44,512	5,05,152 3,26,388

Notes: 1. Data is provisional & hence subject to revision.

2. # Only New Schemes where allotment is completed

3. Figures in RED denote figures for the corresponding period of the previous year.

4. @ There has been an increase in the number of AMCs to 3, due to inclusion of a new AMC-Mirae Asset Global Investment Management (I) Private Ltd.

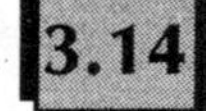

3.14 GLOSSARY

Advisor

It is an organisation employed by a mutual fund. It gives professional advice on the fund's investments and to supervise the management of its assets.

Asked or Offering Price

A mutual fund's shares can be purchased at a price. It is called the asked price. The asked or offering price means the current net asset value (NAV) per share plus sales charge, if any. For a no-load fund, the asked price is the same as the NAV.

Asset Allocation Fund

A fund generally spreads its portfolio among a variety of investments, including domestic and foreign stocks and bonds, government securities, gold bullion and real estate stocks. This gives small investors far more diversification than they could get allocating money on their own.

Automatic Reinvestment

This service is offered by most mutual funds whereby income dividends and capital gain distributions are automatically invested into the fund by buying additional shares.

Balanced Fund

The mutual fund that maintains a balanced portfolio, generally 60% bonds or preferred stocks and 40% common stocks is known as balanced fund.

Bid or Sell Price

The price at which a mutual fund's shares are redeemed (bought back) by the fund. The bid or redemption price means the current net asset value per share, less any redemption fee or back-end load.

Bond Fund

A mutual fund whose portfolio consists primarily of corporate or Government bonds. These funds generally emphasise income rather than growth.

Bond Rating

System of evaluating the probability of whether a bond issuer will default. Various firms analyse the financial stability of both corporate and government bond issuers. Ratings range from AAA or AA (extremely unlikely to default) to D (currently in default). Bonds rated BBB or below are not considered to be of investment grade.

Capital Appreciation Fund

A mutual fund that seeks maximum capital appreciation through the use of investment techniques involving greater than ordinary risk, such as borrowing money in order to provide leverage, short-selling and high portfolio turnover.

Capital Gains Distributions

Payments to mutual fund shareholders of gains realised on the sale of portfolio securities.

Capital Growth

A rise in market value of a mutual fund's securities, reflected in its NAV per share. This is a specific long-term objective of many mutual funds.

Certificate of Deposit

Interest-bearing, short-term debt instrument issued by banks and thrifts.

Closed-end Investment Company

An investment company that offers a limited number of shares. They are traded in the securities markets, usually through brokers. Price is determined by supply and demand. Unlike open-end investment companies (mutual funds), closed-end funds do not redeem their shares.

Commercial Papers

Short-term, unsecured promissory notes with maturities no longer than 270 days. They are issued by corporations, to fund short-term credit needs.

Common Stock Fund

Open-end investment companies whose holdings consist mainly of common stocks and usually emphasise growth.

Confirm Date

The date the fund processed your transaction, typically the same day or the day after your trade date.

Contingent Deferred Sales Charge (CDSC)

A fee (or back-end load) imposed by certain funds on shares are redeemed within a specific period following their purchase. These charges are usually assessed on a sliding scale, such as four per cent to one per cent of its redeemed, with the fee reduced each year the units are held.

Custodian

The bank or trust company that maintains a mutual fund's assets includes its portfolio of securities or some record of them. Provides safekeeping of securities but has no role in portfolio management.

Daily Dividend Fund

This term applies to funds that declare their income dividends on a daily basis and reinvest or distribute monthly.

Deferred Compensation Plan

A tax-sheltered investment plan to which employees of State and local Governments can defer a percentage of their salary.

Distributor

An individual or a corporation serving as principal underwriter of a mutual fund's shares/buying shares directly from the fund, and reselling them to other investors.

Diversification

The policy of spreading investments among a range of different securities to reduce the risks inherent in investing.

Rupee-Cost Averaging

The technique of investing a fixed sum at regular intervals regardless of stock market movements. This reduces average share costs to the investor, who acquires more shares in periods of lower securities prices and fewer shares in periods of high prices. In this way, investing risk is spread over time.

Exchange Privilege (or Switching Privilege)

The right to transfer investments from one fund into another, generally within the same fund group, at nominal cost.

Ex-Dividend Date

The date on which a fund's Net Asset Value (NAV) will fall by an amount equal to the dividend and/or capital gains distribution (although market movements may alter the fund's closing NAV somewhat). Most publications which list closing NAVs place an "X" after a fund's name on its ex-dividend date.

Expense Ratio

The ratio of total expenses to net assets of the fund. Expenses include management fees, the cost of shareholder mailings and other administrative expenses. The ratio is listed in a fund's prospectus. Expense ratios may be a function of a fund's size rather than of its success in controlling expenses.

Global Fund

A fund that invests in both Indian and foreign securities.

Growth Fund

A mutual whose primary investment objective is long-term growth of capital. It invests principally in common stocks with significant growth potential.

Income Dividend

Payment of interest and dividends earned on the fund's portfolio securities after operating expenses are deducted.

Income Fund

A mutual fund that primarily seeks current income rather than growth of capital. It invests in stocks and bonds that normally pay high dividends and interest.

Index Fund

A mutual fund that seeks to mirror general stock market performance by matching its portfolio to a broad-based index, most often the S&P CNX Nifty index.

International Fund

A fund that invests in securities traded in markets outside India.

Investment Company

A corporation, partnership or trust that invests the pooled money of many investors. It provides greater professional management and diversification of investments than most investors can obtain independently. Mutual funds, or "open-end" investment companies, is the most popular form of investment company.

Investment Objective

The financial goal (long-term growth, current income, etc.) that an investor or a mutual fund pursues.

Junk Bond

A speculative bond rated BB or below. "Junk bonds" are generally issued by corporations of questionable financial strength or without proven track records. They tend to be more volatile and higher yielding than bonds with superior quality ratings. "Junk bond funds" emphasise diversified investments in these low-rated, high-yielding debt issues.

Load

A sales charge or commission assessed by certain mutual funds ("load funds") to cover their selling costs. The commission is generally stated as a portion of the fund's offering price, usually on a sliding scale from one to 8.5%.

Load Fund

A mutual fund that levies a sales charge up to 6%, which is included in the offering price of its shares, and is sold by a broker or salesman. A front-end load is the fee charged when buying into a fund; a back-end load is the fee charged when getting out of a fund.

Low-load Fund

A mutual fund that charges small sales commission, usually 3.5% or less, for the purchase of its shares.

Management Fee

The amount a mutual fund pays to its investment adviser for services rendered, including management of the fund's portfolio. In general, this fee ranges from 0.5% to 1% of the fund's asset value.

Money Market Fund

A mutual fund that aims to pay money market interest rates. This is accomplished by investing in safe, liquid securities, including bank certificates of deposit, commercial paper, government securities and repurchase agreements.

Mutual Fund

An open-end investment companies that buys back or redeems its shares at current net asset value. Most mutual funds continuously offer new shares to investors.

Net Asset Value Per Share

The current market worth of a mutual fund share. Calculated daily by taking the funds total assets securities, cash and any accrued earnings deducting liabilities, and dividing the remainder by the number of shares outstanding.

No-load Fund

A commission-free mutual fund that sells its shares at net asset value, either directly to the public or through an affiliated distributor, without the addition of sales charges.

Payable Date

The date on which distributions are paid to shareholders who do not want to reinvest them. This date can be anywhere from one week to one month after the Record Date.

Payroll Deduction Plan

An arrangement between an employer and a mutual fund, authorised by the employee, through which a specified sum is deducted from an employee's salary to buy shares in the fund.

Portfolio Turnover Rate

The rate at which the fund's portfolio securities are changed each year.

Prospectus

An official document that each investment company must publish, describing the mutual fund and offering its shares for sale. It contains information required by the Securities and Exchange Commission.

Record Date

The date the fund determines who its shareholders are; "shareholders of record" who will receive the fund's income dividend and/or net capital gains distribution.

Redemption Fee

A fee charged by a limited number of funds for redeeming, or buying back, fund shares.

Redemption Price

The price at which a mutual fund's shares are redeemed (bought back) by the less expensive fund. The redemption price is usually equal to the current net asset value per share.

Regional Fund

A mutual fund that concentrates its investments within a specific geographic area, usually the fund's local region. The objective is to take advantage of regional growth potential before the national investment community does.

Reinvestment Date (Payable Date)

The date on which a share's dividend and/or capital gains will be reinvested (if requested) in additional fund shares.

Reinvestment Privilege

A service that most mutual funds offer where by a shareholder's income ' dividends and capital gains distributions are automatically reinvested in additional shares.

Sector Fund

A fund that operates several specialised industries sectors portfolios under one umbrella. Transfers between the various portfolios can usually be executed by telephone at little or no cost.

Short Selling

The sale of a security which is not owned by the seller. The "short seller" borrows stock for delivery to the buyer, and must eventually purchase the security for return to the lender.

Speciality Fund

A mutual fund specialising in the securities of a particular industry or group of industries or special types of securities.

Systematic Investment Plans

In case of Systematic Investment Plans, instead of a lump sum amount, investor invests a pre-specified amount in a scheme at pre-specified intervals at the then prevailing NAV.

Systematic Withdrawal Plans

Many mutual funds offer withdrawal programs whereby shareholders receive payments from their investments. These payments are usually drawn from the fund's dividend income and capital gain distributions, if any, and from principal only when necessary.

Underwriter

The organisation that acts as the distributor of a mutual fund's shares to broker/dealers and the public.

Variable Annuity

A type of insurance contract that guarantees future payments to the holder, or annuitant, usually at retirement. The annuity's value varies with that of the underlying portfolio securities, which may include mutual fund shares. All money held in the annuity accumulate tax deferred.

Voluntary Plan

A flexible plan for capital accumulation, involving no specified time frame or total sum to be invested.

Yield

Income or return received from an investment, usually expressed as a percentage of market prices, over a designated period. For a mutual fund, yield is interest or dividend before any gain or loss in the price per share.

Zero Coupon Bond

Bond sold at a fraction of its face value. It appreciates gradually, but no periodic interest payments are made. Earnings accumulate until maturity, when the bond is redeemable at full face value. Nonetheless, interest is taxable as it accrues.

3.15 REVIEW QUESTIONS

Short Answer Questions

1. Define mutual fund.
2. Define Net Asset Value (NAV)
3. What is meant by balanced fund?
4. Describe the gilt fund.
5. Describe about Money Market Mutual Fund.
6. What are the features of an Index Fund?
7. Who is benchmarking in mutual fund?
8. What is ELSS? How do you link it with Section 88 of Income Tax Act?
9. What are the rights of Mutual Fund holder?
10. How is a capital gain of mutual fund treated?
11. Explain about the organisational structure of UTI.
12. What is the main aim of UTI?
13. How has Government classified the UTI schemes now?
14. What is Asset Management Company?
15. What do you mean by Asset under Management (AUM)?

Essay Type Questions

1. Give an account about evolution of Mutual Fund in the world and India.
2. Discuss the rationale of investment companies. Do they outsmart the market?
3. What is meant by mutual funds? What are the advantages of professionally managed portfolio?

4. What are the disadvantages of Mutual Fund Investment to the investor?
5. Give an account of the various types of mutual funds available in the Indian capital market.
6. Distinguish between Treynor and Sharpe indices of Portfolio Performance. Which do you recommend? Why?
7. Explain the Jenson index of portfolio performance.
8. Describe about Eugene Fama's contribution towards fund performance.
9. What is the difference between closed-end and open-end funds?
10. Point out the main RBI guidelines on mutual fund.
11. What is risk? Explain various risks involved in Mutual Fund Investment.
12. Describe about mutual fund organisation.
13. Explain the roles of different players of Mutual Fund.
14. Make an account of the performance of Mutual Funds in India.

❋ ❋ ❋

CHAPTER

4

Lease Financing

Objectives

The student, after studying the chapter, should be able to:

- Explain the term Lease.
- List down the various types of Leasing.
- Make a historical account of Leasing.
- Record accounting entries of Leasing.
- Identify various statutory legislations of Leasing.
- Evaluate the Leasing services in general.
- Examine critically the Indian market for Leasing.

Structure:

4.1 INTRODUCTION

Definitions

The Transfer of Property Act, 1882 (as amended in 1952) describes Lease as follows:

"A Lease of the movable property is a transfer of a right to enjoy such property, made for a certain time, expressed or implied, or in perpetuity, in consideration of a price paid or promised or of money, a share of crops, service or any other thing of value, to be rendered periodically or on specified occasions to the transferor by the transferee, who accepts the transfer on such terms."

The transferor is called the lessor, the transferee is called the lessee, the price is called the premium and the money, share, service or other thing to be rendered is called the rent.

Definition: Section 105 of the above Act defines a lease as follows:

"A Lease is a transfer of a right to enjoy the property. The consideration may be price or rent. The rent may be either money, or share of crops, service of anything of value, to be rendered periodically by the transferee to the transferor."

4.2 EVOLUTION OF LEASING

Leasing in the context of financial services denotes Equipment Leasing. The concept and practice of leasing is not an innovation of the late 20th century. There are historical evidences to show that the practice of leasing was found even five centuries earlier. Such leases were for leasing land, agricultural tools, animals and ships, as documented in the Sumerian and Greek civilisations.

These operators found leasing a viable alternative for enhanced operations as they were desperately short of their own funds. They could not also rely upon conventional sources of funds.

The unparalleled success of Rail Road companies highlighted the importance of equipment leasing as a tool for promoting capital formation.

In the post-Second World War era, European rail companies also took to equipment leasing on a large scale. In the early sixties, this practice of equipment leasing has gained popularity and it is believed that approximately 25% of all business equipments in terms of value are leased.

The later half of 19th century bore witness to this practice as the Rail Road operators in the USA leased rail cars and locomotives.

The practice of Equipment Leasing is of recent origin in India. Equipment leasing took roots only in the eighties. Equipment leasing includes — leasing of plant and machinery, office equipments, automobiles, ships and aircrafts.

Leasing at Present

Nowadays, leasing of large-scale manufacturing facilities, power projects and construction projects has become very common. The range of business assets leased today has led to several offers being made to meet the different needs of the consumers.

Leasing today has come to stay as a popular form of asset based-financing.

"Equipment lease is a contractual arrangement where the lessor of equipment transfers the right to use the equipment to the lessee for an agreed period of time in return for rental."

When lease period is over, the asset reverts back to the lessor except where renewal of contract or transfer of ownership to the lessee is provided.

The lessee with a lease proposal approaches a leasing company, who is a financial intermediary. The lessee decides on the specification of the equipment, its supplier, price, terms of guarantee and warranty, and delivery period. The lessor (the leasing company) and the lessee negotiate the terms such as: duration of the lease, terms and conditions relating to usage, lease rentals, maintenance and insurance of the equipments.

On mutually agreeable terms, a lease contract is entered into, and the lessor buys the equipment and delivers it to the lessee. The lessee bears the cost of insurance and the maintenance of the asset.

The lease agreement is different from the hire-purchase agreement or a Conditional Sales Agreement.

Hire-Purchase Agreement

An agreement under which goods are let on hire and the hirer has an option to purchase them in accordance with the terms of the agreement.

Conditional Sales Agreement

"A transaction which provides the seller with full ownership right in the asset until the user has satisfied all the terms and conditions of the agreement at which time the title passes automatically from the seller to the buyer (user)."

The difference between a lease transaction and other asset financing plans is that a lease contract cannot provide for a transfer of ownership from the lessor to the lessee while other asset-based financing plans have this feature.

4.3 CLASSIFICATION OF LEASE

A lease financing transaction can be differently classified on the basis of differences we find in the following terms and conditions.

- Numbers of parties to the transaction.
- Extent to which risks and rewards of ownership are transferred.
- Domiciles of the equipment manufacturer, the lessor and the lessee.

Considering the differences in the above criteria, we have the following classifications:

- Finance Lease and Operating Lease.
- Sale and Lease Back and Direct Lease.
- Single Investor Lease and Leveraged Lease.
- Domestic Lease and International Lease.

Finance Lease

The financial evaluation and the accounting of leases differ in a financial lease from an operating lease. The difference is based on the extent to which the risks and rewards of ownership are transferred from the lessor to the lessee.

Definition

A lease is defined as a finance lease if it transfers a substantial part of the risks and rewards associated with ownership from the lessor to the lessee.

The International Accounting Standards Committee prescribes the criteria to determine whether there is a transfer of a substantial part of the ownership-related risks and rewards.

They are:

(a) The lease transfers ownership of the asset to the lessee by the end of the lease term; or

(b) The lessee has the option to purchase the asset at a price which is expected to be sufficiently lower than the Fair Market Value (FMV) at the date, the option becomes exercisable that, at the inception of the lease it is reasonably certain that the option will be exercised; or

(c) The lease term is for a major part of the useful life of the asset. The title may or may not be transferred eventually; or

(d) The present value of the minimum lease payments is greater than or substantially equal to the FMV of the asset at the inception of the lease. The title may or may not be transferred eventually.

These are largely based on the criteria laid down by the Financial Accounting Standards Board (FASB) of the USA.

The FASB has defined certain cut-off points for criteria (c) and (d) above.

As per the FASB definition,

If the lease term exceeds 75% of the useful life of the asset or if the present value of the minimum lease payments exceeds 90% of the FMV of the asset, at the inception of the lease, the lease will be classified as 'Financial Lease'.

For determining the present value, the discount rate to be used by the lessor will be the rate of interest implicit in the lease and the discount rate to be used by the lessee will be its incremental borrowing rate. In the Indian context, criteria (a) and (b) above are inapplicable, because, inclusion of any one of these conditions in the lease agreement will make the agreement being treated as a Hire Purchase Agreement. Hence, a lease can be classified as a finance lease only if any one of criteria (c) and (d) are satisfied.

In a finance lease, the lessee is responsible for repair, maintenance and insurance of the asset. The lessee also undertakes an extreme obligation to pay rental regardless of the condition or the suitability of the asset. A finance lease, which prevails over the entire useful life of the equipment, is called a "full payout lease".

4.3.2. Operating Lease

The International Accounting Standard Committee defines an operating lease as:

" any lease other than a finance lease".

An operating lease has the following characteristics:

1. The lease term is significantly less than the economic life of the equipment.
2. The lessee enjoys the right to terminate the lease at short notice without any significant penalty.
3. The lessor usually provides the operating know-how, supplies the related services and undertakes the responsibility of insuring and maintaining the equipment, in which case the operating lease is called a 'Wet Lease'.

An operating lease where the lessee bears the cost of insuring and maintaining the leased equipment is called a 'Dry Lease'.

An operating lease does not shift the equipment-related, business and technological risks from the lessor to the lessee.

The lessor structuring an operating lease transaction has to depend upon multiple leases or on the realisation of substantial resale value (on the expiry of first lease), to recover the investment cost plus reasonable rate of return thereon.

Hence, to deal in operating leasing, one requires an in-depth knowledge of the equipments leased, and the resale market for such equipment. (The existence of a resale market is a pre-requisite for operating lease). In our country, as the resale market for most of the used capital equipments is not active, operating leases are not very popular.

Nevertheless, this form of lease is ideal for firms engaged in sunrise industries with a high degree of technological risk.

4.3.3. Sale and Lease Back

In this form of lease, the owner of equipment sells it to a leasing company, which, in turn, leases it back to the seller of the equipment, who then becomes the lessee.

The 'Lease Back' arrangement in this transaction can be in the form of either a finance lease or an operating lease, e.g., the sale and lease back of safe deposit vaults practiced by commercial banks.

The banks sell the safe deposit vaults in its custody to a leasing company at a market price, which is substantially higher than the book value.

The leasing company then offers these lockers on a long-term lease to the bank. This results in the following benefits to the bank:

1. It is able to unlock its investment in a low income yielding asset.
2. It is able to enjoy the uninterrupted use of the lockers (to be leased to its customers).
3. It can invest the sale proceeds of the safety lockers (not subjected to the Reserve Ratio requirements) in high-income yielding commercial loans.

This 'sale and lease back' arrangement is an easily available source of funds for the expansion and diversification programmes of a firm where high-cost short-term debt has been used for capital investments in the past; the sale and lease back gives an opportunity to substitute the short-term debt by medium-term finance (provided the lease back arrangement is a finance lease).

For the leasing company offering sale and lease back arrangement, it is difficult to establish a fair market value of the asset being acquired as the resale markets are virtually absent.

The Income tax authorities may disallow the claim for depreciation on the FMV, if they view that FMV is not fair.

4.3.4. Direct Lease

A direct lease can be defined as any lease, which is not a 'sale and lease back transaction'.

A direct lease can be of two types:

(a) Bipartite lease, and

(b) Tripartite Lease

Bipartite Lease: In a Bipartite Lease, there are two parties to the transaction—equipment supplier-cum-lessor and the lessee. It functions like an operating lease with built-in facilities like upgradation of the equipments (Upgrade Lease) or improvement in the original equipment configuration.

The lessor undertakes to maintain the equipment and even replaces the equipment that is in need of major repair with the similar functioning equipment (Swap Lease).

All these add ones to the lease agreement are possible as the lessor is the manufacturer or dealer of the equipments covered by lease.

Tripartite Lease: It involves three different parties — the equipment supplier, the lessor, and the lessee. Most of the equipment lease transactions fall under this category. A variant of this type of lease is the sales-aid-lease, where the equipment supplier arranges for lease finance, where the customer is short on liquidity.

In this form of lease:

1. The equipment supplier may provide a reference about the customer to the leasing company.
2. The equipment supplier can negotiate the terms of the lease with the customer and complete the necessary paperwork on behalf of the leasing company.
3. The supplier can take the lease on his own account and discount the lease receivables with the designated leasing company. So, the leasing company owns the equipment and obtains an assignment of the lease rentals.

This form of lease has recourse to the supplier in case of default by the lessee, either to buy back the equipment from the lessor on default or providing a guarantee on behalf of lessee.

4.3.5. Single Investor Lease

The lessor (the leasing company) funds the entire investment by raising a judicious mix of debt and equity. The debt funds raised by the leasing company are without recourse to the lessee, i.e., in the event of the default by the leasing company on its debt-servicing obligation, the lender cannot demand payment from the lessee.

4.3.6. Leveraged Lease

The leasing company (equity investor) invests in equipments by borrowing large investments with full recourse to the lessee without any recourse to it.

The lender (loan participant) gets an assignment of the lease and the rentals to be paid by the lessee and a first mortgage on the leased assets. This transaction is routed through a trustee to take care of the lender and the lessee.

Loan Participant: A leveraged lease entitles the lessor to avail the shields on depreciation, other capital allowances on the entire investment cost, though, a substantial part of the investment cost is funded with non-recourse debt.

So, the return on equity (profit after tax divided by net worth) tends to be high. For, the lessee, the rate of interest is less than that of a straight loan as the lessor extends the tax benefits to the lessee in the form of lower rental payments. This lease is usually preferred for leasing investment-intensive assets like aircraft, ships, etc.

Chart 4.1

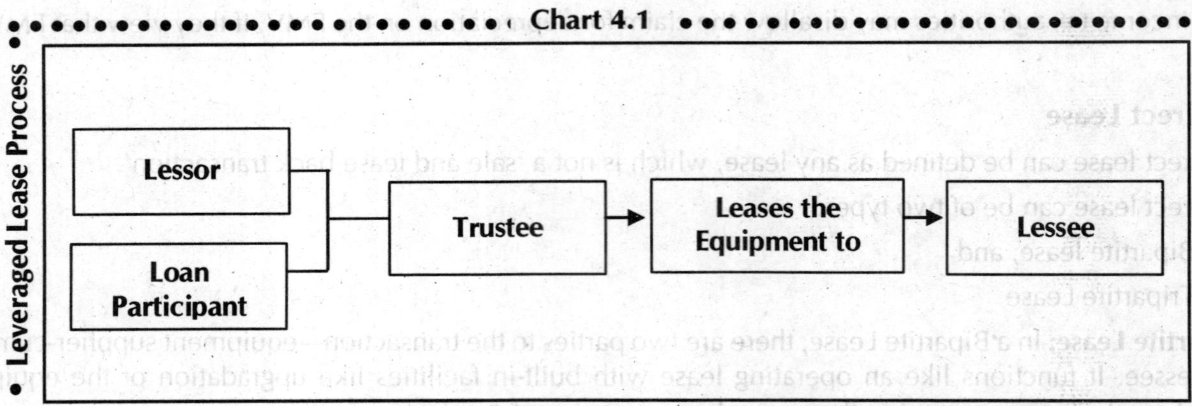

4.3.7. Domestic Lease and International Lease

If all parties to the lease transaction — the equipment supplier, lessor and lessee — are domiciled in the same country, it is a domestic lease.

If the parties to the lease agreement are living in different countries, the lease is an international lease.

An international lease transaction proposes:

1. An understanding of the political and economic climate; and
2. A knowledge about the tax and other regulatory framework governing these transactions in the respective countries, the payments to be effected in different currencies and hence knowledge about exchange rate variation.

As a result, international lease is exposed to country risk and currency risk.

4.4 ACCOUNTING TREATMENT OF LEASE

4.4.1 Accounting for Lease transaction: Lessor Perspective

Assets under financial leases should be disclosed as "assets given on lease" as a separate section under the head "fixed assets" in the balance sheet of the lessor. The classification of the assets should correspond to that adopted for other fixed assets.

Lease rentals should be shown separately under gross income in the income statement of the relevant period. It is appropriate that against the lease rental a matching lease annual charge is made to the income statement, which represents recovery of the net investment over the lease period. This charge is calculated by deducting the finance income for the period from the lease rental for the period. The annual lease charge would comprise minimum statutory depreciation.

There would be a lease equalisation charge where the annual lease charge is more than the minimum statutory depreciation.

There would be a lease equalisation credit where the annual lease charge is less than the minimum statutory depreciation. This would require a separate Lease Equalisation Account (LEA) with a corresponding debit or credit to Lease Adjustment Account (LAA). The LEA should be transferred every year to the income statement. Statutory depreciation must be shown separately in the income statement. Accumulated statutory depreciation should be deducted from the original cost of the leased asset on the balance sheet of the lessor to arrive at the net book value.

Balance standing in the LAA should be adjusted in the net book value of the leased assets. The amount of adjustment in respect of each class of fixed asset could be shown in the main balance sheet or in a schedule.

The finance income should be calculated by applying the interest rate implicit in the lease to the net investment in the lease during the relevant period. Some lessors use a simpler method of calculating it by apportioning the total finance income from the lease in the ratio of minimum lease payments outstanding during each of the respective periods comprising the lease term.

Leased asset for an operating lease should be depreciated on a basis consistent with the lessor's normal depreciation policy.

In the case of a sale and lease back transaction, if the rentals and sale price are established at fair value, profit or loss is normally recognised immediately. If the sale price is below fair value, profit or loss is recognised except that if loss is compensated by future rentals at below market price, it is deferred and amortised in proportion to the rental payments over the useful life and *vice versa*.

4.4.2. Accounting for Lease transaction: Lessee's Perspective

A lessee should disclose assets taken under a finance lease by way of a note to the accounts, disclosing the future obligations of the lessee as per the agreement.

Lease rentals should be accounted for on an accrual basis over the lease period to recognise an appropriate charge in this respect in the income statement, with a separate disclosure thereof. The appropriate charge should be worked out with reference to the terms of the lease agreement, type of asset, proportion of lease period to the life of the asset as per technical or commercial evaluation and other such considerations.

The excess of lease rentals paid over the amount accrued in respect thereof should be treated as prepaid lease rental and *vice versa*.

In the case of operating lease, the aggregate lease rental payable over the lease term should be spread over the term on straight-line basis irrespective of the payment schedule as per the terms and conditions of the lease.

4.5 REGULATORY AUTHORITY

There is no specific Act or legislation governing leasing in India. All legislations or Acts referring to assets and management of assets encompass leased assets, either in terms of assets held by the lessor or joined with assets for which payment in full has not been received. Some of the Acts include:

Companies Act, 1956

Consumer Protection Act, 1986

Easements Act, 1882

Foreign Exchange Regulation Act, 1973, now replaced with Foreign Exchange Management Act, 2000

Hire Purchase Act, 1972

Income Tax Act, 1962

Indian Contract Act, 1872

Indian Stamp Act, 1899

Manufacturing and Other Companies (Auditor's Report) Order, 1988

Motor Vehicles Act, 1988

Recovery of Debts due to Banks and Financial Institutions Act, 1993

Registration Act, 1908

Reserve Bank of India Act, 1934

Sale of Goods Act, 1930

Sick Industrial Companies (Special Provisions) Act, 1985

Transfer of Property Act, 1882

Reserve Bank of India's (RBI) Supervision of NBFCs

Following large-scale asset liability mismatches in the market, the Reserve Bank of India (RBI) amended its RBI Act in 1997 to weigh various assets and off-balance sheet items for their risk. The RBI also provided requirements for providing for bad debts and credit concessions.

The RBI has also proposed the following supervisory measures to track the performance of NBFCs. NBFCs that do not conform to the requirements may find their registrations cancelled on 5 February 2003, the RBI has said that NBFCs not having a minimum Net Owned Fund (NOF) of ₹ 25 lakhs as on 9 January 2003, would not be allowed to continue with their business.

Off-site Monitoring

Annual reporting forms (returns) have been revised to focus on core assets and income. These returns are to be certified by the company auditors. Large NBFCs with asset bases exceeding US$ 23 million must also furnish three years of operations data in the annual returns.

On-site-inspection

There is a need for periodic inspection of NBFCs, especially those suspected of unhealthy financial positions or non-compliance of prudential requirements. A new manual to elicit correct financial position and to point out violations of requirements or directions is under preparation.

External Audit

Auditors must certify important returns of NBFCs. Certified Public Accountant (CPA) firms are engaged to conduct special examinations of certain NBFCs, which are suspected of poor financial strength or violations of regulations. Reports prepared by the CPA firms on NBFCs operations are scrutinised further by the RBI's Department of Supervision.

Note that information provided in annual tax returns and other required reports must conform to specified accounting and taxation practices.

Regulations Affecting the Leasing Industry

The leasing industry in India is regulated by The Reserve Bank of India (RBI). The leasing industry comes under the overall category of non-banking finance companies (NBFCs) which could be of various types such as Leasing and Hires Purchase (HP), Housing Finance Company, Investment Company, Loan Company, Residuary arid Non-banking Company, etc.

Until very recently, the RBI used to be mainly concerned with the liability side of the NBFCs including the Leasing Industry. There are norms laid down by the RBI in terms of the amount of borrowings that could be raised by the leasing company. However, the RBI has been progressively concentrating on the asset side of the balance sheet. Currently, for a company to be considered as a leasing company, at least 51% of the total assets have to be leased assets and 33% of the total income should be obtained from Leasing Operations.

The RBI has broadly asked the leasing companies to comply with three requirements, namely,

1. Registration with the RBI,
2. Credit Rating, and
3. Certain prudential norms.

The above determines the borrowing power of the company.

In case the company meets all the above stated (three) norms, there is no overall ceiling for the borrower. The borrowing limit gets reduced progressively for companies, which do not satisfy all the above stated norms.

Capital Adequacy Framework

1. The RBI has also laid down capital adequacy norms for all NBFCs including leasing companies. Currently, the norm is at 8%. Besides, the RBI has laid down a Statutory Liquidity Reserve norm of 12.50% p.a. to be met by the leasing companies.
2. Every NBFC must maintain a minimum capital ratio of Tier I and Tier II funds of 12% before March 31, 1999. Tier I funds are owned funds excluding reserves created out of revalued assets after deducting accumulated loss balance and book value of intangible assets. Tier II capital includes preference shares, revaluation reserves discounted at 55%, general provision and loss reserves, hybrid debt and subordinated debt. In any case, Tier II capital cannot exceed Tier I capital.
3. The degree of credit risk exposure attached to off-the balance sheet items have been expressed as a percentage of the credit conversion factor to enable the working out of an aggregate to reckon the minimum capital ratio.
4. The liquidity ratio is to be prescribed to the leasing companies to avoid a mismatch of assets and liabilities.
5. Every NBFC must classify their assets as standard assets, sub-standard assets, doubtful assets and loss assets to enable provisioning.

6. As far as the laws governing the leasing contract is concerned, the lease contract clearly states that apart from the interest of the lessor in respect of the ownership of the asset and the benefit thereof in terms of availing depreciation and the collection of the lease rentals, all the other risks and rewards associated with the assets are posted to the account of the lessee. Thus, things such as keeping the asset in good and proper condition, maintaining and repairing the machine, etc. have to be done by the lessee. The lessor has the right to demand the return of the asset or to ask the entire lease rentals to be paid immediately in case he feels that there is danger of default in the repayment by the lessee.

4.6 ADVANTAGES OF LEASING

The following are the advantages of equipment leasing:

1. Flexibility: Leasing can be a flexible financing arrangement as the lease rentals can be structured in a manner that squares with the cash flow pattern anticipated by the lessee.

If a constant cash flow from the project in which the leased assets are employed, the lease rentals can be evenly spread over the lease term. If an increasing cash flow is anticipated, the lease rentals can be gradually stepped up. For a project with gestation period, the lease rentals can be arranged with a deferred period.

2. Leased with User-oriented Variants: Several changed versions of lease agreements are designed to cater to the needs of the lessee, e.g., Upgrade lease and Swap lease — to hedge the risk of obsolescence or replacement of old equipments with a new one. These are leases, which provide all services related to the usage and maintenance of the asset, *e.g.,* A full service car lease, with the lessee paying a pre-determined charge for the use of car, gives an entire spectrum of services from the provision of drivers to breakdown maintenance.

3. Tax-based Benefits: Leasing provides a firm with no capacity to absorb the investment-related tax shelters like depreciation, an opportunity to use the equipments without the cost involved.

A lessor who can absorb these tax shelters can acquire the assets and lease them to the firm at a lower lease rental. A cross-border lease helps in exploiting multiple tax shelters to the benefit of both the lessor and the lessee.

4. Less Paperwork and Quick Disbursement: A lease arrangement requires less paperwork for the lessee and involves a shorter time from submission of proposal and the disbursement of funds.

5. Convenience: When a firm plans to use an asset for a very short time, the decision to lease provides convenience.

Example:

A fleet of cars required by a firm for a week is met easily by leasing rather than buying them on Monday and selling on Saturday. Buying and selling also involves search costs, legal charges, selling commission, etc., which will be more than the rentals paid for a short-term lease.

6. Financing for the Total Requirements: A hire purchase agreement calls for down payments differing from 15% to 25%.

Equipment leasing does not require paying a high margin as other financing schemes, while lease rentals are paid monthly in advance, the first installment is treated as down payment.

Example:

A lease rental of ₹ 30 per thousand rupee per month in advance is treated as a down payment of 3.0% of the asset cost.

7. Scope for Better Use of Own Funds: Leasing is a convenient way of acquiring non-income generating assets like air conditioners, office equipments and vehicles. Own funds can be deployed for more productive uses.

8. Off-balance Sheet Financing: Secured loans and the assets acquired out of these loans are shown in the balance sheet of the borrower. Though a finance lease is non-cancellable, and its full payout features resemble secured loan, to be repaid over a period of time, it need not be disclosed in the balance sheet of the lessee. The financial commitments and the value of the assets acquired under a finance lease are not shown in the final accounts. This feature known as "off-balance sheet financing" is seen as a unique benefit as leasing over other form of financing. The non-disclosure of finance leases in the financial statements of lessee, conceals relevant information and so International Accounting Standards Committee (IASC) recommended the practice of capitalising finance leases in the books of the lessee.

9. Miscellaneous Benefits: A small-scale unit (SSI) on the verge of losing its SSI status by its investment exceeding its prescribed limit can escape de-recognition of SSI status by taking care of investment requirements through leasing. Closely held companies find leasing a convenient method of equipment financing as it does not dilute its control.

4.7 DISADVANTAGES OF LEASING

Some defects of leasing as an asset-based financing method are given below:

1. Lease contracts may have terms restricting use of leased assets resulting in underutilisation of operating capacity.
2. Since, most of the equipment lease transactions are finance leases, the chances of the lessee disinvesting is restricted. The non-cancellable nature is a disadvantage where equipments have uncertain technology and market life.
3. 'Off-balance sheet financing' through leasing exposes the firm to high financial risks as they tend to be highly geared (high debt-equity ratios).
4. In an imperfect financial market, and different methods of leasing and owning by tax authorities, leasing may be costlier than other forms of borrowing.

4.8 LEASE MARKET IN INDIA

Leasing is an emerging method for financing the acquisition of assets in India. It has a large number of players, both in the formal and informal sectors. In India, leasing is used mainly by the industry to acquire assets.

The main formal players in the market are the financial institutions, commercial banks, foreign financial institutions, manufacturers and Non-Banking Financial Companies (NBFCs); individuals and families handle leasing in the informal market.

Market Size

The leased asset base in India's organised sector is estimated at three to four per cent of the total gross fixed capital formation. It is 22% in most developing countries.

1. The reason for the slow growth of leasing finance in India is due to high rate of depreciation allowed in India.
2. Hire purchase system has an edge over leasing with respect to tax exemption in India from the points of lessor and lessee.
3. Financial institutions make loans with favourable terms to companies to assist them in establishing themselves in the market. The financial institutions have a low cost of capital and can offer cheap loans. It is a time-consuming process. Only few companies prefer leasing to avoid time-consuming process of availing loans from financial Institutions.
4. The typical Indian attitude is to own an asset rather than to lease it.

5. A leasing company belonging to a group of companies, obtains a loan from a financial institution, buys equipment required by the group of companies, and then leases the equipment to the companies. The group of companies not only benefit from their ability to obtain financing at a low interest rate, but also from the tax concessions accruing from the loan interest expense. The depreciation on the leased equipment and the lease rental expense are also subject to tax exemption. Most industrial groups in India exploit these provisions in the tax law.

Slowdown

In 1997-98, the total base of leased assets (excluding real estate) in India in the formal sector was estimated at approximately US$ 37.0 billion. This figure represents 7.6% nominal growth from the 1996-97 level of US$ 34.0 billion. The latter figure was up approximately 20% from US$ 28.5 billion in 1995-96. The slowdown is due to three reasons:

1. The growth rate of Indian industries now is staggering around 4%. Investment by Indian corporates and foreign direct investment have slowed considerably.
2. The market has been slowing since 1996. Clients began defaulting on payments. Consequently, a number of lease financing companies faced a severe asset-liability mismatch. That led to a repayment crises and bankruptcy. However, even today, there are over 38,000 estimated players in the market.
3. Since 1996, most existing leasing companies have become more conservative in their lending practices following the collapse of several leasing and hire-purchase finance companies.

Players in the Leasing Market

Financial Institutions (FIs)

FIs are term lending institutions. There are over 10 such institutions handling project finance on an all-India basis and over 20 State-level institutions. While FIs have over 30% of the market, it is not their main line of business.

Commercial Banks

Although banks have been in the leasing market for some time, it is not a priority activity for them either. However, State Bank of India, India's largest commercial bank, decided to enter the market in 1997. This has altered market dynamics considerably because State Bank of India has a very large deposit base from savings accounts and deposit accounts, leading to the lowest cost of capital amongst all players.

Chart 4.2

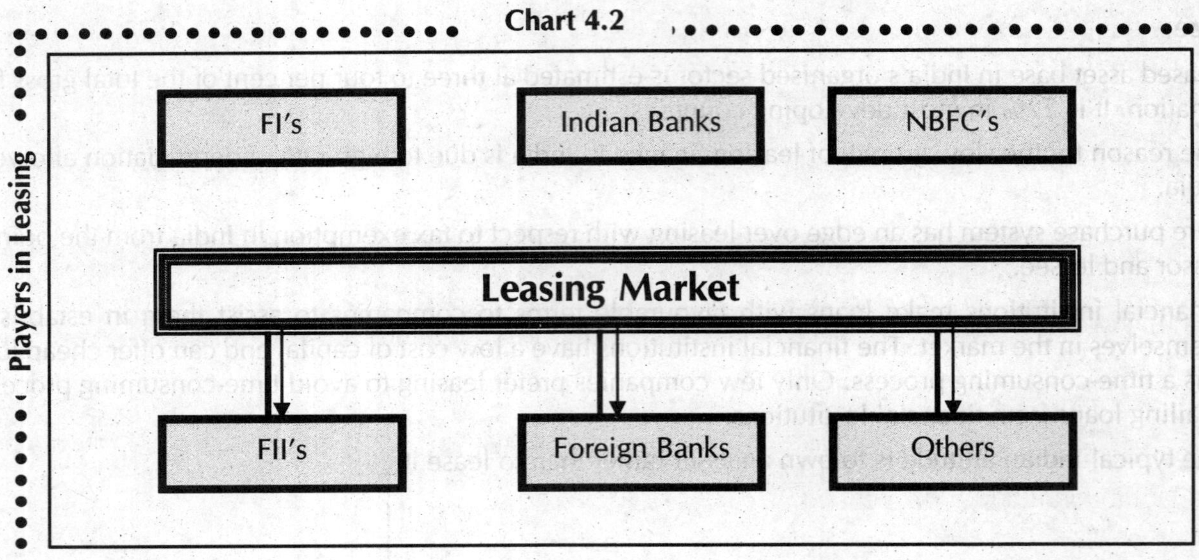

Foreign Banks

Thus far, foreign banks have played a very limited role in the leasing market. A few foreign banks, such as ABN-Amro and ANZ Grindlays, have organised aircraft leasing for private airlines.

The following information is available for Citicorp Securities & Investment, the financial services arm of Citibank; it had leased assets worth US$ 6.7 million in 1996-97.

Non-banking Finance Companies (NBFCs)

Indian finance companies that do not fall into any of the above categories are labelled NBFCs. The strength of NBFCs lies in their ability to capture market niches either bypassed or overlooked by other financial institutions.

FIs and Banks

This has led NBFCs to gain over a 50% share of the leasing market. On the other hand, 70% of NBFCs' business originates with leasing and hire-purchase activities. Their reliance on leasing increased after the recession hit their non-fund businesses.

In 1998, Anagram Finance and ITC Classic merged with the Industrial Credit and Investment Corporation of India (ICICI), a leading all-India FI. In addition, Twenty-First Century Finance merged with Centurion Bank. Although all of the companies recorded profits in 1996-97, fears of a harder recovery and squeezed margins led them to the decision to exit the NBFC segment of the market.

Foreign Institutional Investors (FIIs)

Although there are no legislative barriers that prevent FIIs from entering the leasing market, the only FIIs with measurable involvement in the market are the US company GE Capital and the Japanese company Orix Corporation. Both these companies are not engaged in direct leasing activities.

4.9 LEASING SCENARIO

When First Leasing Company of India was started in Chennai in 1973, equipment leasing, as an industry, had its birth.

The need for financial services was not felt in the 70s and early 80s and so this line of activity did not take roots.

The public sector financial institutions like IDBI, IFCI, ICICI and several State finance companies catered to the needs of term loans and the commercial banks looked after the working capital requirements at easier terms.

The need for alternative source of financing was not felt and so the 20th Century Leasing Limited started its operation only in 1979.

There was a change in the scenario in the early 80s — the credit squeeze announced by the RBI and the implementation of Tandon and Chore Committee norms on Maximum Permissible Bank Finance (MPBF) for working capital made the manufacturing companies set apart a portion of long-term funds for working capital.

The paucity of funds for working capital requirements made the companies seek out alternative sources of funding their capital expenditure plans.

Equipment leasing was seen as a viable alternative because of:

I. Easy documentation,

II. Fewer restrictive terms and conditions,

III. Absence of convertibility clause that may dilute ownership and control, and

IV. Availability of hundred per cent finance.

The existing leasing companies started performing well because of increased demand and this paved the way for active investors' participation in equity stocks of these companies. As a result of this upsurge in the leasing business by the end of 1985, there were about 300 leasing and finance companies in this industry. The enhanced demand lured the financial institutions and commercial banks to enter this industry. In 1983, the ICICI entered this industry, followed by Industrial Reconstruction Bank of India (IRBI) and a host of State finance corporations. IDBI also joined the list of operators.

In 1983, with an amendment to the Banking Regulation Act of 1949, commercial banks were allowed to promote subsidiaries specialising in equipment leasing and financial services, but not in hire purchase.

SBI was the first commercial bank to have its subsidiary — SBI Capital Markets Limited — which started functioning in 1986.

Canara Bank established Can Bank Financial Services Limited, Punjab National Bank, promoted PNB Financial Services Limited. Some commercial banks promoted subsidiaries with equity participation from financial institutions.

The Infrastructure Leasing and Financial Services Limited (ILFS) was one such promoted by Central Bank of India, HDFC and UTI.

The International Finance Corporation Washington (IFCW) and a host of multinational banks entered the leasing industry as co-promoters.

The IFCW promoted two leasing companies with commercial banks and finance companies in the private sector.

1. The India Equipment Leasing Limited (IEL) at Chennai with equal equity participation from State Bank of India and Sundaram Finance.
2. The Leasing Corporation of India, at Mumbai, with equal equity participation from the Bank of India and the Twentieth Century Finance Corporation Limited.

The first foreign bank to participate in the equity of a leasing company was the Standard Chartered Bank. It promoted the Cholamandalam Investment and Finance Company in Chennai, with Tube Investments of India Limited, a constituent of Murugappa Group. Foreign banks began offering the service of lease brokering to their corporate clientele as an agent of the corporate customer. The bank locates the lessor who presents a lease package to suit the requirements of the customers. The bank receives a commission for its services.

There were no entry barriers and this opened the floodgates for a large-scale entry of private sector companies, financial institutions and commercial banks into the industry. This created stiff competition and resulted in a steep fall in the lease rates.

The lease rate on a five-year non-cancellable lease had declined from ₹ 32 ptpm (per thousand per month) to ₹ 25 ptpm, by 1985-86. There was excess pressure on the profit margins with increase in the cost of funding leases; several State Governments imposed a sales tax on lease rentals, which further aggravated this problem.

Hence, several small leasing companies in the private sector either closed down or diversified by adding related activities like bill discounting to their portfolio. Some others diversified into unrelated areas like manufacturing.

The Strongest Leasing Companies

Based on their performance in 1996-97 and 1997-98, the following NBFCs are rated the strongest in the leasing market:

1. Sundaram Finance Limited
2. Cholamandalam Investors and Finance Company Limited
3. Ashok Leyland Finance Limited

4. Kotak Mahindra Finance Limited
5. Tata Finance Limited

These companies have strong balance sheets, which should be able to see them through the prevailing tough times. The main industries focused on (through leasing and hire-purchase) by these companies are:

(a) Manufacturing — over 70%
(b) Transportation cars — over 10%
(c) Office equipment — over 5%
(d) Transportation — commercial vehicles — over 5%

All of these companies are rated best for deposit collection; hence, their cost of capital is lower. Until October 1997, all of the above cited companies were rated AAA by the major credit rating agencies.

Table 4.1 Income Statements of Top Five Leasing Companies, 1996-97 *(US $ million)*

Company	Exchange Rate	Income	Interest Exp.	Depreciation	PAT
Sundaram Fin. (1997-98)	40	114.6	51.2	23	19
Cholamandalam	38	36.6	14.5	9	5.8
Ashok Leyland	38	72.2	43.7	10	9
Kotak Mahindra	38	95	51.9	18.6	7.9
Tata Finance	38	109	62	14.7	13

Note: Dollar conversions are at the given average exchange rate during March-April (Financial year-end).

References: India Leasing Yearbook 1998, Centre for Monitoring Indian Economy, 3rd Revised Edition, Business Line.

From the leasing industry point of view, 1980s experienced a rapid growth in investment in leased assets.

The annual investment in leased assets, which are at ₹ 50 crores at the year 1983, increased to ₹ 900 crores by 1990; registering a growth of more than 50% p.a.

The liberalisation measures announced in the Industrial Policy Statement of 1991 enhanced the growth rate maintained at the same level.

The removal of investment limits in the MRTP Act and permission to allow 51% foreign equity in Indian companies helped the process of capital formation with private sector to an extent.

The main industry sectors that use the leasing option are, according to an American study:

(a) Manufacturing — domestic and imported equipment — over 50% of the market.
(b) Transportation — commercial and personal vehicles — over 15% of the market.
(c) Construction — over 15% of the market.
(d) Office equipment — over 10% of the market.
(e) Others, including medical, agricultural, educational institutions, etc.

4.10 INDIAN CONTEXT OF STRUCTURED LEASE

Salient Features of Structured Lease in India

1. The leases structured in the Indian context are only 'finance lease'.
2. Operating leases are very limited as the resale market for the used capital equipment is Nil.
3. Lease agreements do not provide for transfer of ownership to the lessee either during the lease period or at the end of the lease, as it will turn out to be a hire-purchase transaction from the tax angle.
4. The lease rentals are structured to recover the entire investment cost during the primary period. Lease rentals for the secondary period are very nominal, e.g., Lease rates.

   Lease rates are governed by various factors like the tax, rate of depreciation, availability of capital allowances and the marginal tax rate.

   Table 4.3 **Lease Rates**

Primary Period (years)	Lease Rates (in ₹ ptpm)
3	36-38
5	26.5-28
8	19-21

   The lease rate for the secondary period is around ₹ 0.51 ptpm and so the rental during the secondary period is called the 'pepper-corn consideration'..
5. Lease rentals are payable in equated monthly installments at the beginning of every month with exceptions dependent on lessee's requirements and projected cash flows.
6. Equipment lease transactions are mostly 'direct lease'.
7. These leases are provided for a wide range of equipments from industrial plant and machinery, computers, other office equipments and vehicles.
8. Equipments lease are generally for capital investments not exceeding ₹ 100 lakhs. Most lessors' view leasing as a kind of substitute finance for meeting unplanned capital expenditure or for getting non-productive assets.
9. Project leasing is also done on a limited scale. The Infrastructure Leasing and Financial Services Limited (ILFS) has provided leases for power plants, effluent treatment plants and power transmission lines. It has provided the lease finance of ₹ 2 crores to Madhya Pradesh Government for road construction. The State Government levies and collects road toll and uses the proceeds to pay the lease rentals. Until the investment cost is fully recovered, the ownership of the lands on which the road is laid will vest with ILFS. This is the first public infrastructure project funded by a finance lease.
10. The regulatory and tax framework lay certain conditions on taxing of cross-border lease transactions even though the EXIM Policy of 1985-86 permits leasing company to undertake leasing of imported equipments, after fulfilling certain criteria.
11. The Shipping Credit and Investment Company of India (SCICI) has proposed having a cross-border lease option to the Indian Shipping companies for financing acquisition of ships. Here, the ships will be acquired by group foreign investors and offered on a long-term lease with a purchase option to the Indian shipping companies — with necessary amendment of Merchant Shipping Act, 1938 to enable acquiring an interest in Indian ships.

4.11 GLOSSARY

Advance Payment

Pay beforehand or up front.

Broker

An agent who brings two parties together, enabling them to enter into a contract to which he is not a principal. His remuneration consists of a brokerage, which is usually calculated as a percentage of the sum involved in the contract but may be fixed according to a tariff. Brokers are used because they have specialised knowledge of certain markets or to conceal the identity of a principal, in addition to introducing buyers to sellers.

Deposit

1. A sum of money paid by a buyer as part of the sale price of something in order to reserve it. Depending on the terms agreed, the deposit may or may not be returned if the sale is not completed.
2. A sum of money left with an organisation, such as a bank, for safekeeping or to earn interest or with a broker, dealer, etc., as a security to cover any trading losses incurred.
3. A sum of money paid as the first instalment on a hire-purchase agreement. It is usually paid when the buyer takes possession of the goods.

Depreciation

1. An amount charged to the profit and loss account of an organisation to represent the wearing out or diminution in value of an asset. The amount charged is normally based on a percentage of the value of the asset as shown in the books; however, the way in which the percentage is used reflects different views of depreciation. Straight-line depreciation allocates a given percentage of the cost of the asset each year, thus suggesting an even spread of the cost of the asset over its useful life. Reducing- (diminishing-) balance depreciation applies a constant percentage reduction first to the cost of the asset and subsequently to the cost as reduced by previous depreciations. In this way, reducing amounts are charged periodically to the profit and loss account; by this method, the depreciated value of the asset in the balance sheet may approximate more nearly to its true value, in that many assets depreciate more quickly early and more slowly later in their life. Thus, depreciation is principally a means of allocating the cost of an asset over its useful life.
2. A fall in the value of a currency with a floating exchange rate relative to another. Depreciation can refer both to day-to-day movements and to long-term realignments in value. For currencies with a fixed exchange rate, a devaluation or revaluation of currency is required to change the relative value.

Finance Broker

A broker who arranges finance.

Hire Purchase

System of purchase by paying in installments.

In Advance — Before the start of the period.

In Arrears — Total unpaid debt, debts not paid by the due date.

Interest

The charge made for borrowing a sum of money. The rate of interest is the charge made, expressed as a percentage of the total sum loaned, for a stated period of time (usually one year). Thus, a rate of interest of 15%

per annum means that for every ₹ 100 borrowed for one year, the borrower has to pay a charge of ₹ 15, or a charge in proportion for longer or shorter periods.

In simple interest, the charge is calculated on the sum loaned only, thus I = Prt, where I is the interest, P is the principal sum, r is the rate of interest, and t is the period. In compound interest, the charge is calculated on the sum loaned plus any interest that has accrued in previous periods. In this case I = P [(1 + r) to the nth power – 1], where n is the number of periods for which interest is separately calculated. Thus, if ₹ 500 is loaned for 2 years at a rate of 12% per annum, which is compounded in quarterly bases, the value of n will be 4 × 2 = 8 and the value of r will be 12/4 = 3%. Thus, I = 500 [(1.03) to the 8th power – 1] = ₹ 133.38, whereas on a simple interest basis, it would be only ₹ 120. In general, rates of interest depend on the money supply, the demand for loans, government policy, the risk of non-payment as assessed by the lender and the period of the loan.

Lease Broker

Any broker who arranges a lease between a lender and a lessee. (See 'broker')

Lease Purchase

A variation of leasing, according to which, the goods become the lessee's property.

Leasing

Hiring equipment, such as a car or a piece of machinery, to avoid the capital cost involved in owning it. In some companies, it is advantageous to use capital for other purposes and to lease some equipment, paying for the hire out of income. The equipment is then an asset of the leasing company rather than the lessor. Sometimes, a case can be made for leasing rather than purchasing, on the grounds that some equipment quickly becomes obsolete.

Lender – The person or institution, that grants a loan.

Lessee – A person who is granted a lease; tenant.

Lessor – A person granting a lease; landlord.

On-balance Sheet

Any financial expenditure that shows on a company's balance sheet.

Off-balance Sheet

Under the right circumstances, a lender (such as APT Finance) can arrange an "operating" lease where the asset is leased out for long-term rent, and not a "Cap-Ex" transaction, and so it is an "off" balance sheet item.

Operating Lease – Essentially long-term rent, not a capital expense transaction.

Present value (PV) – The selling price at the time of sale, *i.e.*, now.

Refinancing

The process of repaying some or all of the loan capital of a firm by obtaining fresh loans, usually at a lower rate of interest.

Residual Value

The expected selling price of an asset at the end of its useful life.

Tax Allowances

Sums, which are deducted from, total income to arrive at taxable income.

Term – A specified period of time.

4.12 REVIEW QUESTIONS

Short Answer Questions

1. Define the term Leasing.
2. Distinguish between Lease and Term Loan.
3. What is the difference between Lease and Mortgage?
4. Differentiate the Lease from Hire-purchase.
5. Distinguish between Financial Lease and Operating Lease.
6. What is Sale and Lease Back?
7. Explain the term Direct Lease.
8. How do you know that a lease is a single investor lease?
9. Describe the process of Leveraged Lease.
10. Distinguish between Domestic Lease and International Lease.
11. Who are the players of Leasing in India?
12. List out five major companies involved in leasing in India.
13. What are legislations governing leasing in India?
14. How is accounting done for financial lease with respect to lessor?
15. How is accounting done for financial lease with respect to lessee?

Essay Type Questions

1. Explain the concepts of Leasing and Hire-purchase.
2. Differentiate among Operating Lease, Financial Lease and Lease and Sales back.
3. Why companies go for leasing rather than purchasing equipment?
4. Describe the various legal provisions that govern the leasing business in India.
5. What is the market potential for leasing in India?
6. Explain the roles played by different players in the Lease Market in India.
7. What steps are involved in a lease arrangement?

❋ ❋ ❋

PROBLEMS IN LEASING

Problem No.1

Reliance Equipment corporation is considering to lease an equipment which has a purchase price of ₹ 3,50,000. The equipment has an estimated economic life of 5 years. As per the Income Tax Rules, a written down depreciation at 25% is allowed. The lease rentals per year are ₹ 1,20,000. The company's marginal tax rate is 50%. If the before-tax borrowing rate for the company is 16%, should the company lease the equipment?

Solution:

In this case, the firm has two option: (i) to take the equipment on lease, and (ii) to purchase the equipment by borrowing funds @ 16%. Both the option have been evaluated as follows:

Lease Option: In this case, the firm shall be paying annual lease rental of ₹ 1,20,000 for 5 years. Given the tax rate of 50%, the tax shield will be ₹ 60,000 and the net cash outflow will be ₹ (1, 20,000 – 60,000) = ₹ 60,000 only. The present value of annuity of ₹ 60,000 @ 8% for 5 years is 60,000 × PVIFA (8%, 5 years) = 60,000 × 3.993 = ₹ 2,39,580.

If the firm buys the asset, there will be an outflow of ₹ 3,50,000 at the time of purchase. However, the firm shall have a tax deductibility of depreciation. So, there will be an inflow in terms of tax shield of depreciation, which can be calculated as follows:

	Year 1	Year 2	Year 3	Year 4	Year 5
Depreciation @25% W.D.V.	₹ 87,500	₹ 65,625	₹ 49,219	₹ 36,914	₹ 27,686
Tax Shield @ 50%	43,750	32,813	24,609	18,457	13,843

The Salvage Value after year 5 is taken as nil.

The present value of cash flows of buying option is:

Year	Cash flow	PV Factor	PV
0	– 3,50,000	1.00	35,00,00
1	+43,750	0.926	+ 40,513
2	+32,813	0.857	+28,121
3	+24,609	0.794	+ 19,540
4	+18,457	0.735	+ 13,566
5	+13,843	0.681	+ 9.427
	– 2.38.833		

So, the firm has present value of outflow in both the cases. In lease, the present value is ₹ 2,39,580 whereas in buying option, the present value is ₹ 2,38,833. Since the present value of outflows is lesser in buying option, the firm should buy the asset instead of leasing.

It may be noted that: (i) The discount rate has been taken at 8% which is after tax cost of debt. (ii) There is an implied assumption that the firm does not take a loan for buying the equipment. This is based on the fact that the repayment schedule is not given. It is based on this assumption that neither repayment nor the interest payment have been considered in buying option.

Problem No. 2

ABC Company Ltd. has *two* financial options in respect of procuring an equipment for utilising the same for 5 years costing ₹ 10,00,000. The *two* options are:

Option I: Borrow ₹ 10,00,000 at an interest rate of 15%. The loan is repayable at 5 year-end instalments. The equipment could be sold at the end of its 5 year economic life at a realisable value of ₹ 1,00,000.

Option II: Lease in the asset for a period of 5 years at yearly rental of ₹ 3,30,000 payable at year-end.

The rate of depreciation allowable on the equipment is 15%. The company has to pay Income Tax @ 50% and has a discounting rate of 16%. Capital gain or loss is to be ignored. Evaluate the *two* options and give your opinion.

Solution:

The two options before the company can be evaluated as follows:

Option I – Purchase of equipment out of borrowed funds: In this case, the company shall have to pay interest every year, together with the repayment of part of the borrowing. The company, however, will get a tax shield for both the interest paid as well as for depreciation. The resultant cash flows may be evaluated as follows:

Year (1)	(2)	Interest @ 15% (3)	Depreciation @ 15% (4)	Int.+Dep. WDV (5)	Tax Shield on Int.+ Dep.	Repayment outflow (1+5–4)	Net Cash PV @ 16%
(1)	₹ 1,50,000	₹ 1,50,000	₹ 3,00,000	₹ 1,50,000	₹ 2,00,000	₹ 2,00,000	–1,72,400
(2)	1,20,000	1,27,500	2, 47,500	1,23,750	2,00,000	1,96,250	–1,45,814
(3)	90,000	1,08,375	1,98,375	99,188	2,00,000	1,90,812	1,22,310
(4)	60,000	92,120	1,52,120	76,060	2,00,000	1,83,940	–1,01,535
(5)	30,000	78,300	1,08,300	54,150	2,00,000	1,75,850	– 83,705
(5) Scrap Value							+1,00,000
							+47.600
		Net Present Value of Outflows					5,78,164

Option II: In this case, the company has to pay a lease rental of ₹ 3,30,000 on which tax shield will be ₹ 1,65,000. So, the annual net outflow will be ₹ 1,65,000 only for 5 years. The PV AF for 16% for 5 years is 3.274. The PV of outflows may be ascertained as follows:

PV of outflows = ₹ 1,65,000 × 3.274

= ₹ 5,40,210

Since the PV of outflows is lower in leasing option, it is better for the firm to take the equipment on lease.

Problem No. 3

ABC Machine Tool Company is considering the acquisition of a large equipment to set up its factory in a backward region for ₹ 12,00,000. The equipment is expected to have economic useful life of 8 years. The equipment can be financed either with an eight year term loan at 14% interest, repayable in equal instalments of ₹ 2,58,676 per year, or by an equivalent amount of lease rental per year. In both cases, payments are due at the end of the year. The equipment is subject to the straight-line method of depreciation. Assuming no salvage value, and 50% corporate tax rate. Which of the financing alternatives should it select?

(Ans.: Purchase Option: NPV of outflows: ₹ 7,52,088.
Lease Option: ₹ 7,72,177
The firm should borrow the funds and purchase the machine)

Problem No. 4

A company is thinking of installing a Machine. It has to decide whether the machine is to be purchased outright (through 14% borrowings) or to be acquired on lease rental basis. The firms is in the 50% tax bracket. The other available details are:

Buying Option:

Purchase Price	₹ 20,00,000
Expected Economic Life	6 Years

Depreciation Straight-line Method

Salvage Value ₹ 2,00,000

Lease Option:

Lease Charges (to be paid in Advance) ₹ 4,00,000

Maintenance Expenses To be borne by the lessor

Payment of Loan: 6-year equal annual instalment of ₹ 5,14,271.

You are required to advice the company as to whether it should purchase or lease the machine?

(Ans.: Purchase Option: NPV of outflows: ₹ 11,51,526
Lease Option: ₹ –10,86,800
The firm should lease the machine)

Problem No. 5

A person wishing to take on lease an office premises, has been given two options by the landlord. The options are:

Option I: Lease period 18 years, Initial non-refundable deposit of ₹ 2,00,000. A yearly rent of ₹ 60,000 to be increased by 10% every 5th year of tenancy.

Option II: A yearly rent of ₹ 1,00,800 to be increased by 10% every 5th year of tenancy. Lease period 18 years. You are required to give your views on the alternatives from the point of view of the tenant. The rate of discount is to be taken at 18%. The present value of ₹ 1 payable at the end of the each year at 18% starting from year 1 to year 18 are as follows: 1.0, 0847458, 0.718184, 0.608631, 0.515789, 0.437109, 0.370432, 0.313925, 0.266038, 0.225456, 0.191064, 0.161919, 0.137220, 0.116288, .098549, 0.083516, 0.070776, and 0.059980.

(Answer: The net present value of excess cost of Option II over Option I is ₹ 72,987. Therefore, option I should be accepted by the tenant. Under this option he will be able to save an amount of ₹ 72,987 in terms of NPV.)

Problem No. 6

ABC Co. Ltd. is faced with two options as under in respect of acquisition of an asset value of ₹ 1,00,000:

(a) to acquire the asset directly by taking a Bank Loan of ₹ 1,00,000 repayable in 5 year-end installments at an interest of 15%

(b) to lease the asset at rentals of ₹ 320 per ₹ 1,000 of the asset value for 5 years payable at year end.

The following additional information is available:

(i) The rate of depreciation of the asset is 15% W.D.V.

(ii) The Company has an effective tax rate of 50%.

(iii) The Company employs a discounting rate of 16%.

You are to indicate in your report which option is more preferable to the company. Restrict calculation over a period of ten years.

Solution:

Evaluation of Bank Loan Option

(Figures in ₹)

	Yr. 1	Yr. 2	Yr. 3	Yr. 4	Yr. 5	Yr. 6	Yr. 7	Yr. 8	Yr. 9	Yr. 10
Repayment	20,000	20,000	20,000	20,000	20,000	—	—	—	—	
Int. @ 15%	15,000	12,000	9,000	6,000	3,000	—	—	—	—	—
Depreciation	15,000	12,750	10,838	9,212	7,830	6,655	5,657	4,808	4,087	3,487
Tax saving on										

Int. & Dep.	15,000	12,375	9,919	7,606	5,415	3,327	2,829	2,404	2,043	1,737
Net CF	–20,000	–19,625	–19,081	–18,394	–17,585	3,327	2,829	2,404	2,043	1,737
PVF(16%,n)	.862	.743	.641	.552	.496	.410	.354	.305	.263	.227
PV	–17.240	–14.581	–12.234	–10.154	– 8.370	1.364	1.001	733	537	395
Total present value of inflows										58.546

The net cash flow (Net CF) = (–Repayment — Interest) + Tax saving
= Repayment + Interest – Tax saving

Evaluation of Leasing Option

(Figures in ₹)

	Year 1	Year2	Year 3	Year4	Year5	NPV
Lease Rent	–32,000	–32,000	–32,000	–32,000	–32,000	
Tax savings (50%)	16,000	16,000	16,000	16,000	16,000	
Net cash outflows	–16,000	–16,000	–16,000	–16,000	–16,000	
PVF(16%, n)	0.863	0.743	0.641	0.552	0.476	
Net Present Value	–13,808	–11,888	–10,256	–8,832	–7,616	–52,400

The net present value of outflows in leasing is lower than bank loan and should be accepted. In this case, the NBL (Net Benefit of Leasing) to be company is ₹ 6,146, *i.e.*, –52,400 – (–58,546).

Problem No. 7

Beta Limited is considering the acquisition of a personal computer costing ₹ 50,000. The effective life of the computer is expected to be five years. The company plans to acquire the same either by borrowing ₹ 50,000 from its bankers at 15% interest per annum or by lease. The company wishes to know the lease rentals to be paid annually which match the loan option. The following further information is provided to you:

(a) The principal amount of the loan will be paid in five annual equal installments.

(b) Interest, lease rentals and principal repayment are to be paid on the last day of each year.

(c) The full cost of the computer will be written off over the effective life of computer on a straight-line basis and the same will be allowed for tax purposes.

(d) The company's effective tax rate is 40% and the after tax cost of capital is 9%.

(e) The computer will be sold for ₹ 1,700 at the end of the 5th year. The commission on such sales is 9% on the sale value and the same will be paid.

You are required to compute the annual lease rentals payable by Beta Limited which will result in indifference to the loan option.

Answer:

Sale value: ₹ 1,700 – 9% Commission = ₹ 1,547.

Since the asset is already fully depreciated, this may be treated as capital gain and so taxable at 40%. The net inflow therefore, would be ₹ 1,547 – Tax @ 40% = **₹ 928.**

Lease Rentals = ₹ 33,832/3.899 = ₹ 8,680 (after tax)

In order to find out the annual lease rental (before tax), the following calculations is to be made:

Lease rental (before tax) = ₹ 8,680/(1 – 0.4) = ₹ 14,467

Therefore, Beta Ltd. may be indifferent between the loan option and the lease option so far as the annual lease rental is ₹ 14,467.

Problem No. 8

ABC Ltd. is considering to buy a machine costing ₹ 1,10,000 payable ₹ 10,000 down and balance is payable in 10 annual equal installments inclusive of interest chargeable at 15%. Another option before it is to acquire the assets on a lease rental of ₹ 5,000 per annum for 10 years. As a finance manager, decide between these two options that:

(i) Scrap value of ₹ 20,000 is realisable if the asset is purchased.

(ii) The firm provides 10% depreciation on straight-line method on the original cost.

(iii) The tax rate is 50% and after tax cost of capital in 15%.

Solution:

Option 1 - To Buy the Asset: In this option the firm has to pay ₹ 10,000 down and the balance ₹ 1,00,000 together with interest @ 15% is payable in 10 annual equal installments. The annuity amount may be calculated by dividing ₹ 1,00,000 by the PVAF for 10 years at 15% *i.e.*, Annual repayment = ₹ 1,00,000/5.019 = ₹ 19,925.

The cash flows of the borrowing and purchase option may be evaluated as follows:

Year	Installment	Interest	Repayment	Balance
1	₹ 19,925	₹ 15,000	₹ 4,925	₹ 95,075
2	19,925	14,261	5,664	89,411
3	19,925	13,412	6,513	82,898
4	19,925	12,435	7,490	75,408
5	19,925	11,311	8,614	66,794
6	19,925	10,019	9,906	56,888
7	19,925	8,533	11,392	45,496
8	19,925	6,824	13,101	32,395
9	19,925	4,859	15,066	17,329
10	19,925	2,596	17,329	—

Installment (1)	Interest (2)	Dep. (3)	Tax Shield (4) 50% of (2+3)	Net CF (1–4)	PVF(15%, n)	PV
₹ 10,000	—	—	—	—	—	₹ 10,000
19,925	₹ 15,000	₹ 11,000	₹ 13,000	₹ 6,925	.870	6,025
19,925	14,261	11,000	12,631	7,294	.756	5,514
19,925	13,412	11,000	12,206	7,719	.658	5,079
19,925	12,435	11,000	11,718	8,207	.572	4,694
19,925	11,311	11,000	11,156	8,769	.497	4,358
19,925	10,019	11,000	10,510	9,415	.432	4,067
19,925	8,533	11,000	9,767	10,158	.376	3,819
19,925	6,824	11,000	8,912	11,013	.327	3,601
19,925	4,859	11,000	7,930	11,995	.284	3,407
19,925	2,596	11,000	6,798	13,127	247	3.242
Present value of total outflows						53,806
Salvage Value (after tax)		—	10,000		247	+2.470
Net present value of outflows						51.336

It may be noted that: (i) depreciation of ₹ 11,000 has been provided for all the years. This is 10% of the original cost of ₹ 1,10,000, and (ii) The asset is fully depreciated during its life of 10 years, therefore, the book value at the end of 10th year would be zero. As the asset is having a salvage value of ₹ 20,000, this would be capital gain, and presuming it to be taxable at the normal rate of 50%, the net cash inflow on account of salvage value would be ₹ 10,000 only. This is further discounted to find out the present value of this inflow.

Option 11- Evaluation of Lease Option: In case the asset is acquired on lease, there is a lease rent of ₹ 15,000 payable at the end of next 10 years. This lease rental is tax deductible; therefore, the net cash outflow would be only ₹ 7,500 (after tax). The PVAF for 10 years @ 15% is 5.019. So, the present value of annuity of ₹ 7,500 is:

Present value of annuity of outflow = ₹ 7,500 × 5.019 = ₹ 37,643

If the firm opts to by the asset, the present value of outflow comes to ₹ 51,336; and in case of lease option, the present value of outflows comes to ₹ 37,643. Hence, the firm should opt for the lease option. In this way, the firm will be able to reduce its costs by ₹ 13,693, *i.e.*, ₹ 51,336 - ₹ 37,643. This may also be referred to as Net Benefit of Leasing.

Problem No. 9

DLP Pvt. Limited is considering the possibility of purchasing a multipurpose machine which cost ₹ 10,00,000. The machine has an expected life of 5 years. The machine generates ₹ 6,00,000 per year before depreciation and tax, and the management wishes to dispose the machine at the end of 5 years which will fetch ₹ 1,50,000. The depreciation allowable for the machine is 25% on written down value and the company's tax rate is 50%. The company approached a NBFC for a five-year lease for financing the asset which quoted a rate of ₹ 28 per thousand per month. The company wants you to evaluate the proposal with purchase option. The cost of capital of the company is 12% and for lease option, it wants you to consider a discount rate of 16%.

Answer:

Purchase Option: ₹ 4,60,000

Lease Option: ₹ 4,32,000

Since the present value of purchase option is higher, the company should go in for purchase rather than leasing.

Problem No. 10

ABC Company has decided to acquire a ₹ 5,00,000 pulp control device that has a useful life of ten years. A subsidy of ₹ 50,000 is available at the time the device is acquired and placed into service. The device would be depreciated on straight-line basis and no salvage is expected. The company is in the 50% tax bracket. If the acquisition is financed with a lease, lease payments of ₹ 55,000 would be required at the beginning of each year. The company can also borrow at 10% and debt payments would be due at the very beginning of each of the ten years. What is the present value of cash outflow for each of these financing alternatives, using the after-tax cost of debt? Which alternatives are preferable?

Solution:

SCHEDULE OF DEBT PAYMENT

End of Year	Total Payment	Interest Outstanding	Principal Amount
0	₹ 66,578	0	₹ 83,422
1	66,578	₹ 38,342	3,55,186
2	66,578	35,519	3,24,137
3	66,578	32,413	2,89,962
4	66,578	28,996	2,52,380
5	66,578	25,238	2,11,040
6	66,578	21,104	1,65,566
7	66,578	16,557	1,15,545
8	66,578	11,555	60,522
9	66,578	6,056	–

Initial amount borrowed = ₹ 5,00,000 – ₹ 50,000 = ₹ 4,50,000.

This amount of ₹ 4,50,000 is the amount which together with interest at the rate 10% on outstanding amount is repayable in equal installments *i.e.*, annuities in the beginning of each of 10 years. The PVAF at the rate 10% for 9 years is 5.759 and for the year 0 it is 1.000. So, the annuity amount may be ascertained by dividing ₹ 4,50,000 by (5.759+ 1.000).

So, Annual payment = 4;50,000 / 6.759= 66,578
Amount owed at time 0= ₹ 4,50,000-66,578 = ₹ 3,83,422

SCHEDULE OF CASH OUTFLOW: DEBT ALTERNATIVE

(1) End of Year	(2) Debt Payment	(3) Interest	(4) Dep.	(5) Tax Shield [(3)+(4)] 0.5	(6) Cash Outflows (2) – (5)	(7) PV of (6) at 5%
0	₹ 66,578	0	0	0	₹ 66,578	₹ 66,578
I	66,578	₹ 38,342	₹ 50,000	₹ 44,171	22,407	2 1,340
2	66,578	35,519	50,000	42,759	23,819	21,604
3	66,578	32,413	50,000	41,206	.25,372	21,916
4	66,578	28,996	50,000	39,498	27,080	22,279
5	66,578	25,557	50,000	37,619	28,959	22,690
6	66,578	21,104	50,000	35,552	31,026	23,152
7	66,578	16,238	50,000	33,279	33,299	23,665
8	66,578	11,555	50,000	30,777	35,801	24,230
9	66,578	6,056	50,000	28,028	38,550	25,043
10	—	0	50,000	25,000	–25,000	–15,348
				Total Present value of Outflows = ₹ 2,57,149		

End of Year	Lease Payment	Tax Shield	Cash Outflows	PV at 5%	PV
0	₹ 55,000	0	₹ 55,000	1	₹ 55,000
1-9	₹ 55,000	27,500	27,500	7.108	1,95,470
10	0	27,500	–27,500	0.614	–16,885
					₹ 2,33,585

The present values of cash outflow are ₹ 2,57,149 and ₹ 2,33,585 respectively under debt and lease alternatives. As under debt alternatives the cash outflow would be more, the lease is preferred. It may be noted that the repayment of loan as well as payment of lease rental is made in the beginning of the years. So, at the end of year 10, there will not be any payment in either option, but the tax benefit of depreciation for year10 as well as of lease rentals paid in the beginning or year 10, will be available only at the end of year 10.

Problem No. 11

ABC consultants Ltd. is studying the acquisition of an asset valued ₹ 1,00,000. The supplier offers two schemes:

(a) to sold the asset on credit payable in 5 year end instalments at an interest of 15%. Or,

(b) to lease in the asset at yearly rentals of ₹ 320 per ₹ 1,000 of the asset value for 5 years payable at year end.

The buyer firm provides depreciation @ 15% W.D.V. The firm belongs to a class where the effective tax rate is 50%. It has a policy of evaluating the proposed sales @ 16%.

You are to indicate in your report which option is more preferable to the company. (Restrict calculations over a period of ten years for buying option.) The payment of lease rental may be considered as an annuity.

Answer:

Option I: To acquire the asset on Lease basis: PV of outflow (16,000 × 3.274) = ₹ 52,384

Option II: Buying Option: Net Present Value = ₹ 58,548

The leasing option is better because the PV of outflows in lease is lower at ₹ 52,384 as against the PV of Outflows of ₹ 58,548 in case of buying option.

Problem No. 12

An industrial unit desires to acquire a diesel generating set costing ₹ 20 lakhs which has an economic life of 10 years at the end of which the asset is not expected to have any residual value. The unit is considering the alternative choices of:

(a) taking the machinery on lease, or

(b) purchasing the asset outright by leasing a loan.

Lease payments are to be made in advance and the lessor requires the asset to be completely amortised over its useful period and the asset will yield him a return of 10%.

The cost of debt is worked at 16% per annum. The lender requires the loan to be repaid in 10 equal annual installments, each installment becoming due at the beginning of the year. Average rate of income tax is 50%. It is expected that the operating costs would remain the same under either method. The firm follows straight-line method of depreciation. As a financial consultant, indicate what your advice will be.

Answer:

Option I: To acquire the asset on Lease basis: Net Present Value = ₹ –11.51.651

Option II: Procuring the asset out of borrowed funds: Net Present Value ₹ – 13,28.670

The PV of outflows in leasing option is lower at ₹ 11,51,651. So, the firm should procure the asset on lease basis.

Note: It may be noted that the cost of debt is given as 16%. This rate is used to calculate the interest charge for different years on the basis of loan amount outstanding in the beginning of the year. However, the rate of discount has been taken at 8% which is equal to after tax cost of debt, *i.e.*, 16% (1 – .5) = 8%, In the leasing option, the lease rental is calculated by taking the PVAF @ 10% because the lessor requires a rate of return of 10%. The PV of cash flows for the lease has again been taken @ 8% only.

CHAPTER 5

Hire Purchase

Objectives

The student, after studying the chapter, should be able to:

- Define Hire Purchase.
- List out the features of a Hire Purchase agreement.
- Be familiar with the evolution of the Hire Purchase in India.
- State the difference between Hire Purchase and Lease.
- Be aware of the legal aspects.
- Be familiar with the Motor Vehicles law on Hire Purchase.
- Be aware of the basic tax treatment.
- Have knowledge of Depreciation allowance.
- Be familiar with the accounting for Hire Purchase transactions.

Structure:

5.1 Introduction
5.2 Features of Hire Purchase
5.3 Evolution of Hire Purchase
5.4 Hire Purchase and Lease Compared
5.5 Sources of Law on Hire Purchase
5.6 Motor Vehicles Law on Hire Purchase
5.7 Problems in the Indian Hire Purchase Industry
5.8 Conclusion
5.9 Glossary
5.10 Review Questions

5.1 INTRODUCTION

Hire purchase is one of the various asset-based financing plans offered by the finance companies. In India, the road transport operators have dominated the market for hire purchase and hire purchase has been always associated with financing of commercial vehicles. However, in the recent years, hire purchase has become a means of financing equipment also.

A hire purchase can be defined:

"as a contractual arrangement under which the owner lets his goods on hire to the hirer and offers an option to the hirer for purchasing the goods in accordance with the terms of the contract."

According to the Hire Purchase Act, 1972, an agreement, which fulfills the following conditions, is a hire purchase agreement:

(I) The possession of the goods is delivered by the owner thereof to a person on condition that such person pays the agreed amount in periodic installments;

(II) The property in such goods is to pass to such a person on the payment of the last of such installment; and

(III) Such person has the right to terminate the agreement at any time before the property so passes. Therefore, the two distinct aspects of a hire purchase transaction are:

  (a) The option to purchase the goods at any time during the term of the agreement; and

  (b) The right available to the hirer to terminate the agreement at any time before the payment of the last installment.

Thus, a hire purchase transaction is one where the hirer (user) has, at the end of the fixed term of hire, an option to buy the asset at a token value. In other words, financial leases with a bargain buyout option at the end of the term can be called a hire purchase transaction.

5.2 FEATURES OF HIRE PURCHASE

The main features of a hire purchase arrangement are as follows:

1. The hire-vendor (the counterpart of lessor) gives the asset on hire to the hirer (the counterpart of lessee).
2. The hirer is required to make a down payment of around 20% of the cost of the equipment and repay the balance in regular hire purchase installments over a specified period of time. These installments cover interest as well as the principal repayment. In some cases, the finance company that gives hire purchase finance insists that the hirer give a deposit, which may be around 20% of the cost of the asset. The deposit carries interest and is returnable at the end of the hire purchase period.
3. When the hirer pays the last installment, the title of the asset is transferred from the hire-vendor to the hirer.
4. The hire-vendor charges interest on a flat basis. This means that a certain rate of interest (usually around 10%) is charged on the initial investment (made by the hire-vendor) and not on the diminishing balance.
5. During the currency of the contract (hire period) the hirer can opt for an early repayment and purchase the asset. The hirer exercising this option is required to pay the remaining amount of hire purchase installments (installments which have not fallen due) less an interest rebate.
6. Theoretically, the hirer can exercise the cancelable option and cancel the contract after giving due notice to the finance company.

5.3 EVOLUTION OF HIRE PURCHASE

Hire purchase is of British origin — the device originated much before leases became popular, and spread to countries, which were then British dominions. The device is still popular in Britain, Australia, New Zealand, India, Pakistan, etc. Most of these countries have enacted, in line with United Kingdom, specific laws dealing with hire purchase transactions.

The British concept of hire purchase has, however, been there in India for more than 6 decades. Development of hire purchase took two forms: (a) Consumer durable and (b) Automobiles.

Consumer durables hire purchase was promoted by the dealers in the respective equipment. Thus, Singer Sewing Machine Company, or Murphy radio dealers would provide installment facilities on hire purchase basis to the customers of their products.

The other segment that developed very fast is hire purchase of commercial vehicles. The dealers in commercial vehicles as well as pure financing companies sprang up. The value of the asset being good and repossession being easy, this branch of financing activity flourished fast, although until recently, most of automobile financing business was in the hands of family-owned businesses.

The first hire purchase company is believed to be Commercial Credit Corporation, successor to Auto Supply Company. While this company was based in Chennai, Motor and General Finance and Installment Supply Company were set up in North India. These companies were set up in the 1920s and 1930s.

These companies were set up predominantly to finance the road transport sector. The volume of hire purchase business was around ₹ 635 crores in 1987-88, out of which automobiles accounted for 55%. About 25% of the sale of commercial vehicles is accounted for by hire purchase today. It is estimated by the Federation of Hire Purchase Association that the stock-on-hire or hire purchase companies comprising corporate and non-corporate entities would be approximately ₹ 300 crores now.

The institutions engaged in hire purchase business in organised sector include commercial banks, cooperative banks, State Finance Corporations, Rational Small Industries Corporation and the unorganised sector, comprise of a large number of partnership firms and individuals.

NSIC supplies machinery to the small-scale industry under hire purchase. The IDBI indirectly participates in financing hire purchase by way of rediscounting Usance bills. ICICI also has discounting scheme of Usance bills under hire purchase scheme.

5.4 HIRE PURCHASE AND LEASE COMPARED

Essentially, asset-based financing in India particularly by non-banking financial companies is split into two documentation modes — Lease and Hire Purchase. These two are technically different instruments, but in essence, there is not much difference between the two, except for the caption.

In spite of the substantive similarity, historically, there has been a diametric separation between these two forms. The assets, usually subject matter of hire purchase, have been different from those generally leased out. Leasing has been used mostly for plant and machinery, while Hire Purchase has commonly been used for vehicles. Even the players have been different.

The reasons for this diametric distinction are more historical than logical. Hire purchase, essentially a British form, entered India during the colonial era, and thrived as almost the only form of external finance available for commercial vehicles. For the financiers, as witnessed world-over, commercial vehicles were the natural choice for several asset-features 'he/she loves' lasting value, ready secondary market, self-paying feature, etc. Hence, the industry of hire purchase became synonymous with truck financing. The motor vehicles laws gave the surest legal protection to a financier. The financier would not have to carry any of the operational risks of a motor vehicle, and yet, any transfer of the vehicle would not be possible without the financier's assent.

Leasing, essentially an US innovation entered the country significantly in the early 80s. It was propagated as an alternative to traditional modes of industrial finance. Besides, the early motivation (which continues with a number of players even now) of leasing was capital allowances, more significantly the investment allowance, which was not available for transport vehicles. Hence, the leasing from historically clung to industrial plant and machinery.

For several years, there was no lease of vehicles, because the motor vehicles law protection was not applicable to a lease. There was no investment allowance on vehicles, and for reciprocal reasons, there was no hire purchase of industrial machinery.

These reasons have vanished over time since —

- The motor vehicles law now treats leases and hire purchase at par from the viewpoint of financier protection.
- Investment allowance has been abolished, and hence, there are no predominant tax preferences to a lease.
- The RBI treats lease and hire purchase at par. It has stopped giving a distinctive classification to leasing and hire purchase companies,
- The accounting norms lead to the same effect on pre-tax income, as also balance sheet values, be it a lease or hire purchase transactions.

Therefore, income tax and sales tax treatment apart, there is not much that is different between lease and hire purchase. The choice between the two is largely open, subject to tax consequences.

From legal rights and obligations viewpoint, there is no difference between lease and hire purchase transactions. Both are viewed as bailment transactions. Accordingly, most of the common laws applicable to hire purchase transactions are also applicable to leases, and *vice versa*.

The difference between the two is principally the non-existence of option to buy in case of lease transactions. In other words, lease transactions carrying an option to buy, explicitly or implicitly, will be treated as hire purchase transactions. This may lead to differences in taxation treatment, but there is no appreciable difference in legal rights of parties.

Hire purchase is decisively a financial lease transaction. However, in some cases, it is necessary to provide the cancellation option in hire purchase transactions by statute: that is, the hirer has to be provided with the option of returning the asset and walking out from the deal. If such an option is embedded, hire purchase becomes significantly different from a financial lease: the risk of obsolescence is shifted to the hire-vendor. If the asset were to become obsolete during the pendency of the hire term, the hirer may off-hire the asset and close the contract, leaving the owner with less than a full payout.

5.5 SOURCES OF LAW ON HIRE PURCHASE

Hire purchase is essentially a hiring transaction — transaction in which possession of goods is handed over along with the right to use, for a stated period and for consideration.

Hiring transactions are species of bailment in contract law — therefore, the transactions of hire purchase are governed by the common law of contracts dealing with bailment transactions.

Contracts law, being common law, is codified in the Indian Contracts Act, 1872 but is enriched by history of precedents from both English and Indian Courts. Notably, the common law of contracts in India is based largely on the British legal principles, which have largely been accepted as applicable to?

Therefore, the principal sources of applicable law on hire purchase transactions are Sections 148 to 171 of the Indian Contracts Act dealing with bailment, and a long series of Court rulings, principally on hire purchase transactions, but of late, on lease transactions as well.

The law of hire purchase, essentially with a view to standardise procedures and eliminate malpractices, on the lines of the English Hire Purchase Act, was enacted in 1972. However, the Act has not been enforced yet. In the meantime, there has been an attempt to amend it and make it applicable. Reportedly, the Law Commission is again considering it fit to amend and implement the law, but unfortunately, over years, there have been so much change in commercial reality of hire purchase business that the concepts and calculations relevant in 1972 have become absolutely redundant.

Requirements of a Valid Hire Purchase Agreement

Both lease and hire purchase, to be valid, must be valid bailment transactions. Therefore, all the preconditions of a valid bailment will be applicable to lease and hire purchase transactions too.

The requirements for a valid hire purchase agreement are the same as those in case of a lease, but there is an additional requirement about an option to terminate the hiring by returning the goods, mentioned above.

A hire purchase agreement should contain:

1. The price of the goods to which the agreements relate.
2. The cash price at which the goods would have been available to the hirer if he had agreed to purchase them for cash.
3. The date on which the agreement shall be deemed to have commenced.
4. The number of installments by which the hire purchase price is payable.
5. The amount of each installment, the date of payment or the mode of payment, the person to whom and the place at which payment has to be made.
6. The description of the goods in such manner as sufficiently to identify?

Warranties and Conditions

The implied warranties in a hire purchase agreement are :

1. The owner gives a warranty that the hirer shall have and enjoy the quiet possession of the goods.
2. The owner warrants that the goods are free from any charge or encumbrances in favour of any third party at the time when the property in the goods is to pass to the hirer.

The implied conditions in every hire purchase agreement are:

1. There is a condition as to title that the owner has the right to sell the goods at the time when the property/ s to pass to the hirer.
2. The goods should be of merchantable quality. If the goods have been sold for self-use, they should be reasonably fit for the purpose for which they have been produced and marketed.
3. Implied conditions as to fitness for hirer's purpose. This arises when hirer explicitly or impliedly informs the owner the purpose for which the goods are required.
4. Where the goods are let in reference to a sample, the implied condition on the part of the owner is that the bulk of the goods should correspond with the quality of goods in the sample.
5. Where the goods are delivered under their description, the implied condition is that the goods should correspond with the description.

Rights and Obligations of the Hirer

Rights

Converting the transaction into sale: The hirer has been given the right to convert the transaction into a sale at any time he chooses. If he wants so, he has to pay up the balance of hire purchase price as reduced by rebate to which he is entitled.

Terminating a hire purchase agreement: The hirer can terminate a hire purchase agreement at any time before the final payment falls due. It is essential that he must give notice about his intention to terminate a contract. In these circumstances, he will have to return the goods to the owner; he will also pay the installment of the price which has fallen due up to the time of termination.

Appropriating a payment: If the hirer is indebted to the owner in respect of more than one transaction and he makes a payment which is not sufficient to meet his obligations or liability under the different agreements, he may appropriate the payment to whatever agreement or more than one agreement as he likes. If the hirer does not make any such appropriation, the owner gets the right to apply the payment to the agreements in the order of their time.

Assignment and transmission of hirer's right: The hirer has been given the right to assign his right, title and interest under the hire purchase agreement. He can do so, with the consent of the owner of the goods. However, if the owner withholds his consent without any justified cause, then assignment can be made without his consent. However, the rights of hirer are capable of passing by operation of law to his legal representative who will then be liable in the same manner as the hirer.

Duties

The duties of a hirer under the hire purchase Act are as below:

1. The hirer is under an obligation to pay the hire charges in accordance with the agreement and to comply with the terms of the agreement.
2. The hirer is under an obligation to take care of those goods he took through the hire purchase agreement. Here the hirer is bound to take as much care of the goods delivered to him as a person of ordinary prudence would take of his own goods of the same bulk, quality and value under similar circumstances.
3. There is an absolute liability upon the hirer, irrespective of whether he was negligent or not, if he makes any use of the goods which is not according to the conditions of the agreement.
4. The owner may ask the hirer in writing to give information about the whereabouts of the goods. If he fails to do so without any reasonable cause, he is punishable with fine which may extend to ₹ 200.

Rights and Obligations of the Hire Vendor

Rights

Termination of Agreement: The owner can terminate a hire purchase agreement in case the hirer makes more than one default in the payment of hire purchase installments. The owner must give one week's notice where the hire is payable at weekly or lesser intervals and two weeks in other cases. In case, the hirer pays up the amount together with due interest within the notice period, the owner shall not be entitled to terminate the contract.

The rights of an owner on termination of a contract are:

1. The owner can retain the already paid hire charges and can recover the arrears due up to the date of the termination.
2. The owner has the right to forfeit the initial deposit if the agreement so permits?
3. The owner can enter the premises and seize the goods. However, "protected goods" cannot be seized without the intervention of the court?
4. The owner has been given the right to recover the possession of the goods either by an application under Section 20 of the hire purchase agreement or through suit.
5. Owner has the right to recover damages for non-delivery of goods, in case the hirer makes delay in returning the goods.

Recovery of the "Protected Goods": In case the hirer pays the statutory proportion of the price of the goods, then the goods covered by the Hire Purchase Act are changed into 'Protected Goods'. The owner does not have the right to seize the protected goods. The owner can recover the protected goods either by making an application or by filing a suit.

Duties

While enjoying all the rights of ownership, the owner may virtually escape from all obligations relating to the goods — conditions of fitness, quality, usefulness for purpose, or any damages on account of defects in goods, can be effectively avoided by a disclaimer clause in the agreement backed by evidence that the owner was not involved in selection of the goods nor did he influence the hirer's decision as to the goods or the supplier.

While being owner of the goods, he may completely distance himself from obligations relating to the operation and use of the goods. This issue is very comfortably settled in India though there is a raging controversy on this point in number of other markets. The owner is not in effective possession and is not the user of the goods. The hirer cannot be taken to be the agent of the owner.

Few Cases

A bus given on hire purchase collided with a tree and killed several people. Hire purchase financier as owner was not responsible. The driver of the bus was not to be taken as agent and the financier a "master" [Sundaram Finance Ltd. vs. D.G. Nanajappa and Others].

A truck given on hire purchase was found carrying opium. The financier cannot be held responsible as the misuse of the vehicle could not have been with his consent and there was no possibility of the financier having control over the actual use by the hirer [Great Finance (P) Ltd. vs. the State].

While the owner of the asset has been held not to be responsible for misuse, he still claims right to be notified before confiscation of his asset [Pradeep and Co. vs. Collector of Customs 1973].

5.6 MOTOR VEHICLES LAW ON HIRE PURCHASE

Motor vehicles law in India contains specific provisions relating to lease and hire purchase transactions. In respect of all motor vehicles, registration with motor vehicles authorities is compulsory.

The motor vehicle is given a registration certificate, which contains the name of the "owner". Owner, for the purposes of the motor vehicles law, is defined as the person effectively using the asset — obviously, therefore, the name of the lessee/hirer is reflected as owner there. The name of the legal owner, *viz.*, the lessor or hire-vendor, is reflected merely by way of an endorsement.

However, it is a clear understanding of the law that neither the name on the registration certificate, nor the endorsement therein, has any reflection on the legal ownership of the vehicle.

It is also provided that no transfer of a motor vehicle bearing the endorsement of a lease or hire purchase shall be permitted without the no-objection letter of the lessor or hire-vendor.

Basic Tax Treatment of Hire Purchase and Lease Transactions

The tax treatment of hire purchase transactions in India is based on whether the hire purchase qualifies as a lease or will be treated as hire purchase transactions.

If the transaction is treated as a lease, the lessor shall be eligible for depreciation on the asset. The entire lease rentals will be taxed as income of the lessor. The lessee, correspondingly, will not claim any depreciation and will be entitled to claim the rentals as expense.

If the transaction is a hire purchase or conditional sale transaction, the hirer will be allowed to claim depreciation. This is based on an old Circular of the Department issued in the year 1943. The financing charges inherent in hire installments will be taxed as the hire-vendor's income and allowed as the hirer's expense.

In case of hire purchase transactions, the hire-vendor pays tax on the income inherent in hire installments, not on the whole of the hire rentals. Thus, tax is charged only on the income, and not the inflow.

There are no well-defined rules on determination of income in case of hire purchase transactions—therefore, accounting method adopted by the taxpayer will generally be followed. Thus, either of the straight-line, sum-of-digits, actuarial or IRR basis can be adopted for income allocation.

Depreciation Allowance on Hire Purchase

The 1943 Circular of the Department allows depreciation in case of hire purchase to the hirer of the asset.

Inspite of the old Circular, there have been problems occasionally in claiming depreciation. There have been problems on the part of the hirers in getting depreciation allowed; and there has been a unique case where the financier has claimed depreciation in a hire purchase transaction [AP Paper Mills].

However, in general, Departmental Circulars are understood as binding on lower tax authorities, and, therefore, the Circular can be safely treated as decisive.

A lease qualifying as true lease will entitle the lessor to claim depreciation. The taxpayer claiming depreciation should own the asset. No doubt, the lessor owns the asset, but it is not legal ownership alone that is sufficient; the lessor must establish himself to be the beneficial owner as well. It is on the failure of the condition of beneficial ownership that the legal owner in case of hire purchase is not allowed depreciation.

The lessor's beneficial ownership of the leased asset is proved essentially by the right of reversal of the asset at the end of the lease period — this highlights the significance of proving that the lessor has a substantive and not merely notional or technical right of reversal of the asset.

When a movable property becomes a permanent fixture to land not belonging to the lessor, the lessor ceases to be the legal owner of such fixture. This basic legal tenet is common in England and India. Such an intent is even reflected from the recent Supreme Court ruling in First Leasing Company of India where the Supreme Court distinguished a lease from hire purchase on the ground whether the transfer of right to use in a lease resulted into a permanent effective right of use being transferred, preparatory to a sale.

The other condition for depreciation is that the taxpayer should be using the asset. It is understood clearly that the taxpayer uses the asset in the business of leasing; hence, it is on the strength of the lessor's use that depreciation is claimed and not on the strength of the lessee's use. Use or its absence by the lessee should not, therefore, cast any implication on the lessor's depreciation claim.

Depreciation is allowed in India on a pooling basis: all assets eligible for the same rate of depreciation under a particular class of assets will be treated as one pool, or block of assets. Acquisition of fresh assets is treated as addition to the block and the sales or transfers, whatever be their transfer consideration, are netted off from the block. Therefore, no regard is given to the profit or loss on the sale of an individual asset.

Accounting for Hire Purchase Transactions

It is an international issue — accountants have been concerned about for almost 50 years now.

The concern springs up from the essential accounting rule that transactions ought to be recorded as per their intrinsic substance, and not merely based on their legal form. The legal form of every lease transaction is an asset renting transaction. However, in substance, many lease transactions, particularly financial lease transactions, create for the hirer or lessee an interest in an asset almost similar to assets, which are bought and a liability to pay to the lessor almost similar to those in a loan transaction. Similarly, for the lessor, though he apparently receives a rental income, the substance of his receipts is closer to recovery of principal and interest on outstanding principal, than an income by hiring out assets.

Thus, accounting standards on lease accounting are concerned with —

(a) Distinguishing leases between financial transactions and asset-renting transactions based on the substance of the lease; and

(b) Having found the substance, in applying a finance-based accounting if the substance is found to be a financial transaction, and an asset-renting based accounting, if the substance is not plain financing.

This is the essence of accounting standards on leasing in most countries — the basic approach underlying FASB-13 (USA), or IAS-17 (International Accounting Standards Committee) or SSAP-21 (UK).

Indian and International Accounting Standards Compared

International accounting standards adopt what is known as finance accounting approach to financial lease transactions. That is, based on the substance of the transaction, a financial lease is recorded as a financing transaction both in the books of the lessor and the lessee. The lessee will accordingly capitalise the asset though the lessor owns it. The lessee will also record a corresponding liability for payments to the lessor, as if it were loans and not lease. The lessor will bifurcate rentals into principal and interest, and take only the latter as his income. The lessee will also treat the interest component as the expense.

While the International Accounting Standards were concerned about the distortions that would be caused on the lessee's financial statements if financial leases were not recorded in the above manner, in India, the concern was essentially the lessor's financial statements. The distortions in lessor's reported income — which was the chief issue in India, is understandable in view of the low penetration ratios of leasing as a percentage of total industrial assets at that time.

Hence, Indian Accounting Standards did not make any substantial change to the way a lessee will account for a lease — in other words, leaving lessee's accounting virtually untouched, it made provisions only for the lessor's accounting.

Thus, in India:

1. The lessor would continue to put the asset on his Balance Sheet; the asset will be off-the-lessee's-Balance Sheet.
2. The lessor would continue to book rentals as income. The lessor would also depreciate the asset in his books.
3. However, there will be an extra debit or credit to the revenue statement so that the net impact on the lessor's income statement is only to take the finance charges to the income statement.
4. The lessee would only make a disclosure of the lease liabilities by way of a note to the balance sheet.

Finance Leases in India

The Guidance Note on Lease Accounting adopts the full payout test for differentiating between financial and operating leases. It may be noted that international accounting standards distinguish between a lease and a financing transaction based on the substance of the lease. If substantively, the entire risks and rewards incident to ownership of an asset is transferred to the lessee, the lease is taken as a financial transaction. Besides this general test, there are four quantitative tests:

(a) Transfer of title to the lessee.

(b) Option to buy at a bargain price,

(c) Full payout test, that is, if the whole or substantially the whole of the asset cost is recovered by the lessor by non-cancellable lease rentals and residual value, and

(d) Lease term test, that is, if the right of the lessee to continue the lease covers the whole or substantially the whole of the economic life of the asset.

While International Accounting Standards do not make any distinction between financial leases and hire purchase transactions, the Guidance Note on lease accounting does not apply to hire purchase transactions. Hire purchase accounting is governed more by convention than by a well-coded statement. Some guideline is available in Accounting Standard on Fixed Assets Accounting, which provides that assets taken on hire purchase, deviating from the legal ownership of the assets, will be put on the balance sheet of the hirer.

Thus, in case of hire purchase transactions, India follows the international accounting standards — the asset is put on the balance sheet of the hirer, with a corresponding liability, and the hire installments are broken into principal and interest, with the latter being taken as the hire-vendor's income and the hirer's expense. The only notable question is the manner of allocation of the interest or finance charges over period.

There are 3 methods usually in vogue:

Straight-line splitting, that is, equally over the tenure of hire: Sum-of-digits or sum-of-values-digits, that is, in proportion to the number of installments or the value of installments (in case of unequal installments) outstanding.

Capital recovery method: The Straight-line method results into an equal, and hence, unfair distribution of finance charges over time, since the interest cannot be equal in the face of a declining sum invested.

Sum-of-digits and Capital recovery approaches: Of the sum-of-digits approach and the IRR or capital recovery approach, the former is an over-simplified approach, belonging to the era when technology for exact determination of the IRR and splitting of rentals was not available. Therefore, there is no rationale in sticking to the sum-of-digits approach.

The difference between these two approaches may be noted. Under the sum-of-digits approach, the interest recognised declines linearly over time. Under the capital recovery approach, the interest declines in a curvilinear fashion — the decline is lesser in the beginning and precipitates over time. Hence, the sum-of-digits approach leads to income inflation towards the beginning of the lease.

5.7 PROBLEMS IN THE INDIAN HIRE PURCHASE INDUSTRY

Taxation

The leasing and hire purchase companies in India pay central sales tax, service tax of 5%, local sales tax of 4% to 14% and income tax. The industry has been asking for the removal of either sales or service tax since they are subject to both sales as well as service tax. Of late, the government has recognised these activities as sale, and hence service tax on hire purchase or lease transactions is totally unjustifiable.

Shortage of Low-cost Funds

There is an acute shortage of low-cost funds available to hire purchase and leasing companies in the light of the stringent RBI norms. The industry feels that the banks are meeting out step-motherly treatment. This has squeezed the industry's margins to the minimum.

Slow Market Growth

In 1997-98, the total base of leased assets (not including real estate) in India in the formal market was estimated at US$ 37.0 billion. This value represents nominal growth of 7.6% from 1996-97 when the value of leased assets totalled US$ 34.0 billion. The latter figure was up 20% from US$ 28.5 billion in 1995-96.

A global recession has resulted in a decline in India's industrial growth -rate. From a high of 8% in 1993-94, the current industrial growth rate is hovering around 4 percent. Investment by Indian corporates and foreign direct investment have slowed considerably. Reduced growth has effected the leasing market directly, because it is geared primarily to the industrial market.

Less Number of Players

Between 1991-94, when financial markets were booming, a large number of companies entered the leasing and hire purchase markets with little regard for the quality of clients. Since 1996, with the market slowing, clients began defaulting on payments. Consequently, a number of lease financing companies faced a severe asset-liability mismatch, which led to a repayment crisis and bankruptcy.

Increasing Conservatism in the Market

Since 1996, most existing leasing companies have become more conservative in their lending practices following the collapse of several leasing, and hire purchase finance companies. Companies that were somewhat conservative to begin with have weathered the crisis and have become more conservative.

The government, in response to the above problems, has begun to increase its regulation of the market to ensure better compliance and prudent business practices. The step-up in regulation included stricter requirements for deposit mobilisation, capital adequacy, and registration and de-registration of NBFCs and periodic performance reviews to ensure that only financially sound companies are in the market.

5.8 CONCLUSION

Leasing and hire purchase are tested methods for financing the acquisition of assets in India. It has a number of players, both in the formal and informal sectors. In India, leasing is used mainly by industry to acquire assets.

The main formal players in the market are the financial institutions, commercial banks, foreign financial institutions, manufacturers and non-banking financial companies (NBFCs). Individuals and families handle leasing in the informal market.

The leased asset base in India's formal sector is estimated at 3% to 4% of the total gross fixed capital formation as against 22% in most developing countries according to studies by the Centre for Monitoring the Indian Economy (CMIE) in 1997-98. The main reason for this anomaly is the high rate of depreciation allowed in India. Most, for-profit companies in India prefer to purchase assets as opposed to leasing them, in order to claim depreciation to offset taxable profits. Depreciation rates vary from 20% for ships to 60% on computers. If companies have a problem of raising the funds to purchase equipment outright, then hire purchase and term loan options help balance companies in balancing its cash flows. The tax benefits of depreciation are available to owners (of blocks of assets used for business purposes).

In the case of leasing, leasing companies receive the tax benefits of depreciation, while the lessee receives the tax benefits accruing from lease rental expenses paid. However, in case of hire purchases or term loans for the acquisition of assets, lessees receive tax deductions for the depreciation and the interest component of the loan repayment. The tax benefits from lease rentals are higher in the first few years, but the cost of the rental could constitute a large percentage of the lessee's profits.

Often, financial institutions make loans with favourable terms to companies to assist them in establishing themselves in the market. The financial institutions have a low cost of capital and can offer cheap loans. Hence, term loans are one of the preferred options for raising funds. However, the process of obtaining a loan from financial institutions is a time-consuming process due to the extensive checks on company costs, profits and the profitability of prospective projects for which the loan is being acquired. Some companies in need of funds on an immediate basis circumvent the time-consuming process of obtaining a loan from a financial institution by resorting to leasing.

A number of companies have also started in-house leasing companies to benefit from all of the advantages described above. A leasing company belonging to a group of companies, obtains a loan from a financial institution, buys equipment required by the group of companies, and then leases the equipment to the companies. In this case, the group of companies not only benefit from their ability to obtain financing at a low interest rate, but from the tax benefits accruing from the loan interest expense, the depreciation on the leased equipment and the lease rental expense. Most industrial groups in India exploit these provisions in the tax law.

5.9 GLOSSARY

Bailment

The delivery of goods by one person to another for some specific purpose upon a contract according to which the goods are returned after the purpose is accomplished.

Capital Recovery Method

The method of allocation of the interest or finance charges where the interest declines in a curvilinear fashion over time.

Condition

A stipulation essential to the main purpose of the contract. It gives rise to a right to treat the contract as repudiated or broken.

Hire Purchase Agreement

An agreement under which goods are let on hire. Here, the hirer has an option to purchase them in accordance with the terms of agreement and includes an agreement under which possession of goods is delivered by the owner thereof to a person on the condition that such person pays the agreed amount in periodical installments, and the property in the goods is to pass to such person on the payment of last such Installment, and such person has a right to terminate the agreement at any time before the property so passes.

Hirer

The person who obtains possession of the goods under hire purchase agreement. It also includes a person to whom the hirer's rights or liabilities under agreement have passed by assignment or by operation of law.

Owner

The person who delivers or has delivered possession of goods to a hirer under the hire purchase agreement.

Straightline splitting

The method of allocation of the interest or finance charges equally over the tenure of hire.

Sum-of-digits or Sum-of-values-digits

The method of allocation of the interest or finance charges in proportion to the number of installments or the value of installments (in case of unequal installments) outstanding, the interest declining linearly over time.

Warranty

A stipulation collateral to the main purpose of the contract. Its breach gives rise to a claim for damages but not to a right to reject the goods and treat the contract as repudiated or broken.

5.10 REVIEW QUESTIONS

Short Answer Questions

1. Define Hire Purchase.
2. Explain the two distinct factors in hire purchase transaction.
3. What are the rights of hirer?

4. What are the duties of hire vendor?
5. Briefly explain the treatment of tax under hire purchase system.
6. How would you treat the depreciation of asset in hire purchase system?
7. Give brief account about accounting standards of dealing with hire purchase.
8. What is Capital Recovery Method in hire purchase?
9. Explain the possession of title over the property in hire purchases.
10. Who are the main formal players of hire purchase in India?

Essay Type Questions

1. What are the salient features of a hire purchase agreement?
2. What are the differences between a lease and hire purchase?
3. Briefly trace the evolution of hire purchase in India.
4. What are the Acts that are relevant to hire purchase?
5. State the essential requisites of a valid hire purchase agreement.
6. What are the implied conditions and warranties in a hire purchase?
7. Describe the rights and duties of the hirer and hire vendor.
8. Describe the tax treatment of hire purchase.
9. How is depreciation allowed on an asset acquired through hire purchase?
10. Explain the accounting concepts in hire purchase.

❋ ❋ ❋

CHAPTER 6

Factoring

Objectives

The student, after studying the chapter, should be able to:

- Make a historical account about Factoring in the world, in Asia and in India.
- State the meaning of the term 'Factoring' and its mechanism.
- Identify the various types of Factoring.
- Realise the importance of Factoring in India.
- Appreciate the relationship between Factoring and Forfaiting.
- Familiarise himself with Kalyanasundaram Committee Report and the RBI Guidelines.
- Discuss the future scenario of Factoring in India.

Structure:

6.1 EVOLUTION OF FACTORING

6.1.1 Factoring Then and Now

The modern form of factoring originated in the US in the 1890s. Then the factors or agents in the textile and clothing industry started offering European (mainly UK) exporter debt collection services as well as advance payments against goods sold. Factoring remained very much a small-scale business until the 1960s when banks and other financial institutions started entering the industry. From then, the industry grew rapidly and it is today a US$ 500 billion a year business.

According to industry estimates, the UK has overtaken the US as the world's largest market, recording business volumes of approximately US$ 100 billion in 1998. Now, almost all UK clearing banks have factoring subsidiaries or divisions. This has facilitated the growth of the industry.

Factoring in Asia

Factoring was introduced in Asia in the 1970s. Its popularity only took off in the late 1980s. This coincided with the rise of the Asian economies. Since then, the value of business handled by factoring concerns has risen steadily. Over the five years before 1997, annual domestic and export business factored volumes grew by 25% and 50% respectively.

The recession in Asia over the past two years has had far-reaching effects on all sectors of the economy. Therefore, there has been rising demand for factoring, which does not require tangible security such as property. On the other hand, in markets such as Indonesia, Thailand and Malaysia, mounting losses from non-performing loans forced many banks and finance companies to scale back on their factoring businesses.

The largest Asian factoring markets comprise of Japan, South Korea, Hong Kong, Singapore and Taiwan. Of these, factoring in Hong Kong and Taiwan is a relatively recent development. Japan, by virtue of the size and sophistication of its economy, is Asia's largest factoring market. However, many factoring operations have been affected by the protracted economic slowdown and industry growth has been impeded by write-offs of unrelated business or problems faced by their parent companies.

Factoring growth in Taiwan has been based on its position as a premier semi-conductor and electronics manufacturer, whose largest trading partner is the US. Hong Kong, on the other hand, has leveraged its position as a financial and transportation hub, handling much of the trade and business flows originating from China.

The Singapore market has seen relatively slow but consistent growth. Like Taiwan, electronics manufacturing and trading were the cornerstones of Indian industry's initial development. The government also played a part in promoting the facility by setting up financing schemes for qualifying small and medium manufacturers.

Before 1997, South Korea was the second largest factoring market in Asia. Most of the business was generated from bilateral trade with Japan. This has virtually disappeared as recession hit both markets but, recently, with recovery in its economy, trade volumes are climbing again with the factoring business.

Exporters and importers are often in conflict over the way they prefer to trade. The buying power of importers has increased over recent years, and the adoption of e-commerce to streamline supply-chain management is likely to further strengthen the move to open-account terms.

Exporters, however, continue to require financing and hence factoring and other forms of receivables financing are poised for significant growth in Asia. The ability to provide solutions to exporters and importers trading in the electronic environment will be a critical success factor for financial institutions in the new millennium.

Factoring in India

The Working Group on Money Market (Vaghul Committee) had observed that introduction of factoring services could largely solve the financial problems of the small-scale suppliers. Reserve Bank of India (RBI) had perceived factoring as one of the measures to assist small suppliers with timely finance and collection of receivables. A committee was constituted under the chairmanship of Kalyanasundaram (1987-88) to examine the feasibility of factoring services in India. It suggested operational modalities of launching factoring service. This note discusses the salient features of factoring. It also tried to analyse its relevance in the context of the changing financial scenario and the development of financial services industry. He predicted that there was a vast scope of business potential through factoring which he estimated at around ₹ 4,000 crores.

RBI while accepting the recommendations of the Committee advised banks to take up factoring activity through a subsidiary. The Government of India has since declared 'Factoring' as an activity, which could be undertaken by Banking Companies under Banking Regulation Act, 1949. However, the service never really took off in India and the turnover from this business in the year 1999-2000 stood at ₹ 1,500 crores.

The limited geographical reach of the factoring units has not helped either. There are only two factors that do a reasonable amount of business. They have some kind of a branch network — SBI Factors with five branches, and Canbank Factors with seven branches. The two have a market share of around 45% each, with the balance 10% being shared by Foremost Factors, Wipro Factors and Integrated Factors.

However, this potential is currently limited by the lack of legislation relating to the assignment of receivables. This situation is in part responsible for the fact that the total volume of business registered by factoring companies forms only a tiny proportion of the overall credit extended by the banking sector. As this is the case, at a local level, individual branches of banks perceive factors as competitors and discourage their clients from turning to factoring.

6.2 MEANING OF FACTORING

Factoring is essentially a financial service designed to help firms manage their trade credit or receivables effectively. It is, in fact, a way of offloading a firm's receivables and credit management on to the factoring agency or the factor. Factoring involves an outright sale of the receivables of a firm to another firm specialising in the management of trade credit, called the factor. Under a typical factoring arrangement, a factor collects the accounts on the due dates, effects payments to its client firm on these days (irrespective of whether it has received payment or not). The factor assumes the credit risks associated with the collection of the accounts. For rendering these services, the factor charges a fee. It is usually expressed as a percentage of the total value of the receivables factored.

Factoring is defined as an asset-based means of financing by which the factor buys up the book debts of a company on a regular basis, paying cash against receivables, and then collects the amounts from the customers to whom the company has supplied goods. Thus, factoring provides firms with a source of financing its receivables and also eases the process of collecting the receivables.

The definition of factoring is as follows:

"Factoring means an arrangement between a factor and his client which includes at least two of the following services:

Finance, Maintenance of accounts, Collection of debts, Protection against credit risk."

Factoring is the time-honored and increasingly-utilized financial tool that speeds up client cash flow and helps avoid the problems that slow-paying customer can create for fast-growing companies. Factoring provides quick and convenient funding to growing companies who need capital to expand their business. To do this, factors purchase clients' creditworthy accounts (receivable) at a small discount and fund client with immediate cash.

Reasons to Factor

(a) It helps to obtain a source of working capital.

(b) It increases sales.

(c) It expands client's business or fills more orders.

(d) It eliminates the risk of credit losses on client's customers.

(e) Factor has a professional credit checking and collection payment system.

(f) It has flexible funding programme that increases as seller increases his sales (the goal of factoring).

(g) It helps to pay suppliers timely or take cash discounts or increase credit limits with suppliers.

(h) It facilitates to have funds for payroll and taxes.

(i) Clients can extend credit to customers on large orders without having to ask them pay Cash on Delivery (COD).

(J) It helps to buy equipment or inventory on demand.

Factoring vs. Receivable Finance

In reality, there are few differences between factoring and receivable finance. There are four key separations between the two forms of financing:

1. With receivables financing, a lender is actually lending (not purchasing) against receivables, which are reported to them on what's called a borrowing base certificate. With factoring, the factor is actually purchasing receivables (not lending) submitted to them. A factoring client will actually deliver original or copies of invoices to the factor to be purchased.
2. The lender will not monitor the progress of the receivables. A factor has an interest in the progress (collection) of those receivables.
3. There is limited or no credit assistance. The lender is making a loan against receivables. Ultimately, the lender will look to other collateral to make them compensate in the event of a loss. Factors make a credit evaluation on every invoice purchased. Because of this, the likelihood of collecting a valid receivable is very high.
4. Both the lender and the factor will have dominion over the receivables. It means the proceeds of the invoices will go to a lockbox, which is controlled by the lender or factor. However, a factor typically has greater protection under Article (9) of the Uniform Commercial Code. Because a factor will inform the clients' customer of the Notice of Assignment of the Receivable, this typically gives a factor a greater degree of protection, should default occur.

A nice feature of factoring is that most factors provide other ancillary services which go far beyond the borrowing base a receivables financing line provides a business.

6.3 MECHANISM OF FACTORING

When a firm receives an order from a buyer, a credit approval slip is written and immediately sent to factoring concern for a credit check. The factoring agency gives his decisions rather quickly as he maintains elaborate credit files on selected companies. If sale is approved by the factoring agency, then the goods are dispatched and invoice is early marked with an inscription notifying the buyer that his account has been sold and payment is made direct to factoring agency. The firm receives about 80% of invoice value as soon as firm issues invoice. In return to these services, the factoring agency receives about 0.75-3% of invoice value as commission. The concept of factoring can be easily understood with the help of the Chart 6.1.

Chart 6.1

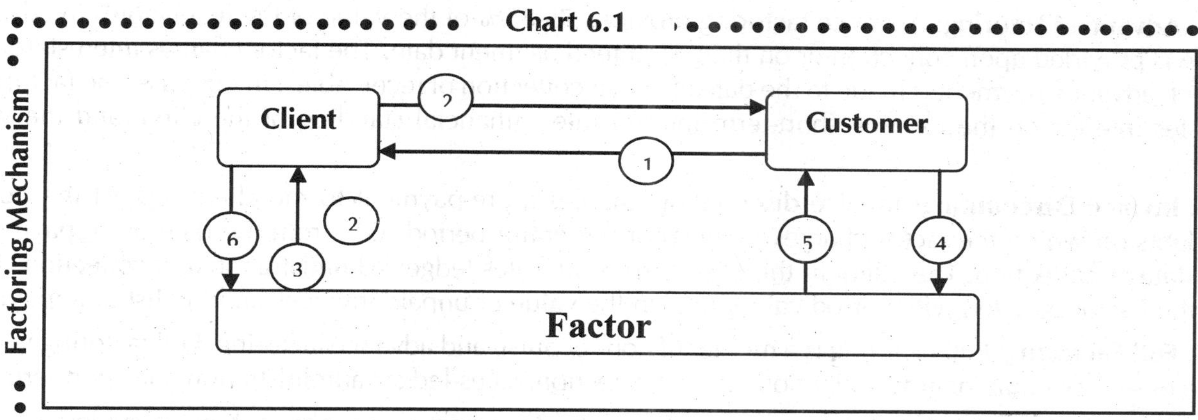

The concept of factoring consists of six stages:

1. In this stage, the client concludes a credit sale.
2. Here, the client sells the customer's account to the factor and notifies the same to the customer.
3. A partial payment is made by the factor after adjusting commission and interest in advance against the account purchased.
4. Customer's account is maintained by the factor and he undertakes any follow-ups for payment.
5. Any amount due from the customer is remitted to the factor.
6. On due date, the factor makes the final payment to the client.

The factor charges a stipulated fee for services offered by him. In cases where the factor has to make an immediate part payment against the debt purchased, a higher rate of interest is charged. The interest charged is calculated on the basis of the time period between the date of advance payment and the date of actual collection. In cases where interest charge is collected upfront, a discount charge is said to be collected.

6.4 TYPES OF FACTORING

Depending upon factoring arrangements, factoring can be categorised into different forms:

1. Recourse Factoring
2. Non-recourse Factoring
3. Advance Factoring
4. Invoice Discounting
5. Full Factoring
6. Bank Participation Factoring
7. Supplier Guarantee Factoring
8. Cross-border Factoring
9. Maturity Factoring

1. Recourse Factoring: The Factor buys receivables on the condition that the loss arising from non-recovery of receivables will be borne by client.

2. Non-recourse Factoring: The Factor is not allowed any recourse if the debt purchased by him turns out to be a bad one in non-recourse factoring. The factor charges a higher commission since he has to bear all the losses in this type of factoring. This type of factoring is most common in the US and UK.

3. Advance Factoring: Advance factoring provides 75-85% of the value of the receivables in advance. The balance is provided upon collection or on the guaranteed payment date. The factor charges interest from the day on which advance payment is made to the date of actual collection of receivables. In this case, the factor generally calculates interest on the existing short-term interest rates, financial standing of the client and the volume of turnover.

4. Invoice Discounting: Invoice discounting enables a pre-payment to the client against the purchase of book debts on which the factor charges interest for the entire period, i.e., from the date of prepayment to the actual date of collection. The client in this case carries out sales ledger administration and collection. The client keeps the Factor updated with periodical reports on the value of unpaid invoices and the list of unpaid debts.

5. Full Factoring: Full factoring is a merger of non-recourse and advance factoring. Full factoring incorporates a range of services that include collection, credit protection, sales-ledger administration and short-term finance.

6. Bank Participation Factoring: In cases of advance factoring, a commercial bank provides an advance to the client against receivables deposited by him with the factor.

7. Supplier Guarantee Factoring: This type of factoring involves a factor to approve extending of credit by an importer/distributor to a customer. The distributor, after receiving credit approval from the factor, makes arrangements for shipping the goods directly to the customer. The factor follows the customer, collects the due amount, and after deducting his commission, makes a final payment to the distributor.

8. Cross-border Factoring: Cross-border factoring involves four parties in the transaction — an exporter, an export factor, an import factor and an importer. The exporter enters into an agreement with the export factor in his country and assigns him export receivables as and when they arise. Payments against factored debts are made in a similar fashion to that of domestic factoring. The export factor enters into an agreement with the factor in the country in which the import factor resides and enters into a contract with him assigning him the tasks of credit checking, sales ledgering and collection, for payment of a stipulated fee.

9. Maturity Factoring: Maturity factoring involves no financing, only services. The factor provides the client with a credit guarantee for all customers, whose orders are approved prior to shipment, thus shielding the client from any bad debt losses. It is then the factor's responsibility to collect the net sales proceeds from customers. On the average due date for each month's sales, the factor turns over the accumulated funds to the client. No interest is charged, since the client has taken no advances against his sales prior to the date when they have theoretically matured and been paid. In fact, the factor remits to the client whether or not he has actually received payment from the client's customers. For all these services, the client pays a fee or service charge computed as a commission on net sales factored.

6.5 SIGNIFICANCE OF FACTORING IN INDIA

Factoring can play an important role in any developing economy. In India, factoring can play an important role in development of small-scale industries and thus help in employment generation, as SSI are labour-intensive industries. The importance of factoring can be summarised as below:

1. In small-scale industries, the small-scale industries suffer from variety of problems, which undermine their efficiency. One of the important problems faced by these units is inadequate working capital often caused by delayed collection of accounts receivable and bad debts. Most of these units face cash flow problems because of their inability to recover the receivable in time and therefore need factoring services.
2. **Export Traders.** Export traders may go for factoring services on account of the availability of additional services like sales ledger maintenance and collection of accounts receivable. The services provided by factoring agency may be extremely useful to small-scale exporters and new entrants.
3. **Prevention of Industrial Sickness.** The incidence of industrial sickness in India has been on the rise during the last decade. According to rough estimates, the loss of production due to sickness in the

country is around ₹ 4,000 crores. Many of these medium and small units may not have been in red if they had been able to recover their dues in time. Most of these units face cash flow problems because of mounting overdue accounts and therefore need factoring services.

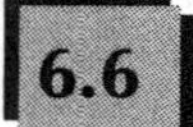

6.6 FINANCIAL ASPECTS OF FACTORING

To use the services of a factor, one should meet two types of expenses. They are:

(a) Factoring commission, and

(b) Interest on (funds) advances.

(a) Factoring Commission. The factor provides the administrative services. He bears the credit risk. For which, he is entitled to receive a commission. The commission charged is usually 2-4% of the face value of the receivables factored. The rate varies according to the services he renders. For example, the commission for recourse factoring is lower than the commission for non-recourse factoring.

(b) Interest on Funds Advances. The factor is also entitled to receive an additional remuneration, the interest, on advances drawn by the firm against uncollected and non-due receivables. It is a practice to advance up to 80-85% of the outstanding receivables. For which, he is entitled to receive 2-4% above the base rate. This, generally, works out to near the interest rate of bank overdrafts.

The cost of factoring varies, from 15-20% to 16-20% (Singh, 1988), 15.6% to 16.0% (SBI Monthly Review, 1989), and the margins in which the factors will have to operate would be extremely narrow. The strategy of factors, therefore, must be to carve out a niche in the services segment, namely, receivables management and generate revenues by way of commission rather than concentrate on lending and financing activities where the margins are low.

6.7 ADVANTAGES

Factoring offers the following advantages from the firm's point of view:

(a) There will be no liquidity problem if firms effectively use the factoring services. The factoring improves the cash flow.

(b) Factoring is invaluable as it leads to a higher level of activity resulting in profitability.

(c) Division of work is effectively carried out if a firm hires a factor. The management has more time for planning, running and improving business.

(d) Factoring also helps the firms to explore and exploit opportunities.

(e) The improved cash flows and speedy collection will bring down the cost of debt. This will contribute towards cost savings.

While a factor provides related financing and services only, a banker render comprehensive financing. However, factoring as a financial option against receivable scores over bank finance on many counts.

6.8 DISADVANTAGES

1. Factoring could prove to be costlier to in-house management of receivables. Large firms having access to similar sources of funds function like factors, themselves as they have large size of business and well-organised credit and receivable management. Therefore, there is no need for factor services separately.
2. Factoring is perceived as an expensive form of financing and also as finance of the last resort. This tends to have a negative effect on the creditworthiness of the company in the market.

6.9 FORFAITING

It is a technique of trade finance, which has attracted growing interest in the banking sector and the financial press of export-oriented countries over the last years. This is certainly due to the fact that in many cases it has proven to be the most efficient instrument when it comes to export finances.

Definition of Forfaiting

"Forfaiting is the term generally used to denote the purchase of obligations falling due at some future date, arising from deliveries of goods and services — mostly export transactions — without recourse to any previous holder of the obligation."

The forfaiter will deduct interest (discount) in advance for the whole period of credit and disburse the net proceeds immediately. The exporter thus virtually converts his credit-based sale into a cash transaction. His sole responsibilities are manufacturing and delivery of the goods, thus creating a valid payment obligation of the importer.

Historical Development of Forfaiting

The origins of the forfaiting market lie in changes in the world economic structure during the early sixties, when trade between Western and Eastern Europe was re-established. The growing importance of trade with developing countries in Africa, Asia and Latin America boosted the forfaiting market to an international level.

Advantages of Forfaiting

100% Risk Cover:

The forfaiter fully covers the following risks associated with any export:

Country Risk (Political and Transfer Risk): He absorbs the full political risk without recourse or residual liability. Extraordinary state measures or political incidents like war, revolution, invasion or civil unrest, which could block or unable payments. It is an inability or unwillingness of states or other official bodies to effect payment in the currency agreed upon — including the risk of moratorium.

Currency Risk: Floating exchange rates can have the effect of changing the contract value by a considerable amount when converted into the exporter's own currency, and can lead to a loss for the eventual holder of the claim.

Commercial Risk: It is simply an inability or unwillingness of the obligor or guarantor to fulfill its obligations on due date.

Interest Rate Risk: All forfaiting cost (discount, days of grace, and commission) are binding and remain unchanged during the whole financing period.

Instant Cash: They allow clients to generate instant cash, which relieves clients' balance sheet and improves liquidity. His credit sale is transformed into a cash sale.

Flexibility and Simplicity: Simple documentation is generally achieved even for tailor-made financing solutions. Complete credit administration and collection including relevant costs will be handled by the forfaiter.

Forfaiting vs. Factoring

The following are the difference between factoring and forfaiting:

1. The terms factoring and forfaiting have been mixed up frequently. Factoring is suitable for financing several and different smaller claims for consumer goods with credit terms between 90 and 180 days, whereas forfaiting is used to finance capital goods exports with credit terms between a few months and seven years.

2. Factoring only covers the commercial risk, whereas forfaiting additionally covers the political and transfer risk.
3. Factoring can be with recourse or without recourse depending upon the terms of transactions between the seller and factor. Forfaiting is without recourse to the exporter. All risks are taken over by the forfaiter.
4. Cost of factoring is usually borne by the seller while the cost of forfaiting is borne by the overseas buyer (importer).
5. In factoring, the business can avail of services at a pre-determined price for a whole set of jobs. In forfaiting, structuring and costing is on case-to-case basis.

General Aspects of Forfaiting

Repayments of Amounts: Most likely repayment will be by periodic installments. Where debt is evidenced by promissory notes or bills of exchange, a series of drafts will be issued, usually at six month intervals. Forfaiting applies to amounts of approx. US$ 5,00,000 and above.

Currency: The debt is normally denominated in US Dollars, German Marks or Swiss Francs, although in principle any other currency may be possible as well. Since the cost of forfaiting is for the most part determined by the forfaiter's funding cost, a weak currency would make such a forfaiting transaction just too expensive. It is essential that payments be made in effective currency. This means that the debtor may not pay in another (e.g., his local) currency. To ensure this, the drafts will always carry the effective clause.

Discounting: The forfaiter will discount the drafts after the exporter has delivered the goods to the importer and handed over the required documents to the forfaiter. The discount (interest) will be deducted from the face value (nominal) of the drafts and the resulting net proceeds will be paid out immediately.

Types of Instrument

Promissory Note or Bill of Exchange: The great majority of forfaitable obligations take the form of either promissory note issued by the debtor in favour of the beneficiary or bills of exchange drawn by the beneficiary on and accepted by the debtor. These drafts will generally be guaranteed by a bank aval or a separate bank guarantee of the debtor's bank. The first reason for the predominance of these forms of debt instrument is a matter of familiarity. Long experience in dealing with such paper has led to considerable ease of handling by all parties and generally facilitates a quick and uncomplicated transaction.

The second advantage is the internationally agreed legal framework based upon the International Convention for Commercial Bills established by the Geneva Conference of 1930; this provides a clear code of practice which was later adopted by the laws of most trading countries.

"Without Recourse" Clause: By transferring the drafts, the exporter also transfers his claim to the forfaiter. This is done by an endorsement on the back of the draft, the exporter being the endorser and the forfaiter being the endorsee.

A sample endorsement would read: "Please pay to the order of forfaiter without recourse — signed exporter." This clause excludes the endorsee's right of recourse against the previous holder of the draft — the main characteristic of forfaiting.

"Effective or Net of Deduction" Clause: All drafts should bear this clause which ensures that payment may only be effected in the currency agreed upon and not in any local currency. The clause will read "effective ' payment to be made in United States Dollars only, without deduction for and free of any tax, impost, levy or duty present or future of any nature." A draft hearing this clause is issued "in international format".

Book Receivables or Letters of Credit with deferred payment clause can be forfaited as well. However, transactions tend to be more complex, since all maturities are evidenced by a single document, made out in favour of the beneficiary. The obligation is often not transferable without specific permission from the obligor.

Forms of Bank Security

Guarantee and Aval: Drafts will generally be guaranteed by a bank aval or a separate bank guarantee. The guarantor will usually be an internationally active bank resident in the importer's country and able to ascertain the importer's creditworthiness first-hand. This security is important for the exporter, as it confirms the client's ability to fulfill his obligations. Guarantees and avals are essentially similar, both being in their simplest form a promise to pay a certain sum on a given date in the event of non-payment by the original debtor. In the case of a guarantee, the promise takes the form of a separate document signed by the guarantor setting out in full all conditions relating to the transaction, whereas an aval is affixed and duly signed directly on each promissory note or bill of exchange.

An aval makes the avalising bank primary obligor where a guarantee does not. Besides, an aval is transferable by nature but a guarantee must state that it is unconditional and fully transferable. The simplicity and clarity, together with its inherent abstractness and transferability, makes an aval the preferred form of security for forfaiting.

Export Risk Insurance: Claims covered by export credit agencies (ECA), e.g., EXIM Bank, ERG and Hermes, may of course also be forfaited. The discount rate would be reduced accordingly. Unlike an ECA, the forfaiter will be able to purchase the total claim without restriction.

Technical Aspects of Forfaiting

Cost

Discount Rate: The claims will be discounted at an all-in-discount rate. The rate is usually quoted as margin over LIBOR (funding cost) and is made up of the following:

1. Cost of covering commercial, country and interest rate risk; and
2. Cost of funds based on the Euro market rates (LIBOR)

Grace Days: Grace days are added to each maturity when calculating interest. These will compensate for delays in payment that are common in certain countries.

Commitment Fee: Exporters will often need a forfaiter's firm commitment to purchase a claim long before the delivery of goods. A commitment fee will then be charged from the day of commitment until disbursement.

6.10 FACTORING IN CURRENT ERA

The concept of 'Factoring' has been recently evolved in India. Kalyanasundaram Study Group appointed by RBI has submitted a report on factoring in 1989. Based on Committee's report, the RBI has issued guidelines for factoring services in 1990.

Kalyanasundaram Committee Report

The main recommendations of Kalyanasundaram Committee are:

(a) To introduce factoring services complementary to the services provided by banks.

(b) To introduce exports factoring to finance export trade.

(c) To make factoring business viable proposition within a period of two or three years.

(d) To direct the factors to offer their services to all industries and all sectors in the economy.

(e) To insist the factors in mixing various sources of funds to keep the cost of funds as low as possible.

(f) To restrict them to fix the cost not exceeding 13.5% per annum, so that the reasonable spread is available.

(g) To allow factoring organisation to raise funds from the Discount and Finance House of India Limited as also other approved financial institutions, against their Usance promissory notes covering receivables factored by them.

(h) To price the financing services around 16% per annum.

(I) To have the aggregate price for all order services not exceeding 2.5% to 3% of debt services.

(j) To select promoter institutions or groups of individuals with good track record in financial services to enter the field in the beginning.

(k) To allow, initially, the organisations to promote on zonal basis.

(l) To advise the commercial banks to have subsidiaries in handling factoring services.

(m) To insist the Small Industries Development Bank of India (SIDBI) in association with one or more commercial banks to take up factoring services.

(n) To recommend the bank branches to educate the business community about the nature and scope of factoring services and the benefits accruing therefrom.

(o) To insist the factoring organisations to have well-organised networking through computers.

(p) To insist the Central Government and RBI to initiate appropriate measures immediately for setting up specialised agencies for credit investigation for monitoring factors.

(q) To provide for proper linkage between banks and factoring organisations so that the suppliers would be able to get financial services from both banks and factors.

(r) To insist the factors to provide financial services to Small Scale Industries (SSI), which is beneficial to both factors and SSI units.

(s) To insist Government of India to ratify and accept the Unidroit Convention on international factoring.

(t) To involve Export Credit and Guarantee Corporation (ECGC) to be eminently suitable for handling export financing.

(u) To allow competition for ensuring satisfactory service to the exporters.

(v) To recommend the Government to create and foster an environment for promoting factoring services by initiating proper legislation and granting appropriate exemptions.

RBI Guidelines

Following the recommendations of the Working Group, the Government has notified that factoring is a form of business in which banks can engage.

The statutory framework now enables the banking companies to carry on factoring business and set up subsidiaries or invest in companies jointly with other banks. The RBI is of the view that in the public interest and in the interest of banking policy, some guidelines should govern the conduct of such business by the banking companies. Therefore, the RBI has issued the following guidelines as early as 1990:

1. For the present, banks shall not themselves undertake directly (*i.e.*, departmentally) the business of factoring. While banks may invest in shares of other factoring companies within the limits specified, with Reserve Bank's prior approval, they shall not act as promoters of such companies. Banks may set up separate subsidiaries to invest in factoring companies jointly with other banks with prior approval of the RBI. Banks desirous of doing so should apply to the Chief Officer, Department of Banking Operations and Development, Reserve Bank of India, Central Office, Mumbai, in the form specified for the purpose.
2. A factoring subsidiary or joint venture factoring company may undertake factoring business and such other activities as are incidental thereto. They should not engage themselves in financing of other companies or concern engaged in factoring.
3. Investment of a bank in the shares of factoring companies inclusive of its subsidiary carrying on factoring business shall not in the aggregate exceed 10% of the paid-up capital and reserves of the bank.
4. Any application to be made to the RBI in connection with the setting up of the subsidiaries of the joint venture factoring companies shall require prior clearance of the Reserve Bank of India.

5. Banks setting up subsidiaries of investing in joint venture factoring companies for the purpose of carrying on factoring business should furnish such information in such form and at such time as the RBI may require from time to time.

Besides enabling banks to take up factoring service, RBI has got the Banking Regulation Act, 1949 amended and allowed SBI and Canara Bank to take up factoring services on Feb. 27, 1990 on experimental basis by establishing subsidiaries. Accordingly, both these banks have their factor subsidiaries incorporated and launched the services.

6.11 FACTORING INSTITUTIONS IN INDIA

"We are looking at factoring as a prospective business area but things are at a preliminary level right now," ICICI Bank Chairman P.V. Maiya said. The nascent factoring market in the country has an annual potential of ₹ 10,000-15,000 crores for receivables finance. Though the statement of Mr. Maiya holds good, the limited geographical reach of the factoring units has not helped in any way. In 1988, a Reserve Bank of India committee, headed by Mr. C.S. Kalyanasundaram, recommended that factoring services be introduced in the country in view of the "vast scope of business potential", estimated at around ₹ 4,000 crores. However, the service never really took off in India and the turnover from this business in 1999-00 stood at ₹ 1,500 crores.

There are only two factors that do a reasonable amount of business. They have some kind of a branch network — SBI Factors with five branches, and Canbank Factors with seven branches. The two have a market share of around 45% each, with the balance 10% being shared by Foremost Factors, Wipro Factors and Integrated Factors. The brief account about existing factoring organisations are given below:

SBI Factors and Commercial Services Limited

SBI, the premier bank in India, responding to the call given by RBI started its factoring subsidiary in 1991. SBI Factors & Commercial Services Limited was jointly promoted by SBI and its associate banks (State Bank of Indore and State Bank of Saurashtra) along with Small Industries Development Bank of India and Union Bank of India. SBI Factors being the pioneers of factoring in india have played a pivotal role in popularising the concept of factoring in India. At present, it has 5 branches at Mumbai, Vadodara, Pune, Delhi and Coimbatore.

SBI Factors have so far financed over 300 clients out of which about 40% of clients are from Small Scale Industrial Sector. On a sample analysis, it is observed that, due to follow-up of receivables. made by SBI Factors, the collection period of clients has shown an improvement and their cash flow has also improved. Further, the quick sanction of limits has helped the clients to execute their orders in time and improve their sales. Also as their credit sales are converted to cash sales, they are able to avail of cash discount on their purchases resulting in further profitability.

Canara Bank Factors Limited

Canara Bank Factors Limited got RBI approval as subsidiary of Canara Sank in August 1991. It has been operating in south zone. It has a paid-up capital of ₹ 10 crores contributed by Canara Bank, Andhra Bank and Small Industries Development Bank of India in the proportion of 6 : 2 : 2 and rendering same services as SBI FACS.

Canbank Factors, India's largest factor by market share, have released their annual accounts for the year ended March 31, 2001. Turnover has increased by 21% from ₹ 732 crores in the previous year to ₹ 887 crores in the year ended March 31, 2001. The company introduced an export factoring service in December 2000 and there is optimism that their entry into the realm of international factoring will present "tremendous development opportunities in the future".

Canbank Factors accounts for approximately 40% of India's factoring market according to estimates provided in the Chairman's statement. In 1999, Canbank had a market share of 48%. Total income also increased over the period. The increase in total income was 6.86% from ₹ 22,74,72,848 to ₹ 24,30,78,147.

An increase in profit before tax (PBT) was recorded too. For the year ended March 31, 2001, PBT stood at ₹ 10.77 crores compared with ₹ 10.49 crores in the previous year. These figures were achieved in spite of the fact that deceleration was recorded in the rate of manufacture and in growth of capital goods.

Future of Factoring in India

New Legislation: Factoring is fairly a new venture in the Indian Financial Market. One of the bottlenecks is that there is no proper legislation, which would infuse a new blood in the factoring market. The Union Cabinet has taken a decision to float a new legislation soon. The Union Cabinet is expected to clear shortly fresh guidelines governing factoring services. The Ministry of Small Scale Industries has formulated draft legislation seeking to remove hurdles to the development of factoring business.

Letter of Disclaimer (LoD) and Letter of Notification (LoN): The issue of LoDs and LoNs was proving to be one of the major dampeners to the development of factoring in the country. Banks consider factors as rivals and refuse to issue LoDs and, likewise, big clients refuse to accept LoNs issued by factors to avoid making payment. Factors also find it difficult to compete with banks in terms of cost of financing. The Ministry, according to sources, has simplified litigation procedures, underlined the importance of the Letter of Disclaimer (LoD) and the Letter of Notification (LoN) to the business, and added incentives to draw more players into it.

Importance of recognising non-recourse factoring: The new legislation is also likely to allow factoring without recourse and credit insurance. Currently, the factoring service available is only with recourse.

Viable stamp duty: However, an important deterrent in factoring of stamp duty has not been dealt with in the legislation. Many factoring units compromise on security without going into the process of registering their subject, thus mostly relying on good faith. These units do not have any guarantee under law.

Indoctrination: Many traders and manufacturers, particularly belonging to small-scale and medium sectors are not fully aware of the concept of factoring. Therefore, it is important to educate them about the types of services provided by these factoring agencies. Again, due to entrance of foreign banks in India, the margins for Indian public sector companies are reducing at a very high rate. Therefore, to diversify their operations, factoring can be a good investment.

6.12 REVIEW QUESTIONS

Short Answer Questions

1. Define factoring.
2. What are the reasons to avail the services of a factor?
3. List out the factoring packages.
4. Explain recourse factoring. How do you differentiate recourse factoring from non-recourse factoring?
5. What do you mean by maturity factoring?
6. What is factoring commission?
7. Explain the term forfaiting.
8. Differentiate factoring from forfaiting.
9. List out five major recommendations of Kalyanasundaram Committee.
10. Can a commercial bank undertake directly the factoring business? If not, how can a bank undertake the factoring business?
11. Explain the term Letter of Notification (LoN).
12. What is Letter of Disclaimer (LoD)?

Essay Type Questions

1. Give an account about the evolution of factoring business in India.
2. What are the various services rendered by a factor to a client?
3. Describe the various types of factoring.
4. What are the advantages and disadvantages of availing the services of factoring?
5. Which sector in India uses the services of factor effectively? Why?
6. Distinguish between factoring and forfaiting.
7. List out the features of forfaiting.
8. Explain the main contents of Kalyanasundaram committee report.
9. What are the main guidelines of RBI towards factoring services in India?
10. Describe in detail about the growth of factoring business in India.
11. What are future challenges with respect to factoring business in India?

CHAPTER 7

Capital Market

Objectives

The student, after studying the chapter, should be able to:

- Distinguish between primary and secondary market.
- Discuss organisation and functioning of primary and secondary markets.
- State the role and functions of stock exchanges in the capital market.
- Identify the weaknesses of stock markets in India.
- Describe the reforms initiated by authorities.
- Explain the procedures for new issue.
- State the regulations in a particular context.

Structure:

7.1 INTRODUCTION

Some sectors in an economy generate surplus. Some others are deficit-generating units. At sectoral level, Corporates and Governments are deficit-generating units while household sector generally generates surplus in India. The statements given above are true only at aggregate levels. What do the surplus-generating units do with their surpluses or savings? There are two alternatives before these surplus-generating units. They can either hold it as liquid cash or invest. Keeping the liquid cash with them is due to meet the speculative, precautionary and transaction needs. They can, on the other hand, invest in different avenues.

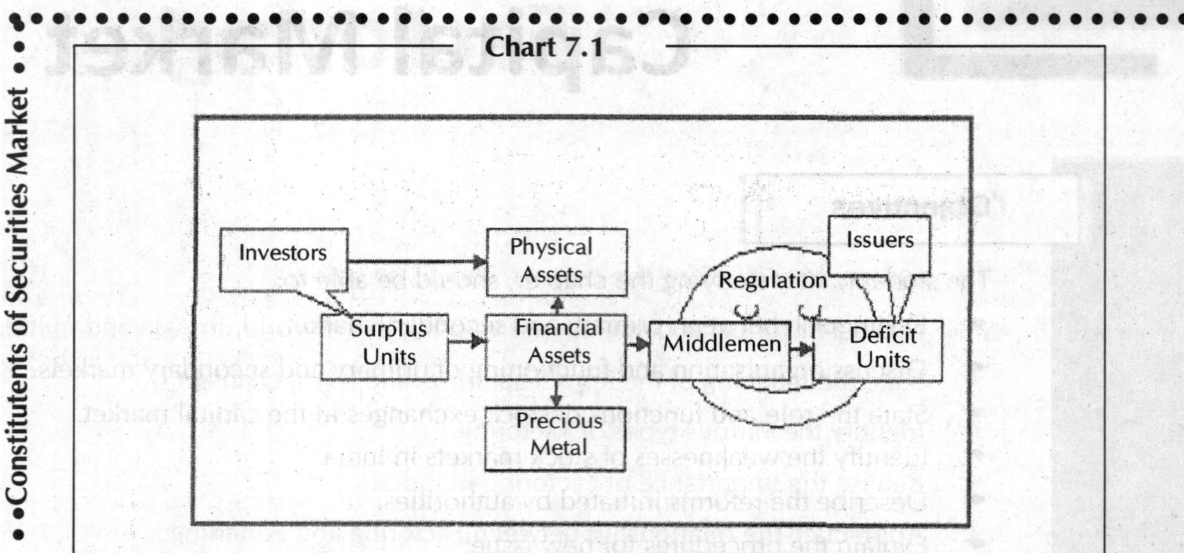

They may invest either on physical asset or precious metal like gold, silver, etc. and in financial assets like shares, debentures and units of UTI mutual funds.

Financial assets are paper assets. Deficit-generating units issue these paper assets to surplus-generating units in exchange for their savings. It is for this reason that the surplus-generating units are generally called investors. The deficit-generating units are called issuers. These investors and issuers constitute two important elements of the securities market (Refer to Chart 7.1). The third critical element of markets is the intermediaries. They act as conduits between the investors and issuers. The regulatory body constitutes the last but very significant element of securities markets. Therefore, there are four important elements of securities market namely investors, issuers, intermediaries and regulators.

There are different relationships existing among these four constituents. Based on the relationship, the market is classified as primary and secondary. Based on the maturity period, securities are divided into short-term and long-term. Based on the issuers, they are classified as government securities or industrial securities. Government securities are called gilt-edged securities. Investors or portfolio managers must know each segment of the securities market to invest.

7.2 PRIMARY MARKET

It is a market for new issues of shares, debentures and bonds. The investors apply directly to the issuer for allotment. They pay application money to the issuer's account. The transactions in the primary market result in new capital formation.

7.2.1. Players in a Primary Market

1. Issuers may be Corporations, the Government or Mutual Funds; they start the whole process of raising funds. Funds are raised through public issues, rights issues, or through private placement and preferential allotments.
2. Instruments are the means through which issuers raise funds, such as debentures, equity shares, warrants, etc.
3. Intermediaries are those who facilitate the flow of funds from a person who has excess funds to the person who needs it. They help the issuer to raise funds by issuing securities through selected instruments. Examples of financial intermediaries are banks, investment companies, insurance companies, development financial institutions, NBFCs, Mutual Funds, pension funds, etc.
4. Investors invest their surplus money in securities issued by issuers. The investor may be an individual, corporate, financial institution, foreign institutional investor, etc.

7.2.2. Mobilisation from Primary Market

The momentum witnessed in the primary market since 2005-06 increased further in 2006-07. Strong macroeconomic fundamentals, favourable investment climate, encouraging corporate results, and buoyant secondary market performance supported by institutional investors encouraged a number of companies to raise capital from the primary market. Besides several large companies, many small and medium-sized corporates accessed the primary market and mobilised resources through public and rights issues. Apart from the conventional modes, Qualified Institutions' Placement (QIP) was also used by many listed companies to meet their financing requirements. During 2006-07, 124 companies accessed the primary market and raised ₹ 33,508 crores through public and rights issues compared to 139 companies which had raised ₹ 27,382 crores in 2005-06. Even though the number of companies accessing the primary market was lower, the amount mobilised was higher in 2006-07 as compared to the previous year. Of the 85 public issues, 77 were Initial Public Offerings (IPOs) and eight were Follow on Public Offerings (FPOs) . Resources raised through IPOs and FPOs were ₹ 28,504 crores and ₹ 1,293 crores, respectively. The average size of the public issues increased from ₹ 226 crores in 2005-06 to ₹ 351 crores in 2006-07. The average size of IPOs increased from ₹ 138 crores to ₹ 370 crores during the same period. The share of IPOs in the total resource mobilisation was 85.1% in 2006-07 as compared to 40.0% in 2005-06. The amount mobilised through rights issues declined from ₹ 4,088 crores in 2005-06 to ₹ 3,711 crores in 2006-07. Due to introduction of QIP in 2006-07, the resources raised through FPO route declined from 45.1% in 2005-06 to 3.9% in 2006-07. As per the data made available by NSE and BSE, four companies only at BSE and 21 companies both at NSE and BSE raised ₹ 4,963 crores at BSE and ₹ 4,530 crores at NSE through the QIP route. The private sector companies dominated the resource mobilisation from the primary market in 2006-07. There were 122 issues from the private sector companies and only two issues from the public sector. The private sector and the public sector raised ₹ 31,728 crores and ₹ 1,779 crores respectively. The public sector issues were from Power Finance Corporation Ltd. (a financial company) and Indian Bank.

New issue market (Primary Market) is dealt in another section of the same chapter.

7.2.3. Method of Issuing Securities

Issues are made either at par or at premium in the primary market.

'Par' means that the securities are issued at the face value. 'At premium' means that the securities are issued at a price more than its face value. This may be due to the reputation of the issuer, which is contributed by many factors. Issuer fixes the price for his security by coping with stipulation laid down by Securities and Exchange Board of India (SEBI). Pricing the new issues is regulated under guidelines on Capital issues. It is known as Guidelines for Disclosure and Investor Protection issued by SEBI.

The following steps are to be taken by the issuer before entering capital market:

(a) Issues are to be advertised in the newspapers announcing the proposed public issue. Advertising can also be made through mass mailing. The general practice is that the prospectus, application forms and other information regarding new issues are distributed to the investing public.

(b) The advertisement must contain the risk involved in the business of issuers.

Book Building

Book Building is basically a capital issuance process used in Initial Public Offer (IPO). It is a process used for marketing a public offer of equity shares of a company. The Book Building process allows for price and demand discovery. The cost of the public issue is reduced. The time taken to complete the entire process is also reduced. It is a mechanism where, during the period for which the book for the IPO is open, bids are collected from investors at various prices. Bids are probable price offered by the possible buyers of shares. Such bids are above or equal to the floor price. The process aims at tapping both wholesale and retail investors. The offer or issue price is then determined after the bid closing date based on certain evaluation criteria.

The Process

A company that is planning an initial public offer (IPO) appoints a category-I Merchant Banker as a book runner. Initially, the company issues a draft prospectus, which does not mention the price. However, the draft prospectus gives other details about the company with regards to issue size, past history and future plans among other mandatory disclosures. After the draft prospectus is filed with the SEBI, a particular period is fixed as the bid period and the details of the issue are advertised. The book runner builds an order book, that is, collates the bids from various investors, which shows the demand for the shares of the company at various prices. For instance, a bidder may quote, that he wants 50,000 shares at ₹ 500 each while another may bid for 25,000 shares at ₹ 600 each. Prospective investors can revise their bids at any time during the bid period, that is, the quantity of shares or the bid price or any of the bid options. Usually, the bid must be for a minimum of 500 equity shares and in multiples of 100 equity shares thereafter. The book runner appoints a syndicate member, a registered intermediary who garners subscription and underwrites the issue. On what basis is the final price decided? On closure of the book, the quantum of shares ordered and the respective prices offered are known. The price discovery is a function of demand at various prices, and involves negotiations between those involved in the issue. The book runner and the company conclude the pricing and decide the allocation to each syndicate member. Book building is a good concept and represents a capital market, which is in the process of maturing.

Difference between shares offered through book building and offer of shares through normal public issue:

Features	Fixed Price process	Book Building process
Pricing	Price at which the securities are offered/allotted is known in advance to the investor.	Price at which securities will be offered/allotted is not known in advance to the investor. Only an indicative price range is known.
Demand	Demand for the securities offered is known only after the closure of the issue.	Demand for the securities offered can be known every day as the book is built.
Payment	Payment is made at the time of subscription whereas refund is given after allocation.	Payment is made only after the allocation of shares.

Guidelines for Book Building

Rules governing book building is covered in Chapter XI of the Securities and Exchange Board of India (Disclosure and Investor Protection) Guidelines 2000.

7.3 SECONDARY MARKET

It is a market for the secondary sale of securities. In other words, the market where existing securities are traded is referred to as the secondary market or stock market. In the stock market, securities of government, semi-government, and other public bodies as well as shares and debentures issued by joint stock companies are traded.

The secondary market differs from the primary market in a fundamental sense. In primary markets, the investor exchanges his savings for securities issued by deficit units primarily for gaining expected return. The secondary market provides liquidity to the investor, since he can trade his securities at any time. The secondary market is therefore primarily aimed to liqudify the investment made in the primary market and thereby performs a complementary role. Investors may have and aim to ensure both liquidity and profitability, for which he has to deal with both primary and secondary market.

7.4 TYPE OF SECURITIES TRADED

Based on the issue, the securities may be divided into three types. They are:

(a) Industrial Securities

Industrial and commercial undertakings of private and public sector issue these securities.

(b) Government Securities

Central and State Governments, Municipalities and Public Utilities issue these securities. These are generally risk-free securities. They fetch low return when they are compared with industrial securities.

(c) Financial Intermediaries Securities

Financial intermediaries are the third important group. The securities issued by financial institutions and banks would fall, in terms of risk-return features, somewhere in between the industrial securities and government securities.

Based on maturity, securities may be classified into two types. They are short-term and long-term. They have different names also. They are called money market securities and capital market securities. Treasury, bills, and commercial papers certificate of deposit are some short-term securities. Common share, preferred stock, bonds and debentures are long-term or capital market securities.

Based on settlement of deals, securities may be classified into forward securities and cash securities. By paying badla charges, one can shift free settlement from one date to the other specified shares, 'A' scrip, etc. are two examples for forward securities. Non-specified shares or Beer scrips are known as cash securities.

Secondary Market in 2003

Daily Turnover in BSE and NSE has averaged ₹ 11 bn and ₹ 22 bn respectively in the first fortnight of March 2003. Average daily volumes traded on BSE were 64 mn shares, while that on NSE were ₹ 129 mn.

7.5 STOCK MARKET IN INDIA

With small beginnings in the early 19th century, India's stock market has risen to greater heights. By 1990, India had 19 stock exchanges. By 1999, the number of stock exchanges has risen to 23. There were around 9877 listed companies. This evokes one's interest to know about the origin and growth of stock market in India.

7.5.1 Origin and Growth

Stock exchanges of India in a rudimentary form originated in 1800 and since they have developed through six broad phases. The Stock exchange, Mumbai, popularly known as "BSE", was established in 1875 as "Native Share and Stock Brokers Association", as a voluntary non-profit making association. It has evolved over the years into its present status as the premier stock exchange in the country. It may be noted that the Bombay Stock Exchange is the oldest one in Asia, even older than the Tokyo Stock Exchange, which was founded in 1878.

1866-1900

The shares were actively traded in stock exchange of Bombay between 1866-1900 due to rapid industrial activities. It led to formation of a regulated market for securities. A share market was established in Bombay then. Still it is a leading stock exchange and the most organised stock exchange in India. The Native Share and Stock Brokers Association, a voluntary organisation, was set up in 1887. The brokers laid down their code of conduct. They mobilised funds for government securities issued by Bombay Port Trust and the Bombay Municipality. A similar organisation was initiated at Ahmedabad in 1894.

1901-1913

Share investment took a different direction due to the influence of Swadeshi Movement of Mahatma Gandhi during this period. It encouraged indigenous trading. It motivated the business class to start industrial enterprises. Calcutta became another major centre of share trading. Coal boom injected a new blood in the stock market between 1904 and 1908. Therefore, the stockbrokers of Calcutta started a stock exchange in Calcutta. Due to involvement of British in the World War, the existing enterprises in steel and cotton textiles, woollen textiles, tea and engineering goods expanded. New enterprises were floated. Another stock exchange was initiated at Madras in 1920.

During 1935-1965

This period was a consolidation period for existing exchanges in India. Industrial development planning played the pivotal role of expanding the industrial and commercial base of the country in this period. Two more stock exchanges were set up at Hyderabad in 1943 and at Delhi in 1947. Seven stock exchanges were functioning in the major cities of the country at the time of Independence.

Twelve more stock exchanges were set up between 1946 and 1990.

1992 Onwards

The number of stock exchanges increased to 23 and number of listed companies to 9,877 in 1999.

It is equally important to know that the network of Indian stock; exchanges is spread throughout the length and breadth of the country.

7.5.2. Role and Functions

The major roles played by a stock exchange in a country are:

(a) The stock exchange provides a marketplace for purchase and sale of securities. It ensures the free transferability of securities. It is the essential basis for the joint stock enterprise system. The private sector economy depends fully on stock exchanges for marketing their securities at any time.

(b) The stock exchange provides the linkage between the savings in the household sector and the investment in corporate economy.

(c) The stock exchanges provide a market quotation of the prices of shares and bonds. It is a sort of collective judgment reached by many buyers and sellers at a time. It makes a stock exchange an input provider for predicting economic trend. It serves as a barometer, not only of the state of health of individual companies, but also of a nation's economy as a whole.

(d) The stock exchanges in India serve the joint sector units and also to some extent public sector enterprises.

(e) Another important function that stock exchanges in India discharge is of providing a market for gilt-edged securities. Central Government, State Government, Municipalities, etc. issue gilt-edged securities.

7.5.3. Membership, Organisation and Management

The stock exchanges are highly organised and smooth functioning network in the world. The membership of stock exchanges initially comprised of individuals and partnership firms. Then the corporate bodies were allowed to become members.

7.5.4. Qualifications

The qualifications for becoming an individual member of a Stock Exchange in India are:

(a) Minimum age of 21.

(b) Citizenship of India: The Governing Board may, in suitable case, relax this condition.

(c) Not been adjudged bankrupt or insolvent.

(d) Not compounded with his creditors.

(e) Not been convicted of an offence involving fraud or dishonesty.

(f) Not engaged as principal or employee in any business other than that of securities.

(g) Not been, at any time, expelled or declared a defaulter by any other Stock Exchange.

(h) Either matriculate or has the 10 plus 2 years qualification. Generally, however, preference is given to professionally qualified persons.

7.5.5. Experience

Minimum 2 years' experience as a partner or authorised clerk or apprentice with a member of the Exchange or in other connected areas in capital market.

Table 7.1 **Stock Exchange and their Forms**

Forms of Organisation	Name of the Stock Exchange
1. A Voluntary Non-profit making Association of persons	(a) Bombay Stock Exchange
	(b) Ahmedabad Stock Exchange
	(c) M.P. (Indore) Stock Exchange
2. Public Limited Companies	(a) Calcutta Stock Exchange
	(b) Delhi Stock Exchange
	(c) U.P. Stock Exchange
	(d) Ludhiana Stock Exchange
	(e) Cochin Stock Exchange
3. Company Limited by Guarantee	(a) Chennai Stock Exchange
	(b) Hyderabad Stock Exchange
	(c) Pune Stock Exchange

Source: Official Directory of Bombay Stock Exchange

A partnership firm as such is not eligible to become member of the Exchange. A company, seeking membership of the Exchange, should have a minimum paid-up capital of ₹ 30 lakhs. Besides, minimum of its two directors should be appointed as designated directors, fulfilling the criteria for individual members, except the criteria relating to citizenship.

The applications for membership submitted by the applicants fulfilling various criteria as discussed above, are scrutinised by the Membership Committee appointed by the Exchange and the Committee recommends the same to the Governing Board. The Governing Board then elects the applicants. After paying the requisite fees, the applicant is admitted as the member of the Exchange and the Exchange then forwards application to SEBI for registration. After getting SEBI registration, a member is required to comply with the requirements of network connectivity, insurance, maintenance of minimum capital, opening of accounts with Clearing House and Clearing Bank etc., and thereafter, he is allowed to commence business on the Exchange.

Bombay Stock Exchange has the following structure. A Governing Board comprising of 9 elected directors (one-third of them retire every year by rotation), two SEBI nominees, seven public representatives and an Executive Director is the apex body, which decides the policies and regulates the affairs of the Exchange. The Executive Director as the Chief Executive Officer is responsible for the day-to-day administration.

As of now, there are 23 exchanges in India. Each has its own structure. The following features can be noticed with respect to their structure and management:

1. The size of the membership varies from 69 to 650.
2. The entrance fee is different for different stock exchanges.
3. The internal management rests in a governing board.
4. The governing bodies of stock exchanges have government nominees, whose number generally does not exceed three.
5. The broker-members are highly influential in stock exchanges. SEBI makes these stock exchanges powerful to make bye-laws.
6. Governing bodies can admit, punish, censure and expel any member, any partner, any remisier, and authorised clerk and employee.
7. Governing bodies have the power to make, amend, suspend and enforce rules, bye-laws, and regulations and supervise the entire functioning of a stock exchange.

7.5.6. Listing of Securities in Exchange

A stock exchange facilitates trading of a security. The company issuing the security has to seek permission of the exchange for allowing its security to be listed in the exchange. This process is called listing of the security in that exchange, for which the company has to pay a listing fee to the exchange. This fee differs from exchange to exchange.

The following are the information required to list a company in a recognised stock exchange.

1. The company provides all relevant information on its business activities, financial performance and so on to the exchange.
2. The company undertakes to abide by the conditions stipulated by the respective stock exchange
3. The kind of information to be supplied, the periodicity of such information, disclosure norms, etc. is specifically laid out in an undertaking executed by the company and the exchange. This undertaking is commonly called the Listing Agreement.
4. The reason behind the listing agreement is to provide relevant information to the investors who trade in securities.
5. Non-disclosures attract suspension or delisting of securities of companies.

6. The person responsible for such misconduct will be prosecuted.
7. An exchange also has the right to permit non-listed securities for trading. This is for the benefit of investors spread across the country. With investors spread across the country, in order to avoid such an eventuality, popular securities are permitted to be traded by different exchanges. Such securities are called Permitted Securities.

7.5.7. Execution of Trades in an Exchange

The market mechanism in an exchange can be broadly classified into two. They are:

1. Dealer Market

It is the market where dealers are intermediaries. They buy stocks into inventory and sell stocks from the inventory. The Over the Counter Exchange of India (OTCEI) operates a dealer market.

2. Auction Market

In an auction market, all orders to buy or sell securities are channeled to a central location and a market-clearing price is determined by means of set of rules or algorithm. The algorithm determines the priority of different offers to buy or sell. For example, the order matching algorithm of the National Stock Exchange specifies a Price-Time Priority, *i.e.,* if two orders are received at the same time, the order with a better price gets priority and if two orders of the same price are received, the order that has been received first gets priority.

Types of Auction Market

Auction market can be continuous or discrete.

Continuous Auction Market: Buy and sell orders are received throughout the trading hours in the continuous market. They are matched as per the set algorithm. All changes (except OTCEI) operate continuous auction markets and investors can trade during specified trading hours. For example, the National Stock Exchange permits trading between 9.30 a.m. and 4.00 p.m. During this period, investor orders are matched in the central computer in Mumbai.

Discrete Auction Market: Buy and sell orders are accumulated and at a particular time, a single price is set to clear the market according to pre-determined rules. Such markets are also called call markets. Opening prices on large markets are set using this process. Call markets can be operated one or more times a day or can be operated for a set of securities. The exchange as a rule does not interfere in the price discovery process. However, at times, exchange authorities do not allow certain orders to be executed. Typical of these is the restriction on price movements – the price of a security cannot fluctuate more than 10% in a day and more than 25% in a settlement period. Such price freezes are stipulated to curb excessive volatility.

The trading system of an exchange is designed to provide maximum information to investors relevant for trading. Such information pertains to the quantum of buy or sell orders already existing in the system, the prices offered, price movement during the day, details of the order placed, details of trades control, etc.

7.5.8. Trading System

The stock markets in India have gone through a virtual transformation from the days of the hue and cry halls and the days of small groups of brokers controlling the Sensex. Now, technology rules the roost and transparency has become the benchmark.

The major exchanges at the present moment are the National Stock Exchange (NSE) and the Bombay Stock Exchange (BSE). Delhi, Calcutta and Chennai (Madras) also have Stock Exchanges where all transactions are completed on a Computer Trading Terminal. The difficult part is deciding on which shares to buy and which shares to sell.

7.5.9. Placing the Order

Clients have to open an account with a member of the exchange. The members are brokers and dealers as mentioned earlier. When clients want to trade in futures, they instruct members to execute orders in their account. The trade details are reported to the clearing house. If a member of the exchange is also a member of clearing house, then he directly deposits the margins with the clearing house. If he is not a member then he should route all transactions through a clearing member for maintaining margins. The members have to maintain security deposits. Brokers act as agents buying and selling securities for others, for which they are entitled to receive brokerage commission at stipulated rates. Dealers act as principals buying and selling securities on their own accounts.

Once the transaction has been completed, the Broker should inform the investor about it. He should confirm his quantity and price (market rate and the net rate). He should then give investor a contract note. This note confirms the sale or purchase. It should state the time of order confirmation, the market rate, the commission charged and the net rate. It should also state the taxes, which are levied on each transaction. One copy of this contract note should be given to investor, and the other signed copy returned to the Broker.

Members are permitted to deal only in listed securities. However, with the approval of the Governing Body, they can deal in listed securities of other exchanges.

7.5.10. Steps in Trading

A person wants to buy or sell 1000 shares of Wipro through National Stock Exchange. He follows the following steps to acquire such shares:

1. The person goes to a broker located in his place. The person introduces himself or herself to the broker. He gives all information about himself or herself to the broker. These particulars are filled in the form supplied by the exchange. The form is called the client registration form. It serves as the basis for the person to trade in the exchange through that broker.
2. The person enters into an agreement with the broker then as specified by the exchange. This agreement is called the client-member agreement.
3. The person gives, thereafter, his order his writing to the broker for the purchase or sale of 1000 shares of Wipro at market price per share prevailing on that day".
4. The broker retains the investor's order in his record. He places the order in his computer system. The order is transmitted through the computer networking system of the exchange at Mumbai. The broker gets an order confirmation slip from the exchange that the order has been received.
5. The computer now matches the order as per the matching algorithm (as we see in the previous section). A trade confirmation slip is generated. It consists of details of the trade executed. The investor has to pay necessary margin money to the broker.
6. The broker will issue a contract note to the person for all such orders executed during the day. This will tell the obligation of the investor in terms of amount to be paid and/or the shares to be delivered.
7. The investor will have to pay the amount due and deliver the shares and receive the shares purchased or amount realised on a specified day.

7.5.11. Types of Delivery

There are three types of contracts permitted by the stock exchanges.

(a) Spot Delivery

The delivery as well as payment is made on the same day as the date of contract or at the most the next day.

(b) Hand Delivery

The delivery and payment are made within the time and date stipulated at the time of entering into bargain. The time shall not exceed 14 days following the date of contract.

(c) Special Delivery

The delivery and payment are made within anytime exceeding 14 days from the date of contract when entering into a bargain. However, the Governing Body or President should permit it.

In the matter of delivery, equity share trades are classified into two groups. They are deliver orders and receive orders. For these groups, there now exists a computerised system of settlement. These orders are issued first and last party respectively. Delivery in respect of the first group passes through the clearing house. In the case of the other group, the delivering member hands over directly to the receiving member named in the Receive order, the share certificates with duly executed transfer deeds. Such deliveries should be effected before 2 p.m. on the prescribed day, which is generally Thursday.

7.5.12. Clearing House

A clearing house was established in Bombay in 1921. It receives delivery and payment on behalf of the customers. All the banks of the country are its members. It guarantees payments. It returns shares to the concerned bank if a member defaults. Clearing houses cost huge amount of money to the Bombay Stock Exchange. The services are tendered in the interest of the investing public. The clearing operations were introduced in Calcutta in 1944 and in Madras and Delhi in 1957.

7.5.13. Dealing of Various Securities in Stock Exchanges

Dealing in government securities are transacted between 12 noon and 3 p.m. on the Bombay Stock Exchange. Institutional investors and brokers largely transact the government securities. The business is settled through banks. The documents are delivered through banks against payment at the contract rate with interest accrued to the date of delivery.

Dealing in shares are also transacted between 12 noon and 3 p.m. The bargains are entered into by words of mouth but seldom any serious mistakes occur. We will see about settlement in detail in the next section.

7.6 SETTLEMENT CYCLE

7.6.1. Settlement and Settlement Cycle

Settlement refers to the process in which traders who have made purchases make payments while those who have sold shares deliver them. The exchange ensures that buyers receive their shares either in the physical or the demat form. Similarly, sellers who have delivered shares to the exchange receive payment for the same. The process of settlement is managed by stock exchanges through Clearing House (CH) entities, formed specifically to ensure that the process of settlements takes place smoothly. SEBI introduced a new settlement cycle known as the rolling settlement cycle from Jan. 12, 2000.

7.6.2. BSE Settlement Cycle

The BSE settlement cycle is similar to that of the NSE. However, the schedule or trading and settlement days is different. It starts on day 1 (Monday) and ends on day 5 (Friday). The settlement takes place on day 11 (Thursday), day 12 (Friday), and day 13 (Saturday). The examples stated for NSE settlement cycles apply to BSE settlement cycles as well except that there is change in days.

Table 7.2 **BSE Settlement Cycle at a Glance**

Day	Activity
Monday to Friday	Trading on BOLT and daily downloading of statement showing details of transactions and margin statement, at the end of each trading day.
Saturday	Carry Forward Session (for 'A' Group Security and downloading of money statement).
Monday	Marking the mode of delivery — physical or demat.
Wednesday	Pay-in of physical securities.
Thursday	Delivery of securities in the Clearing House as per prescribed time slots up to 1:00 p.m. only. Debiting of members' bank accounts having payable position at 5:00 p.m. Reconciliation of securities delivered and amount claimed.
Friday	Pay-out (Physical securities only).
Saturday	Funds pay-out.

7.6.3. Rolling Settlement Cycle

SEBI introduced a new settlement cycle known as the 'rolling settlement cycle'. This cycle starts and ends on the same day. And the settlement takes place on the 'T+5' day. It is five business days from the date of the transaction. Hence, the transaction done on Monday will be settled on the following Monday and the transaction done on Tuesday will be settled on the following Tuesday and so on. Hence, unlike BSE or NSE weekly settlement cycle, in a rolling settlement cycle, the decision has to be made at the conclusion of the trading session, on the same day. Rolling settlement cycles were introduced in both exchanges on January 12, 2000.

Internationally, most developed countries follow the rolling settlement system. For instance, both the US and the UK follow a rolling settlement (T+3) system, while the German stock exchanges follow a T+2 settlement cycle.

7.6.4. Advantages of Rolling Settlements

(a) In rolling settlements, payments are quicker than in weekly settlements. Thus, investors benefit from increased liquidity.

(b) From an investor's perspective, rolling settlement reduces delays.

(c) This also reduces the tendency for price trends to get exaggerated. Hence, investors not only get a better price but can also act at their leisure. Currently in India, T+3 system is followed.

The National Stock Exchange was the first to introduce rolling settlement in the country. Rolling settlements require electronic transfers funds and demat facilities, with respect to securities being traded. Suppose a trader wants to buy a stock on a Monday, the first day the of new BSE settlement cycle, with the intention of selling it on the Thursday which lie on same week. In the current weekly settlement system, the trader needs to just pay up the margin. On Thursday, when the position is squared, the trader would take home the profit or pay up for the loss. However, in a rolling settlement, the trader will have to make the complete payment for the outstanding long position on Monday. On Thursday, the squaring up position is a separate transaction altogether where the trader would deliver the shares he had purchased on Monday. Hence, in the current system, traders who hope to profit from a price rise or decline in the five-day period play a very active role in the market, thereby making the current spot market more of a five-day futures market. On the other hand, under the rolling settlement, the role of traders who treat the spot market as a five-day futures market is marginalised as each of their transactions necessarily results in delivery of shares and a receipt of payments.

7.7 BADLA TRADING

Badla is the price payable by the buyer to carry over his speculative purchase to the next settlement. This system helps traders to carry forward businesses without taking deliveries of stocks purchased. It helps to have large volumes on the exchanges and impart liquidity in stocks.

In the badla system, a position (either a short sale or long purchase) is carried forward. In the event of a long purchase, the investor may want to carry forward the transaction to the next settlement cycle and for doing so, he has to compensate the seller. The 'seedha badla' financier enters the market to lend money to the investor for a return. This is measured as interest on the funds made available for one settlement cycle, *i.e.*, one week or a longer period in case of a book closure badla system. Similarly, 'undha badla' or a 'contango' charge is a return paid by the stock borrower to the stock lender. In a short sale, when the investor wants to carry forward the transaction to the next settlement cycle, he has to borrow the stocks to compensate the other party in the contract. The charge paid on the borrowed stock is called a 'contango' charge or "share badla'.

7.7.1. Vyaj Badla

Sometimes the lender lends money to the borrower through the clearing house. This transaction is called Vyaj Badla. The lender takes up the delivery of the shares from the original buyer at a standard rate (average or hawala rate) and sells the same in the next settlement back to him at a standard rate plus finance charge, to pay for the stock for that particular period. Vyaj Badla is not speculation since the financier or the investor is not taking any investment position in the market. His role is that of a financier and he steps into the shoes of the buyer only for funding the delivery at a pre-determined rate.

7.7.2. The Badla Mechanism

The Badla session is held every Saturday in Mumbai, Delhi and Ahmedabad and on Thursday at the Calcutta Stock Exchange. The outstanding positions of various stocks are listed along with the quantities outstanding. Depending on the demand and supply of money, the carry forward rates are determined. If the market is over-bought, i.e., there is more demand for funds, it results in Vyaj badla. However, when the market is oversold, or when in a particular stock the short position is more, the Undha badla applies.

7.7.3. Hawala and Badla Rates

The hawala rate is the price at which buyers and sellers settle their speculative transactions at the end of the settlement on any exchange. It becomes the basis for buy and sell for the investor opting for carry forward during the next settlement. This price is fixed by taking the weighted average of trades in the last half-an-hour of trading on the settlement day for securities in the carry forward list, also known as A group or specified group. This price is significant because for a speculative buyer or a seller, the hawala rate is the standard rate for settling his trade and for carrying forward business to the next settlement.

By Friday (which in case of BSE is the settlement day), if ₹ 90 were the weighted average price in the last half an hour, the buyer would have to carry forward his trade at ₹ 90. He then settles at ₹ 90 and enters into a contract at ₹ 90 plus badla charges for the next settlement.

7.8 DEMATERIALISATION

Demat is the commonly used abbreviation of Dematerialisation. It is a process whereby securities like shares and debentures are converted from the "material" (paper documents) form into electronic form and stored in the computers of an Electronic Depository.

One surrenders material securities registered in his name to a Depository Participant (DP). These are then sent to the respective companies who cancel them after dematerialisation and credit his Depository Account with the DP. The securities on dematerialisation appear as balances in the Depository Account. These balances are transferable physical shares. If at a later date he may wish to have these "Demat" securities converted back into paper certificates, the Depository can help to revive the paper shares.

7.8.1. Procedure for the Dematerialisation of Securities

Check with a DP as to whether the securities the investor holds can be dematerialised. Then open an account with a DP and surrender the share certificates.

7.8.2. Rematerialisation

Rematerialisation (Remat) refers to the process of conversion of securities held in the electronic form back to the physical form. In remat, the Registrar and Transfer Agent issue share certificates to the investor. Once the securities are being rematerialised, the DP account of the investor is debited with the quantity and the value of respective securities. The investor becomes the registered owner of the securities. His name is added in the "Register of Shareholders" kept with the Registrar and Transfer Agent and the name of the depository is deleted. How is the access of Rematerialisation initiated? The investor submits the Rematerialisation Request Form (RRF) to the Depository through his DP. The depository further sends the request to the Registrar and Transfer Agent of the company. The company after verifying the details dispatches the share certificates directly to the investor. You have frequently come across the word 'depository' in this section. The next section explains what a depository is and how it functions.

7.8.3. Depository

According to the Depositories Act, 1996:

"Depository is an organisation where the securities of a shareholder are held in the form of electronic accounts in the same way as the bank holds money."

The depository holds the electronic custody of securities and also arranges for the transfer of ownership of securities on settlement dates. A Depository is a securities "bank", where dematerialised physical securities are held in custody, and from where they can be traded. This facilitates faster, risk-free and low-cost settlement. A Depository is akin to a bank and performs activities similar in nature.

At present, there are two depositories in India, National Securities Depository Limited (NSDL) and Central Depository Services (CDS). NSDL was the first Indian Depository. It was inaugurated in November 1996. NSDL was set up with an initial capital of ₹ 124 crores, promoted by Industrial Development Bank of India (IDBI), Unit Trust of India (UTI), National Stock Exchange of India Ltd. (NSEIL) and the State Bank of India (SBI).

7.8.4. Depository Participant (DP)

NSDL carries out its activities through business partners — Depository Participants (DPs), Issuing Corporates and their Registrars and Transfer Agents and Clearing Corporations or Clearing Houses. NSDL is electronically linked to each of these business partners via a satellite link through Very Small Aperture Terminals (VSATs). The entire integrated system (including the VSAT linkups and the software at NSDL and at each business partner's end has been named the "NEST" (National Electronic Settlement and Transfer) system. The investor interacts with the Depository through a Depository Participant of NSDL. A DP can be a bank, financial institution, a custodian or a broker.

7.8.5. Performance of Depositories in India

The progress of NSDL is a tribute to India's and Indian people's ability to adapt to change. Indians no longer think that stuffing share certificates under the pillow is the best way to store wealth. From a mere 8,000 investor accounts opened with NSDL — the country's first depository— in the month of March 1998, these investor accounts have crossed the 50,000 mark by August 1998. From more than 563 cities in the country and 35 cities from overseas, investors have joined a silent revolution to rid the Indian capital markets of fake, forged or stolen shares and to help it to move to a paperless form of trading. Since the year 1996, NSDL has dematerialised more than 256 crores shares worth ₹ 40,900 crores. The figures of shares delivered in "demat" form as compared to the percentage of the total delivery is very encouraging. The next best competitor of NSDL is the BSE's Central Depositories Services Ltd.

7.8.6. The Depositories Act, 1996

The paper-based ownership and transfer of securities has been a major drawback of the Indian Securities markets since it often resulted in delay in settlement and transfer of securities and also led to "bad delivery", theft, forgery, etc. The Depositories Act, 1996 was, therefore, enacted to pave the way for smooth and free transfer of securities.

7.9 PLAYERS IN THE SECONDARY MARKET

The players in the secondary capital market include the following:

1. General Investor Public
2. Companies
3. Mutual Funds
4. Indian Financial Institutions
5. Foreign Institutional Investors
6. Non-resident Indians
7. Brokers
8. Sub-brokers

7.9.1. General Investor Public

India's national savings are voluminous, with one of the largest per capita saving rates in the world. The General Investor Public plays a major role in the stock market. Popularly referred to as small investor, the investor had been investing traditionally in tax saving scheme offered by the government like NSC VIII, etc. But in recent time, investors have been increasingly evincing interest in the stock markets. A bulk of the investment in the stock market made by the small investors is routed through the mutual funds. Equity shares and convertible debentures continue to remain popular among these investors.

7.9.2. Companies

Most of the companies having surplus funds will be investing these funds in the money markets. Generally, these companies favour inter-corporate deposits and commercial paper. But for long-term needs, companies tap capital markets. These companies, which have made investments using their surplus funds, are required to make disclosures about the same in their annual reports. Generally, companies are not regular players in the capital market. Some finance or investment companies operating portfolio management schemes for clients or companies with stock market operations as their main objective, however, are regular players in the secondary market.

7.9.3. Mutual Funds

Mutual Funds pool the funds of the investors and invest them in a well-diversified portfolio. Fund managers and investment consultants take the selection of companies for investment for maximising returns in investments. Recently, many private sector mutual funds like Kothari Pioneer Mutual Fund and CRB Mutual Funds have been started. All the mutual funds in the country are regulated in accordance with the provisions laid down in the SEBI (Mutual Funds) Regulations, 1993. The regulations are related to mutual funds from option trading, short selling or carrying forward transactions in securities. Mutual Funds constitute the single largest player in the stock market.

7.9.4. Indian Financial Institutions

Indian Financial or Investment Institutions play a major role in the capital markets. UTI, LIC and GIC are the institutions operating in the public sector. These institutions have huge investible funds estimated at around ₹ 1,00,000 crores. Generally, financial institutions partake the share capital of various companies. By their active buying and selling of securities from the secondary market, the financial and investment institutions maintain a balance in the market.

7.9.5. Foreign Institutional Investors

Foreign Institutional Investors (FIIs) have been allowed by SEBI to operate in the Indian markets. It is believed that FIIs have invested about $ 2 billion in the capital market. FIIs have picked up stocks with an eye on the long-term gains. The presence of FIIs in the stock markets is considered as a big boost to the market sentiments. Such purchases will be effected by the off-market deals. Block transactions arranged by brokers between FIIs and large shareholders like government financial institutions are termed off-market deals. These deals are also permitted by SEBI. FIIs have been dealing with UTI for a large number of transactions.

Foreign brokers will have to transmit orders to a member of the stock exchange and only the members will be allowed to execute such orders. SEBI registered foreign brokers on the condition that, they operate only on behalf of FIIs. The entry of foreign brokers is expected to give a further fillip to the present investment trends. In December 1993, SEBI has allowed the entry of foreign brokers into the stock exchanges. James Capital, Kleinwort Benson, Credit Lyonnaise Securities and Martin Partners have incidentally become the first set of foreign brokers to get permission from SEBI to operate on behalf of foreign institutional investors.

7.9.6. Non-resident Indians

Non-resident Indians (NRIs) also invest sizeable funds in the Indian stock markets. A NRI is permitted to subscribe freely to any new issue of shares or debentures of any company provided the company is not engaged in real estate business. However, the NR has to give an undertaking that he does not seek repatriation of the same. A NRI can also appoint any resident in India as his agent with appropriate power shares or debentures in the market. NRIs benefit because they can acquire securities at a low price and purchase the reserved shares offered by some companies. Also, without the prior permission of RBI, NRIs are allowed to gift their shareholdings to close relatives.

7.9.7. Brokers

The number of stock brokers has increased, with the increase in the number of stock exchanges, especially during the last decade. It is estimated that there are about 8,000 listed companies in the stock exchange. The number of active stock brokers dealing in the securities all over the country is about 5,500. Since November 1992, corporate entities are also allowed as members of the stock exchange. Subject to the recommendations of the government, financial institutions and subsidiaries of banks in the public sector were also allowed to become members of stock exchanges. The increase in the number of players in the stock market naturally increases the liquidity in the stock market. Though, we still follow the open cry system on our trading floors, on majority of the exchanges more than 90,000 transactions are executed during each day's trading session.

7.9.8. Sub-brokers

With explosion of capital market activity and equity culture spreading in the remote corners of the country, the number of sub-brokers operating also increased heavily. According to an estimate, around 60,000 sub-brokers are operating in the country at present.

Sub-brokers enter into deals with member-brokers of the exchanges. They can trade on their own account or on behalf of the investors. The number of sub-brokers allowed to enter into the trading ring on behalf of a member-broker of exchange is limited. In Bombay Stock Exchange, the number of sub-brokers entering into the trading ring (called authorised clerks) is seven, whereas in other regional stock exchanges, it is four.

7.10 WEAKNESSES OF STOCK EXCHANGES IN INDIA

The Indian stock exchanges have had the following problems:

1. Unprecedented booms and crashes lead to rampant speculative activities. This does not reflect a very healthy state of affairs.
2. Insider trading is rampant on Indian stock exchanges. Insider trading means operating on information, which is price-sensitive and not available to the public. Potential source of information is people working in these companies.
3. Demand and supply forces in the stock market are not allowed to act freely. It is highly dominated by large financial firms, big brokers and operators. Therefore, it is oligopolistic in structure. In an oligopoly market, only few sellers prevail.
4. There are limited forward trading activities in the stock exchanges.
5. The major problem areas include settlement periods, margin system and carry forward (badla) system.
6. The recent development of the primary market has created serious problems of interfacing with the secondary market. The secondary market should be re-oriented as to discharge the new responsibilities cast on it by the recent developments.
7. Indian stock market has still fragmented regulation even with the arrival of SEBI. There is multiplicity of administration.
8. The primary markets are not ignited enough to cope with changes taking place in the financial system.
9. Poor disclosure in prospectus is still rampant.
10. Even with the world of dematerialisation, investors face problems of delays (refund, transfer, etc.)
11. FIIs are now permitted to invest in unlisted securities and corporate and Government debt. Still there is some wall separating the foreign institutional investors to invest in Indian securities.
12. Stock Exchanges are run as brokers' clubs. Management is still dominated by brokers.
13. Poor disclosures by mutual funds are the main problem in the mutual fund industries. Net asset value (NAV) is not revealing the real picture about the performance of the fund.

7.11 REFORMS IN INDIAN SECURITIES MARKET

The development in Indian securities market since 1992 can be summarised as follows:

1. Capital Issues (Control) Act of 1947 was repealed and the office of Controller of Capital Issues was abolished. Control over price and premiums of shares were removed. Companies are now free to raise funds from securities markets after filing prospectus with the Securities and Exchange Board of India (SEBI).
2. The power to regulate stock exchanges has been delegated to SEBI by the Government.
3. SEBI introduces regulations for primary and other secondary market intermediaries and brings them within the regulatory framework.

4. Reforms by SEBI in the primary market include improved disclosure standards, introduction of prudential norms, and simplification of issue procedures. Companies are required to disclose all material facts and specific risk factors associated with their projects while making public issues.
5. Listing agreements of stock exchanges have been amended to listed companies such that these companies are required to furnish their annual statement showing variations between financial projections and projected utilisation of funds in the offer document and actual figures. This is to enable the shareholders to make comparisons between performance and promises.
6. SEBI introduces a code of advertisement for public issues to ensure fair and truthful disclosures.
7. Disclosure norms further have strengthened by introducing cash flow statements.
8. New issue procedures have been introduced. Book building for institutional investors is introduced to bring down the costs of issue.
9. SEBI introduces regulations governing substantial acquisition of shares and takeovers and lays down conditions under which disclosures and mandatory public offers are to be made to the shareholders. Regulations were further revised and strengthened in 1996.
10. SEBI reconstitutes the governing boards of the stock exchanges and introduces capital adequacy norms for broker accounts. Private mutual funds are permitted and several such funds have been already set up. All mutual funds are allowed to apply for firm allotment in public issues. This is to reduce issue costs.
11. Regulations for mutual funds have been revised in 1996, giving more flexibility to fund managers while increasing transparency, disclosure, and accountability.
12. Over the Counter Exchange of India has been formed.
13. National Stock Exchange (NSE) has been established as a stock exchange with nation-wide electronic trading.
14. Bombay Stock Exchange (BSE) introduces screen-based trading. 15 stock exchanges now have screen-based trading. BSE has been granted permission to expand its trading network to other centers.
15. Capital adequacy requirement for brokers has been enforced.
16. System of mark-to-market margins has been introduced in the stock exchanges.
17. Stock lending scheme has been introduced.
18. Transparency is brought about in short selling.
19. NSE has set up the National Securities Clearing Corporation Ltd.
20. BSE is in the process of implementing a trade guarantee scheme.
21. SEBI strengthens surveillance mechanisms and directs all stock exchanges to have separate surveillance departments.
22. SEBI strengthens enforcement of its regulations.
23. SEBI begins the process of prosecuting companies for mis-statements and ensures refund of application in several issues on account of mis-statements in the prospectus.
24. Indian companies are permitted to access international capital markets through Euro issues.
25. Foreign direct investment has been allowed in stock broking, asset management companies, merchant banking and other non-bank finance companies.
26. Foreign institutional investors (FIIs) are allowed access to Indian capital markets on registration with SEBI.

7.12 NEW GENERATION STOCK EXCHANGES

7.12.1. Over the Counter Exchange of India (OTCEI)

Over the Counter Exchange of India (OTECI) has been promoted by a consortium of leading financial institutions in India. The financial institutions include Unit Trust of India (UTI), Industrial Credit and Investment Corporation of India (ICICI), Industrial Development Bank of India (IDBI), Industrial Financial Corporation of India (IFCI), Life Insurance Corporation of India (LIC) and others. OTCEI is a recognised Stock Exchange under the Securities Contracts (Regulation) Act, 1956. It is set up to provide small and medium-sized companies access to the capital markets and to investors for a convenient mode of investments. It is a ringless electronic national exchange listing an entirely new set of companies which otherwise will not be listed on other stock exchanges. The companies listed on any other exchanges cannot be listed on OTCEI. The OTCEI Exchange can list companies with issued capital ranging from ₹ 30 lakhs to ₹ 2 crores.

Features of OTC

(a) OTCEI is ringless. Instead of having a localised trading ring likes other traditional exchanges, OTCEI has a network of counters linked by electronic communication systems. OTCEI operations are fully computerised. In a stock exchange transaction, there are four components:

(i) An offer

(ii) Acceptance of the offer

(iii) Settlement

(iv) Documentation

(b) On the traditional stock exchanges only and in some cases may be computerised. In the case of OTCEI with its electronically linked counters, all the above components are computerised.

(c) OTCEI has national jurisdiction, unlike the other exchanges, which have local jurisdiction.

(d) Only OTCEI has an exclusive list of companies. Securities of companies listed on OTCEI are not permitted to be listed on other exchanges.

(e) OTCEI permits to trade on its exchanges, a list of equity and debentures.

(f) Listing requirements of OTCEI are different from those of the other stock exchanges.

(g) The public offer method of OTCEI is different from that of the other exchanges.

Advantages to Investors

(a) OTCEI removes the illiquidity by instituting a new breed of operators called compulsory market markers.

(b) The OTCEI seeks to give the investor price vision by continuously displaying current security prices on screens installed at each OTCEI counter. In OTCEI, delivery or payment will be within a week's time.

(c) At the OTCEI counter, the investor's orders are executed immediately because, if there are no buyers or sellers, as the case may be, the compulsory market makers are obliged to deal with the investor. Besides, through the electronically linked OTCEI counter, the investor can contact compulsory market makers for any security.

(d) Every security listed on the OTCEI has a sponsor. This sponsor, who has been mentioned above as the compulsory market maker, is a member of OTCEI, which is involved with the sponsored security from the project stage. The sponsor appraises the Issue Company's project, values the company's securities, purchases them at the valued price or sells them to the public. Once market trading in the securities begins, the sponsor has to offer buy and sell quotes for them daily, for a period of eighteen months.

Players in the OTCEI Market

(a) There will be a few Registrars and Custodians registered with OTCEI and the listed companies can choose any one of these. There will be a running agreement with these registrars and custodians to ensure that there are no delays in transfers of securities.

(b) OTCEI will also have a few affiliated banks to speed up payments (especially inter-city ones). OTCEI intends to offer investors the option of opening an account with an affiliated bank with the power of operating the account being given to OTCEI.

Future Plans

1. Increasing the dealer network countrywide.
2. Proposal to allow 'Options' trading on OTCEI.
3. Consolidation of different trading documents (CR, SCS, and TD) into a single self-contained document.
4. Automated Banking.

7.12.2. National Stock Exchange of India

The National Stock Exchange (NSE) considered as a rival exchange to the Bombay Stock Exchange (BSE). It is India's leading Stock Exchange covering more than 160 cities and towns across the country. It provides modern fully computerised trading system designed to offer investors across the length and breadth of the country a safe and easy way to invest or liquidate investment in securities. It was incorporated in November 1992. Then it was recognised as a Stock Exchange in April 1993, went live for debt markets in June 1994 and commenced capital market operations in November 1994.

Today the National Stock Exchange (NSE) is the largest exchange in India with a network that trades 1400 equity stocks and 500 debt securities. It has over 1000 trading members. The companies listed on NSE are selected, based on their paid-up capital, market capitalisation, dividend payment and a good track record. The criterion is meant to ensure that only companies that meet certain standards are listed. The list is reviewed at periodic intervals. From 26th December 1996, the NSE has started trading in depositary scripts. Its debt market operations average 270 crores (US$ 75 million) a day and capital market operations average more than ₹ 1,200 crores (US$ 340 Million) a day.

Listing Requirement

The companies should meet the following requirements for listing on NSE:

1. A company should have a minimum paid-up capital of ₹ 10 crores.
2. It should have a market capitalisation of ₹ 50 crores.
3. All the listed companies should provide unabridged balance sheets to the shareholders of the company.
4. All the listed companies have to compare the actual financial performance with that of the projections made by them at the time of becoming public.
5. Once depository is created, it is necessary for companies to immobilise their share certificates.

Eligibility Criteria for Trading Membership

For Wholesale Debt Market Segment

Individuals, subsidiaries of banks and institutions are eligible for membership. The whole-time directors or the dealers should possess at least two years' experiences in any activity related to banking of financial service. The applicant must possess net worth of ₹ 2 crores.

For Capital Market Segments

Individuals, registered firms, corporate bodies and institutions are eligible for membership. The minimum net worth requirements prescribed are as follows:

(a) Individual and registered firm: ₹ 75 lakhs

(b) Corporate bodies: ₹ 100 lakhs.

The minimum prescribed qualification is graduation and two years' experience in dealing in capital markets must be fulfilled by:

(a) minimum two directors, in case the applicant is a corporate

(b) minimum two partners, in case of partnership firm

(c) individual in case of individual or sole proprietary concern

Common to Both the Segments

The applicants must be engaged solely in the business of securities and must not be engaged in any fund-based activities. The minimum paid-up capital for a corporate body should be ₹ 30 lakhs.

Wholesale Debt Market Segment

It is a facility for institutions and corporate bodies to enter into high value transactions in instruments such as government securities, treasury bills, public sector bonds, unit 64 of UTI, commercial papers and certificate of deposit.

Entities on the Wholesale Debt Market (WDM) Segment

There will be two types of entities in the system (1) Trading members are the recognised members of the exchange and (2) Participants are the organisations directly responsible for the settlement of trades. Participants will include trading members who will settle trades executed on their own account and on behalf of those clients who are not direct participants.

Capital Market Segments (CM)

It covers trading in equities, convertible debentures, etc., and retail trade in debt instruments like non-convertible debentures. Securities of medium and large companies with nation-wide investor base will be traded on the NSE. These will include securities that are traded today on other stock exchange. The identity of the trading member placing the order is not disclosed in the NSE computer trading system. The system provides complete transparency of trading operations.

Order Matching

Orders are matched automatically by the exchange computer system. All orders received are stacked in price-time priority. Subject to the conditions placed on an order by the trading member, the computer system will automatically search for best match. As soon as it finds a suitable match, the deal is struck.

NSE Trading System

The trading member can enter various types of order depending upon his requirement. These conditions are broadly of three categories, *viz.*, time-related conditions, price-related conditions and volume-related conditions.

Time Conditions follow the day order. A day order as the name suggests is an order, which is valid for the day on which it is entered. If the order is not matched during the day, at the end of the trading day, the order will get cancelled automatically.

Price Conditions follow on-stop order. On-stop or stoploss (OS) order allows the trading member to place an order, which gets activated only when the market price of the relevant security crosses a threshold price. Until then, the order does not enter the market.

Volume Conditions allow the trading members to disclose only a part of the order value to the market. For example, an order of 1000 with disclosed value conditions of 200 will mean that 200 is released into the market. After this is traded, another 200 is automatically released and so on till the full order is executed. The exchange may set a minimum disclosed volume criteria from time to time.

Clearing and Settlement System

Wholesale Debt Market Segment: In line with automation of trading facilities, the post-trade facilities for clearing and settlement of trades are also automated. Confirmed trades executed on the NSE are processed further at the clearing house, where participant's obligations for funds and securities would be drawn up each day and conveyed to the respective participants or settlers.

Capital Market Segment: Automated clearing, book entry transfer and a depository mechanism is envisaged for capital market clearing and settlement. NSE is at present using the physical delivery settlement procedure. A weekly trading and settlement cycle is being followed.

Salient Features of Settlement

Identification of Custodian Trades: Trades will be segregated into: (i) Trades to be settled by Trading Members and (ii) Trades to be settled by Custodians and Clearing Member Banks or Institutions. At the end of each trading day, NSE clearing system will inform trading members and custodians of their obligations through a daily report and at the end of the trading period, the trading members and custodians will receive their final obligation report. This report will contain information on: (i) Security-wise obligation to deliver and/or receive and (ii) Funds obligation to pay or to receive for each member and custodian.

Custodial Trades Identification: The clearing system will identify custodial trades based on the custodial client ID code entered by the trading member during order entry and segregate the custodial trades from the member trades. It is therefore important for a trading member to enter custodial client code correctly during order entry. The system will check for valid codes and reject those, which are not registered with NSE. Members will be informer about any change in the list of custodial client on a regular basis.

Settlement Procedure

Authorised Clearing House Representatives/Clearing Assistants: Each member can appoint three authorised representatives to deliver and receive securities through the clearing house. A member should make an application for designating these authorised representatives. The exchange will issue an identity card to these representatives. The authorised representatives shall display this ID card on their person at all times they are in the clearing house premises. This ID card is non-transferable and must be surrendered immediately to the clearing house upon cessation of employment of any of the authorised representative. Any loss or theft of this ID card should also be promptly informed to the clearing house.

Delivery at the Allotted Time: The delivering member should deliver all his delivery lots to the clearing house on the pay-in day for securities. The clearing house will knowledge the delivery of a copy of the delivery slip.

Receipt at the Allotted Time: The receiving member should collect the documents from the clearing houses on the payout day for securities. Receiving members will be allotted time slots for collecting documents from the clearing house. The authorised representative should produce an authorisation letter for receiving the documents from the clearing house. The receiving member or his authorised representative will be required to acknowledge receipt of the documents on the copy of the receipt statement.

NSE Settlement Cycle

The National Stock Exchange (NSE) settlement cycle is a weekly cycle. It begins on Wednesday (Day 1) and ends on the following Tuesday (Day 7). There are therefore 5 trading days in the weekly settlement cycle, as trading does not take place on Saturdays and Sundays. All the trades, which take place from and during the weekly cycle (Day 1-7), are settled on the following Monday, Tuesday and Wednesday (Day 13, 14, and 15). All securities are delivered to the NSE Clearing House (CH) on Monday (Day 13) and all payments are made on Tuesday (Day 14). The CH makes the payment and delivery of shares to brokers on Wednesday (Day 15), who would then transfer it to their clients. This means that if an investor buys a share on any day from Day 1-7 (Wednesday to Tuesday), the payment will have to be made to the CH on Day 14. Shares will then be delivered to investor's broker on Day 15, and subsequently will be transferred to investor's demat account on Day 16.

7.13 REGULATION OF STOCK EXCHANGES

All stock exchanges were subject to self-regulation from their own management bodies, i.e., Board of Governors till 1956. However, after that, it is changed to three-tier regulation.

1. Constitution of India lists the subject of 'Stock Exchanges and Future Markets' under the exclusive authority of Central Government. Central Government through Ministry of Finance regulates the stock exchanges primarily through Securities Contract (Regulation) Act, 1956 (SCRA).
2. The Securities and Exchange Board of India (SEBI) also regulates the stock exchanges in order to protect the interest of investors and to promote the development of security markets in India.
3. In addition, all stock exchanges have their own separate rules, bye-laws and regulations, which are exercised through their Governing Councils.

7.13.1. Role of Ministry of Finance in Regulation

The Stock Exchange Division of Ministry of Finance has its Head Office at Delhi and Branch offices at Mumbai and Kolkata. This Division:

(a) Links government and stock exchanges
(b) Keeps a close watch on the operations of the stock exchanges
(c) Advises in case of untoward developments and crisis
(d) Ensures the compliance of listing provisions
(e) Ensures smooth functioning of the stock exchanges
(f) And issues licenses to brokers and dealers in securities and also in areas beyond the jurisdiction of recognised stock exchanges.

7.13.2. Role of SEBI in Regulation

The Central Government also set up an apex body called the Securities and Exchange Board of India (SEBI), which is headed by a Chairman. The government is also empowered to nominate four members to constitute top management team of the SEBI. This body acquires a wide rules, regulations and guidelines for promoting, developing, stabilising and strengthening the security markets in India.

Few rules and regulations of SEBI are given below:

1. SEBI (Portfolio Managers) Rules and Regulations, 1992.
2. SEBI (Stock Brokers and Sub-brokers) Rules and Regulations, 1992.
3. SEBI (Insider Trading) Regulation, 1992
4. SEBI (Merchant Bankers) Rules and Regulations, 1992.
5. SEBI (Mutual Fund) Regulations, 1993.
6. SEBI (Underwriters) Rules and Regulations, 1993.
7. SEBI (Registrars to Issue and Share Transfer Agents) Rules and Regulations, 1993.

8. SEBI (Debentures Trustee) Rules and Regulations, 1993.
9. SEBI (Bankers to an Issue) Rules and regulations, 1993.

Few guidelines are given below:

(a) Free pricing of shares
(b) Disclosures and Investors' Protection
(c) Registration of Foreign Institutional Investors (FII)
(d) Allotment of shares
(e) New financial instruments
(f) Credit rating fixed return bearing securities.

1. The Securities and Exchange Board of India Act, 1992 (hereinafter referred to as "The SEBI Act") is deemed to have come into force on January 30, 1992. Relatively a brief Act containing only 35 sections, the SEBI Act governs all the stock exchanges and the securities transactions in India.

2. A Board by the name of the Securities and Exchange Board of India (SEBI) consists of one Chairman and five members, two from the department of the Finance and Law of the Central Government, one from the Reserve Bank of India and two other persons. It has its head office in Bombay and regional offices in Delhi, Calcutta and Madras. The Board has been constituted under the SEBI Act to administer its provisions. The Central Government has the right to terminate the services of the Chairman or any member of the Board. The Board decides all questions in its meeting by majority vote with the Chairman having a second or casting vote.

3. Section 11 of the SEBI Act provides that it shall be the duty of the Board to protect the interest of investors in securities and to promote the development of and to regulate the securities market by such measures, as it thinks fit. It empowers the Board to regulate the business in Stock Exchanges. SEBI regulates the working of stock brokers, sub-brokers, share transfer agents, bankers to an issue, trustees of trust deeds, registrars to an issue, merchant bankers, underwriters, portfolio managers, investment advisers and so on. SEBI also registers and regulates the working of collective investment schemes including mutual funds, to prohibit fraudulent and unfair trade practices and insider trading, to regulate takeovers, to conduct inquiries and audits of the stock exchanges, etc.

4. As all Stock Exchanges are required to be registered with SEBI under Section 12 of the SEBI Act. All the stock brokers, sub-brokers, share transfer agents, bankers to an issue, trustees of trust deed, registrars to an issue, merchant bankers, underwriters, portfolio managers, investment advisers and such other intermediaries who may be associated with the Securities Markets are obliged to register with the Board.

5. The Board has the power to suspend or cancel such registration. The Board is bound by the directions given by the Central Government from time to time on questions of policy and the Central Government has the right to supersede the Board. The Board is also obliged to submit a report to the Central Government every year, giving true and full account of its activities, policies and programmes. Any one aggrieved by the Board's decision is entitled to appeal to the Central Government.

6. The Central Government uptil now has framed ten Rules by virtue of Section 29 of the SEBI Act.

7. The Board empowered by Section 30 of the SEBI Act has till now with the previous approval of the Central Government made twelve regulations.

7.13.3. Regulation of Intermediaries

Eligibility to be a Participant

Participants in the Indian capital market are required to register with SEBI to carry out their businesses. These include Stock brokers, sub-brokers, share transfer agents, bankers to an issue, trustees of a trust deed, registrars to an issue, merchant bankers, underwriters, portfolio managers, investment advisers, and other such intermediaries who may be associated with the securities market in any manner.

Stock brokers are not allowed to buy, sell, or deal in securities, unless they hold a certificate granted by SEBI. At the end of March 1997, they numbered 8,867.

Each stockbroker is subject to capital adequacy requirements consisting of two components

(a) Basic minimum capital and

(b) Additional or optional capital related to volume of business

The basic minimum capital requirement varies from one exchange to another. A SEBI regulation requires stock brokers of BSE or NSE to maintain a minimum of ₹ 5,00,000 (about $ 14,000), which is the largest requirement among the stock exchanges.

However, BSE and NSE require their respective members to deposit with them larger amounts. The additional or optional capital and the basic minimum capital combined have to be maintained at 8% or more of the gross outstanding business in the exchange. The gross outstanding business means the cumulative amount of sales and purchases by a stock broker in all securities at any point during the settlement period. Sales and purchases on behalf of customers may not be netted but may be included to those of the broker.

There is no mandatory qualification test for stock brokers and other market participants in India, unlike other countries such as Japan, United Kingdom, and United States.

Sub-brokers

Most stock brokers in India are still relatively small. They cannot afford to directly cover every retail investor in a geographically vast country and in such a complex society. Thus, they are permitted to transact with sub-brokers as the latter play an indispensable role in intermediating between investors and the stock market.

An applicant for a sub-broker certificate must be affiliated with a stock broker of a recognised stock exchange. A sub-broker application may take the form of sole proprietorship, partnership, or corporation.

There are two major issues concerning sub-brokers in the Indian capital market:

(i) Majority of sub-brokers are not registered with SEBI; and

(ii) The function of the sub-broker is not clearly defined.

No sub-broker is supposed to buy, sell, or deal in securities, without a certificate granted by SEBI. Nevertheless, there were only about 2,593 sub-brokers registered with SEBI as of end-June 1997, while the number of stock sub-brokers in India was estimated in the range of 50,000 to 200,000 (End of 1998).

The Indian law defines a sub-broker as any person, not being a member of a stock exchange, who acts on behalf of a stock broker as an agent, or otherwise, to assist the investors in buying, selling, or dealing securities through such a stock broker. Based on this definition, the sub-broker is either a stock broker's agent or an arranger for the investor. Thus, legally speaking, the stock broker as a principal will be responsible to the investor for a sub-broker's conduct if a sub-broker acts as his agent. However, the market practice is different from this legally defined relationship. In reality, the stock broker, in general, issues a contract note of a transaction even to a registered sub-broker, thus treating the latter as counterparty. This implicitly denies the stock broker's privity with the investor.

NSE does not officially allow its members to transact with end-investors through a sub-broker. This is probably because NSE has liberal membership criteria and its computerised trading network can easily provide geographically scattered stock brokers with direct access to trading on NSE. Nevertheless, many trading members of NSE have been using registered and unregistered sub-brokers.

To sort out this confusion, SEBI enforced the following measures in March 1997:

1. Initiation of criminal actions on complaints received against unregistered sub-brokers in suitable cases;
2. Revival of the institution of "remisier" under rules and bye-laws of the stock exchanges; and
3. Prohibition of stock brokers in dealing with unregistered subbrokers or unregistered remisiers after 1 June 1997 (this deadline was later extended to 1 July 1997).

In spite of these actions, the confusion has remained. There is a need to address the basic issue of clarifying the role of the sub-broker and to operationally define its relationship with the stock brokers.

Merchant Bankers

Under the old regulations, there were four categories of registered merchant bankers with different minimum net worth requirements. Under the new regulations, the categories were abolished. Among other provisions, a merchant banker applicant is required to have a minimum net worth of ₹ 50 million.

The new regulations have drawn a clear-cut line between the merchant banker and the non-banking finance company (NBFC). Under the old regulations, a merchant banker is permitted to carry out fund-based activities such as deposit taking, leasing, bill discounting and hire purchasing. The new regulations no longer allow a merchant banked to engage in these fund-based activities except for those related exclusively to the capital market such as underwriting.

The merchant banker is required to cease such activities within two years. Correspondingly, an existing NBFC performing merchant banking activities is required to relinquish such activities after a certain period of time.

The merchant banking industry in India has many problems, the main ones being that there are too many merchant bankers, and that they are considered to be relatively incompetent.

Only 20 merchant bankers account for 60-85% of the merchant banking business, while 148 of them are in business only on paper. In May 1997, a substantial number of merchant bankers were found to be professionally imprudent or negligent (Endos, 1998). SEBI listed 134 merchant bankers of Categories I, II, and III who broke their underwriting commitments for possible disciplinary actions. Of this number, 95 were in Category I. Furthermore, there have been records of listing delay or rejection of initial public offerings (IPOs) in the recent past. One must know that three out of four categories of merchants bankers have been abolished now.

7.13.4. Fragmentation of Regulatory Authorities

The present functions and powers of regulatory agencies for the securities market seem to be fragmented. SEBI is the primary body responsible for regulation of the securities market, deriving its powers of registration and enforcement primarily from the SEBI Act.

1. There was an existing regulatory framework for the securities market, provided by the Securities Contract Regulation (SCR) Act and the Companies Act, administered by the Ministry of Finance and the Department of Company Affairs (DCA) of the Ministry of Law, respectively.
2. SEBI has been delegated most of the functions and powers under the SCR Act, and shares the rest with the Ministry of Finance.
3. It has also been delegated certain powers under the Companies Act.
4. RBI also has regulatory involvement in the capital market regarding foreign exchange control liquidity support to market participants and debt management through primary dealers.

Table 7.3 Capital Adequacy Requirement for Merchant Banker Applicant (Old Regulations)

Category	Minimum Amount of Net Worth (₹ million)
I	50
II	5
III	2

Source: Endo (1998).

5. It is RBI and not SEBI that regulates primary dealers in the Government securities market.
6. However, securities transactions that involve a foreign exchange transaction need the permission of RBI.

So far, fragmentation of the regulatory authorities has not been a major obstacle to effective regulation of the securities market. Rather, lack of enforcement capacity by SEBI has been a more significant cause of poor regulation. But since the Indian stock markets are rapidly being integrated, the authorities may follow the global trend of consolidation of regulatory authorities or better coordination among them.

7.13.5. Self-regulatory Body

Self-regulatory organisations (SROs) have been adopted in many countries to regulate various participants in the securities market. The SRO's bye-laws and codes of conduct bind members. Through the SEBI Act of 1992, SROs were introduced in the Indian capital market, but they are not yet operational.

A clear regulatory framework has yet to be set up, and relevant market participants are not ready to regulate themselves for professional purposes. The only securities-related SROs in India whose regulatory frameworks have been well established and which are actually functioning are the recognised stock exchanges. Participants in the Indian capital market seem to have successfully preserved the spirit and practice of self-regulation or self-governance in the old stock exchanges such as BSE. However, it is true that the old stock exchanges have been rife with vested interests of member brokers who are not fully friendly to investors.

7.14 REVIEW QUESTIONS

Short Answer Questions

1. List out different types of securities based on issuer in the primary market.
2. List out different types of securities based on maturity of primary market.
3. What are the basic constituents of the securities market?
4. Write a note on different types of securities market.
5. Write a brief note on the management of stock exchanges in India.
6. Briefly discuss the recent trends in the development of primary market.
7. What is OTCEI?
8. Which securities are called risk-free?
9. Who is an intermediary in the stock market?
10. Is experience required to be a member of a stock exchange?
11. Who are the constituent members of Bombay Stock Exchange?
12. What is Sauda?
13. Distinguish between spot delivery and hand delivery.
14. Explain the role of clearing houses in stock market operations.
15. Describe settlement procedures.
16. What is a badla transaction?
17. Write a short note on arbitration procedure.
18. List out the players in the secondary market.

19. Briefly explain the trading mechanism of OTCEI.
20. What is the role of the self-regulatory body?
21. List out the types of new issues.
22. Write a note on the role of issue manager.

Essay Type Questions

1. What were the broad phases of the growth of stock exchanges in India?
2. Explain the role and functions of stock exchanges in the capital market?
3. Describe the features of stock exchanges in India.
4. Discuss the procedures for listing a security in a stock exchange.
5. Write an essay in detail on the trading system in the Indian-stock exchanges.
6. Describe settlement cycles in various stock exchanges in India.
7. Evaluate the rolling settlement cycle.
8. Critically examine the mechanism of badla trading.
9. What is Arbitration? Explain the procedures in detail.
10. Who are the players of secondary market? Briefly describe their roles.
11. What are the problems faced by the stock exchanges in India?
12. 'Stock Market reformation is a continuous process.' Comment and evaluate the statement in the Indian context.
13. Explain the trading mechanism prevailing in the OTCEI.
14. Describe the stock market regulation in India.
15. What are procedures of initiating initial public offer (IPO)?

❋ ❋ ❋

CHAPTER 8

Venture Capital

Objectives

The student, after studying the chapter, should be able to:

- Make a historical account about venture capital in India and in the world
- Describe the mechanism of venture capital cycle and apply it
- Adopt an organisation suitable for venture capital services
- Identify the various types of investors in venture capital segment
- Choose the venture capital stage for a particular business
- Evaluate the venture capital scenario in India

Structure:

8.1 INTRODUCTION

An entrepreneur cannot always depend on banking finance to realise his business goals. He knows his limitation. For example, if he has a new idea in the field of motor mechanism, he has to convince the banker that his idea can be realised and the potential customers will accept the product. Bankers many a time cannot be convinced. Therefore, there exists 'non-bankable gaps' that arise during the growth of his or her business. Some giant business will come forward to help these thousands of firms leverage new opportunities by providing seed and growth capital. Venture capital represents the major source of growth for private equity investment around the world.

Definitions of venture capital are all very similar. The Organisation for Economic Cooperation and Development (OECD) (1996) defines venture capital as follows:

"Capital provided by firms who invest alongside management in young companies that are not quoted on the stock market. The objective is high return from the investment. Value is created by the young company in partnership with the venture capitalist's money and professional expertise."

Venture capital is a private equity investment in entrepreneurial companies used to finance the working capital requirement and asset needs of growing businesses. People often use terminologies like 'high return' and 'growth' when they mention about venture capital. Some people use venture capital and private equity interchangeably. Venture capital means an early stage investment in USA and it also includes later stage investment.

Meaning

Venture Capital is money provided by professionals who invest alongside management in rapidly growing companies.

Venture Capital derives its value from the brand equity, professional image, constructive criticism, domain knowledge, and industry contacts. They bring to table at a significantly lower management agency cost.

A Venture Capital Fund (VCF) strives to provide entrepreneurs with the support they need to create for an up-scalable business with sustainable growth, while providing their contributors with outstanding returns on investment, for the higher risks they assume.

Venture Capital Funds generally:

(a) Finance new and rapidly growing companies;
(b) Invest in typically knowledge-based, sustainable, up-scaleable companies;
(c) Purchase equity or quasi-equity securities;
(d) Assist in the development of new products or services;
(e) Add value to the company through active participation;
(f) Take higher risks with the expectation of higher rewards;
(g) Have a long-term orientation.

Problems and confusion emerge when the terms "venture capital" and "private equity" are being used. In the USA, "venture capital" refers to early stage investment, in Europe, it also includes later stage investment.

8.2 EVOLUTION

R.S. Bhat, the chairman of Bhat Committee highlighted the problems of new entrepreneurs and technologists in setting up industries in 1972. The concept of Venture Capital was introduced in India by the All India Financial Institutions in 1975.

The Risk Capital Foundation (RCF) sponsored by the Industrial Finance Corporation of India (IFCI) was inaugurated. The purpose of establishing the institution was to supplement promoters' equity with a view to motivate technologists and professionals to promote new firms. Industrial Development Bank of India (IDBI) introduced Seed Capital Scheme in 1976. Till 1984, the concept of venture capital was known as 'Risk Capital' and "Seed Capital'. The objectives of risk capital were different to those understood under venture capital today.

The Central Government announced the Technology Policy Statement in 1983. It laid down guidelines towards technological self-reliance through commercialisation and exploitation of technologies developed in the country. The Policy Statement stressed the importance of venture capital.

Apart from IFCI and IDBI, all other all-India financial institutions took decision in 1984 to allocate funds for providing assistance. The assistance was in the form of venture capital. ICICI launched a Venture Capital Scheme to encourage new technocrats in the private sector in new fields of high technology with inherent high risk in 1986.

ICICI undertook administration of Programme for Application of Commercial Technology (PACT) aided by USAID with the initial grant of US$ 10 million in 1986. It resembled the nature of venture capital financing for specific needs of the corporate sector industrial unit.

The Central Government created the Venture Capital Fund. It became operational with effect from 1-04-1986. The general administration is with Industrial Development Bank of India. A Research and Development levy is imposed on all payments made for purchase of technology from abroad including royalty payments, lump sum payments for foreign collaboration and payment of designs and drawings under the R&D Cess Act, 1986. The levy provides source for funding the Venture Capital Fund. IDBI was made the nodal agency to operate this fund. ICICI sponsored Technology Development and Information Company of India Ltd. (TDICI) in 1988. Venture Capital operations of ICICI were taken over by TDICI with effect from 1 July, 1988.

Central Government announced guidelines for the establishment and functioning of venture capital activities in November 1988. These guidelines allowed the private sector to operate in the venture capital financing industry.

Risk Capital Foundation (RCF) was renamed Risk Capital and Technology Finance Corporation Ltd. in 1988. It took over the activities of RCF in addition to the administration of the other schemes of financing technology development and managing venture capital fund.

Unit Trust of India (UTI) sponsored 'Venture Capital Unit Scheme' known as VECAUS in 1989. UTI has sponsored VECAUS-I and appointed TDICI as its manager. During 1990, UTI sponsored VECAUS-II that is also being managed by TDICI. During 1991, UTI launched VECAUS-III and appointed RCTC as Fund Manager.

Many new venture capital funds were sponsored after the Government of India guidelines in November 1988. ANZ Grindlays Bank, a foreign bank, set up the first private venture capital fund in 1987. It was called India Investment Fund. It came out with the Second Investment Fund subsequently in 1989. This was the only foreign bank, which had the Venture Capital Fund operational in India. The contributions to the fund have been made by Non-resident Indians (NRIs).

Other Venture Capital Funds, which were established during the period, are:

(a) Canbank Venture Capital Fund (CVCF) in October, 1989

(b) Credit Capital Venture Fund (I) Ltd. (CVF) in January, 1990

(c) APIDC Venture Capital Ltd. in October, 1990

(d) Gujarat Venture Finance Ltd. (GVFL) in November, 1990

(e) 20th Century Capital Corporation Ltd. (TCCCL) in August, 1991

(f) Indus Venture Capital Management Ltd. (IVCML) in October, 1991

(g) IL & FS Venture Corporation in 1991

(h) IFB-Venture Capital Finance Ltd. (IFB-VCFL) in November, 1992

(i) SIDBI-Venture Capital Fund (SIDBI-VCF) in April 1994 etc.

All the above venture capital funds or management companies are members of Indian Venture Capital Association (IVCA).

Current Trends in India

(a) Capital is pouring into private equity funds.

(b) Average ticket size of VC investment is increasing.

(c) First-generation entrepreneurs are finding easier to raise funds.

(d) Investors are demanding non-financial value additions.

(e) Most states are setting regional VC funds.

(f) VC firms are getting professionalised.

(g) Incubators and serial entrepreneurs are germinating.

(h) VC firms are getting specific industry focused.

(i) Competition is stretching valuations.

8.3 MECHANISM OF VENTURE CAPITAL — HOW IT WORKS?

The flow of venture capital from the investor to a Start-up Company and back can be thought of as a cycle that runs through several phases. Following is a schematic overview of these different phases (Refer to Chart 8.1):

(A) Raising of venture fund.

(B) Investing in, monitoring of, adding value to firms.

(C) Exiting successful companies; returning capital to investors.

Raising the Money

An entrepreneur has to raise money for investment. Money can come from a variety of sources: institutional investors (public and private pension funds, insurance companies, banks, and foundations), wealthy individuals, corporate investors, government agencies, or endowments of academic institutions. Venture capitalists raise funds into a "blind pool". This means that investors do not know for which purpose their money will be used when they make the investment. Hence, the money has been raised by venture capitalists. They explore whether the business plans have the potential to grow into successful companies if the answer is yes, the business plan is then financed by venture capital. Likewise, innovators and businesspeople try to find a VC firm that would fund their business idea. Only very few proposals out of several hundred will be selected. Fund-raising and picking the right business plan are usually parallel and ongoing processes.

Invest and Oversee

The money is being invested in a newly created technology firm. These companies very often produce only one product. It is the goal of venture capitalists to develop this start-up business into a stable, growing and profitable company. Constant monitoring is the key. Very often, the venture capitalist sits on the board of the company and is involved in strategic decision-making. High net worth individuals and experienced businessmen not only provide capital but also contribute their business experience and leadership to successfully build a new business.

Chart 8.1

Venture Capital Cycle

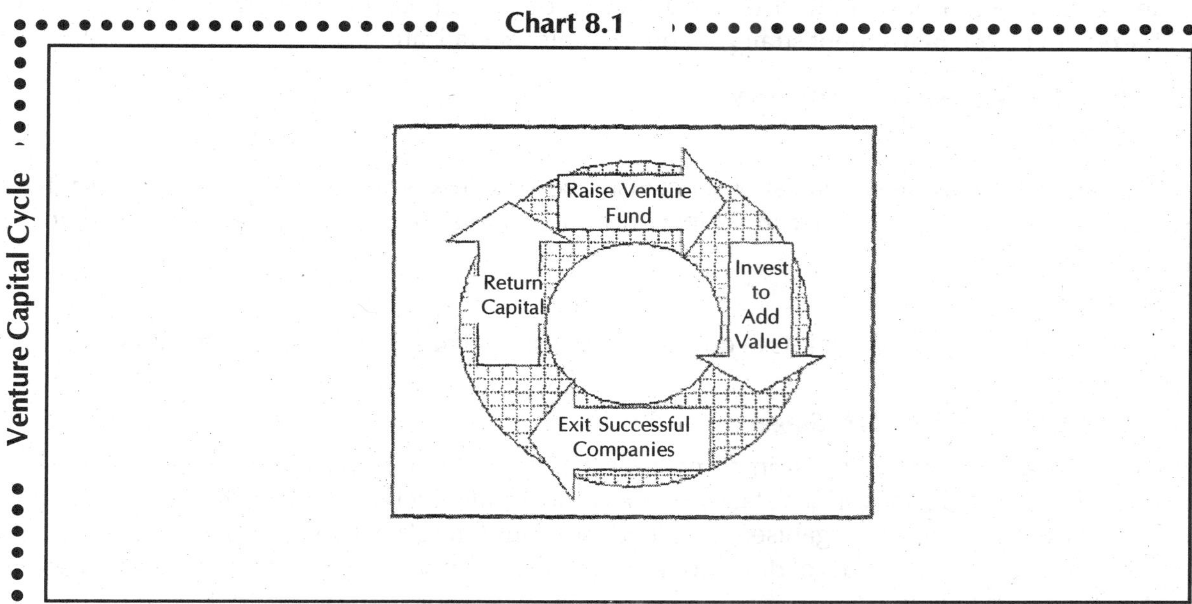

Managing the Exit

Assuming the venture capitalist hits gold and the company turns into a success, it is time for him to cash on the gains. Different exit strategies are available. Floating the company on the stock market (initial public offering or IPO) is a very common exit. Other options include selling the company in question and distribute the gains to the investors.

8.4 VENTURE CAPITALIST

The typical venture capitalist is that of a wealthy financier who wants to fund start-up companies. The perception is that a person who has developed a new product needs capital. Thus, if they cannot get capital from a bank or from their own pockets, they seek the help of a venture capitalist.

Venture capital and private equity firms, in fact, are pools of capital. It is typically organised as a limited partnership. It, in turn, invests in companies that represent the opportunity for a high rate of return within five to seven years. The venture capitalist may look at several opportunities before investing in only a few selected companies with favourable investment opportunities. Venture capitalists are not simply passive financiers. They foster growth in companies through their involvement in the management, strategic marketing and planning of their investee companies. They are entrepreneurs first and financiers second.

Even individuals may be venture capitalists. While this type of individual investment did not totally disappear, the modern venture firm emerged as the dominant venture investment vehicle. However, in the last few years, individuals have again become a potent and increasingly larger part of the early stage start-up venture life cycle. They are called 'Angel Investors'. These "angel investors" will mentor a company and provide needed capital and expertise to help develop companies. Angel investors may either be wealthy people with management expertise or retired businessmen and women who seek the opportunity for first-hand business development.

Types of Venture Capitalist

Venture firms come in various sizes from small seed specialist firms of only a few million dollars under management to firms with over a billion dollars in invested capital around the world. The common denominator in all these types of venture investing is that the venture capitalist is not a passive investor. He has an active and vested interest in guiding, leading and growing the companies they have invested in. They seek to add value through their experience in investing in tens and hundreds of companies. The types of venture investors are classified based on: (a) the investment strategy, and (b) their specialisation.

8.4.1. Based on the Investment Strategy

(a) Generalists

Venture capitalists may be generalist or specialist investors depending on their investment strategy. Venture capitalists can be generalists, investing in various industry sectors, or various geographic locations, or various stages of a company's life.

(b) Specialists

Alternatively, they may be specialists in one or two industry sectors. They may seek to invest in only a localised geographic area.

(c) Venture Capitalists of Early Stage

Venture firms generally will invest in companies that are in their initial start-up modes. Venture capitalists will also invest in companies at various stages of the business life cycle. A venture capitalist may invest before there is a real product or company organised (so called "seed investing"). He or she may provide capital to start up a company in its first or second stages of development known as "early stage investing". An early stage investment takes seven to ten years to mature.

(d) Venture Capitalists of Expansion Stage Financing

These venture capitalists may provide needed financing to help a company grow beyond a critical mass to become more successful. This kind of financing is called expansion stage financing.

(e) Later Stage Investors

The venture capitalist may invest in a company throughout the company's life cycle. Therefore, some funds focus on later stage investing by providing financing to help the company grow to a critical mass to attract public financing through a stock offering. Alternatively, the venture capitalist may help the company attract a merger or acquisition with another company by providing liquidity and exit for the company's founders. A later stage investment may only take a few years, so that the appetite for the investment life cycle must be congruent with the limited partnerships' appetite for liquidity.

(f) Turnaround Investors

At the other end of the spectrum, some venture funds specialise in the acquisition, turnaround or recapitalisation of public and private companies that represent favourable investment opportunities.

(g) Diverse Investors

There are venture funds that will be broadly diversified and will invest in companies in various industry sectors as diverse as semiconductors, software, retailing and restaurants.

The venture industry gets a lot of attention for its high technology investments. Venture capitalists also invest in companies such as construction, industrial products, business services, etc. There are several firms that have specialised in retail company investment and others that have a focus in investing only in "socially responsible" start-up endeavours.

(h) Synergetic Venture Investment

Some venture firms are successful by creating synergies between the various companies they have invested in.

Example

One company has a great software product. However, it does not have adequate distribution technology. It may be paired with another company or its management in the venture portfolio that has better distribution technology.

8.4.2. Based on their Specialisation

The "venture funds" available could be from:

(a) Incubators

An incubator is a hardcore technocrat who works with an entrepreneur to develop a business idea. He prepares a company for subsequent rounds of growth and funding. "Infinity" is an example of incubators in India.

(b) Angel Investors

An angel is an experienced industry-bred individual with high net worth. Typically, an angel investor would:

(a) Invest only in his chosen field of technology.

(b) Take active participation in the day-to-day running of the company.

(c) Invest small sums.

(d) Not insist on detailed business plans.

(e) Sanction the investment upto a month.

(f) Help the company for "second round" of funding.

Business angels generally invest smaller amounts of venture capital in earlier stage companies compared with venture capital firms. Many companies find business angels through informal contacts. But for others, finding a business angel may be more difficult. The details of individual business angels are rarely available. Both the companies are seeking finance and business angels can register with companies, which aim to make productions that result in investment, frequently known as "business introduction services", "informal private investor services" or "business angel networks". In Britain, the BVCA "has list of such companies in its *Sources of Business Angel Capital*, which is published annually.

The IndUS Entrepreneurs (TIE) is a classic group of angels like: Vinod Dham, Sailesh Mehta, Kanwal Rekhi, Prabhu Goel, Suhas Patil, Prakash Agarwal and K.B. Chandrashekhar. In India, there is a lack of home-grown angels except a few like Saurabh Srivastava and Atul Choksey (ex-Asian Paints).

(c) Venture Capitalists (VCs)

VCs are organisations raising funds from numerous investors and hiring experienced professional managers to deploy the same. They typically:

(a) Invest at "second" stage.

(b) Invest over a spectrum of industry.

(c) Have hand-holding "mentor" approach.

(d) Insist on detailed business plans.

(e) Invest into proven ideas and businesses.

(f) Provide "brand" value to investee and act as.

(d) Private Equity Players

They are established investment bankers. They:

(a) Invest into proven or established businesses.

(b) Have "financial partners" approach.

(c) Invest between USD 5 and 100 million.

8.5 TYPES OF VENTURE CAPITAL FIRMS

Some venture capital firms manage a range of funds including investment trusts, limited partnerships and venture capital trusts. For a company looking to raise venture capital is concerned, only those investment preferences which match its requirements should be approached. The source of a venture capital firm's funds is of relevance only, if it affects the terms at which a venture capital firm offers one.

There are several types of venture capital firms. Like a mutual fund company, a venture capital firm may have more than one fund in existence. A venture firm may raise another fund, a few years after closing the first fund in order to continue to invest in companies and to provide more opportunities for existing and new investors. It is possible for a successful firm to raise six or seven funds consecutively over the span of ten to fifteen years. Each fund is managed separately. It has its own investors or limited partners and its own general partner. These funds' investment strategy may be similar to other funds in the firm. However, the firm may have one fund with a specific focus and another with a different focus and yet another with a broadly diversified portfolio. This depends on the strategy and focus of the venture firm itself.

(a) Limited Partnership Firms

Most mainstream firms invest their capital through funds organised as limited partnerships in which the venture capital firm serves as the general partner. The venture capital firm will organise its partnership as a pooled fund. That is, a fund is made up of the general partner and the investors are limited partners. These funds are typically organised as fixed life partnerships, usually having a life of ten years. Each fund is capitalised by commitments of capital from the limited partners. Once the partnership has reached its target size, the partnership is closed to further investment from new investors or even existing investors so the fund has a fixed capital pool from which it makes its investments.

(b) Independent Venture Firms

The most common type of venture firm is an independent venture firm that has no affiliations with any other financial institution. These are called "private independent firms".

(c) Affiliates or Subsidiaries

Venture firms may also be affiliates or subsidiaries of a commercial bank investment bank or insurance company. They make investments on behalf of outside investors or the parent firm's clients. Still other firms may be subsidiaries of non-financial, industrial corporations making investments on behalf of the parent itself. These latter firms are typicals called "direct investors" or "corporate venture investors".

(d) Affiliates of Government

Other organisations may include government affiliated investment programs that help start-up companies either through Central or State Government programmes. One common vehicle is the State Finance Corporation of India.

(e) Corporate Venturing

One form of investing that was popular in the 1980s and is again very popular is corporate venturing. This is usually called "direct investing" in portfolio companies by venture capital programmes or subsidiaries of non-financial corporations. These investment vehicles seek to find qualified investment opportunities that are congruent with the parent company's strategic technology or the one that provides synergy or cost savings.

These corporate venturing programmes may be loosely organised programmes affiliated with existing business development programmes. Or it may be self-contained entities with a strategic charter and mission to make investments congruent with the parent's strategic mission. There are some venture-firms that specialise in advising, consulting and managing a corporation's venturing programme.

Difference between Corporate Venturing and Other Types of Venture Investment

The typical distinction between corporate venturing and other types of venture investment vehicles is that corporate venturing is usually performed with corporate strategic objectives in mind while other venture investment vehicles typically have investment return or financial objectives as their primary goal. This may be a generalisation as corporate venture programmes are not immune to financial considerations, but the distinction can be made.

The other distinction of corporate venture programmes is that they usually invest their parent's capital while other venture investment vehicles invest outside investors' capital.

8.6 BENEFITS OF VENTURE CAPITAL

(a) Venture-backed companies have been shown to grow faster than other types of companies. This is made possible by the provision of a combination of capital and experienced personal input from venture capital executives, which sets it apart from other forms of finance.

(b) Venture capital can help you achieve your ambitions for your company and provide a stable base for strategic decision-making.

(c) The venture capital firms will seek to increase a company's value to its owners, without taking day-to-day management control. Although you may have a smaller "slice of cake", within a few years your "slice" should be worth considerably more than the whole "cake" was to you before.

(d) Venture capital firms often work in conjunction with other providers of finance and may be able to help you to put a funding package together for your business.

8.7 VENTURE CAPITAL VS. DEBT

		Venture finance	Debt finance
1.	Objective	Maximum Return 2-5 years	Interest payment
2.	Holding Period	Common shares, convertible bonds, options, warrants	Short/Long term Loan
3.	Instruments		Factoring, leasing
4.	Pricing	P/E Ratio net tangible assets	Interest spread
5.	Collateral	Very rare	Yes
6.	Ownership	Yes	No
7.	Control	Minority shareholders, rights protection, board members	Increased leverages
8.	Exit	Selling their shares back to the management	
9.	Mechanism	Selling the shares to another investor. A trade sale, where the whole company is sold to another and the company achieving a stock market listing	
10.	Risk	The venture capital firm often faces the risk of failure just like the other shareholders	The company may be liquidated through receiver

8.8 VENTURE CAPITAL FUNDS VS. MUTUAL FUNDS

There is often confusion among investors about the differences between venture capital funds and equity-focused mutual funds. While most investors recognise that venture capital funds invest in private companies and mutual funds predominantly invest in publicly listed companies, other differences appear less obvious. This confusion is hardly surprising given that venture capital investing has historically been confined to a small group of wealthier investors.

But there are some important distinctions of which anyone thinking of investing in venture capital should be aware. These include:

(a) The amount of information that is publicly available on potential investments and the industry segments in which they operate.

(b) The direct influence that such funds have over the management of the companies in which they are invested.

(c) The ease in which managers can sell portfolio investments.

These distinctions have a significant impact on the way these funds are managed and the experience that portfolio managers need in order to be successful.

Information "Under-load"

A venture capitalist relies on a unique set of skills. VC Funds that invest in public companies have greater access to a standard pool of public information. There are many different types of mutual funds, focusing on many market sectors, and each with their own style of investing. But the one thing that they have in common is that the public companies in which they invest are legally required to disclose specific financial information on a quarterly basis and also make announcements about events that are likely to have a significant (material) impact on company performance and its stock price. In addition, relevant information the majority of public companies have a readily accessible track record from which a manager draw when making an investment decision.

Funds that invest in Private Companies Often have Information "Under-load"

Private companies and public companies do not operate under the same insure requirements. And because many of the companies in which venture capital funds invest are so young — often consisting of only a business plan at the earliest (seed) stage of funding — the portfolio manager must draw on a very wide range of skills in order to analyse potential investment. Many of these private companies are also bundling into entirely new or rapidly developing markets. So, the venture capital portfolio manager must be able to assess a very broad range of market factors that will influence the development of these new industries.

In Addition, a Venture Capitalist Has to Exercise Very Extensive Due Diligence

A venture capitalist has to meet with management to probe their background and the company's financial reliability. He has to rely heavily on experience, detailed analyses and sometimes instinct before closing a deal. This process is usually more comprehensive than the one conducted by a mutual fund manager.

An Influential Partnership

Venture capitalists can steer the direction of a company. Venture capital funds and the average mutual fund influence the direction of a company in very different ways.

Mutual Funds as Shareholder

As a shareholder in a public company, a mutual fund has a similar role in directing company business as other individual shareholders would, although its influence will increase in proportion to its stake in the company. Shareholders generally have the right to elect company directors and vote on other important issues that are tabled by the board of directors, but may have little direct impact on the success of that company.

Venture Capitalist as Director

As a requirement for extending financing to a privately held company, the venture capital fund that takes the lead in an investment will often be granted a seat on the board of directors. Directors play a large and crucial role in the management of a company. The main purpose of the board of directors is to oversee the operations of the company. This includes helping to appoint senior management, naming the members of the executive and finance committees, and advising senior management on company policy and strategy. In bringing their outside expertise and experience to a company, introducing potential customers and partners, and attracting top senior management talent, the venture capitalist plays an important part in ensuring the success of an investment.

The Liquidity Event

A VC may take a long time in recovering its Capital/Investments. One of the most significant differences between private and public equity is the speed at which a fund is able to realise capital gains on its investment.

Mutual Funds Usually Invest in Liquid Investments

Public companies tend to have very liquid investments, and so it is easy for a mutual fund to exit those investments at short notice. Liquidity means that there are enough shares available to allow relatively large share transactions without making a significant impact on the share price. The more liquid a stock, the easier it is to trade.

Venture Capital Funds Invest in Liquid Investment

As venture capital funds are invested in private companies, there is no readily available market for their shares when a portfolio manager wants to sell the investment. For a manager to "cash on" his investment, there has to be a liquidity event. Liquidity events include taking a company public through an IPO (initial public offering) or an acquisition by or merger with another company. This can often be a slow and deliberate process requiring a different management style to that of a mutual fund. A venture capitalist, by necessity, has to invest for the long-term and has a much greater stake in the outcome of each portfolio company. As outlined in this section, there are notable disparities between venture capital funds and mutual funds. The hands-on way in which a venture capital fund is managed is fundamentally different from the management of a mutual fund and requires much more than a singular type of skill set to be successful. It includes specialised industry and business experience, and the ability to spot long-term industry trends. In fact, it can be argued that it is the dissimilarities that make venture capital such a useful asset to own as a small part of a diversified investment portfolio. In purchasing shares in a venture capital fund, an investor is buying a truly unique type of investment; tapping the exciting investment avenues.

8.9 TYPES OF INVESTORS

Informal Investors

Angel investors are usually self-made millionnaires between the ages of 40 and 60. As one might suspect, they tend to be well-educated and savvy investors. They may invest on their own or along with a syndicate (group) of angel investors. Most angels share a common desire to help fledgling entrepreneurs and their local communities.

Sources of Informal Investors

Informal investors can be difficult to find. Unlike professional VCs, informal investors do not solicit businesses for investment proposals. Entrepreneurs must actively seek angel investors and convince them to invest.

Entrepreneurs should begin their search for investors with the people closest to them. Would any friends, family, business associates, etc. be interested in investing in their company?

It is generally easier to negotiate favourable terms with friends, family and business associates. Therefore, they may be just the right investors for seed financing. Moreover, it is important to have the support of friends and family in any venture. If they detect operational or ethical deficiencies in the business concept or strategy, it is important that they have an opportunity to voice their concerns before the venture is launched. Involving trusted friends and family in the business as company shareholders may provide entrepreneurs with much-needed support that may be hard to find from other investors during difficult times.

"Who you know is more important than what you know." Anyone who has ever searched for a job understands this. Unfortunately, when it comes to raising capital, few entrepreneurs know the right people. Angel investors tend to keep their investment activities and the amount of their investable assets private; complicating the venture capital process. If money is what makes the world go around, then referrals represent the axis or source of rotation. Accountants, attorneys, bankers, business associates, university professors, financial advisors, and business owners know who are in the market to make venture capital investments. These individuals not only know informal investors, but they can also provide invaluable insight and suggestions that may, with any luck, be followed by a referral and personal introduction to an investor.

If all else fails, entrepreneurs should search the directories of law and private placements firms. These firms syndicate investment packages for networks of private investors. It is probable that they have worked with hundreds, if not thousands, of formal and informal investors.

Finding the "Right" Investor

Finding the "right" investor involves more than sourcing and convincing a venture capitalist to commit equity to the firm. Many entrepreneurs with operations financed with venture capital may challenge by characterisation of "angel" investors and refer to venture capitalists as "vulture" capitalists who add nothing of value to the firms they finance. In many cases, this 'negative label is' deserved, but angels very often add value in ways that go beyond financial assistance. For instance, angels may help companies in the following ways:

(a) Assist in business strategy development.

(b) Attract human and financial capital to fill remaining and anticipated resource gaps.

(c) Serve on the firm's board of directors.

(d) Provide contacts with important stakeholders.

(e) Provide access to information, people, and institutions.

Entrepreneurs can expect to give up a large equity stake in their firms (typically 30% to 70%) and some control for venture capital. The difference between entrepreneurs who call their private investor(s) "angels" or "vultures" is the value-added service they receive.

Segments of Formal Investors

The merchant banking subsidiaries of investment banks, insurance companies, industrial companies, and bank holding companies drive the formal venture capital market. These institutions create and manage venture capital funds for various investors, including: wealthy individuals, pension plans, insurance companies, bank holding companies, endowments, and foreign investors. Investors place investments with venture capital funds in the hopes of earning above average returns. In return, venture capital firms earn annual management fees (1.5% to 2.5% of the fund) and a percentage of the capital gain from the sale of portfolio companies' stock. As a general rule, the general partner (venture capitalist) earns about 20% of the capital gains for managing the fund and the limited partners (investor base) receive 80% for providing the capital.

8.10 VENTURE CAPITAL FUND STAGES

A venture capital fund has five stages in its life. Venture capital funds begin with the general partner's conception of the fund and targeting of the investment opportunity. Once the goals and scope of the fund are established, the VC firm conducts fund-raising activities until the fund is sufficiently capitalised by investors. This typically lasts 6 months to a year. During the investment stage, venture capitalists' source, screen, evaluate, value, negotiate, and structure deals with businesses seeking venture capital. The firm who receive venture capital become portfolio companies in the VC fund, where they will remain until they are harvested by their investors. Typically, this stage lasts 3 to 7 years. The fifth and final stage is the closing of the fund and distribution of the portfolio's capital gains to investors. See Chart 8.2.

Chart 8.2

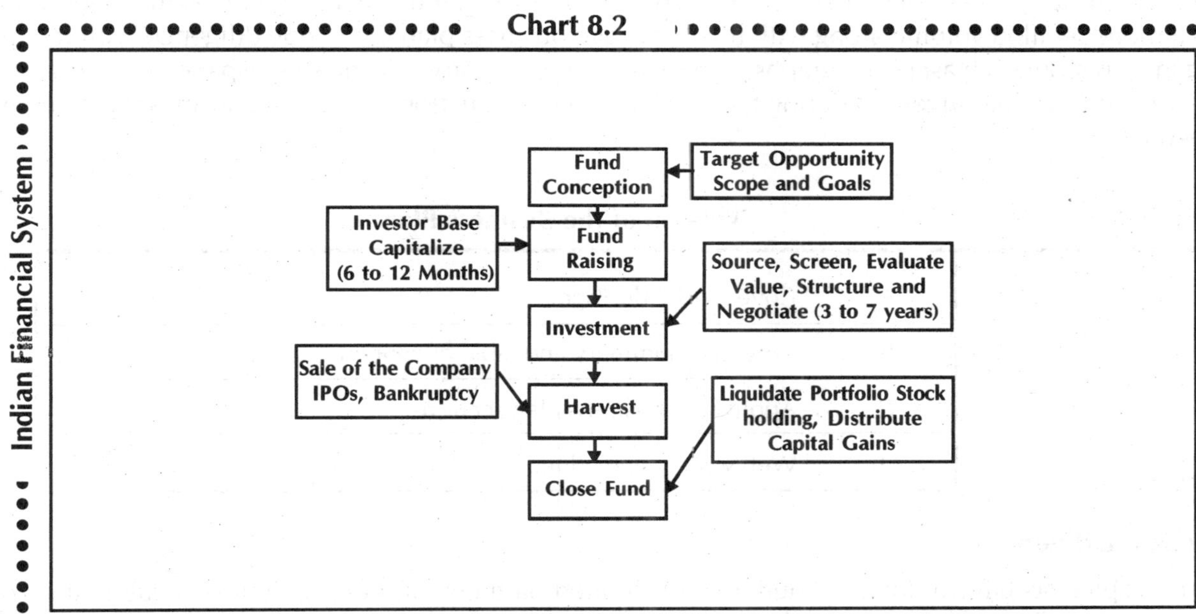

Entrepreneurs are only involved in two of the five stages — investment and harvest. Therefore, let us examine these stages in detail.

Investment

The investment stage of a VC fund is a six-step process. General partners must source, screen, evaluate, value, structure, and negotiate deals during this stage in the fund's development. Each step is addressed below.

Source

"Sourcing" refers to locating venture capital sources. It is the entrepreneur's responsibility. Venture Capital divisions of commercial and investment banks are the best sources for formal venture capital funding. The Directory of Venture Capital Clubs is probably the best sourcing tool for start-ups looking for venture capital. Unfortunately, such guides do not exist for informal investors.

Screen

First impressions can make or break a deal. Venture capitalists get their first impression of the firm and its management team from the business plan. Entrepreneurs are often surprised to learn that only 10% to 20% of the business plans submitted to formal investors are actually read. It is simply impractical for venture capitalists to read every plan they receive. After reading a few dozen business plans, investors learn how to "judge a book by its cover."

To survive the initial screening, the business plan must possess the following:

(a) An investment opportunity that interests the investor. Every venture capitalist begins the screening process with an idea of what they are looking to invest in. Is the firm in a "hot" industry? What stage of development is the firm in; are they requesting seed, first round, second round, or third round financing? Does the firm's investment proposal meet the VC's financing requirements? Does the firm have satisfactory growth rates? Does management have enough experience? The list of questions goes on.

(b) A good overall appearance of business plan. The business plan should have a plastic spiral binding capable of withstanding abuse. Contained within the binding should appear a pair of cover sheets of a single colour and a business plan of approximately forty pages, produced on a 26 pound stock.

Quite often, entrepreneurs have trouble keeping the business plan down to forty pages. It is important to remember that it usually takes a second or third draft of the plan to hit the target length. In some cases, it is useful to provide a more detailed volume along with the forty-page business plan. This "due diligence" volume contains supporting information, such as: phonographs, market research, industry statistics, newspaper articles, references, tax returns, etc. that will aid investors during the due diligence (evaluation) stage if the business plan survives the initial screening.

Table 8.1 **Skeleton of the Business Plan**

A	Cover and Title Page.
B	Executive summary and table of contents.
C	Applicable business plan sections.
D	Well written and edited.

Evaluate (Due Diligence)

Venture capitalists have a fiduciary duty to their limited partners for thoroughly investigating the potential business investments. Everything must be checked and verified to assess the investment opportunity relative to the risk involved. Management must be prepared to support every assumption, estimate, and claim they have made. Additionally, management will be asked to provide some important aspects as shown in Table 8.2.

Table 8.2 **Contents of the Evaluation Report**

(a)	Personal and business references
(b)	Resumes and personal financial statements
(c)	The firm's articles of incorporation, bye-laws or memorandum, and minute book
(d)	Corporate tax returns and financial statements for the last three years, if applicable
(e)	Copies of leases and contracts with all stakeholder groups
(f)	Lists of equipment owned and to be purchased
(g)	Brochures and adverting materials
(h)	Industry studies and market research
(i)	Photos of proprietary products and products under development and letters of support from future customers

These materials are used to help the venture capitalist assess the venture's value as well as its degree of risk. Venture capital is a high-risk, high-return investment. As such, venture capitalists must determine a venture's strategic and market feasibility; especially in relationship to management's ability to see the business plan through. Most VC evaluations revolve around four fundamental areas: management, marketing, products, and financial opportunity.

Most venture capitalists agree; that the most important criterion for investing in a business is the firm's management team. An "A Team" with a "B Product" has a better chance of receiving venture capital funding than a "B Team" with an "A Product." VCs must be confident in management's ability to implement the firm's business plan. Absolutely, the last thing a venture capitalist wants is to invest in a firm with weak management that ultimately needs replacement. Not only does this jeopardise the venture, but it diverts the VC's attention from other portfolio companies.

The management team must be just that, a team. Venture capitalists took for firms with 3 to 6 people running the business rather than a single individual. They must possess complementary skills and a proven track record. Most importantly, management must have integrity.

Venture capitalists try to visualise how the outside world perceives the company and how the company sees the outside world. Firms base their marketing strategy on these assumptions. Unfortunately, entrepreneurs tend to be overly optimistic, skewing their financial projections. Venture capitalists must, therefore, assess the accuracy of the firm's assumptions and determine whether the firm's market scope is appropriate.

If the venture capitalist is confident in the firm's management, agrees that a need exists, and believes that the firm is capable of reaching its target market, the venture capitalist will examine the firm's market offerings to ascertain the likelihood of mass consumer appeal. Mass consumer appeal requires certain strategic underpinnings to be present in the firm's offerings. First, the products or services should have many proprietary features that differentiate them from competitor offerings. Second, the products or services should fit with the firm's overall generic strategy. And lastly, the fate of the company should never ride on the success of one product of a product line which is present or in development stage. Only after the venture capitalist has determined returns will the fund manager begin to value the firm. In addition to assessing the investment opportunity, the VC will analyse the various risks that may jeopararre the investment. A few of the most important risks are outlined below:

(a) If the firm is an early stage business with a limited financial history, it may be difficult for the VC to estimate the firm's future performance. Just as important are the strategic uncertainties associated with new businesses that, have yet to prove their ability to withstand the five competitive forces within their industry.

(b) New products and technological changes pose a potential risk. The speed of change requires companies to anticipate and respond to changes at an ever-increasing rate. Uncertainties exist as to whether the firm is capable of changing and otherwise new direction will be the right one. Change sets the stage for huge returns and huge losses. A new product or product line may be just what the firm needs to boost sales. However, consumers may reject the firm's new products and successful products, or business strategies may be imitated by competitors.

(c) Start-ups are particularly dependent on a few key managers and employees. The risk here is that the loss of one or more of these people may create conditions where the firm is no longer able to effectively compete against its rivals. In fact, some managers or employees may leave the firm to enter into direct competition against the firm. Investors usually require their portfolio companies to carry keyman insurance on their top executives and non-compete or non-disclosure agreements with management and employees.

(d) The final objective of every venture capital investment is the harvesting of the portfolio companies. For investor capital gains to be realised, the venture capitalist must transfer ownership of the Portfolio Company's stock from the VC fund. This may occur through an outright sale of the company, a public offering, or bankruptcy. If the venture capitalist believes that the fund may have difficulty in exiting its investment, then the investment proposal will be rejected. Liquidity is absolutely essential.

Business Valuation, Structure and Negotiation

At this point in the investment process, the venture capitalist will have the information needed to value the firm. There are literally dozens of accepted ways to value a private firm. A venture capitalist may use a multiple of cash flows, sales, earnings, EBIT, EBITDA, or a combination therein to value the firm. The multiple(s) used by one or more of the above methods is determined during negotiations. Naturally, the venture capitalist will want to use a very low multiple in order to buy into the firm as cheaply as possible. Meanwhile, the entrepreneur will want a high multiple to support a higher valuation of the firm. Other valuation approaches may include the discounted cash flow method, First Chicago method, venture capital method, or a proprietary valuation method.

Before negotiations, the venture capitalist will calculate a range of values within which a firm's worth is estimated. The valuation will be based on a range of multiples and proforma estimates. For instance, the venture capitalist may determine that based on recent venture capital investments within the same funds, that the firm should be valued using an EBITDA multiple somewhere between 5 and 7. Assuming the firm had an EBITDA (earnings before interest, taxes, depreciation, and amortisation) of ₹ 1 million, the firm's value would fall between ₹ 5 million and ₹ 7 million. Current and expected market conditions throughout the holding period will influence the choice of multiple to use.

Both parties should enter the negotiations with an idea of what the firm is worth. Many inexperienced entrepreneurs have entered negotiations unprepared to discuss the value of the firm and, as a result, have been "taken for a ride."

As many entrepreneurs have found, valuing a firm is no simple task. The venture capitalist is a trained business appraiser intent of bringing down the price of the company's stock. So, it is important that the management team feel confident in its own valuations. Therefore, it is suggested that management have the firm valued by a third-party prior to entering negotiations and that the third-party, preferably a CPA, be present at the meeting along with the firm's attorney. "Valuation and Structuring the Deal: The Venture Capital Approach" by Dr. William Petty will help the reader understand how businesses are commonly valued.

Venture capitalists determine the amount of share ownership they will require based on their annual required rate of return (ROR), the expected holding period of the investment, and the value of the firm. Let us assume a business owner approaches a venture capitalist requesting ₹ 500,000 for 5 years. In 5 years, the firm is expected to be worth ₹ 4 million. The VC has a required rate of return of 30%. How much stock ownership will the venture capitalist bargain for? Answer: 46.4%.

To solve, use the following equation:

Future value of investment	₹ 500,000 × (1.3)	₹ 1/856,465
		0.464
Future value of business	₹ 4,000,000	₹ 4,000,000

Although venture capitalists may seek returns as high as the ones displayed in Table 8.3, a 25% to 35% ROR will interest most venture capitalists, regardless of the company's stage or expected holding period.

The focus of every venture capital negotiation is the valuation of the firm and the amount of stock ownership the VC will receive for placing an investment, must as important, however, are the legal and financial control issues that spell out the rights and obligations of the parties to the transaction. Venture capitalists can be persuaded to reduce their required rate of return if they perceive their risk has been adequately reduced, by including terms that favour investors. The following are some of the major points that should be addressed during negotiations that will affect the structure of the deal:

Factors that affect the investor's rate of return, which among others are: the number, type, features, and mix of stocks. Venture capitalists typically invest in common stock, stock plus debt unit, stock warrant, convertible debt, and preferred stock.

Table 8.3 **Rates of Return Sought by Venture Capital Investors**

Stage	ROR (%) Annual	Typical Holding Expected Period (year)
Seed and start-up	50-100+	10+
First stage	40-60	5-10
Second stage	30-40	4-7
Expansion	20-30	3-5
Bridge and mezzanine	20-30	1-3
Leveraged buyouts	30-50	3-5
Turnarounds	50+	3-5

(a) Factors that affect the *liquidity* of the investment, including the amount and timing of conversions, takedowns, and implementation of exit strategies.

(b) The rate and timing of interest or dividend payments on debt and preferred shares.

(c) Factors affecting the investor's *control* of the firm. The extent of the investor's representation on the board of directors and ability to alter the composition of management are important.

(d) The terms of management's employment, *viz.*, salaries, bonuses, profit sharing and stock option plans, vesting schedules and rights, and non-complete agreements.

(e) Affirmative covenants.

Affirmative covenants spell out everything the entrepreneur agrees to do as long as the investor's stock remains outstanding. Table 8.4A shows some standard affirmative covenants.

Table 8.4A **Affirmative Covenants**

(a)	Provide financier with monthly financial and operating reports
(b)	Provide all documents filed with government agencies
(c)	Provide annual bugets
(d)	Inform investors of adverse changes
(e)	Maintain negotiated financial ratio
(f)	Conform all accounting practices to generally accepted accounting standards
(g)	Provide venture capitalist with access to the facilities, books, and records of the organisation
(h)	Pay company taxes
(i)	Conduct activites in accordance with applicable laws and regulations
(j)	Inform venture capitalist when board meetings will occur so their representative(s) may be in attendance
(k)	Maintain equipment and property
(l)	Maintain life insurance on key executives of the firm
(m)	Maintain sufficient capitalist the right of first refusal on future stock offerings
(n)	Inform venture capitalist in the event of default on loans or leases

(f) Negative Covenants

Negative covenant spells out *everything* the entrepreneur agrees not to do as long as the investor's stock remains outstanding. Table 8.4B shows some standard negative covenants.

Table 8.4 B **Negative Covenants**

(a)	Management will not change control of the company
(b)	Management will not assign, sell, or transfer its shares in the firm
(c)	Management will not alter the firm's business scope
(d)	The company's business form will not be changed. For instance, the firm cannot change its status as a company to a partnership
(e)	The company will not relocate its place of business
(f)	The company will not liquidate, merge, or sell its assets
(g)	Additional stock will not be issued. This prevents dilution of investor ownership
(h)	The company will not invest or speculate in non-company related ventures or activates
(i)	The company will pay no cash or stock dividends
(j)	The company will not transact business with its own members
(k)	The company will not expend funds in excess of prescribed limits for brokerage fees, loans to employees and shareholders, equipment, and capital improvements.

(g) The payment of accounting, consulting, and legal fees incurred during the course of the venture capital transaction. Businesses are often expected to pay these expenses, which typically run 2% to 3% of the amount received at closing.

Harvest

Exit strategies are planned prior to the venture capitalist's investment. Venture capitalists are in the business of investing, not running or operating a company. There will come a day in every portfolio company's life when the investors will want to "cash out" of their investment. Planning for the exit, or as some call the "harvest", begins on Day 1 Venture capitalists will not invest in a company unless they possess contractual rights to control the timing and method of their exit. In the business plan, management should propose an exit strategy for two reasons. First, it tells the venture capitalist that management understands investor objectives; and secondly, it allows management to set direction and tone for future exit negotiations.

There are three basic ways a venture capitalist can cash out — company can be sold, taken public, or liquidated in bankruptcy. The approaches are discussed below:

Sale of the Company

The quickest and easiest way for a venture capitalist to harvest the investment is through the sale of the company. Typically, the venture capital fund will sell its shares back to the company or entrepreneur. As a general rule, most VCs transfer stock ownership in their portfolio companies back to the company in one of the following four ways:

(a) Cash

Nothing even comes close to approaching cash for stock. Cash is 100% liquid and there is no risk of default. Investors may accept as much as 10 to 30% less for their stock in an average-performing portfolio company if they receive all cash. Remember that, "cash received today is better than cash to be received tomorrow."

(b) Notes

Venture capitalists generally will not sell their positions in a firm for long-term notes alone; some up-front cash will be required. In the venture capital industry, long-term notes are commonly called "paper." For many VCs, paper has proved to be a fitting name. If the buyer defaults, "paper" is all the VC will ever get. Therefore, VCs will include a risk premium in the price of their stock for notes.

Buying back stock with notes is made more expensive for yet another reason. VCs must have cash to invest in new firms. If a portfolio company ties up a substantial sum of money for a number of years, the VC partners suffer an opportunity cost. Whereas the fund could have been earning 20% to 30% on a new investment, the fund is financing a company stock purchase at 8% to 15%, depending on current interest rates. Ideally, the firm will be able to raise all the cash if it needs to buy back its outstanding shares from other sources.

(c) Puts and Calls

Exits by puts and calls are negotiated up-front. These are options that entitle their holders to buy or sell stock at prices established by predetermined formulas. In a put and call arrangement, the investor receives the right or option to sell his or her stock in the company at a predetermined price. The company, in turn, receives the right or option to buy back stock from the VC; again, at a predetermined price.

The predetermined option price is based on an agreed upon formula. It may be something as simple as a pre-arranged cash amount, multiple of sales, percentage of sales, or multiple of cash flows.

There are literally hundreds of potential puts and call formulas. The most commonly used, however, is the price/earnings ratio. Using this approach, the VC selects a popular P/E ratio of a publicly traded firm in the same industry. This ratio is then multiplied by the earnings per share of the Portfolio Company to arrive at a price per share in which the company can be bought or sold.

(d) ESOP

Employee's Stock Option Plans (ESOP) are sometimes used to finance company stock buybacks. ESOPs are very similar to pension and profit-sharing plans, except that they only invest in their company's stock. Over time, employers are able to contribute a significant sum of cash that is held in the trust until it buys stock. These tax-deductible contributions allow firms to repurchase their own stock with before-tax dollars. If the ESOP has insufficient cash for a buyback of the company's shares from the VC fund, the ESOP may be able to borrow the difference from a commercial lender based on its financial projections.

Other companies and investors may also be interested in purchasing the VC's equity stake in the Portfolio Company. Conglomerates may propose to acquire the entire company to increase their industry presence. Corporate acquirer may want to purchase a majority interest (51% or more) in the company so that it can exercise control over the firm. This exit method not only offers investors a way of cashing out, but so to the entrepreneur as well.

There are six ways in which outside companies and investors can purchase a portfolio company:

Table 8.5 **Possible Purchase Consideration**

(a)	*Stock for cash*
(b)	*Stock for notes*
(c)	*Stock for stock*
(d)	*Assets for cash*
(e)	*Assets for notes*
(f)	*Assets for stock*

Again, the VC's preferred method of exit is stock for cash. Stock for stock may also provide a quite lucrative approach for harvesting the investment. By engaging in a "stock swap" the VC does not have to recognise its capital gains in the Portfolio Company. It sells its stock. This has the advantage of deferring the payments taxes.

Asset purchases are very similar to stock purchases. Rather than formally buying the firm's stock, the acquirer purchases the firm's underlying value - its assets. Asset transfers, however, are less desirable because the seller experiences double taxation in cases where the firm's assets are sold above book value.

Usually, both the Portfolio Company and the VC will have a buy-sell agreement protecting each other's interests. In a buy-sell agreement, the portfolio company agrees that should a *bona*fide offer to buy out he venture capital partner be made, the company must either buy the VC's stock on the same terms and conditions as the sales offer, or allow the VC to sell its stock. This provides the VC a backdoor exit strategy if a forced exit is required to liquidate the investor's position in a portfolio stock thus allowing the VC fund to be closed. Additionally, the buy-sell agreement protects the Portfolio Company against an unwanted sale of a competitor.

Initial Public Offering

The most prestigious of all exit strategies is the initial public offering (IPO). If all goes well, an IPO can make a firm's shareholders phenomenally rich. However, this implies a high degree of risk. There are no assurances that the public offering will be a success. Even if IPOs are timed perfectly, it is anyone's guess how the market will react. This choice of exit is not for everyone. Firms reporting income after tax under ₹ 1 million, with growth rates below 30% to 60% will draw no interest from underwriters. Moreover, the larger underwriters typically will not touch an IPO under ₹ 25 million. Since underwriters generally avoid selling more than 50% of a firm's stock in an IPO, the firm should have at least a ₹ 25 million pre-IPO valuation.

There are many advantages and disadvantages associated with making an initial public offering. First, some of the advantages:

(a) Liquidity

Two identical companies, one private and the other public, will be valued quite differently by investors. Private companies have discounted valuations because of their illiquidity. In other words, private companies are more difficult for investors to convert into cash than companies sold publicly over an exchange. This results in a higher cost of capital and greater ownership dilution for private companies. Whereas private firms must go to the private markets to raise additional capital, public firms have the choice of going to the public marketplace as well, where they will encounter less operational restrictions and relaxed financing terms.

(b) Enhanced ability to raise capital

As a firm grows, it requires additional financing. The public market allows firms to raise equity more quickly and with less ownership dilution than private placements.

(c) Personal wealth

Quite simply, going public can make a firm's shareholders rich.

(d) Competitive advantage

Public companies are able to raise capital more quickly than their private competitors, allowing them to respond to changes faster.

(e) Prestige

The firm's stakeholders take public companies, as a general rule, more seriously. It is easier to recruit and retain employees with stock option plans. The availability of multiple equity sources allows public companies to negotiate better financing packages with lenders and investors.

The advantages of going public are real; however, so are the disadvantages. The major disadvantages of going public are as follows:

1. Expensive

The initial and ongoing expenses of going public are substantial. Underwriters typically receive 5% to 10% of the offering for their services, with 8% as the norm. Therefore, an underwriter with an 8% discount on a ₹ 25 million offering will receive ₹ 2 million. In addition to the underwriter's commission, the firm's own legal fees will typically run between ₹ 250,000 and ₹ 600,000. Accounting fees may approach ₹ 200,000 for the certification of the firm's financial statements and review of the prospectus. Finally, printing the prospectus may cost ₹ 100,000 to ₹ 350,000 depending on the number of copies, length, type of paper, and colour of the documents. In total, a ₹ 25 million offering will likely to cost a business between ₹ 2 and ₹ 3 million, or approximately 8% to 12%.

Ongoing expenses for going public may run from ₹ 50,000 to ₹ 100,000 annually. Regulatory reporting requirements require public firms to print and distribute quarterly and annual reports, proxy statements, and stock certificates. Additional accounting and financial personnel must often be hired to assist the firm in meeting disclosure requirements. Furthermore, issue officers and directors of the corporation will need to carry liability insurance.

2. Disclosure

The disclosure requirements mandated by the government, particularly the Securities and Exchange Commission, open a company's operations and financial status to public scrutiny. Employees, customers, suppliers, and competitors can collect important information about the company that can be used to the firm's disadvantage.

3. Shortsighted decision-making

Shareholders expect their stock to increase in value. If the company's earnings do not meet investor and analysts' quarterly expectations, the stock price will fall. This often leads executives to make shortsighted decisions that may have serious consequences in the future.

4. Loss of control

Unlike private businesses, public companies are always at risk to a hostile tender offer. Aggressive competitors and corporate raiders may attempt to purchase a controlling interest in the firm. If this happens, they may *eject new board members and replace the company's management*. The threat of a corporate takeover can be reduced, however, by inserting anti-takeover defenses in the firm's charter.

5. Lawsuits

Numerous disclosure requirements and strict insider trading laws open the firm to shareholder class action lawsuits. If shareholders believe that a material event was not disclosed or that a disclosure was misleading, they may file suit.

Bankruptcy

Bankruptcy is the exit of last resort. It usually occurs when a firm breaches a covenant in a loan agreement. The firm may enter a workout period; however if this fails, the lender will accelerate the payment of the loan. With little or no cash to service its debt, the firm may be forced to sell its assets. Depending on the amount of a firm's debt, the firm or its creditors may purse relief through bankrupt.

According to the US bankruptcy code, equity investors are not paid until all creditors receive payment. To make matters worse, assets are usually liquidated well below book value. For instance, accounts receivable may be sold for 50% of book value, and inventory, equipment, and fixtures may be sold for 20% to 30% on the dollar. Specialised machinery, worth thousands of dollars, may be sold for virtually nothing. In these conditions, investors may lose their entire investment.

8.11 VENTURE CAPITAL SCENARIO IN INDIA

Between 2000 and 2001, there has been a change in the overall environment for VC investing. According to various estimates, VC Investment in India increased from less than US$ 5 million in 1995 to around US$ 350 million in 2000. Overall committed funds are reportedly in excess of US$ 1 billion. Prior to 1997, the AIFIs, multilateral development agencies and SCBs contributed the most to the pool of funds available for VC investment. However, over the last few years, the major source of increased VC funding have been the foreign institutional investors, primarily VC funds raised overseas and investment banking arms of foreign banks. Concurrently, there has been a declining role of AIFIs, SCBs and multilateral development agencies.

The growth in VC funding in India can be attributed to various factors. In the late 1990s, the GoI became increasingly aware of the benefits of VC Investments. VC is a critical component in the success of entrepreneurial high technology firms and the development of many new technologies, including software and the Internet. As a result, favourable regulations were passed regarding the ability of various facial institutions to invest in VC, tax treatment for VC funds were liberalised. The procedures were simplified. India has the second largest English speaking scientific and technical manpower in the world. As compared with developed economies, wages are lower in India for trained engineers and scientists. India boasts of a software-industry. It became visible in the world scene during the mid-1990s. Software exports creased from US$ 1.1 billion in FY1997 to US$ 6.2 billion in FY2001. The recent IT-led boom coupled with the entry of angel investors (especially NRIs) and venture capitalists has also led to the boom in the VC industry. Some Indian software firms became significant successes and were able to list on NASDAQ. Further, during the last twenty years, Many Indian engineers immigrated to the US and began their own high technology firms. Some of them were extremely successful and some used their wealth to become angel investors or venture capitalists. Finally, India has a relatively well-developed stock market that can handle IPOs from high technology firms.

As in the US, technology enterprises and especially Internet related companies have attracted the predominant share of VC funding in India. Nearly 70% of the VC investments in India have been directed into IT and IT-related products, business to consumer (b2c) electronic commerce (e-commerce) service firms, ERP, accounting software, Internet and Internet-related products. Other major sectors which have attracted VC funding include industrial products, biotechnology, food and food processing, and pharmaceuticals.

An estimated 60% of the VC investments in India are in start-ups. By contrast, early-stage financing attracted only 23% of VC financing in the US during 2000, as compared with expansion/later stage financing (74%). In Europe, nearly 41% of amount invested during 2000 was towards buyouts, followed by expansion financing (37%) and start-up or seed financing (19%). In Asia, nearly 70% of venture capital in Asia goes to later-stage financing as compared with around 20% in start-ups. However, start-ups include many new ventures promoted by established state or family-run businesses.

Prospects

Considering the pattern of VC investments in India to date, the prospects of many start-ups (and the venture capitalists that financed them) will depend on the growth of IT, Internet and e-commerce in India. These sectors in turn have become increasingly reliant on an adequate, cheap and efficient telecommunications infrastructure. Only a high quality telecommunications system allows the development of global e-commerce by Indian firms who aim to sell their products in the international markets through the use of the Internet. Few Indians have access to a fixed telephone (3.2 per 100 inhabitants), PC (0.45 per 100 inhabitants) and, the Internet (0.2 subscriptions per 100 inhabitants). At end-September 2001, the user base in India was approximately 5 users per 1000 inhabitants. On the same date, India had an estimated 0.05 Internet hosts per 1000 inhabitants. The growth of the IT and software industry is also critically dependent on the sustained growth of the US markets. An estimated 62% of India's software exports were to the North American (predominantly the US market) and a downturn in the US economy could adversely affect many Indian IT start-ups. Many dotcom ventures now face a bleak prospect, again it is expected that only few of them will survive in the long-term. This places a question mark on the survival of large number of venture funds that have financed these dotcoms.

In the medium term, it is expected that the VC industry will also witness some weeding out of the smaller players or those, whose funds do not perform well. VC interest is critically dependent on the constant flow of opportunities that have enormous potential for reward. Enterprises in the fast-changing IT and other high technology sectors have traditionally provided and will continue to provide such an opportunity to earn high returns. Prior to the recently increased interest in Internet-related companies, VC funding in India was primarily directed towards IT firms (Mastek, Microland, etc.) and pharmaceuticals (Sun Pharmaceuticals, etc.). This was because only fast-changing industries, which can generate high returns, will attract VC interest. However, over the past two years, technology enterprises and especially Internet-related companies have attracted the predominant share of VC funding in India. Considering the uncertain prospects of many Internet-related start-ups, it is expected that instead of speculative investments at excessive valuations in every 'Internet idea', venture capitalists will now invest cautiously and selectively. Venture capitalists will also seek to increase the diversification of their portfolios, both in terms of industry sectors and stage of development. Investments are expected to increase in IT-related software and services, Internet and communications infrastructure, and media. More VC funding will also expected to be directed towards food processing and the longer-gestating pharmaceutical and biotechnology sectors (where there are always more ideas than funding available for research. Expansion stage companies are also expected to get a greater percentage of total funding, reflecting a reluctance of venture capitalists to invest in new companies and the need to preserve the value of investments in companies already on their portfolios. Venture capitalists will also need to move from the role of primarily providing financing to bringing the type of expertise needed to nurture young entrepreneurial companies (e.g., helping to recruit talent, providing strategic advice and introduction to potential investors, customers, suppliers, etc.).

Despite the tremendous growth during the last few years, the Indian VC industry is still at a nascent stage, especially when compared with the status of the industry in other developed countries. The primary problems facing Indian entrepreneurs and VC investors have been restrictive sources of funding, the risk-averse behaviour of institutional investors, inflexible labour laws, cumbersome exit mechanisms, lack of management talent amongst venture capitalists to nurture early stage companies and a relative dearth of high quality talent willing to leave the safety of secure and well-paid jobs with large companies, to join a start-up.

The various measures that can impact VCs positively can include providing greater flexibility to start-ups to reward employees, reducing entry and exit obstacles for overseas venture capitalists, relaxation of restrictions on offshore investments by domestic VC firms, widening the domestic pool of funds permitted for venture capital investment (pension and insurance funds) and removal of restrictions on venture capitalists regarding the industries in which they are prohibited to invest.

8.12 DECLINE IN INVESTMENTS DURING 2001

VC investments have slowed down significantly across the world during 2001. In the US, VC investment has declined from a peak of US$ 29 million during 2000 (July-September 2000) to US$ 12 billion during 2001 (January-March 2001) and to US$ 10.5 billion during 2001 (April-June 2001). Further, there has been a shift in the pattern of VC investments. Non-Internet-related investments increased from 24% of VC investments in 2000 to 32% in 2001 mainly because of a notable increase in VC investments in the longer-gestation medical or health or biotechnology sector. Over the same period, Internet-related VC investments declined from 76% to 68%. Amongst the Internet-related investments, VC investments (as % of Internet-related investments) have declined in e-commerce and content. However, it has increased in the computer software and services sector, communications and media. Even in India, VC funding has declined. Industry estimates indicate that VC funding during January-March 2001 has declined by as much as 50% over the same period during 2000. The decline is especially significant in ventures in business-to-consumer (b2c), Internet solutions and ERP or accounting software.

The decline in VC funding is because of various factors including the general slowdown in the global economy, depressed state of the stock markets, decline in new capital issues, sharp decline in valuation of technology stocks and venture capitalists spending more time with their current portfolio companies.

It is also due to decline in interest in e-commerce and Internet-related IPOs. Venture capitalists have invested a significant amount into e-commerce and content ventures. Because of competition for deals, many funded companies had received financing at excessive valuations. However, negative cash generation at a majority of these ventures has necessitated a further round of financing.

Ultimately, exit is crucial to venture capitalists and to the growth of high-risk enterprises, which depend on VC funding. Robust Mergers & Acquisitions (M&A) and IPO activity are paramount to successful performance in the VC industry. Considering the decline in interest in IPOs of e-commerce and Internet companies, M&A remain the only opportunity for venture capitalists to earn a return on their significant Internet-related investments. This option has also become limited as parallel to the decline in the stock markets, M&A are at lower valuations than in the past. Reduced valuations for technology stocks, the depressed outlook for IPOs and the need to preserve the value of their investments has forced venture capitalists to keep funding companies they've already invested in. As a result, the investment horizon for venture capitalists has lengthened. Further, bankruptcies at many start-ups are rising, forcing venture capitalists to write-off their investments. Consequently, investors in many VC funds have seen negative returns on their investments as valuations for privately held companies follow the decline in stock markets. Investors are now realising that VC investing involves a large amount of risk, without necessarily commensurate rewards. With significant decline in valuations of high technology stocks, lower exit values on investments have lowered the overall performance of venture capitalists, lowering their capabilities to raise additional funds from investors and reducing the funds available for fresh investments. Many existing venture capitalists are finding it difficult to arrange financing, thereby reducing the availability of VC funding. New VC firms trying to raise first-time funds are also finding it difficult to raise funds.

8.13 PROBLEMS WITH VCs IN INDIA

License Raj

Till recently, mere obtaining a license-ensured profits. Hence, both homegrown VCs and entrepreneurs have minimal risk evaluation skills.

Scalability

Products developed for Indian markets lack economies of scale.

Valuation

Due to the Infotech boom, most companies are pre-positioning their IPOs.

Mindsets

Most VCs, being offshoots of financial institutions, with lending mindset look forward to security in what is essentially a risk venture.

1. Venture Capital investments in calendar year 2001 dropped by 22% to $ 908 million against $ 1.2 billion in 2000, inflows eroded 52% to $ 395 million against $ 825 million in the previous year.
2. The initial success has come from the emerging IT-enabled services (ITES) sector. Ten business process outsourcing companies (BPO) within the ITES space attracted $ 100 million in private equity funding during 2002. While this represents a small percentage of the estimated $ 1.1 billion invested, BPO was the only sector, which saw VC money disbursed across multiple entrepreneurs-led companies.

Enforceability

Lack of legal framework to enforce most of the Standard Affirmative covenants (like option writing) is another hindrance.

Exit

Lack of market width and depth, framework for mergers and acquisitions prevents new ventures.

Returns, Taxes and Regulations

Multiplicity of regulators like SEBI, RBI, Trusts Act, Companies Act, etc., is creating an artificial barrier to ventures.

8.14 GLOSSARY

Buyout Funding

Funds provided to enable an enterprise to acquire another enterprise or product line or business.

Bridge/Mezzanine Funding

Financing for a company expecting to go public usually within 6-12 months; usually so structured to be repaid from proceeds of a public offerings, or to establish floor price for public offer.

Convertible/Equity Related Loan

Loan convertible into equity as per pre-agreed terms.

Equity

Ownership interest in a company, represented by the shares issued to investors.

First Stage Capital

Capital provided to entrepreneur who has a proven product, to start commercial production and marketing, not covering market expansion, de-risking and acquisition costs.

Follow-on/Subsequent/Secondary Public Offer

An offer subsequent to an initial public offering. A secondary public offering can be either an issuer offering or an offer for sale by another investor.

Investment Banks

A firm/company that serves as an intermediary between an issuer of securities and the investing public. They handle the distribution of blocks, of previously issued securities, either through secondary offerings or through negotiations, maintain markets for securities already distributed, and act as finders in private placements of securities.

IPO/Initial Public Offering

Issue of shares of a company to the public by the company (directly) for the first time.

Private Placement

The sale of securities to a small group of investors that is exempt from elaborate requirements of a public issue.

Seed Capital

A small amount of capital provided to an entrepreneur, usually for product development, beta stage development, pilot project, etc. not covering launch expenses, commercial production or marketing; typically provided by angel investors.

Second Stage Capital

Capital provided to expand marketing and meet growing working capital need of an enterprise that has commenced production but does not have positive cash flows sufficient to take care of its growing needs.

Stock/Secondary Market Transaction

Purchase or sale of shares, through a member of a Stock Exchange or privately from another shareholder.

Third Stage Capital

Capital provided to an enterprise that has established commercial production and basic marketing setup, typically for market expansion, acquisitions, product development, etc.

Underwriter

An investment banking firm committing successful distribution of a public issue, failing which the firm would take the securities being offered (i.e. buy) into its own books. Some countries also provide for underwriting on best effort basis.

Venture Capital

Professionals co-invested with the entrepreneur usually to fund an early stage of a more risky venture. Offsetting the high risk the investor takes is the promise of high return on the investment. A venture capitalist not only brings in money as "equity capital" (*i.e.,* without security/charge on assets) but also brings onto the table extremely valuable domain knowledge, business contacts, brand equity, strategic advice, etc. He is a fixed interval investor, whom the entrepreneurs approach without the risk of "takeover".

8.15 REVIEW QUESTIONS

Short Answer Questions

1. Define venture capital.
2. What are three phases of venture capital cycle? Write a short note on each phase.
3. Differentiate the functions of generalists from specialist's venture capitalists.
4. Who is called as diverse investor?
5. Why do we say an investment as a synergetic venture?
6. Which investor is called an incubator?
7. Who is called an angel investor?
8. Write a short note on corporate venturing.
9. Distinguish between venture capital and a debt.
10. Differentiate a mutual fund from venture capital.
11. Who are called informal investors?
12. What are the five stages of venture capital strategy?
13. Give some examples for affirmative covenants of an entrepreneur.
14. Explain about negative covenants with examples.
15. Describe the term "Harvest".
16. Write a short note on ESOP.

Essay Type Questions

1. What are the various stages of evolution of Venture Capital business in India?
2. Explain the mechanism of venture capital with examples.
3. What are the various types of venture capitalists?
4. Describe the types of venture capital firms.
5. What are the benefits of venture capital?
6. "Mutual Fund is a Venture Fund." Evaluate the statement.
7. Describe different types of venture capital investors.
8. How do you find a right investor for your venture?
9. Explain the different states of venture capital fund.
10. Evaluate the present position of venture capital in India.

CHAPTER 9

Insurance

Objectives

The student, after studying the chapter, should be able to:

- Define the word "insurance".
- Apply the principles of insurance and differentiate the types of policies.
- Define the functions of various persons involved in the business.
- State the various provisions of IRDA Act.
- Apply claim settlement procedures in the event of an accident or death.
- Evaluate the performance of Insurance Companies in rendering services.

Structure:

9.1 INTRODUCTION

The function of insurance is to protect one against losses he cannot afford. This is done by transferring the risks of a person, business, or organisation known as, the "insured" to an insurance company, known as the "insurer". The insurer then reimburses the insured for "covered" losses, *i.e.*, those losses it pays for under the terms of the policy.

Every family depends on their leader every day for financial support, food, shelter, transportation, education, and much more. Spouses have plans for their future and dreams for their family: another child, a bigger home, a new business, college education, travel and retirement. Insurance is all about ensuring that one's family has adequate financial resources to make those plans and dreams come true in the event of the breadearners premature death. And just as his spouse and children (as beneficiaries) count on him, he counts on his spouse. That is why coverage for his spouse is also important. This is especially true today, with so many "double income" families.

As the insurance consumer, the insured pays an amount of money, called a premium, to the insurer to transfer the risk. The insurer pools all its premiums into a large fund, and when a policyholder has met with a loss, the insurer draws funds from the pool to pay for the loss. Life is full of unexpected events that can create large financial losses. For example, whenever the insured drives, it is possible that he may have a costly accident. Risks affect him by causing worried about potential loss and how to deal with the consequences. Insurance reduces anxiety over a possible loss and absorbs the financial brunt of its consequences. However, while insurance coverage is essential, how much and what type of insurance people need differs with each individual. He must decide how much risk he is willing to tolerate without insurance. For example, benefits for disability policies typically begin after a waiting period of one to six months. Therefore, he should ensure that he has some form of coverage or financial resources before the policy period begins.

9.2 PRINCIPLES OF INSURANCE

1. PROXIMATE CAUSE

It is the main cause which brings about a loss with no other intervening cause which breaks the chain of events "Cause proxima".

Example:

Firemen remove undamaged stock from a burning building to avoid its involvement in the fire. It is stacked in the open yard and subsequently damaged by rain. Was the proximate cause of the damage the fire or the rain?

If the rain damage occurred before the Insured had an opportunity to protect it, then the proximate cause of the damage would be the fire and fire is covered under a fire policy. However, if the stock was left unprotected for an unreasonably long period, the rain would be a new and independent cause of damage and damage caused by rain may not be covered under a policy.

2. INSURABLE INTEREST

To insure anything, the Insured must have an insurable interest in the subject matter of insurance, i.e., he/she must benefit by its safety or be prejudiced by its loss.

Notes: Insurable Interest may be created either by:

Obligation to Insure

- By Statute
- By Contract
- By Custom

Option to Insure

- Owners
- Mortgagors
- Lesser
- Trustees
- Tenants

Example:

Everyone will have an insurable interest in his/her own personal possessions, e.g., house, car or watch, but your next door neighbours would not normally have an insurable interest in your house.

3. CONTRIBUTION

Although the Insured may effect more than one policy to cover the same property or interest, he/she cannot recover in total more than a full indemnity.

NOTE:

Cover can only arise when the policies:

- Cover the same peril
- Cover the same subject matter
- Are effected by or on behalf of the same Insured

Example:

An insured loses his/her watch whilst on holidays. He/she has holiday insurance which covers the loss. But he/she also has the watch covered under his/her house policy. The cost of the claim should be shared by both policies, i.e., the insured cannot claim twice.

4. INDEMNITY

It is the placing of the insured in the same financial position after a loss as he/she was immediately before the loss. In the event of a claim, the Insured must:

(a) Prove that he/she has sustained a monetary loss

(b) Prove the extent and value of his/her loss

(c) Transfer any rights which he/she may have for recovery from another source to the Insurer, if he/she has been fully indemnified.

The settlement of the loss will be subject to the following limitations:

(a) Sum Insured

(b) Average

(c) Excess/deductible

5. UTMOST GOOD FAITH — UBERRIMAE FIDEI

It is the duty to disclose all material facts relating to the risk to be covered. A material fact is a fact which would influence the mind of a prudent underwriter in deciding whether to accept a risk for insurance and on what terms.

Examples:

Motor: Age of drivers, license status, details of any accidents, claims or convictions, exact model of vehicle, etc.

Household: Construction of house, location of house, *i.e.,* close to river, any previous claims etc.

Duty of Disclosure applies to both the proposer and the Insurer. Duty of disclosure operates at:

(a) Inception — until the date cover is confirmed by the Insurers

(b) Renewal — up to the renewal date

(c) Mid term alterations — until the Insurers confirm cover in respect of the alterations

6. SUBROGATION — STEPPING INTO SHOES

It is the right of an insurance company who has paid a claim to its client to pursue another party who may have caused the incident resulting in the claim.

NOTES:

1. The Insurer must exercise the right of recovery in the name of the Insured (prevents the Insured from obtaining more than one indemnity).
2. Subrogation rights only apply where there is a legal liability under the policy, i.e., where policy cover existed.

Example:

A client makes a claim under his/her own comprehensive policy for the damage done to his vehicle by another person. His/her insurance company pays the claim but pursue the negligent third party for the cost of the claim they have paid.

9.3 TYPES OF POLICIES

1. ENDOWMENT POLICY

An endowment policy covers risk for a specified period, at the end of which the sum assured is paid back to the policyholder, along with the bonus accumulated during the term of the policy. It is this feature, the payment of endowment to the policyholder when the policy's term is complete, that rightly accounts for the popularity of endowment policies. Typically, as one's children grow up and get independently settled, his responsibility to protect the family financially reduces significantly. The focus now shifts to managing a smaller family, perhaps only oneself and his or her spouse, after retirement. This is where the endowment, the original sum assured and the accumulated bonus, received come in handy. One can either use the endowment amount to buy an annuity policy to generate a monthly pension for the rest of his life, or put it into any other suitable investment of his choice. This is the major benefit that an endowment policy offers over a whole life policy of the insured.

2. WHOLE LIFE POLICY

A typical whole life policy runs as long as the policyholder is alive. In other words, risk is covered for the entire life of the policyholder, which is why such policies are known as whole life policies.

The whole life policy sum assured and bonus are payable only to the nominee of the beneficiary upon the death of the policyholder. The policyholder is not entitled to any money during his or her own lifetime, i.e., there is no survival benefit.

Suppose, for instance, you buy a whole life policy at the age of 30, when your children are young and the family needs protection. Conceivably, by the time you are 55 or 60, your children may be well settled, no longer truly needing the protection your whole life policy provides. On the other hand, you would probably require the money for yourself and your wife in your retired life, but this would not be possible since the sum assured is payable only when the policyholder dies.

3. TERM LIFE POLICIES

Term life policies cover risk only during the selected term period. If the policyholder survives the term, the risk cover comes to an end.

A term plan is designed to meet the needs of people who are initially unable to pay the larger premium required for a whole life or an endowment assurance policy, but hope to be able to pay for such a policy in the near future. Hence, they may leave the final decision regarding the plan to a later date, when a better choice can be made. No surrender, loan or paid-up values are granted under these policies because reserves are not accumulated. If the premium is not paid within the grace period, the policy will lapse without acquiring any paid-up value.

However, a lapsed policy may be revived during the lifetime of the life assured but before the expiry of the period of two years from the due date of the first unpaid premium, on the usual terms. Accident and/or disability benefits are not granted on policies under the term plan.

4. MONEY-BACK POLICIES

Unlike ordinary endowment insurance plans, where the survival benefits are payable at the end of the endowment period, money-back policies provide for periodic payments of partial survival benefits during the term of the policy, as long as the policyholder is alive.

An important feature of this type of policies is that in the event of death at any time within the policy term, the death claim comprises the full sum assured, without deduction of any of the survival benefit amounts, which may have already been paid as money-back components. Similarly, the bonus is also calculated on the full sum assured.

5. JOINT LIFE POLICIES

Joint life policies are similar to endowment policies in that they too offer maturity benefits to the policyholders, apart from covering risks like all life insurance policies. But joint life policies are categorised separately as they cover two lives simultaneously. It is, thus, offering an unique advantage in some cases, notably, for a married couple or partners in a business firm.

6. CHILDREN'S INSURANCE POLICIES

Children's insurance policies include those through which parents or legal guardians can provide life insurance for their child from birth. The risk cover commences from the child attaining the age of 12/17/18/21 known as the Date of Risk, and will vest itself on the child upon his or her attaining majority on completion of age 21, if the case demands.

Until the child attains majority, the parents are the owners of the policy and have to pay the premium periodically. It is important that these policies are considered only after the insurance portfolios of the parents have been completed. The family's insurance budget should primarily buy as much life insurance as possible on the lives of the breadwinner and should not be frittered away on the children's lives as their insurance is useless in the event of any premature death of the breadwinner. In fact, those lives should be insured that have maximum economic benefits. Quite often, policies lapse if and when the premium-paying breadwinner of the family dies before the vesting age. After all, the child may not be in a position to continue paying the premiums.

7. PENSION PLAN OR ANNUITIES

An annuity is an investment that one makes, through installments paid over a certain number of years, in return for which he receives a specific sum every year, every half-year or every month, either for life or for a fixed number of years.

After the death of the annuitant or after the fixed annuity period expires for annuity payments, the invested annuity fund is refunded perhaps along with a small addition, calculated at that time. Annuities differ from all the other forms of life insurance discussed so far in one fundamental way — an annuity does not provide any life insurance cover but, instead, offers a guaranteed income either for life or for a certain period.

Typically, annuities are bought to generate income during one's retired life, which is why they are also called pension plans. Annuity premiums and payments are fixed with reference to the duration of human life! Annuities are an investment, which can offer an income you cannot outlive and provide a solution to one of the biggest financial insecurities of old age; namely, of outliving one's income.

8. WOMEN'S POLICY

Women's policy provides funds for women in times of need like education, marriage or sickness, with Guaranteed and Loyalty Additions during the policy term period and after maturity. At present, the sole women's policy available in the market is Jeevan Sneha from LIC.

9. SPECIAL PLANS

Special plans are insurance policy plans available from the national insurance providers to serve the needs of citizens who cannot be commonly classified or segregated. These special plans are designed to satisfy needs ranging from debt clearance in the event of the death of the insured to financial aid in the event of a medical mishap. Special plans also provide financial assistance for handicapped dependants as well as emergency surgery required if and when a medical condition arises.

10. GROUP INSURANCE

Group insurance offers life insurance protection under group policies to various groups such as employers, employees, professionals, co-operatives, weaker sections of society, etc. It also provides insurance coverage for people in certain approved occupations at the lowest possible premium cost. Besides providing insurance coverage, it also offers group schemes to employers that allow the funding of the gratuity and pension liabilities of the employers.

9.4 MAJOR INSURANCE ROLES

Within the life and general industry sectors the major roles are:

1. THE UNDERWRITER

He is employed by insurance companies to assess the risk and dictate the terms of the policy, including the premium. Early in their careers, underwriters worked off to established data but may find themselves assessing risks based just on their skill and experience later in their careers.

2. THE SURVEYOR

The Surveyor is contracted by the insurer to act as an intermediary between the insurance company and the policyholder over claims. The loss adjuster's role is to help settle the claim fairly and speedily. This type of jobs is not popular in India but found elsewhere in the world.

3. THE BROKER

The broker is an independent intermediary, who uses his knowledge and experience to assess the client's risk and finds appropriate policies. A broker must put the interests of a client first even though they receive a commission from the insurance company.

4. THE CLAIMS ADVISER

They are the members of an insurance company's claims department. They are the first part of the call when a claim comes in. They deal directly with the public over the claim and, depending on the complexity of the claim and the adviser's experience, will either resolve or help to process the claim.

5. THE ACTUARY

They provide the formula which is used to calculate premiums and surrender values. The appointed actuary of a company has the legal responsibility of certifying that the millions invested in life insurance policies are safe.

6. THE FINANCIAL ADVISER

Most companies offer investment opportunities to clients, such as endowments and life assurance. Job opportunities exist in sales, consultancy or investment analysis.

9.5 A BRIEF HISTORY OF THE LIFE INSURANCE SEGMENT

The business of life insurance in India in its existing form started in India in the year 1818 with the establishment of the Oriental Life Insurance Company in Kolkata. Some of the important milestones in the life insurance business in India are:

1912: The Indian Life Assurance Companies Act was enacted as the first statute to regulate the life insurance business.

1928: The Indian Insurance Companies Act enabled the government to collect statistical information about both life and non-life insurance business.

1938: Earlier legislation was consolidated and amended by the Insurance Act with the objective of protecting the interests of the insuring public.

1956: 245 Indian and foreign insurers and provident fund societies were taken over by the Central Government and nationalised. LIC was formed under an Act of Parliament, *viz.*, LIC Act, 1956 with a capital of ₹ 5 crores from the Government of India.

The general insurance business in India, on the other hand, can trace its roots to the Triton Insurance Company Ltd., the first general insurance company established in the year 1950 in Kolkata by the British.

9.6 A BRIEF HISTORY OF GENERAL INSURANCE BUSINESS IN INDIA

Some of the important milestones in the general insurance business in India are:

1907: The Indian Mercantile Insurance Ltd. set up the first company to transact all classes of general insurance business.

1957: General Insurance Council, a wing of the Insurance Association of India, framed a code of conduct for ensuring fair conduct and sound business practices.

1968: The Insurance Act was amended to regulate investments and set minimum solvency margins and the Tariff Advisory Committee was set up.

1972: The General Insurance Business (Nationalisation) Act, 1972 was passed as an act of Parliament. It helped the Government to nationalise the general insurance business in India with effect from January 1, 1973. About 107 insurers are amalgamated and grouped into four companies, *viz.*, the National Insurance Company Ltd., the New India Assurance Company Ltd., the Oriental Insurance Company Ltd., and the United India Insurance Company Ltd. GIC was incorporated as a company.

9.6.1. Insurance Sector Reforms

In 1993, Malhotra Committee, headed by former Finance Secretary and RBI Governor R.N. Malhotra, was formed to evaluate the Indian insurance industry and recommend its future direction. Malhotra Committee was set up with the objective of complementing the reforms initiated in the financial sector. The reforms were aimed at "creating a more efficient and competitive financial system suitable for the requirements of the economy keeping in mind the structural changes currently underway and recognising that insurance is an important part of the overall financial system where it was necessary to address the need for similar reforms."

In 1994, the committee submitted the report and some of the key recommendations included in the report are as below:

(1) Structure

Government stake in the insurance companies to be brought down to 50%. Government should take over the holdings of GIC and its subsidiaries so that these subsidiaries can act as independent corporations. All the insurance companies should be given greater freedom to operate.

(2) Competition

- Private companies with a minimum paid-up capital of ₹ 1 bn should be allowed to enter the industry.
- No company should deal in both Life and General Insurance through a single entity.
- Foreign companies may be allowed to enter the industry in collaboration with the domestic companies.
- Postal Life Insurance should be allowed to operate in the rural market.
- Only one State Level Life Insurance Company should be allowed to operate in each state.

(3) Regulatory Body

- The Insurance Act should be changed.
- An Insurance Regulatory body should be set up.
- Controller of Insurance (currently, a part from the Finance Ministry) should be made independent.

(4) Investments

- Mandatory Investments of LIC Life Fund in government securities to be reduced from 75% to 50%.
- GIC and its subsidiaries are not to hold more than 5% in any company. (Their current holdings to be brought down to this level over a period of time.)

(5) Customer Service

- LIC should pay interest on delays in payments beyond 30 days.
- Insurance companies must be encouraged to set up unit-linked pension plans.
- Computerisation of operations and updating of technology to be carried out in the insurance industry. The committee emphasised that in order to improve the customer services and increase the coverage, the insurance industry should be opened up to competition. But at the same time, the committee felt the need to exercise caution as any failure on the part of new players could ruin the public confidence in the industry. Hence, it was decided to allow the competition in a limited way by stipulating the minimum capital requirement of ₹ 100 crores. The committee felt the need to provide greater participation for private players.

9.7 REGULATION OF INSURANCE COMPANIES

The Government of India (GoI) opened the insurance sector to private players on October 24, 2000, thus unraveling a new chapter in this field. This new policy of the GoI is an outcome of India's policy of liberalisation and also the result of its obligation as a signatory to the WTO to conform to its principles and guidelines relating to the reduction of barriers to trade and services. This epoch-making decision has ushered in a new era that has transgressed four decades of complete control by the public sector over the insurance sector [life insurance was nationalised in 1956 by merging 245 private insurance companies to] form the Life Insurance Corporation of India (LIC) while general insurance was nationalised with the formation of the General Insurance Corporation (GIC) in 1972.

This decision of the GoI has been accompanied by a set of laws and regulations governing this domain. Accordingly, the Insurance Regulatory and Development Authority Act, 1999 (the IRDA Act) was enacted with the predominant aim of setting up an autonomous body known as the Insurance Regulatory and Development Authority (the IRDA) to regulate, promote and ensure orderly growth of the insurance industry. Further, the Insurance Act, 1938 has been significantly amended so as to bring it in conformity with the IRDA Act.

The IRDA has a twin role, *i.e.,* regulation as well as development of the insurance sector.

I. Governing legislation

Insurance is a federal subject in India and the legislation that governs insurance in India is:

- The Insurance Act, 1938; and
- The IRDA Act, 1999.

II. Highlights of the IRDA Act

(a) According to the IRDA Act, the Indian promoter may invest either wholly or enter into a joint venture with a foreign insurance company (Foreign Partner). It would be pertinent to note that Foreign direct investment (FDI) has been capped at twenty-six percent (26%). The underlying tone of the 26% FDI cap ensures that the Foreign Partner has a definite say in direction and management. As per Indian Company Law, certain significant items require special resolutions to be passed, which require three-fourth majority in a shareholders' meeting. In light of the aforesaid, the Foreign Partner would have the right to veto or block the passing of such resolutions.

(b) It is relevant to note that for the purposes of calculation of the aforesaid 26% FDI cap, the holdings of the equity in the Indian promoter company held by Foreign Institutional Investors and mutual funds will not be taken into account.

(c) It is pertinent to mention that insurance business can be carried out only by a public company incorporated in India under the Companies Act, 1956.

(d) The IRDA Act has made it mandatory for private insurance companies to sell a percentage of their policies in the rural and social sectors. (The "social sector" as per the IRDA Act includes the unorganised sector and economically vulnerable and backward classes). Accordingly, in the life insurance segment, five per cent (5%) of the policies have to be sold in the rural sector while for the general insurance segment, at least two per cent (2%) of the policies should be sold in the rural sector. The aforesaid obligations have to be undertaken in the first two (2) years of operation of the insurance companies.

(e) Life insurance companies will have to increase their rural business from five per cent (5%) in the first year to fifteen per cent (15%) in the fifth year. In the case of general insurance, the companies have to increase their rural business from two per cent (2%) in the first year to five per cent (5%) in the third year.

(f) The IRDA Act has also prescribed social sector obligations to be undertaken by insurance companies. The companies will have to insure five thousand (5,000) lives in the social sector in the first year. This has to gradually increase every year to twenty thousand (20,000) lives in the fifth year.

(g) The Indian insurance company should have a minimum paid-up equity capital of Rupees one billion (₹ 1,000,000,000) in the event it proposes to engage in life insurance or general insurance business.

(h) The Indian insurance company should have a minimum paid-up equity capital of Rupees two billion (₹ 2,000,000,000) in the event it proposes to engage exclusively in the business of re-insurance.

(i) Distribution through banks

Distribution of insurance products through banks are considered to be the most popular medium as the private players prefer to utilise the wide network of banks for the distribution of insurance policies in India.

(j) Distribution through insurance agents

Insurance agents and development officers provide another vital link in insurance selling and various surveys have proven this aspect. These intermediaries help the insurance companies to keep in touch with policyholders, assist claimants, and act as advisors to those who invest their claim proceeds.

(k) Online distribution

Extensive use of information technology can make the role of these intermediaries more effective and buyer-friendly. The online media is definitely considered to be one of the most effective modes of distribution as a number of websites have already started offering policies online.

(l) Other modes of distribution

Marketing alliances with people/companies having a strong physical presence is gaining popularity and is considered to be a good distribution strategy as well. The reasons why foreign insurance companies have shown such immense interest in forging joint ventures in the Indian insurance sector are not difficult to fathom. A look at the following statistics indicates that the existing insurance market in India in terms of premium income holds a promising future.

Out of an insurable population of 300 million, 50 million people have the capacity to pay a premium of approximately US$ 200 per year, 100 million have the capacity to pay approximately US$ 175 per year and 150 million have the capacity to pay approximately US$ 75 per year. On this basis, the total annual insurance premium would be approximately US$ 40 billion. India has a huge middle-class population of about 300 million who can afford to buy life, health, and disability and pension plan products. Out of this, only 20% of the insurable population has insurance cover, such cover catering to only 25% of their needs and financial capacity. The remaining 80% do not avail of any insurance cover. The life insurance market of India, therefore, remains practically untapped.

The size of the existing insurance market is very large and is growing at the rate of 10% per year. The estimated potential of the Indian insurance market in terms of premium was approximately $ 80 billion in the year 1999. Only 10% of the market share has been tapped by LIC and GIC and the balance 90% of the market still remains untapped. This vast potential can be tapped only by private participation.

The huge life fund can be utilised for financing the infrastructure/industry as well as provide support to other industries in the country. Hence, the insurance industry is likely to play a key role in changing the economic landscape of the country. However, the success of the insurance industry will primarily depend upon meeting the rising expectations of the consumer who will be the real king in the liberalised insurance market in future.

9.8 CLAIMS

Insurance is a financial service. It falls under the purview of Consumer Protection Act. The consumer forums accept complaints from the aggrieved insured and decide such case.

(a) The principle of indemnity is involved in a contract by which one party promises to save the other from a loss.

(b) The insurers too are bound by good faith. They are bound to place a proper interpretation on the terms and conditions of the contract and settle the claim with fairness and equity.

(c) The insurance company may pay the value of the property at the time of the happening of its destruction or the amount of such damage or at its opinion reinstate or replace such property or any part thereof.

Insurance is well covered under Consumer Protection Act. The Consumer forums are helping in claiming for the loss from insurance companies. Besides, the government has been setting up numerous Lok Adalats for speedy disposal of such cases. In those cases where the insurers have admitted the liability and the dispute is only regarding the quantum of the liability, both the parties may resort to an Arbitrator for amicable settlement of the case in lines with Arbitration and Conciliation Act.

9.8.1. Legal Issues on Claims

Insurance claims are settled in accordance with the terms and conditions of the insurance contract entered into between the policyholder and the insurance companies. The settlement of claims plays an important role in generating satisfaction among policyholders and at the same time ensuring the accuracy and impartiality of the information provided by the policyholder and the insurance company at the time of settlement of the claim.

An insurance policy compensates the policyholder against the financial impact that can arise following a loss, damage, destruction of the property, health or life. The policyholder can only make an insurance claim if there has been a loss of the subject matter of the policy. Also, claims are settled depending on the measure of indemnity, which is decided at the time of procuring the policy. Both the parties to the policy are expected to observe good faith and disclose all relevant material information relating to the subject matter of the policy. The person insuring the subject matter, be it property, health or life, must have some insurable interest in the subject matter.

9.8.2. Process of Claims Settlement

(a) Submission of Claim Documents

The submission of all necessary documents forms an integral part of the process of claim settlement in India. The following documents are to be submitted:

(i) Details of the insurance policy

(ii) Claims form issued by the agent or the insurance company

(iii) The original insurance policy document

(iv) Intimation to the insurance in writing and

(v) Estimation of loss to the insurance company

(b) Verification

Upon submission of the documents, the surveyor or company official would verify the documents and prepare an independent report on the assessment of loss or details of death. Moreover, the insurance company after checking the papers shall settle the claim as per the terms and conditions of the policy.

Chart 9.1

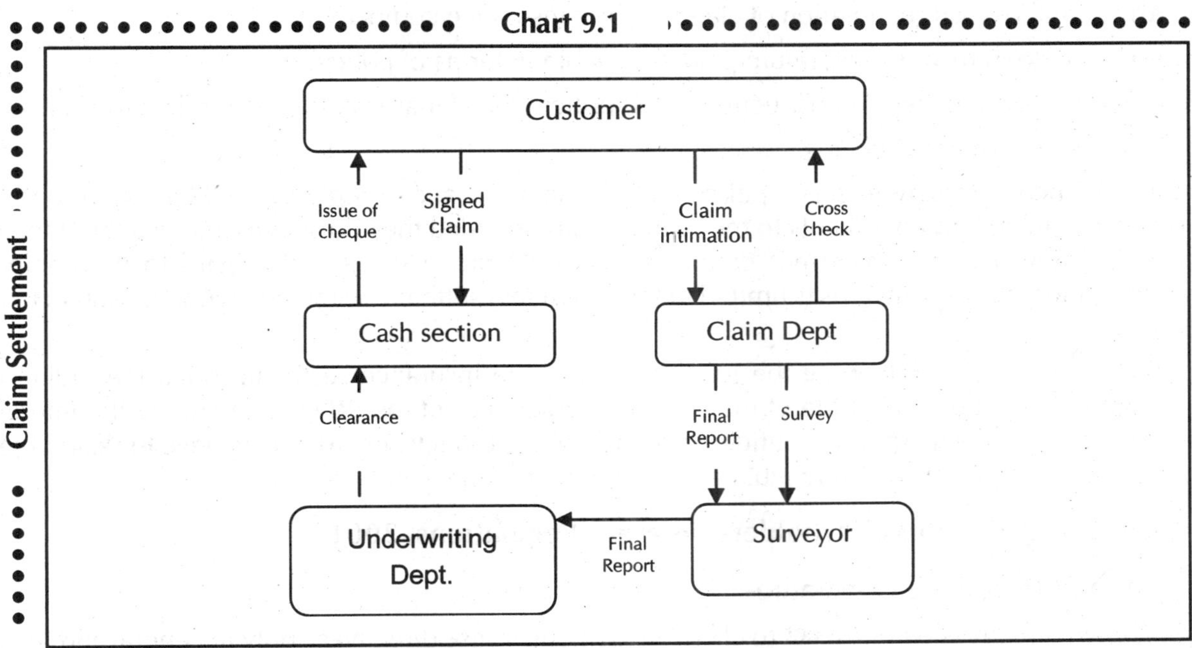

(c) Settlement

If the claim is processed or settled by the insurance company, then the insurance company or the insurance agent issues the; discharge form. However, if the claim is denied by the insurance company, it should be intimated to the policyholder.

(d) Steps to be taken by the Policyholder in case of Non-acceptance of Claims

The policyholder can initiate the following steps:

(i) There are complaint cells usually functioning at the offices of the insurance company. The policyholders can send the written complaints to these officers.

(ii) The policyholder can ask the clause of the contract on which they rely for refusal of claims.

(iii) If the insurance company claims that the policyholder has breached the policy, the policyholder may check the policy to see if there has been a breach as per the terms of the policy.

(iv) Under the law, an insurance company has a legal obligation to inform the policyholder about the restrictions in the insurance policy. This must be done before the policyholder signs the application and the policy is issued. This means that the policyholder must be given a copy of the policy and the terms of the policy must be clear and unambiguous. If these preconditions are not met, it may be possible to retain coverage under the policy.

(v) In case the claimant is dissatisfied with the decision of repudiation of claim, he can approach the claims review committees comprising of senior officers of the insurance company for review of claims objectively.

9.8.3. Regulations Governing Claim Settlement in India

The primary regulations governing the insurance in India are the Insurance Act, 1938, the various regulations and notifications issued by the Insurance Regulatory and Development Authority (IRDA), from time to time. In exercise of the powers conferred by the Insurance Act, 1938, the Central Government by notification, has framed the Redressal of Public Grievances Rules, 1998. These rules apply to both life insurance and general insurance policies. The said rules provide for the appointment of an 'ombudsman' who is conferred the powers to adjudicate and provide redressal in respect of public grievances, in particular for expeditious settlement of personal insurance claims. The range of issues over which the ombudsman is conferred powers to adjudicate is as follows:

(a) Any partial or total repudiation of claims by the insurance company.

(b) Any dispute in regard to premium paid or payable in terms of policy.

(c) Any dispute on the legal construction of the policies insofar as such disputes relate to claims.

(d) Delay in settlement of claims.

If the insurance company rejects a policyholder's claim or fails to reply to it within one month, then the policyholders can take their complaints to the ombudsman provided they do so within one year of the insurance company's rejection and they have not commenced formal proceedings with regard to the complaint. The ombudsman's ability to make awards is limited to the actual loss suffered by the policyholder, subject to a limit of ₹ 20 lakhs.

Apart from the above, following the liberalisation of the insurance sector in India, the Indian insurance market is regulated by the IRDA. One of the important objectives of the IRDA is to protect the interests, of the policyholders so as to increase public confidence in insurance products. In order to achieve the said objective, the IRDA issues various notifications and regulations from time to time.

9.8.4. IRDA (Protection of Policyholders' Interest) Regulations, 2001

(a) Obligation of Insurance Companies

It lays down directives with respect to claim, settlement. These directives apply to general and life insurance polices and aim to specify minimum standards from the point of sale of the policy to settlement of the claim. The main features, as far as claims relating to general insurance policies are concerned, are as follows:

(I) The insurance company must offer a fair settlement of the claim rather than 'try to improperly beat down the claim taking advantage of the policyholder's need for an early settlement'.

(II) The insurance company must make its offer of settlement within 45 days of the receipt of all documents and information asked for, and make payment within seven days of the policyholder's acceptance.

(III) The Board of Directors of an insurance company must, at least once a quarter, review the number of claims notified in the preceding quarter; the number of claims settled and outstanding during that quarter; and an analysis of how long it has taken to settle claims.

(b) Obligation of Policyholders

Obligations are also placed on policyholders. They are expected to state correctly all relevant facts for the grant of a cover and in settlement of claim arising thereunder, and provide all information sought from them by the insurance company to enable the risk to be assessed.

(c) Obligation of Brokers

IRDA (Insurance Brokers and Insurance Consultants) Regulation, 2002 have been framed to protect the policyholders' interest. It is framed to govern the conduct of brokers as and when they are permitted to operate in the Indian market. Under these regulations, the brokers are allowed to maintain proper records of claims and assist in the negotiation of claims.

In spite of the regulations, a major challenge that remains to be addressed is to ensure that the new insurance regulatory regime works towards eliminating corruption and ensuring that claims are processed efficiently and quickly. Efficiency in handling and settling of claims will go to show that privatisation of the insurance sector has been a boon for the claimants and the country.

9.9 CONCLUSION

Indian insurance market size is presently estimated at US$ 66-70 million. By 2005, it is expected to grow five-fold to US$ 377 million. In 2000-01 fiscal years, total premiums stood at US$9933 million which is 0.41% of total global premiums of US$ 2443.6 billion. Total premiums of Indian insurance industry in 2000-01 fiscal were 2.32% of country's GDP. Per capita premium stood at US$ 9.9. Indian insurance market potential could be gauged by the fact that currently about 40-42 million people have been brought under insurance whereas the potential is estimated at 200-250 million. Insurance companies could tap only 5% of Indian middle class segment.

In India, insurance is generally considered as a tax-saving device instead of its other implied long-term financial benefits. Indian people are prone to investing in properties and gold followed by bank deposits. They selectively invest in shares also but the percentage is very small, *i.e.,* 4-5%. Even to this day, Life Insurance Corporation of India dominates Indian insurance sector. With the entry of private sector players backed by foreign expertise, Indian insurance market has become more vibrant.

Indian federal government considers insurance as one of major sources of funds for infrastructure development. The government has identified the following as major thrust areas:

(a) Timely and reliable statistical data and information about policies and markets to instill a degree of credibility;

(b) A code of good practices based on international best practices to raise the standard of Indian insurance sector;

(c) Strengthening of supervision and regulation;

(d) Market participation in decision-making;

(e) High solvency standard and developing alternative channels.

Till end of 1999-2000 fiscal years, two state-run insurance companies, namely, Life Insurance Corporation (LIC) and General Insurance Corporation (GIC) were the monopoly insurance (both life and non-life) providers in India. Under GIC, there were four subsidiaries, *i.e.,* National Insurance Company Ltd., Oriental Insurance Company Ltd., New India Assurance Company Ltd., and United India Assurance Company Ltd. In fiscal 2000-01, the Indian federal government lifted all entry restrictions for private sector investors. Foreign investment insurance market was also allowed with 26% cap.

GIC was converted into India's national reinsurer from December, 2000 and all the subsidiaries working under the GIC umbrella were restructured as independent insurance companies. Indian Parliament has cleared a Bill on July 30, 2002 delinking the four subsidiaries from GIC. A separate Bill has been approved by Parliament to allow brokers, cooperatives and intermediaries in the sector.

Currently, insurance companies, both private and public, have to cede 20% of its reinsurance with GIC. GIC is planning to increase re-insurance premium by 20% which works out at ₹ 3,000 cr. GIC is actively considering entry into overseas markets including West Asia, South-east Asia and SAARC region. To regulate, promote and ensure orderly growth of the insurance business and re-insurance business, a regulatory authority, Insurance Regulatory and Development Authority (IRDA) was set up under IRDA Act, 1999. IRDA is composed of a chairman, five whole-time members and four part-time members. There are four types of Indian insurance business: Life, Fire, Marine and Miscellaneous. In life insurance more than 80% business relates to Endowment Assurance (Participating) and Money Back (Participating). Motor Vehicles insurance is compulsory in India.

Indian insurance industry has ombudsmen in 12 cities empowered to reduce customers' grievances in respect of insurance contracts on personal lives where the insured amount is less than ₹ 20 lakhs.

In the first year of insurance market liberalisation (April 2-December 31, 2001) as much as 16 private sector companies including joint ventures with leading foreign insurance companies have entered the Indian insurance sector. Of this, 10 were under the life insurance category and six under general insurance. Since then, till June, 2002, two more joined the life insurance sector. Thus, in all there are 18 players (12 players belong to life insurance and 6 belongs to general insurance) in the Indian insurance industry till date. (See Appendix 1)

Up to end 2001, 16 insurance players had made a total investment of ₹ 1,910.95 crore including investments made from policyholders' funds. In life category, Allianz Bajaj topped the list with ₹ 147.01 crore closely followed by Om Kotak's ₹ 146.25 crore and ICICI Prudential's ₹ 134.64 crore. In non-life segment, Tata AIG General led the list with ₹ 161.68 crore followed by Reliance General's ₹ 121.86 crore and Royal Sundaram's ₹ 111.86 crore.

Foreign equity in broking firms is capped at 26%. Brokers have been divided into four categories:

- Direct general insurance broker (category I);
- Direct life insurance broker (category II);
- Reinsurance broker (category III); and
- Composite broker (category IV).
- Category wise net worth for insurance brokers is:
- ₹ 25 lakhs for category I and category II;
- ₹ 2 crores for category III; and
- ₹ 3 crores for category IV.

For insurance consultants, net worth is ₹ 10 lakhs.

In India, motor vehicle insurance premium is 2.5% of the vehicle cost against international standard of 6%.

The Indian insurance regulatory authorities have asked the insurance companies operating in the country to take into account the investment income earned on the funds earmarked for outstanding claims, unreported claims and unexpired risks while calculating the underwriting margins. These funds are called technical funds belonging to the policyholders. Hence the income earned on such funds should be considered as contributions from the policyholders of the concerned insurance companies.

9.10 REVIEW QUESTIONS

Short Answer Questions

1. Define insurance.
2. Make a brief historical account about Life Insurance Business in India.
3. Write a note on evolution of general insurance business in India.
4. Write a short note on:
   (i) Insurable Interest
   (ii) Indemnity
   (iii) Proximate Cause
   (iv) Contribution
   v. Utmost Good Faith
   vi. Subrogation
5. What are the different types of insurance policies?
6. Write a short note on:
   (a) Endowment Policy
   (b) Whole Life Policy
   (c) Term Life Policies
   (d) Moneyback Policies
   (e) Joint Life Policies

   (f) Children's Insurance Policies
   (g) Women's Policy
7. What are the major roles played by different persons in Insurance business?
8. Explain about insurance regulation in India in a few sentences.
9. List the legal issues on claims.

Essay Type Questions

1. Discuss the principles of insurance with examples.
2. What are the major roles being played by different persons in Insurance?
3. Explain the procedures of insurance claim in the event of death or an accident.
4. Evaluate the insurance sector reforms of India.

❋ ❋ ❋

CHAPTER

10

Housing Finance

Objectives

The student, after studying the chapter, should be able to:

- State the status of housing finance in India.
- Explain the basic tenets of housing policy in India.
- Trace the institutional framework of housing finance.
- Appreciate the role being played by National Housing Bank in India.
- Evaluate the financial services rendered by the housing financial institutions.

Structure:

10.1 INTRODUCTION

Decisions about housing are among the most important financial decisions most of the people ever have to make. Buying a home is a major commitment, and home payments take a big chunk of the family budget. In the 1970s, home payments took about one-quarter of a family's take-home pay. People bring about 1/3rd of their salary to their home now. Home ownership has a number of advantages over renting. Mortgage payments are like "forced savings", making one's house an investment, not just a place to live. He may have a better quality of life if he buys instead of renting. He can do whatever he wants to the house and feels free to improve or change it to suit his needs. He may enjoy more privacy if he owns his own home. He will have no landlord to let in and perhaps no neighbors nearby to make noise and disrupt his life. Closing costs and mortgage interest are tax-deductible.

Housing is one of the basic human needs of the society. It is closely linked with the process of overall socio-economic development of a country. India, being a highly populated country, there is a great need and scope for the development of Housing Sector. Unfortunately, for some reasons or the other, the housing sector in India has remained underdeveloped in the past. However, it is hoped that there would be improvement in the near future.

10.2 HOUSING FINANCE IN INDIA

Indian consumers had a credit aversion over housing loan traditionally. This attitude has been changed only in the 1990s. Banks have considered it as an opportunity. They come forward to lend housing loan to diversify their risk. Apart from this opportunity, the Retail Asset Portfolio would be distributed over a large number of borrowers as compared to wholesale lending. Retail assets also provide the bank an opportunity to cross-sell liability products to the asset customers and build long-term profitable relationship.

Dr. Y.V. Reddy, Governor, Reserve Bank of India (RBI), said on April, 7 that the year 2003-04 saw an incremental credit off-take of ₹ 1,19,964 crores. He said that the credit expansion has been led primarily by the housing and retail sectors. Bank credit to housing has increased by 33% over the past year. This is a clear sign that the housing sector and especially the home loan sector has been major growth driver for banks. This has been a boon for banks at the time when the credit off-take from the manufacturing sector was stagnating.

The retail lending business is growing at an outstanding rate of over 30% every year. Banks in India have gone a long way since 1990s where the retail portfolio was less than 5% to the current level of around 18%. The proportion of the retail share in the lending portfolio is slated to close in at around 40% by 2005-2006.

10.2.1. Risk in Lending

The risks always accompany growth in lending for home loans. The banks are reporting higher delinquency rates. CRISIL has recently reported a dramatic increase in non-performing loans in the housing loan sector. RBI has warned the banks against growing NPA too fast. There is also talk in some corners that the home loan bubble may one day burst.

10.2.2. Housing Loan — A Lucrative Business

Banks have shifted their focus from traditional base of lending to companies to retail. It serves two purposes. It helps banks to get rid of the excess liquidity. Secondly, it has become a lucrative business for banks. Foreign and private banks initiated the retail lending and the public sector banks followed the suit. In the last three years (2000-2003), the retail asset portfolio of banks has grown at a compound annual growth of 25%. Banks are seeing housing sector a sunrise one. This is due to the fact that first time in the history of human civilisation there is such a large proportion of middle class. A class that is set to grow by the years as India is set to grow at an impressive rate. The reasons for the banks to shift their focus to retail credit are dealt in the next section. The reasons for lending housing loan are given below:

- Poor credit off-take of companies, commercial and other traditionally industrial sector.
- Growing risk of lending to industry on account of recession,
- Growing financial disintermediation process enabling many triple A rated companies to access the market directly,
- Relatively less risk for retail borrowers,
- Rising disposable income and changing lifestyle aspiration of a sizable section of the population,
- Continuous softening of lending rates which has improved the borrowers' ability to repay,
- Increased governmental incentives by way of tax relief or concessions on certain types of loans,
- Improved liquidity with banks following a reduction in Cash Reserve Ratio (CRR) and low credit off-take in the face of continued accretion of deposits,
- Availability of better spread to banks,
- Widespread of risk among large number of borrowers, and
- Developments in technology which have reduced transaction costs on a large number of borrower accounts.

As of now, the share of retail lending of banks in their total lending is not more than 15%. If one takes out the aggressive banks like ICICI Bank and -State Bank of India, the average share of the industry will be lower. For Bank of India, about 20% of the bank's advances are deployed under retail lending.

10.3 HOUSING POLICY

It has been seen that the Government of India, regarding the housing policies has always laid focus on the lowest-income households. Earlier, particularly the middle class, for financing a house took loans from informal sources like their relatives and friends, or try to accumulate money for their dream home, which was realised only after a long wait. The jhuggi or shack dwellers of India spend a considerable amount on building and rebuilding their pregnable dwellings. These dwellings are illegal constructions and with unlawful electric connections. The amount they spend on the construction of these shacks and the unlawful temporary legalisation of these electric connections could easily be spent on repaying a loan on a small terraced pucca and legalised house, if they built it themselves. While finance for housing is usually available for high and middle-income households, there is a general need to widen and deepen the flow of long-term finance at affordable levels to low-income households.

10.3.1. Budget 2000-2001

To boost up housing in India, the Union Government in the 2000-2001 financial years budget proposed a 20% rebate of tax under Section 88 of the Income-tax Act, which would now be available for repayment of principal of housing loans up to ₹ 20,000 per year as against ₹ 10,000 earlier. Earlier, the exemption from tax on long-term capital gains was not available if the capital gain from transfer of capital assets was invested in a house, if one house was already owned. The restriction was removed. Even if the taxpayers own one house, they can make an investment in a new house and claim exemption from capital gains tax on sale of capital assets.

10.3.2. New Housing Finance Companies

In June 2000, the Union government, through National Housing Bank, in order to endorse endowment for escalating housing delivery all over the country, approved 29 new housing finance companies to hasten the national housing programme. The list of 29 housing finance companies was given the go ahead nod by the National Housing Bank.

It is interesting to note that Tata Home Finance Ltd. and Birla Home Finance Ltd. too have joined the housing finance provider's race. Reliance Industries and GE Capital are also likely to storm housing finance market in near future. A boost to the housing finance industry can push up the Indian economy scenario on a large scale. Housing has a tremendous tendency to create income and insist for resources, tools and services. Finances owed to housing arrive in the profile of profits.

10.4 INSTITUTIONAL FRAMEWORK

To give a boost to the housing scenario in India and to narrow down the margin between the housing demand and the availability of houses, The National Housing Bank was set up in the year 1988. This was done by keeping in mind that a home seeker though does have a desire for a house but lacks the resources for construction or buying it. To give an enhancement to private housing finance institutions, the National Housing Bank came into the picture. It is a principal agency to promote housing finance institutions both at local and regional levels and to provide financial and other support to such institutions. While it is important to keep in mind that the National Housing Bank itself does not give loans or finance individuals or a party as such, it is only a corporate body to promote, establish, support or aid the housing finance institutions. The housing finance institutions can be segregated into three categories:

- Public Sector Finance
- Banks
- Private Sector Finance

10.4.1. Housing Finance Organisations

Many organisations of both public and private sectors have entered in the field. For example, Life Insurance Corporation of India and General Insurance Corporation entered the field with various schemes for financing housing units. Housing and Urban Development Corporation (HUDCO), a wholly government-owned enterprise was set up with the objective of housing and urban development as well as infrastructure development in 1970. Another corporation named Housing Development Finance Corporation (HDFC) was set up in private sector in 1977.

Various nationalised and other banks also set up housing finance companies as their subsidiaries such as Canfin Homes Ltd., GIC Griha Vitta Ltd., LIC Housing Finance Ltd., PNB Housing Finance Ltd. and SBI Home Finance Ltd. After 2000, the new generation banks entered the field.

Chart 10.1

Structure of House Financing Industry

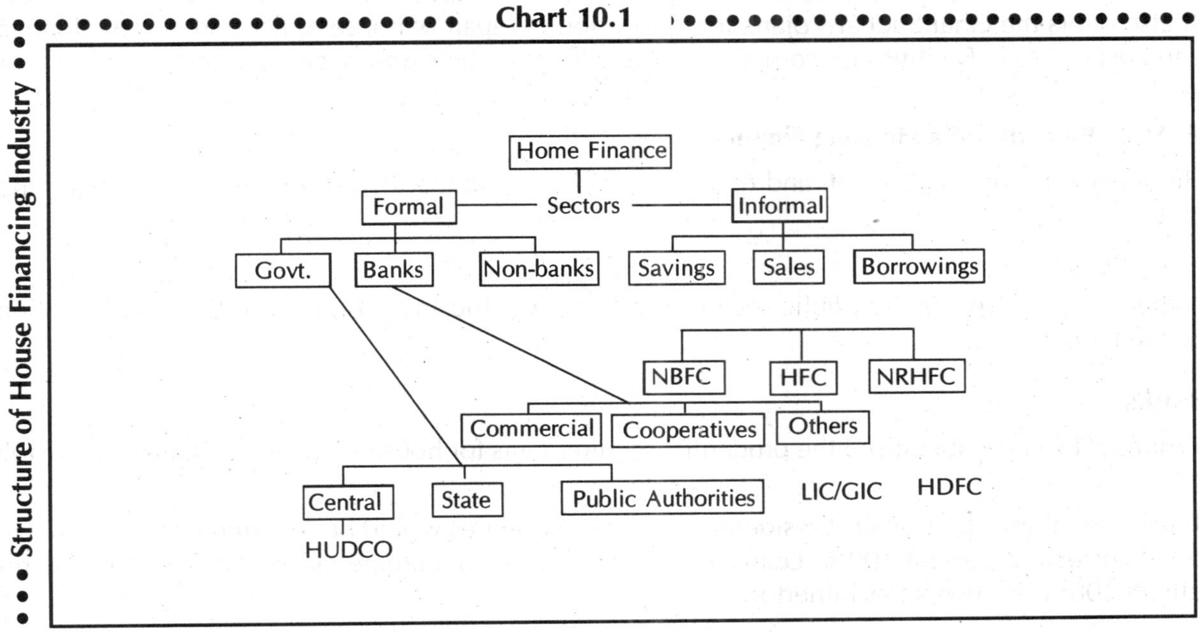

Housing finance industry can be broadly divided into two categories namely formal (organised) and informal (unorganised) sector. The formal sector which comprises of various public and private sector institutions normally finances around 30% of the total funds required in the housing industry. On the other hand, informal sector comprising of household savings, disposal of existing property, borrowing from friends, relatives and money lenders, etc. meets around 70% funds requirement of this industry. The structure of housing finance industry is presented in Chart 10.1.

10.4.2. Public Sector Finance

(a) HUDCO (Housing and Urban Development Corporation Limited)

HUDCO is an influential Government of India enterprise. With the main aim of funding state governments for infrastructure development and the Vision 2002, HUDCO intends to surface as the lone organisation of its kind for dealing with the needs of shelter and infrastructure development in the human settlements.

Since HUDCO entered into the individual housing finance sector, the complete state of affairs has changed. As HUDCO gives housing finance for 11.5% and after deductions the interest rate comes to 8.81%, the war of interest rates has begun.

(b) LICHFL (Life Insurance Corporation Housing Finance Limited)

LIC Housing Finance Ltd. is one of the leading and oldest home funding organisations, which offers one of the finest services in the trade. It has branches all over India. It offers variety of loans like housing finance for new purchases, reconstructions, renovations, NRI housing finance etc. Some of the schemes that LICHFL offers are the Griha Shobha, which is for NRIs, Griha Sudhar, where one can apply for a loan for renovations and repairs in existing houses. Green Channel Facility is meant for professionals like practising doctors, CAs, computer engineers, etc. Lately, LICHFL introduced a new scheme Apna Chikitsalaya, which is especially for medical practitioners for renovating, purchasing or extending their clinic, hospital, laboratory, etc. Then it also has the scheme of Sampurna Griha (A) and (B) for resident Indians.

(c) GICHFL (General Insurance Corporation Housing Finance Limited)

GIC Housing Finance Ltd., a company from the house of General insurance Company, has also emerged as a strong housing finance institution in the recent years.

(d) PNBHFL (Punjab National Bank Housing Finance Limited)

A subsidiary of the Punjab National Bank, PNBHFL offers the Apna Ghar Yojana for construction or buying a house. It also offers the Ghar Sudhar Yojana for renovation or repair of house or flat. It has home loan facilities for NRIs and Line of Credit Facilities for companies to give loans to their employees for construction or renovation of a house.

(e) SBIHF (State Bank of India Housing Finance)

SBIHF offers loan for construction and renovation of houses at the lowest interest rates, which range from 11.5% p.a. to 12.75% p.a.

(f) Others

The other major players in the public sector are the Indian Housing, Corporation Bank Homes, Cent Bank Home Finance Limited, etc.

10.4.3. Banks

Accordingly, RBI also liberalised the prudential requirements for housing finance by banks on the following lines:

(i) Banks extending loans against residential housing properties would be required to assign risk weight of 50%, instead of present 100%. Loans against the security of commercial real estate would continue to attract 100% risk weight as hitherto.

(ii) Investments made by banks in Mortgage Backed Securities (MBS) of residential assets by HFCs, which are recognised and supervised by NHB, would also be assigned a risk weight of 50% for the purpose of capital adequacy. However, investment by banks in MBS of housing assets, which include commercial properties, would attract 100% risk weight.

(iii) Investments by banks in MBS issued by HFCs supervised by NHB will be reckoned for inclusion in the prescribed housing finance allocation of 3.0%.

(iv) Besides, a Working Group was proposed to be set up to suggest modalities for widening the investor base in MBS, improving the quality of assets, creating liquidity for trading in such assets and other related issues.

The details of performance of commercial banks in the housing finance sector during the last three years can be summarised as below:

However, as per the RBI guidelines, direct housing finance up to ₹ 5 lakhs provided per dwelling in semi-urban/rural areas and up to ₹ 10 lakhs provided in urban or metropolitan areas would only be considered eligible for being treated as 'housing finance' under the Annual Housing Finance Allocation. Housing loans beyond these stipulated size limits would not be considered as achievement under the allocated target.

Almost all the banks throughout India provide housing finance, except a few small branches. The major banks that provide loans for housing are Bank of Baroda, Bank of India, Bank of Maharashtra, Bank of Punjab, Canara Bank, Cooperative Banks, Citi Bank NA, Corporation Bank, Dena Niwas, HSBC, ICICI Home Finance, IDBI Bank, IndusInd Bank, Lakshmi Vilas Bank, Punjab National Bank, SBI (State Bank of India), UCO Bank, and many others.

Amongst these, ICICI and SBI are the leaders. ICICI gives the maximum period of 30 years for the repayment of loans. It offers loans ranging from a minimum of ₹ 1 lakh to ₹ 1 crore.

10.4.4. Private Sector Finance

(a) HDFC (Housing Development Finance Corporation)

With the objective of augmentation of housing through the stipulation of housing finance, HDFC was established in 1978 with the support of the Industrial Credit and Investment Corporation of India, the International Finance Corporation (IFC) in Washington and the Aga Khan Fund. Today, HDFC and Housing finance are synonymous. It has become one of the largest home loan providers in India.

The maximum loan HDFC offers is ₹ 250,000 or 85% of the cost of the property. The repayment of the loan is on a monthly basis in equated monthly installments over a period of between 5 and 15 years.

(b) DHFCL (Dewan Housing Finance Corporation Limited)

Dewan Housing Finance Corporation Ltd. is one of the finest preferences in private housing finance sector. Since 1984 in the market, today it has 22 branches all over the country. Union Bank of India has obtained an equity involvement in DHFCL's capital composition. It is interesting to note that DHFCL's shares are listed on Mumbai, Delhi and Ahmedabad Stock Exchanges.

DHFCL offers a Double Protection Plan in the form of 'Free' Accident Risk Cover + Property Insurance to the extent of the loan liability to safeguard the interest of the borrower. It also has a Regressive Payment Scheme for applicants who are due for retirements within 5-10 years and apply jointly with the eligible younger co-applicants.

(c) GHFCL (Global Housing Finance Corporation Limited)

GHFCL, a syndicate of reputed builders, incorporated in June 1994, offers Individual Home Loan Scheme and Home Improvement Scheme. Oriental Bank of Commerce, one of the leading nationalised banks, also participates in the equity of the company.

Table 10.1 **Operations of HDFC**

Year	Loan approval/sactions	Loan disbursements	Housing loan outstanding (end Year)
1	2	3	4
1978-79	7.1	1.3	1.3
1979-80	23.2	9.1	10.1
1980-81	33.3	21.0	29.8
1981-82	46.6	29.8	56.4
1982-83	76.1	47.8	98.5
1983-84	102.9	74.9	161.2
1984-85	134.6	93.2	234.7
1985-86	186.4	145.7	351.8
1986-87	237.5	175.5	484.2
1987-88	305.0	235.3	654.9
1988-89	333.3	255.2	844.9
1989-90	603.0	489.3	1221.8
1990-91	813.8	668.5	1726.9
1991-92	711.9	627.8	2129.9
1992-93	859.1	719.9	2561.7
1993-94	1024.8	889.1	3071.2
1994-95	1494.6	1211.7	3747.6
1995-96	2071.5	1683.6	4740.7
1996-97	2521.7	2100.8	5709.3
1997-98	3251.3	2753.6	6944.1
1998-99	4071.8	3424.3	8219.3
1999-00	5305.1	4492.7	10063.0
2000-01	6879.8	5803.0	13224.7
2001-02	9041.3	7616.6	17169.2
2002-03	11731.6	9950.9	21749.9
2003-04	15215.6	12696.8	27974.3
2004-05	19715.0	16207.0	36011.5
2005-06	25633.7	20679.2	44990.1
2006-07P	33331.7	26178.4	56512.4

P: Provisional.

Note: Data are on July-June basis up to 1987-88 and on April-March basis thereafter.

Source: Housing Development Finance Corporation Ltd.

Table 10.2 Financial Assistance Sanctioned and Disbursed by All Financial Institutions

(₹ in crore)

Year	IDBI		IFCI		ICICI^^		SIDBI		IDBI@	
	Sanctions	Disbursements	Sanctions	Disbursements	Sanctions	Disbursements	Sanctions	Disbursements	Sanctions	Disbursements
1	2	3	4	5	6	7	8	0	10	11
1970-71	69.6	57.6	32.3	17.4	43.9	28.9	—	—	—	—
1971-72	148.9	80.1	28.7	23.3	39.7	30.3	—	—	6.6	1.1
1972-73	96.6	81.7	45.7	28.0	49.4	39.7	—	—	6.1	3.5
1973-74	167.0	137.0	41.9	31.9	61.1	43.5	—	—	7.2	52
1974-75	258.9	203.1	29.2	37.0	62.9	45.4	—	—	7.6	8.0
1975-76	304.6	223.5	51.3	34.7	78.6	61.1	—	—	5.3	4.7
1976-77	539.6	341.4	76.6	54.9	98.7	67.3	—	—	10.0	10.8
1977-78	679.5	410.3	113.4	57.5	108.3	91.6	—	—	10.9	9.1
1978-79	724.8	618.1	138.5	73.5	182.8	109.2	—	—	10.7	12.6
1079-80	1124.6	752.9	137.9	91.0	204.3	135.8	—	—	15.2	12.5
1980-81	1691.3	1258.0	206.6	108.9	314.1	185.3	—	—	19.4	16.9
1981-82	1835.0	1504.3	218.1	169.4	302.4	264.7	—	—	50.4	28.4
1982-83	1926.8	1595.1	230.2	.196.1	392.1	282.2	—	—	62.3	37.9
1983-84	2391.3	1976.3	321.9	224.5	507.6	334.2	—	—	69.5	41.4
1984-85	3354.3	2199.0	415.4	272.9	620.7	392.7	—	—	110.8	54.8
1985-86	3655.6	2798.0	499.2	403.9	708.2	482.2	—	—	75.2	67.8
1986-87	4565.5	3259.0	798.1	451.6	1118.3	695.5	—	—	148.9	94.7
1987-88	5289.2	4004.6	922.6	657.1	1231.7	771.2	—	—	186.5	101.9
1988-89	4411.1	3382.1	1635.5	997.5	1978.1	1085.6	—	—	208.8	116.5
1989-90	7269.1	5121.2	1817.0	1121.8	2850.6	1357.1	—	—	146.6	141.1
1990-91	6278.3	4501.1	2429.8	1574.3	3744.0	1967.5	2408.7	1838.5	234.7	153.9
	(5132.7)	(3613.3)						(1215.3)	(1096.1)	
1991-92	6590.2	5768.8	2421.2	1604.4	4094.9	2351.3	2846.0	2027.4	277.7	185.2
	(5535.2)	(4822.3)					(1357.3)	(1181.9)		
1992-93	9249.4	6710.7	2347.9	1733.4	5771.8	3315.2	2909.2	2146.3	294.3	183.9
	(8601.9)	(6084.0)					(1519.0)	(1291.7)		
1993-94	12086.0	8095.9	3745.9	2163.1	8491.4	4413.3	3356.3	2672.7	425.8	188.6
	(11591.8)	(7702·7)					(2095.5)	(1777.8)		
1994-95	18199.4	10671.8	5719.5	2838.7	14527.9	6879.3	4706.3	3389.8	777.9	397.6
	(17701.2)	(10299.5)					(3323.7)	(2493.3)		
1995-96	16476.4	10605.2	10300.3	4563.3	14594.0	7120.4	6065.6	4800.8	897.3	528.6
	(15873.8)	(10177.6)					(4190.5)	(3441.7)		
1996-97	15634.0	11467.7	7212.3	5157.1	14083.8	11180.9	6485.3	4584.7	816.0	549.6
	(14891.2)	(10798.5)					(4204.0)	(3334.5)		
1997-98	23982.0	15170.0	7693.2	5650.4	24717.5	15806.0	7484.2	5240.7	2061.0	1153.2
	(23608.9)	(14835.1)					(5059.0)	(3839.7)		
1998-99	23744.7	14470.1	4445.2	4819.3	32370.6	19225.1	8879.8	6285.2	2175.2	1688.5
	(23598.1)	(14313.0)					(6674.4)	(4674.8)		
1999-00	26966.5	17059.4	2080.0	3272.1	43522.8	25835.7	10264.7	6063.5	2338.1	1439.6
	(25786.5)	(16036.5)					(8088.4)	(5402.7)		
2000-01	26832.6	17476.9	1766.5	2156.8	55815.2	31664.6	1,0820.6	6441.4	2102.3	1709.8
	(26414.4)	(16894.0)					(10435.0)	(6158.7)		
2001-02	15867.0	11012.5	777.6	1074.4	36229.1	25831.0	9025.5	5910.3	1321.9	1068.0
	(15583.3)	(10710.4)					(8866.3)	(5783.1)		
2002-03	5898.2	6614.9	1960.0	1779.9	—	—	10903.5	6789.4	1206.5	1091.9
	(5898.2)	(6614.9)					(10025.4)	(6121.3)		
2003-04	3937.7	4986.4	1391.6	278.2	—	—	8246.3	4414.2	2412.0	2252.2
2004-05	10700.0[$$]	6183.3[$$]	0	91.3	—	—	9090.6	6187.8	—	—
2005-06P	—	—	0	187.0	—	—	11974.8	9099.8	—	—
2006-07P	—	—	1050.0	550.0	—	—	11184.4	10128.5	—	—
1970-71	—	—	—	—	—	—	—	—	17.8	8.1
1971-72	—	—	—	—	—	—	—	—	23.1	5.3
1972-73	—	—	—	—	—	—	—	—	20.1	14.0
1973-74	—	—	—	—	—	—	—	—	25.9	20.0
1974-75	—	—	—	—	—	—	—	—	43.8	54.1

1975-76	—	—	—	—	—	—	—	—	61.0	27.5
1976-77	—	—	—	—	—	—	—	—	57.1	38.9
1977-78	—	—	0.3	0.1	—	—	—	—	52.7	42.8
1978-79	—	—	0.3	0.2	—	—	—	—	65.5	31.7
1979-80	—	—	0.7	0.5	—	—	—	—	80.0	70.9
1980-81	—	—	0.6	0.5	—	—	—	—	70.0	65.6
1981-82	—	—	0.8	0.8	—	—	—	—	165.5	135.9
1982-83	—	—	0.7	0.7	—	—	—	—	136.5	86.6
1983-84	—	—	0.8	0.6	—	—	—	—	166.8	140.9
1984-85	—	—	2.4	1.0	—	—	—	—	219.9	161.5
1985-86	—	—	2.2	1.7	—	—	—	—	383.6	261.9
1986-87	—	—	2.7	2.7	—	—	—	—	363.8	389.8
1987-88	143.8	60.5	3.7	3.5	—	—	—	—	362.7	342.3
1988-89	312.0	137.9	5.7	4.6	8.1	3.4	—	—	660.2	442.0
1989-90	321.2	225.7	6.1	5.1	12.3	9.5	52.8	12.8	578.0	455.0
1990-91	331.6	167.0	9.8	7.3	11.0	11.4	85.0	39.2	688.0	427.0
1991-92	409.0	170.9	10.6	8.4	16.5	17.8	103.5	48.3	1515.0	1022.0
									(1115.0)	(972.0)
1992-93	760.9	486.3	9.2	10.2	23.4	22.9	125.0	59.8	1740.0	1395.0
									(1090.0)	(-945.0)
1993-94	1698.3	1006.6	7.4	9.4	29.7	22.4	159.5	78.8	1664.0	794.0
									(1464.0)	(594.0)
1994-95	3719.8	1440.7	13.4	13.3	120.3	97.9	229.3	137.2	1790.0	1343.3
									(1540.0)	(1143.3)
1995-96	5049.0	2464.6	29.8	15.4	53.6	47.1	271.6	166.9	2341.9	2529.7
									(2241.9)	(2379.7)
1996-97	—	—	30.5	20.7	16.8	24.6	303.5	182.8	2820.8	2960.6
1997-98	—	—	9.9	18.2	22.6	19.6	320.1	186.8	3472.6	3909.9
1998-99	—	—	10.7	10.4	19.4	18.1	211.2	132.3	4829.6	4824.9
1999-00	—	—	8.1	11.9	155.9	136.2	82.4	111.7	6825.5	5634.3
2000-01	—	—	3.6	3.3	229.9	189.6	105.6	60.6	10867.2	7095.0
2001-02	—	—	3.0	4.1	774.0	778.3	95.4	86.5	6741.5	8914.2
2002-03	—	—	1.5	1.5	390.5	394.0	84.1	94.7	4332.7	6205.8
2003-04	—	—	0	0	379.8	361.3	60.0	34.9	21974.0	15781.6
2004-05	—	—	0	0	—	—	110.6	71.9	9339.9	7954.1
2005-06P	—	—	0	0	—	—	133.0	88.0	15164.6	11199.5
2006-07P	—	—	0	0	—	—	245.4	120.2	18126.9	27017.0

Year	*UTI@@*		*GIC^*		*SFCs*		*SIDCs*		*Total*	
	Sanctions	*Disbursements*	*Sanctions*	*Disbursements*	*Sanctions*	*Disbursements*	*Sanctions*	*Disbursements*	*Sanctions*	*Disbursements*
1	22	23	24	25	26	27	28	29	30	31
1970-71	10.7	5.1	—	—	49.6	33.5	19.3	11.1	254.2	159.9
1971-72	15.0	1.6	—	—	64.1	39.6	23.6	14.4	342.7	191.4
1972-73	9.9	5.6	—	—	78.7	44.7	23.5	16.6	325.9	218.8
1973-74	7.7	7.7	—	—	103.1	54.6	27.9	20.6	446.7	301.6
1974-75	7.0	7.6	—	—	141.8	79.6	33.5	26.7	549.6	425.0
1975-76	7.8	4.9	—	—	155.5	98.8	37.5	26.4	648.3	435.2
1976-77	9.0	6.1	—	—	163.8	105.2	71.8	35.0	988.9	602.0
1977-78	26.5	15.8	—	—	166.1	107.4	87.9	44.8	1224.8	713.0
1978-79	50.7	20.1	—	—	200.7	135.0	98.3	60.1	1404.3	947.5
1979-80	74.8	63.9	66.0	52.0	263.8	184.8	157.7	85.3	2060.5	1352.2
1980-81	40.4	51.0	30.8	44.0	370.5	248.0	216.4	124.6	2926.9	1847.9
1981-82	85.5	62.7	50.1	33.7	509.6	317.7	299.6	191.1	3332.9	2532.0
1982-83	127.5	71.7	92.7	44.7	611.6	404.0	296.6	208.0	3358.5	2468.5
1983-84	165.8	139.3	108.5	84.5	644.9	435.5	364.6	236.5	4166.4	3138.4
1984-85	357.3	236.2	144.1	110.5	743.1	497.7	477.9	297.6	5550.7	3627.9
1985-86	696.6	528.9	153.0	107.3	1009.1	608.5	527.0	364.0	6532.6	4940.0
1986-87	465.0	417.6	153.3	131.6	1210.8	791.9	570.3	425.5	8118.4	5709.1
1987-88	966.0	707.2	98.3	103.5	1305.0	942.5	641.5	448.6	9554.5	7061.1
	(836.0)	(565.8)								
1988-89	1878.1	1054.6	122.6	115.4	1391.1	1055.2	722.1	472.1	11286.7	7700.8
	(1769.1)	(1033.1)								

1989-90	1202.8 (1070.3)	1017.5 (798.5)	211.2	179.6	1514.2	1156.5	691.0	545.2	14400.9	9639.7
1990-91	2809.6 (2296.1)	2241.2 (1713.7)	336.8	170.3	1863.9	1270.8	823.7	598.3	19202.4	12810.1
1991-92	3814.1 (3156.1)	2906.4 (2401.9)	695.5	280.1	2190.3	1536.8	1009.0	678.7	22394.6	16260.0
1992-93	10302.5 (9105.0)	7469.4 (6229.8)	559.3	536.0	2015.3	1557.4	973.1	694.7	33196.1	23150.3
1993-94	8332.6 (7627.0)	6612.4 (5933.1)	824.0	470.3	1908.8	1563.4	917.9	700.8	40987.0	26624.3
1994-95	7522.8 (6628.8)	4791.2 (4516.2)	688.5	379.2	2702.4	1800.9	1588.6	1051.0	59275.3	33568.1
1995-96	3685.7	3006.5	1216.4	965.2	4188.5	2961.1	1951.2	1188.7	64162.7	38649.5
1996-97	3633.1	3237.3	1273.3	925.4	3544.8	2782.7	1811.1	1501.8	54641.2	42656.5
1997-98	4532.8	3557.9	1172.8	1143.8	2926.1	2110.2	1795.1	1416.2	77091.6	53647.9
1998-99	3898.6	3435.9	1314.7$	1386.2$	1864.4	1624.7	2280.5	2176.3	83695.6	58329.5
1999-00	6845.0	5162.1	2141.7$	1967.6$	2395.2	1842.6	1648.2	1741.2	101917.8	68594.1
2000-01	6770.1	4599.9	1046.8$	1097.9$	2911.4	1979.0	2080.1	1664.4	120548.1	75363.6
2001-02	991.0	1269.6	1505.2$	1465.5$	2210.2	1749.6	—	—	75088.5	58734.7
2002-03	307.4	414.7	1325.0	1281.9	1855.9	1454.0	923.7	1250.0	28310.9	26704.6
2003-04	—	—	1223.4	1207.1	1133.8	856.8	—	—	40758.6	30172.7
2004-05	—	—	1063.8	1017.4	—	—	—	—	30403.9	21505.8
2005-06P	—	—	393.0	571.2	—	—	—	—	27665.4	38655.8
2006-07P	—	—	632.3	840.1	—	—	—	—	31239.4	21145.5

P: Provisional.

@ The IRBI was renamed as Industrial Investments Bank of India Ltd. (IIBI) with effect from March 27, 1997.

SCSCI Ltd. was merged with ICICI KLtd. with efect from April 1, 1996.

* RCTC was renamed as IVCF with effect from february 28, 2000.

** TDICI was renamed as ICICI venture Funds Management Company Ltd. with effect from October 8, 1998.

^ Data include general Insurance Corporation of India, New India assurance Company Ltd. United India Insurance Company Ltd. and Oriental Insurance Company Ltd.

$ Includes public sector bonds.

$$ Pursuant to the Industrial Development Bank (Transfer of Undertaking and repeal) Act, 2003, IDBI Act was repealed on October 1, 2004 and the accounting period for FY 2003-04 was extended by six months up to September 30, 2004.

@@ The UTI Act 1963 was repealed in 2002-03 and UTI has been reorganised into two separate institutions. As such UTI ceased to be an AIFI.

^^ Following the merger of ICICI with ICICI Bank in 2002-03, ICICI ceases to be an AIR.

Note: 1. Data in parentheses indicate assistance net of inter-institutional flows which are reckoned for the purpose of total assistance.

2. IDBI's data up to 1989-90 include assistance to small sector.
3. SIDBI commenced operations in April 1990, TDICI in July 1988, IFCI in February 1989 and GIC in 1973.
4. SCICI's assistance for 1987-88 covers the period from January 1987 to March 1988.
5. RCTC's assistance up to 1987 relates to the calendar year; for 1988-89 to January-March and from 1989-90 onwards to April-March.
6. Totals are adjusted for inter-institutional flows.

Source: Report on Development Banking, Industrial Development Bank of India and respective financial nstitutions.

(d) BHFL (Birla Home Finance Limited)

BHFL offers easy title for registration of the property or land purchased and easy upgrade loans for renovation of the existing house, which has been purchased or constructed at least one year ago. The renovation can be in the form of flooring, tiling, plumbing, paint, polish, etc., easy extend loans for extensions of an existing house, easy home loans for outright purchase of a ready built house, easy build loans for construction of house on self-acquired or inherited vacant plot of land, and easy Bridge Loans for purchase of a ready built house, when an individual already owns a property, which would be sold on getting possession of the new one.

(e) Maharishi Housing

Maharishi Housing Finance Corporation Ltd., a company from Maharishi Group, started in 1997 also caters to home loans. One of the key attractions of Maharishi Housing is its 35-year loan repayment scheme.

(f) Others

Other key housing finance providers in the private sector are Sundaram Home Finance, Hometrust Housing, Gruh Finance, Weizmann Homes, GLFL Housing, etc.

10.5 NATIONAL HOUSING BANK

The National Housing Bank was set up in 1988 as a subsidiary of Reserve Bank of India. It is a principal agency promoting housing finance institutions both at local and regional levels and provides financial and other support to such institutions.

10.5.1. Business of the National Housing Bank

The National Housing Bank guarantees the financial obligations of housing finance institutions and underwrites the issue of stocks, shares, bonds, debentures and securities of these institutions. It is responsible for undertaking research and surveys on construction techniques and other studies relating to or connected with shelter, housing and human settlement. It does the business of formulating of one or more schemes, for the purpose of mobilisation of resources and extension of credit for housing. It is also responsible for coordinating with the Life Insurance Corporation of India, the Unit Trust of India, the General Insurance Corporation of India and other financial institutions. Besides providing technical and administrative assistance to housing finance institutions, it acts as an agent of the Central Government, the State Government or the Reserve Bank or of any other authority as authorised by the Reserve Bank.

10.5.2. Borrowings and Acceptance of Deposits by National Housing Bank

The National Housing Bank Act, 1987 defines that the National Housing Bank, for the purpose of carrying out its functions, can issue and sell bonds and debentures with or without the guarantee of the Central Government. It can borrow money from the Central Government and from any other authority or organisation or institution approved by the Government. The details regarding NHB's equity participation in HFCs are given below:

Table 10.3 NHB's participation in equity of HFCs *(₹ in crore)*

Sl. No.	Name of the HFC	Face value	Investment as on 31.03.2002
1	Andhrabank Housing Finance Ltd.	1.90	4.23
2	BOB Housing Finance Ltd.	4.94	4.94
3	Canfin Home Ltd.	0.50	1.75
4	Centbank Home Finance Ltd.	1.60	1.60
5	GRUH Finance Ltd.	0.45	0.85
6	Vysya Bank Housing Finance Ltd.	0.38	0.56
7	Vibank Housing Finance Ltd.	1.20	1.20
	TOTAL	—	15.13

10.5.3. Power to Acquire Rights

The National Housing Bank has the right to acquire, by transfer or assignment, the rights and interests of any housing finance institution in relation to any loan or advance made, or any amount recoverable by such institution, either whole or in part.

10.5.4. Access to Records or Power to Inspect

The National Housing Bank has free access to all records of any housing finance institution, which seek credit facilities from the National Housing Bank. It has access to records of any person who seek credit facilities from such housing finance institutions. On the direction of the Reserve Bank of India, it can inspect at any time the accounts, documents and other books of the financial institutions, to which the Bank has provided loans, advances or granted any financial assistance.

10.5.5. Advisory Services

The National Housing Bank can provide advisory services to the Central and State Governments, local authorities and other agencies, in respect of formulation of overall policies aimed at promoting the growth of housing and housing finance institutions. It can advise the government to bring up a legislation relating to matters having a bearing on shelter, housing and human settlement.

10.5.6. Funds

The National Housing Bank on the advice of the Reserve Bank of India has established a fund called the General Fund, through which all the payments of the National Housing Bank are made.

10.6 MINISTRY OF URBAN DEVELOPMENT

With effect from 9-4-1999, the Ministry of Urban Affairs and Employment came to be known as Ministry of Urban Development. The Ministry located in Nirman Bhawan, New Delhi - 110001, is responsible for formulating policies, monitoring programmes in the areas of urban development and sanitation, and planning and coordinating in matters of Urban Development. These although are subjects covered under the state list; but the Government of India plays a coordinating and monitoring role and also supports these programmes through Central Sector Schemes, Institutional Finance and expertise. In addition to this, the Ministry has been entrusted with the responsibility of planning and coordination in Urban Transport matters in India along with meeting to the demands of Printing and Stationery requirements of all the Central Government Ministries or Departments and stocking and selling of Government publications.

10.6.1. Responsibilities

The Ministry of Urban Development is also responsible for construction and maintenance of Central Government buildings, including residential accommodation, with the exception of those under the Ministry of Defense, Atomic Energy, Railways and Communication. It also manages the Central Government land or property, most of which is confined to Delhi and some other metropolitan cities. These functions are discharged through the agencies of the Central Public Works Department, which has field organisations spread all over the country and Land and Development Office located in Delhi.

10.6.2. National Urban Policy

The Ministry is in the process of formulating a National Urban Policy keeping in view the recommendations of the National Commission on Urbanisation. The Policy will take into account suggestions received from State Governments, State Urbanisation strategy papers prepared in the context of Integrated Development of Small and Medium Towns scheme and the decentralisation reforms as envisaged in the Constitution (74th Amendment Act, 1992). The Planning Commission has constituted a National Task Force on Perspective and Policy in 1995. The recommendations of the Task force will form an important input for the National Urbanisation Policy.

10.6.3. Integrated Development of Small and Medium Towns Scheme

In order to improve economic and physical infrastructure, provide essential facilities and services, and also to slow down the growth of large cities by developing small and medium towns through increased investments in these towns, the centrally sponsored scheme of Integrated Development of Small and Medium Towns (IDMST) was initiated in the year 1979-80. The scheme is being continued with timely amendments and modifications. Investment in the development of small urban centers would also help in reducing migration to large cities and support the growth of surrounding rural areas as well.

10.6.4. Mega Cities Scheme

The Mega Cities Scheme, launched in 1993-94, provides funds to State Government for infrastructure development in the ratio of 25 : 25 through a designated nodal agency and the balance 50% is to be met by the States from financial institutions or accessing the capital market.

10.6.5. Public Grievance Cell

The Department of Administrative Reforms and Public Grievances in the Ministry of Urban Development ensures redress of the grievances of public under the overall supervision of Joint Secretary (Administration) who acts as Director of Public Grievances.

10.6.6. Other Offices under the Ministry

Under its administrative control, the Ministry of Urban Development has three Attached and four Subordinate Offices, one Public Sector Undertaking and five Statutory or Autonomous Bodies.

10.6.7. Exemption of Tax on Income

The National Housing Bank is not liable to pay income tax or any other tax in respect of its income, profits or gains derived.

10.7 HOUSING FINANCIAL SERVICES

10.7.1. Project Finance

In order to facilitate flow of credit into the housing sector, the Bank has formulated schemes to extend project finance to Public Housing and Area Development Agencies. Project loans are provided to public agencies set up by Central or State Governments and authorised to borrow funds, and provide security for the same.

(a) Project Types

The projects financed by NHB fall into three categories:

I. Land Development and Shelter Projects (LDSP) (Costing > ₹ 2 crores)

II. Housing Infrastructure Projects (HIP) (Costing > ₹ 2 crores)

III. Slum Redevelopment Projects (SRP) (Costing > ₹ 25 lakhs) (including EWS and LIG Categories)

(b) Guidelines for Project Finance

Scheme for Guaranteeing Bonds of HFCS

Housing Finance companies depend to a great extent on refinance assistance from NHB. However, the extension of refinance assistance by NHB is constrained by various factors like NHB's own (Net Owned Funds) NOF, HFCs' borrowing power, etc. In addition, in the present liberalised environment, HFCs prefer to raise resources directly from market in order to eliminate the cost of intermediation. Besides NHB refinance, HFCs mainly depend upon term loans from banks and public deposits. Of late, the maturity profile of public deposits has been shortening leading to asset-liability mismatches for HFCs. One way to overcome this problem is floatation of bonds/debentures having a longer maturity period of say five to seven years. To attract the investors at competitively low rates, such bonds/debentures should have sufficiently high rating. Many of the HFCs have not been able to float bonds/debentures because of the lower credit rating from the rating agencies for various reasons including the inherent mismatch between assets and liabilities. NHB's intervention in this area was considered critical and accordingly a scheme was introduced to extend guarantee to the bonds/debentures to be floated by HFCs meeting certain laid down criteria. Under the scheme, NHB will provide top ended guarantee relating to the repayment of principal and interest which will provide necessary credit enhancement and will enable HFCs to acquire higher credit rating leading to competitive pricing of these instruments. The salient features of the scheme are as under:

Scope of the Scheme

The scheme envisages provision of guarantee by NHB to the investors regarding repayment of principal and interest during the top end (say last two years) irrespective of the repayment schedule fixed by the HFC and the guarantee shall not exceed 67% of the total amount to be raised and the interest thereof.

Terms and Conditions for Guarantee

The HFC desirous of availing the guarantee from NHB shall comply with the following terms and conditions:

(i) The bond issue shall carry at least a rating of 'AA' from an approved rating agency. However, the Bank may consider providing the guarantee in the case of an instrument being rated with subject to the HFC meeting the following requirements:

  (a) NOF shall be ₹ 30 crores or more

  (b) Net NPA shall be less than 2%

  (c) The HFC shall have earned profit during the last three years or since its inception if it is in existence for less than 3 years

  (d) The overdue for more than 3 months should not exceed 10% of the aggregate demand for the year

  (e) The promoters and the management of the HFC are found to be satisfactory

  (f) The HFC shall have complied with all the provisions of the Housing Finance Companies (NHB) Directions, 1989 as amended from time to time and all the provisions of the guidelines on prudential norms.

(ii) The maturity of the bonds/debentures shall be for a period of five years to begin with and,

(iii) The market shall determine the coupon rate.

Exposure Norms

For the purpose of extending guarantee to the HFCs, exposure limits will be fixed by NHB along with the annual refinance limit. The aggregate amount of the guarantee in a year can be maximum up to the actual amount of the bond to be floated at a time or the annual refinance limit provided in a particular year, whichever is less. The overall borrowing including the amount to be mobilised through the bond/debenture issue shall not be more than 7 times the NOF of the company.

Minimum Sise of Each Issue

The minimum size for each issue should be ₹ 10 crores and it will be subject to the overall borrowing powers fixed under the Housing Finance Companies (NHB) Directions, 1989, as amended from time to time.

Security

The HFCs desirous of availing the guarantee will have to create a floating charge on the assets equivalent to 125% of the principal amount in favour of NHB. In case the HFC offers any other security in addition to a floating charge for its existing borrowing or is in a position to provide further security, the same shall, also be asked for. In case of the HFCs, where personal or corporate guarantee has been obtained, the same shall be extended to cover the guarantee for the bonds/debentures.

Guarantee Fee

For extending the guarantee, the HFCs shall be charged 75 basis points per year of the amount to be floated as guarantee commission and this shall be payable upfront.

Creation of Reserves

The HFC shall create appropriate bond/debenture redemption reserves as may be laid down under the Companies Act from time to time.

Returns

The HFC shall furnish such returns/information as may be laid down from time to time for the purpose of availing refinance.

10.7.2. New Regulations on Housing Finance (2007)

In pursuance of National Housing Policy of Central Government, Reserve Bank of India has been facilitating the flow of credit to housing sector. During last three years, the housing sector has emerged as one of the sectors attracting a large quantum of bank finance. The current focus of RBI's regulation is to ensure orderly growth of housing loan portfolio of banks

Direct Housing Finance

Direct Housing Finance refers to the finance provided to individuals or groups of individuals including co-operative societies.

Banks are free to evolve their own guidelines with the approval of their Boards on aspects such as security, margin, age of dwelling units, repayment schedule, etc.

Other Guidelines

The following types of bank finance may be included under Direct Housing Finance:

(i) Bank finance extended to a person who is already owning a house in town/village where he resides, for buying/constructing a second house in the same or other town/village for the purpose of self-occupation.

(ii) Bank finance extended for purchase of a house by a borrower who proposes to let it out on rental basis on account of his posting outside the headquarters or because he has been provided accommodation by his employer.

(iii) Bank finance extended to a person who proposes to buy an old house where he is presently residing as a tenant.

(iv) Bank finance granted only for purchase of a plot, provided a declaration is obtained from the borrower that he intends to construct a house on the said plot, with the help of bank finance or otherwise, within such period as may be laid down by the banks themselves.

(v) Supplementary finance

(a) Banks may consider requests for additional finance within the overall ceiling for carrying out alterations/ additions/repairs to the house/flat already financed by them.

(b) In the case of individuals who might have raised funds for construction/acquisition of accommodation from other sources and need supplementary finance, banks may extend such finance after obtaining *pari passu* or second mortgage charge over the property mortgaged in favour of other lenders and/or against such other security, as they may deem appropriate.

Indirect Housing Finance

General

Banks should ensure that their indirect housing finance is channelled by way of term loans to housing finance institutions, housing boards, other public housing agencies, etc., primarily for augmenting the supply of serviced land and constructed units. It should also be ensured that the supply of plots/houses is time bound and public agencies do not utilise the bank loans merely for acquisition of land. Similarly, serviced plots should be sold by these agencies to cooperative societies, professional developers and individuals with a stipulation that the houses should be constructed thereon within a reasonable time, not exceeding three years. For this purpose, the banks may take advantage of various guidelines issued by NHB for augmenting the supply of serviced land and constructed units.

Lending to Housing Intermediary Agencies

Lending to Housing Finance Institutions

(i) Banks may grant term loans to housing finance institutions taking into account (long-term) debt-equity ratio, track record, recovery performance and other relevant factors.

(ii) In terms of NHB guidelines, housing finance companies' total borrowings, whether by way of deposits, issue of debentures/bonds, loans and advances from banks or from financial institutions including any loans obtained from NHB, should not exceed 16 times of their net owned funds (*i.e.*, paid-up capital and free reserves less accumulated balance of loss, deferred revenue expenditure and intangible assets).

(iii) All housing finance companies registered with NHB are eligible to apply for refinance from NHB and will be eligible subject to the refinance policy. The quantum of term loan to be sanctioned to them will not be linked to net owned fund as NHB has already prescribed the above referred ceiling on total borrowing of housing finance companies. A list of housing finance companies registered with NHB may be obtained by the banks directly from NHB or download from www.nhb.org.in.

Lending to Housing Boards and Other Agencies

Banks may extend term loans to state level housing boards and other public agencies. However, in order to develop a healthy housing finance system, while doing so, the banks must not only keep in view the past performance of these agencies in the matter of recovery from the beneficiaries but they should also stipulate that the Boards will ensure prompt and regular recovery of loan installments from the beneficiaries.

Financing of Land Acquisition

In view of the need to increase the availability of land and house sites for increasing the housing stock in the country, banks may extend finance to public agencies and not private builders for acquisition and development of land, provided it is a part of the complete project, including development of infrastructure such as water systems, drainage, roads, provision of electricity, etc. Such credit may be extended by way of term loans. The project should be completed as early as possible and, in any case, within three years, so as to ensure quick recycling of bank funds for optimum results. If the project covers construction of houses, credit extended therefore in respect of individual beneficiaries should be on the same terms and conditions as stipulated for direct finance.

Terms and Conditions for Lending to Housing Intermediary Agencies

(i) In order to enhance the flow of resources to housing sector, term loans may be granted by banks to housing intermediary agencies against the direct loans sanctioned/proposed to be sanctioned by the latter, irrespective of the per borrower size of the loan extended by these agencies and such term loans would be reckoned for the purpose of achievement of their housing finance allocation.

(ii) Banks can grant term loans to housing intermediary agencies against the direct loans sanctioned/proposed to be sanctioned by them to Non-resident Indians also. However, banks should ensure that housing finance intermediary agencies being financed by them, are authorised by RBI to grant housing loans to NRIs as all housing finance intermediaries are not authorised by RBI to provide housing finance to NRIs. Further, such finance granted by banks to housing finance intermediary agencies against the latters' on-lending to NRIs will not be treated as housing finance for the purpose of scheme of yearly allocation of housing finance applicable to banks.

(iii) Banks have freedom to charge interest rates to housing intermediary agencies without reference to Benchmark Prime Lending Rates (BPLR).

Term Loans to Private Builders

In view of the important role played by professional builders as providers of construction services in the housing field, especially where land is acquired and developed by State Housing Boards and other public agencies, commercial banks may extend credit to private builders on commercial terms by way of loans linked to each specific project. However, the banks are not permitted to extend fund based or non-fund based facilities to private builders for acquisition of land even as part of a housing project. The period of credit for loans extended by banks to private builders may be decided by banks themselves based on their commercial judgement subject to usual safeguards and after obtaining such security as banks may deem appropriate. Such credit may be extended to builders of repute, employing professionally qualified personnel. It should be ensured, through close monitoring, that no part of such funds is used for any speculation in land.

Care should also be taken to see that prices charged from the ultimate beneficiaries do not include any speculative element, that is, prices should be based only on the documented price of land, the actual cost of construction and a reasonable profit margin.

It is advised that banks adhere to the National Building Code (NBC) formulated by the Bureau of Indian Standards (BIS) in view of the importance of safety of buildings especially against natural disasters. Banks' may consider this aspect for incorporation in their loan policies.

Housing Loans under Priority Sector

Banks may refer to the Master Circular on Lending to Priority Sectors issued by Rural Planning and Credit Department.

RBI Refinance

Finance provided by the banks would not be eligible for refinance from Reserve Bank.

Construction Activities not Eligible for Bank Credit

Banks should not grant finance for construction of buildings meant purely for Government/Semi-government offices, including Municipal and Panchayat offices. However, banks may grant loans for activities, which will be refinanced by institutions like NABARD.

Projects undertaken by public sector entities which are not corporate bodies (*i.e.*, public sector undertakings which are not registered under Companies Act or which are not Corporations established under the relevant statute) may not be financed by banks. Even in respect of projects undertaken by corporate bodies, as defined above, banks should satisfy themselves that the project is run on commercial lines and that bank finance is not in lieu of or to substitute budgetary resources envisaged for the project. The loan could, however, supplement budgetary resources if such supplementing was contemplated in the project design. Thus, in the case of a housing project, where the project is run on commercial lines, and the Government is interested in promoting the project either for the benefit of the weaker sections of the society or otherwise, and a part of the project cost is met by the Government through subsidies made available and/or contributions to the capital of the institutions taking up the project, the bank finance should be restricted to an amount arrived at after reducing from the total project cost the amount of subsidy/capital contribution receivable from the Government and any other resources proposed to be made available by the Government.

Banks had, in the past, sanctioned term loans to Corporations set up by Government like State Police Housing Corporation, for construction of residential quarters for allotment to employees where the loans were envisaged to be repaid out of budgetary allocations. As these projects cannot be considered to be run on commercial lines, it would not be in order for banks to grant loans to such projects.

REPORTING

Banks should compile the data relating to Housing Finance at half-yearly intervals on the lines of format given in *Annexure 1* and keep it ready for being made available to the bank's internal inspectors/RBI's inspectors.

For the purpose of monitoring the macro-level performance of the commercial banks in disbursement of housing finance, banks should submit, on a quarterly basis, details of disbursements made by them towards housing finance to Department of Banking Supervision, RBI, Central Office, World Trade Centre, Cuffe Parade, Mumbai 400 005, as per the format given in *Annexure 2* within 20 days from the close of the respective quarter.

Housing loans taken over from other banks should not be included in the quarterly statement as disbursements.

Home Loan Account Scheme (HLAS) of NHB

Foreclosure of Loans Obtained from Other Sources

Under the HLAS, a member of HLAS is eligible for a loan after subscription to the scheme for a minimum period of 5 years. The member has to declare while joining the scheme/availing loan that he/ she does not own a house/flat. However, a member may acquire a house or a flat from a public agency/cooperative/private builder by obtaining a loan from a bank at the normal rate of interest or from friends and relatives or through a hire-purchase scheme of Housing Board/Development Authority. Thereafter, when the member becomes eligible for a loan under HLAS, he/she may approach the bank for such a loan to repay the loan(s) raised earlier from other sources.

There is no objection to bank loans under HLAS being utilised for foreclosing loan secured earlier from other sources, as a special case.

Classification of Deposits/Loans under HLAS

Under HLAS, the participating bank is required to accept deposits on behalf of NHB and make use of these deposits by way of refinance under any scheme approved by NHB from time to time. The surplus funds, if any, not so utilised (i.e., excess of deposits over refinance) can either be remitted by the participating bank to NHB or retained by it, subject to compliance with the statutory reserve requirements as under:

(i) The deposits under the HLA Scheme are on a recurring basis; and they should be treated as 'time' liabilities, subject to reserve requirements under Section 42(1) of the Reserve Bank of India Act, 1934 as also under Section 24 of the Banking Regulation Act, 1949 and included under item II(a)(ii) of Form 'A'.

(ii) In terms of sub-clause (ii) of clause (c) of the Explanation to Sub-section (1) of Section 42 of the RBI Act, as amended by Clause 3 of the Second Schedule to the National Housing Bank Act, 1987, 'liabilities' will not include any loan taken from NHB. Hence, the deposits utilised as refinance from NHB should be deducted from the total deposits received under the HLA Scheme while including the amount under item II(a)(ii) of Form 'A'.

Bank's Exposure to Real Estate Sector

While the development of real estate is welcome, there is a need for the banks to curb the excessive risk lending by exercising selectivity and strengthening the loan approval process. Banks should ensure that the borrowers should have obtained prior permission from government, local governments, other statutory authorities for the project, wherever required. While the proposals could be sanctioned in normal course, the disbursements should be made only after the borrower has obtained requisite clearances from the government authorities.

Risk Weight on Housing Finance

Banks extending housing loans to individuals against the mortgage of residential housing properties were required to assign risk weight of 75% on such loans which were fully secured by mortgage of residential properties and investments in Mortgage Backed Securities (MBS) of Housing Finance Companies (HFCs), recognised and supervised by NHB. In view of the fact that banks have been advised from time to time to tighten their credit administration in this area in particular, it has been decided to reduce the risk weight on the residential housing loans to individuals from the existing 75% to 50% as a temporary measure. This dispensation will be applicable for loans up to ₹ 20 lakhs and will be reviewed after one year, keeping in view the default experience and other relevant factors. Similarly, the risk weight for banks' investment in mortgage backed securities, which are backed by housing loans which would now qualify for 50% risk weight, and are issued by the housing finance companies regulated by the National Housing Banks is also reduced from 75% to 50%. In all other cases, it will be 100%. However, the risk weight for commercial real estate exposure has been raised to 125% on July 26, 2005 and further to 150% on May 25, 2006.

Table 10.4 **Refinance Disbursal in 2001-02** (*₹ in crore*)

Institutions	Disbursements during 2001-02	Disbursements during 2001-02	Cumulative during disbursements up to June 30, 2002
Scheduled Banks	86.35	105.67	434.66
Cooperative Sector Institutions	219.15	140.57	1285.89
Housing Finance Companies	719.30	761.98	5530.81
Total	1024.80*	1008.22*	7251.36*

10.8 TYPES OF HOME LOANS

There are a variety of home loans available. They are:

1. Home Purchase Loan	This is the common loan for purchasing a home.
2. Home Improvement Loan	This loan is given for implementing repair works and renovations to your home.
3. Home Construction Loan	This loan is available for the construction of a new home.
4. Home Extension Loan	It is given for expanding or extending an existing home. For example, addition of an extra room, etc.
5. Home Conversion Loan	It is made available for those who have financed the present home with a Home Loan and wish to purchase and move to another home for which some additional funds are required. Through a Home Conversion Loan, the existing loan is transferred to the new home, including the additional amount required, eliminating the need for pre-payment of the previous loan.
6. Land Purchase Loan	It is sanctioned for purchase of land, for both home construction or investment purposes.
7. Bridge Loan	The Bridge Loan is designed for people who wish to sell the existing home and purchase another. The bridge loan helps finance the new home, until a buyer is found for the old home.

8. Balance Transfer Loan	Balance Transfer — Loans help you pay off an existing home loan with a higher interest rate, and avail of a loan with a lower rate of interest.
9. Refinance Loan	This loan helps you pay off the debt you have incurred from private sources, such as relatives and friends, for the purchase of your present home.
10. Stamp Duty Loan	This loan is sanctioned to pay the stamp duty amount that needs to be paid on the purchase of a property.
11. Loans to NRIs	This loan is tailored for the requirements of NRIs wishing to build or buy a home in India.

10.8.1. Some Innovative Home Loan Schemes

1. Step Up Repayment Facility (SURF)

The objective of SURF is to provide the customer with a repayment schedule, which is linked to his expected growth in income. It also helps a customer get a larger amount of loan as compared to the loan under the normal housing loan. The customer can avail of a higher amount of loan and pay lower EMIs in the initial years. Subsequently, the repayment is accelerated proportionately with the assumed increase in his income.

2. Flexible Loan Instalment Plan (FLIP)

This product offers a customised solution to suit the needs of customers whose repayment capacity is likely to alter during the term of the loan. The loan is structured in such a way that the EMI is higher during the initial years and subsequently decreases in the latter part proportionate to the reduced income of the customer. For example, if the husband has 10 years of service left and the wife has 15 years to retire, then a 15-year loan can be structured such that a higher EMI (serviced out of both the incomes) is paid for first 10 years and a lower EMI (serviced out of only wife's income) is paid for first 10 years and a lower EMI (serviced out of only wife's income) is paid for the next 5 years.

3. Balloon Payment

Balloon payment is an enhancement tool, which helps in increasing the loan eligibility of the customer without increasing the EMI by assigning securities like National Savings Certificate (NSC), LIC policies, etc. to HDFC. The present value of the maturity amount of assigned securities is combined with the loan amount to arrive at the enhanced loan eligibility. Under this facility, the EMI is calculated on the net loan amount (*i.e.*, total loan less the present value of the maturity value of the securities).

10.8.2. The Housing Finance Scenario: 2001-2002

1. Though there were certain inherent problems such as scarcity of long-term funding, inelastic supply of land, legal issues related to land mortgaging and foreclosure, but still the housing sector continued to grow robustly during the year 2001-02. The disbursement of housing loans kept a fast pace and the amount disbursed soared high. Both the banking sector and the housing finance companies (HFCs) infused around ₹ 15,000 crores each in the year 2001-02.
2. The NHB modified the Housing Finance Companies (NHB) Directions, 1989 and the same was notified as Housing Finance Companies (NHB) Directions, 2001 on December 29, 2001. The new directions include the guidelines on prudential norms as well.
3. The NHB issued the Guidelines for Asset-liability Management for the HFCs in June 2002.
4. The National Housing Bank (Recovery of Dues of the Approved Institutions) General Regulations, 2002 was notified on May 8, 2002 providing procedure for transfer by sale, lease or otherwise of the mortgaged property by the recovery officer.

5. For the fifth consecutive year, the targets under the Golden Jubilee Rural Housing Finance Scheme of NHB were successfully achieved.
6. NHB introduced a scheme for extending guarantee to the bonds to be floated by the HFCs. This Scheme is aimed at providing credit enhancement for the long-term resource mobilisation instruments of HFCs.
7. The rapid growth in the housing loan sector is likely to continue in 2004-2005. The housing finance market is expected to grow at a compounded annual growth rate of over 30% in the same period.

10.8.3. Future Trends

It is estimated that by 2010 and with the current rate of growth in population, India would require at an average of 2.5 million to 3 million additional dwelling constructions annually. Presently, only a meagre 20% of India's new housing units are financed through formal housing finance institutions, although there is a remarkable prospective to augment the figure of home credit.

With Government's timely intervention, housing finance on its own has become a major industry in India. With the semi-government and nationalised banks, the private sector too has shown a tremendous interest in the race. With various plans to suit one's necessity and with attractive interest rates, these housing finance institutions offer most attractive finance options for home seekers.

10.9 REVIEW QUESTIONS

Short Answer Questions

1. What is the main reason for lending housing loan?
2. What are the preconditions to be fulfilled by one to borrow housing loan?
3. Briefly describe the role being played by the public sector institutions in providing housing loan.
4. Write a note on private sector housing finance.
5. List the various roles performed by NHB.

Essay Type Questions

1. Explain the role of National Housing Bank in house financing. Examine critically.
2. Explain the present position of house financing in India. Give also your suggestions in this regard.
3. Critically examine the House Loan Account Scheme of National Housing Bank.
4. Explain in brief various house financing schemes available in the country.
5. Explain the institutional structure of housing industry along with its weaknesses.

CHAPTER 11

Securitisation

Objectives

The student, after studying the chapter, should be able to:

- State the meaning of the word Securitisation.
- Initiate the process of Securitisation with a financial institution segregating, and then pooling the receivables
- Identify the reason for Securitisation of debt instruments
- Securitise various types of instruments.
- Know pricing strategies for securitised instruments.
- Give an account of Securitisation in India.

Structure:

11.1 INTRODUCTION

Securitisation is the process of transforming assets into securities. A financial institution can convert illiquid assets into capital market instruments by pooling like assets, and then repackaging the underlying cash flows to make them more attractive to investors. By creating securities, a financial institution gains access to financing sources. Therefore, securitisation is a pooling of "homogeneous", "financial", "cash flow producing", "illiquid" assets and issuing claims on those assets in the form of marketable securities. The higher yield associated with these securities attracts investors who are willing to bear incremental credit, prepayment and liquidity risk. The fundamental principle in securitisation is specific identification of risks and allocation of the same to various parties who are best able to manage those risks. As defined by the recent ordinance:

"Securitisation" means acquisition of financial assets by any securitisation company or reconstruction company from any originator, whether by raising of funds by such securitisation company or reconstruction company from qualified institutional buyers by issue of security receipts representing undivided interest in such financial assets or otherwise.

The balance sheet of a bank shows its loans on assets side. Such loans are financed out of deposits collected from numerous investors. Deposit is shown on the liability side of the balance sheet. An increase in loans portfolio of a bank is possible through an increase in deposits or through borrowings from the market. The market borrowings, on the other hand, cannot be used for lending long-term funds. They are meant for meeting day-to-day shortfall. Therefore, the size of loans portfolio of a bank is directly related to its quantum of deposits. Supposing there is a demand for bank loan, it may exceed the amount of deposits collected. What should a bank do? An answer to this question has been found in securitisation of debt. This is a sensible way and involves sale of assets, *i.e.*, sale of existing debt portfolio on a bank's balance sheet.

Example

ABC Bank has lent ₹ 5,00,000/- to buy a car at the rate of interest of 16% to Mr. Prakash. One Mr. Rakesh approaches the bank for another ₹ 5,00,000/- for a four-wheeler loan. The bank has no funds to lend and cannot lend beyond this existing debt-equity ratio of the bank. One way out is to mortgage the asset (old debt/loan of ₹ 5,00,000) in a willing lender's favour and raise resources which can after re-lent (in this case to Mr. Rakesh). It amounts to selling an old loan to create a fresh loan. However, it is difficult, in the absence of a secondary market, to locate such a lender and hence to mortgage the assets. How does one create secondary market for such loan asset? The banks have thought of securitising old debts instead of selling them. This is done by selling old debt in the form of securities of different denominations and varying maturities. These securities are backed by the assets (car) against which earlier loans had been made. Investors buy these securities according to their percentage regarding maturity pattern and return on these securities.

Bond or Debenture Issue vs. Securitisation

Unlike a traditional bond issue, the repayment of funds raised through securitisation is not an obligation of the originator, or the finance company issuing the securitised instrument. In a straight bond or debenture issue, in the event of the company going bust, the investors would have a tough time getting their funds back. However, if one invests in a securitised instrument, investors are assured of interest payments even if the finance company goes bust, as the securitised loans are separated from the finance company's books through a SPV (Special Purpose Vehicle) which holds these assets. At the same time, as securitised instruments can be traded, the investor is provided with liquidity as the securitised bond can be sold in the market.

11.2 PROCESS OF SECURITISATION

The Securitisation process begins with a financial institution segregating, and then pooling receivables. In the usual ABS transaction, a wide variety of asset types are eligible to be pooled, including credit card receivables, auto loans, or consumer installment loans typically, anything other than mortgages. (Mortgages tend to be pooled and sold separately as mortgage-backed securities.) The only requirement is that each asset pool must be homogeneous with respect to credit, maturity, and interest rate risk. Size and diversity of ABS (Asset Backed Securities) asset pools tend to minimise interest rate sensitivity.

After pooling, a financial institution sells the selected assets to a special purpose vehicle. This special purpose vehicle, or SPV, is responsible for both the financial re-engineering of the underlying cash flows and the sale of securities to investors.

While there are various legal and accounting implications of the chosen SPV structure, the originating financial institution is generally looking for a "true sale" of the asset pool. True sale allows the financial institution to remove assets from its books, and obviates its need to hold capital against them. Making the SPV a bankruptcy-remote trust facilitates the financial institution receiving off-balance-sheet treatment. (Bankruptcy-remote means that securities sold from the trust wouldn't be affected by the bankruptcy of the originating financial institution).

Chart 11.1

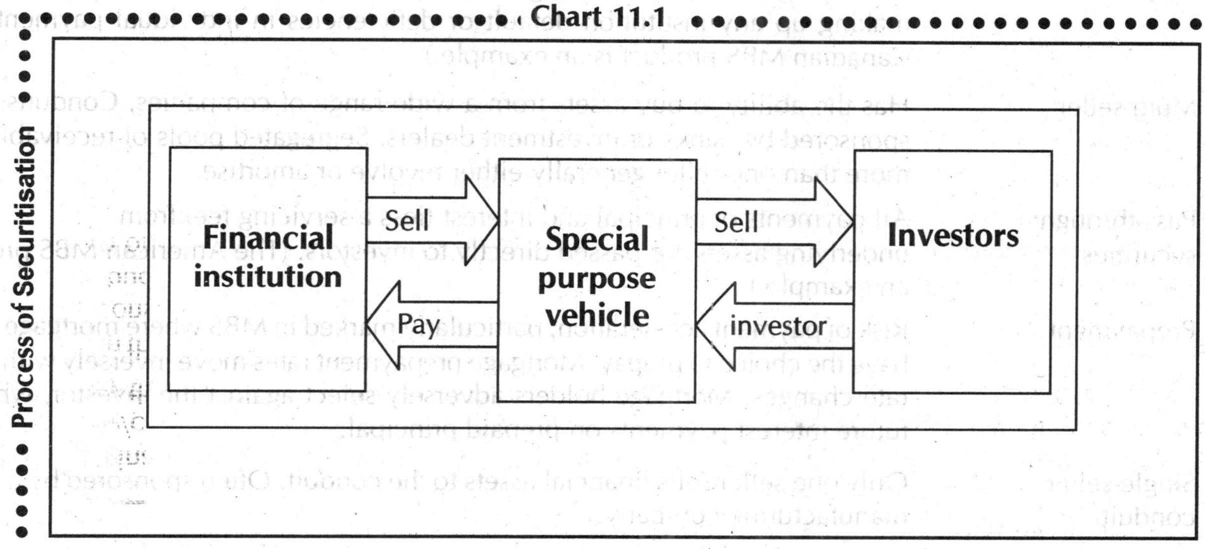

An asset becomes securitised once it is used as collateral for securities issued to investors—hence, the securities are said to be "asset-backed". The cash flows from the underlying pool of assets support the securities (usually bonds) that are sold in the marketplace. Principal and interest cash flows from the selected asset pool are passed on to the investors.

The basic cash flows involved in securitisation transaction are outlined below, with fund transferred from the financial institution to SPV to investors.

11.3 DEFINITIONS

The following definitions should aid familiarity and understanding.

Asset-backed Securitisation (ABS)	Refers to the transformation of illiquid, risky security individual loans into more liquid, less risky securities referred to as asset-backed securities (ABS).
Mortgage-backed Security (MBS)	Interests in a pool of residential mortgages. Mortgage-Backed Security investors securitised receive payments of principal and interest from the pool. Despite the fixed nature of the underlying monthly mortgage payments, the payments made to investors can vary widely. MBS are marked by prepayment risk

	(mortgage holders can prepay early), and therefore are very sensitive to interest rate changes.
Asset-backed commercial paper (ABCP)	Short-term money market ABS, maturity less than 1 year (usually. 30-180 days) Asset-backed Longer-term ABS, maturity longer than one year term debt.
Conduit	Single-purpose trust that buys a financial institution's assets. It raises funds by issuing debt (commercial paper, long- or medium-term notes, subordinated debt).
Collateralised Mortgage Obligation (CMO)	Type of MBS, securitised interests in a pool of mortgages. Structured in tranches (classes) of bondholders with different prepayment and maturity.
Commercial MBS (CMBS)	Securitised interests in a pool of commercial mortgages (e.g., multi-family housing, hotels, office buildings). Modified pass. All payments (less a servicing fee) from underlying assets passed through security directly to the investor, with the financial making up any institution default or deficiencies in individual payments. (The Canadian MBS product is an example.)
Multi-seller	Has the ability to buy assets from a wide range of companies, Conduits usually sponsored by banks or investment dealers. Segregated pools of receivables from more than one seller generally either revolve or amortise.
Pass-through securities	All payments of principal and interest (less a servicing fee) from underlying assets are passed directly to investors. (The American MBS product is an example.)
Prepayment	Risk of payment acceleration, particularly marked in MBS where mortgage holders have the choice to prepay. Mortgage prepayment rates move inversely with interest rate changes. Mortgage holders adversely select against the investor, who loses future interest payments on prepaid principal.
Single-seller conduit	Only one seller sells financial assets to the conduit. Often sponsored by a specific manufacturing company.
Special purpose vehicle (SPV)	Financial intermediary involved in re-engineering the cash flows. Could be a trust or a corporation.
Trust	A charitable trust as SPV keeps the residual funds of the transaction. Not consolidated or taxed with the financial institution. Bankruptcy-remoteness protects investors.

MBS vs. ABS

Besides MBS products securitising residential mortgages, and ABS products securitising just about everything else, there is another difference between the usual MBS and ABS products: Residential mortgage-backed securities have little credit risk. It's common for MBS products to involve residential mortgages that have been either insured or guaranteed by a government body. In such cases, the investor does not take on credit risk. Rating agency investigations are virtually obviated by any government backing of an MBS product.

In ABS transactions, however, rating agencies carefully examine credit risk, and good ratings require credit enhancements to provide a layer of protection. Credit enhancements are often based on a multiple of the selected assets historical losses. The enhancement could take the form of a recourse provision, where the financial institution contractually agrees to cover losses up to a set amount; over-collateralisation, which happens when the underlying asset value is greater than that of the security; prioritisation of claims with senior-subordinated structures; or third-party guarantees, such as letters of credit or liquidity provisions.

 REASONS FOR SECURITISATION

There are three basic reasons why a financial institution wants to securitise assets:

(a) Asset management,

(b) Funding, and

(c) Regulatory performance ratios.

Asset management allows financial institutions to improve asset-liability matching. Securitising minimises any mismatching of cash flows, since enables the exchange of long-term assets, such as mortgages, for cash. Exchanging the long-term assets increases a financial institution's liquidity profile, which, in turn, gives the institution access to new, lowest funding. Additional funding allows the financial institution to grow existing business or expand into new business areas. This additional funding is important as financial institutions continue to see declines in their traditional deposit base, and a surge in the popularity of mutual funds.

Securitisation also affects performance ratios. With markets increasingly aware of declining capital ratios, financial institutions are clamoring to improve their image of strength. If a financial institution secures "true sale" accounting treatment in Securitisation transaction, then securitised assets are removed from their balance sheet. Selling the assets obviates a financial institution from holding regulatory capital against them. This allows the institution to deploy that capital in other ways, and the off-balance-sheet treatment improves return-on-asset (ROA) and return-on-equity (ROE) ratios. Of course, "true sale" requires just that: All rights and interests of ownership should be transferred from the financial institution to the new owner of the asset -the investor.

The sellers also have supplementary benefits of the Securitisation transaction in that their clients (mortgage holders, for example) are unaware of the transaction, and original relationships are maintained. Sellers have no direct relationship with the investors.

11.4.1. Reasons for Purchasing Securitised Assets

On the other hand, there are three basic reasons why an investor wants to purchase securitised assets:

1. asset diversification,
2. attractive returns, and
3. safe investments.

Asset diversification is important for investors who are seeing less volume of traditional choices with a decreased supply of government debt products. It offers additional choice, with a range of maturity and liquidity instrument profiles.

Attractive returns and predictability of cash flows have been realised with investment markets continuing disintermediation trends with a "flight to quality." Securitisation products are filling a need for secure and, in the case of ABS, rated investments.

For MBS products, prepayment risk introduces variability in investor payouts, and higher yields are paid to compensate.

11.4.2. Assets Which can be Securitised

Assets that generate funds over time can be securitised. These include payments under car loans, money due from owners of credit cards, airline ticket sales, toll collections from roads or bridges, and sales of petroleum-based products from oil refineries. In fact, artists have even raised funds by securitising the royalty, they will get out of future sales of their records. For an asset to be securitised, it must fulfill certain conditions. These conditions are:

(a) The cash flows of the asset should be dependable and paid periodically in accordance with a determinable and a demonstrated historical payment pattern.

(b) The asset should be of good quality and readily marketable, either on its own merit or with some form of credit enhancement so that the risk of default is substantially reduced.

(c) The pool of assets must have similar interest payment dates and maturities.

(d) The total amount of assets to be securitised must be large enough to make the transaction a worthwhile proposition keeping in view the high transaction costs involved at the moment in India.

11.5 SECURITISATION INSTRUMENTS

Three types of instruments are used to implement securitisation. These differences are based on maturity characteristics:

1. Pass-through Certificates (Single Maturity Structure)
2. Pay-through Securities (Multiple Maturity Structure)
3. Stripped Securities

1. Pass-through Certificates

The cash flows from the underlying collateral are "passed through" to the holders of the securities in the form of monthly payment of interest, principal and prepayments. In other words, the cash flows are distributed on a pro-rata basis to the holders of the security. Prepayments occur when the holder of an underlying asset prepays the remaining principal before the final scheduled payment month. Any prepayment is also proportionally passed on to the security holders leading to a quicker retirement of their underlying principal. Critical to the pricing of pass-through are the specific features of that particular collateral. All the securities are terminated simultaneously since the last payment on the pool leads to its complete amortisation. Some of the main features of Pass-through Certificates are:

(a) It tells one the ownership rights in the asset backing securities.

(b) Prepayment reflects the payment on underlying mortgage.

(c) It is a self-amortising mortgage. Therefore, whatever amount is amortised, it is passed on to the security holders with repayment.

(d) Prepayment occurs when a house owner makes a payment which exceeds the minimum scheduled amount. It shortens the life of the instrument and skews the cash flows towards the earlier years.

2. Pay-through Securities

The PTS structure overcomes the single maturity limitations of the pass-through certificates. Its structure permits the issuer to restructure receivables' flow to offer a range of investment maturities to the investors associated with different yields and risks. Issuers of asset backed debt are thus freed from the limitations imposed by the pass-through-securities which simply provides a conduit for sale of ownership interests in the receivables. A key difference between traditional pass-through and PTS is the mechanics of principal payment process. In a pass-through, each investor receives a pro-rata distribution of any principal and interest payments (not of servicing) made by the borrower. Because these assets are self-amortising assets, a pass-through, however, does not occur until the final asset in the pool is retired. This results in large differences between average life and final maturity as well as a great deal of uncertainty with regard to the timing of the principal return.

3. Stripped Securities

The securities sold are classified as "interest only" or "principal only" securities under this category. Interest only securities holders are paid back out of interest income only and PO security holders are paid out of principal repayments only. However, these securities are highly volatile in nature and are least preferred by the investors. PO normally increases in value when interest rates go down because it becomes lucrative to prepaid existing mortgager and undertake fresh loans at lower interest rates. As a result of prepayment of mortgages, the maturity period of these securities goes down and investors are returned the money earlier than they anticipated. In contrast, IOs increase in value when interest rates go up because more interest is collected on underlying mortgages. However, in anticipation of a decline in interest rates, prepayment of mortgages declines and maturities lengthen. They are normally traded by speculators who make money by speculating about interest rate changes. These securities, being volatile in nature, have no government backing.

11.6 PRICING OF THE SECURITISATION INSTRUMENTS

Pricing is an important step in the process of securitisation Pricing should be done keeping in mind the investors' expectations and the cost to the seller (the originator).

Most of the deals that have taken place in India have been with Citibank NA as the buyer/investor. Only recently, GE Capital Services Limited has started investing in asset-backed securities on a very limited basis.

There are not many buyers of securitisation instruments as of now, because of which the buyers (basically Citibank) have dictated the price with some negotiation. The price is arrived at in such a manner that it matches the investor expectations and is acceptable to the originator.

After having selected a pool of loans, weighted average rate of return can be calculated for the pool. From this weighted average rate of return after deducting the management fees (which is generally 2% to 2.5% of the amount deal), the legal fees and other expenses, the price (yield) of the instrument can be arrived at. Pricing of the instrument can be done in two ways.

(a) By Working Forward

This is done by calculating the return to the originator and then deducting the expenses from this return to arrive at the rate to be offered to the investor.

(b) By Working Backward

The expectations are taken into consideration and a rate of return to be offered to the investor is arrived at. This should be less than the weighted average rate of return to the organisation and the difference will be the spread that the organisation will get as profit. The instrument can also be priced at a rate at which the organisation has to incur, a loss if that loss can be amortised over a period of time by investing the amount raised through securitisation.

11.7 LEGISLATIONS

There were no laws specially governing securitisation transactions in India before 2002. The Government of India constituted a Working Group on Asset securitisation in July 2000. This Working Group submitted a comprehensive draft securitisation Bill to the Government. The securitisation and Reconstruction of Financial Assets and Enforcement of Security Interest Ordinance, 2002 as the name suggests seems to be all in one law addressing issues of securitisation, the issue of Reconstruction Company and the issue of perfection of security interests. These three issues seem to be unrelated and this form of mixing these unrelated issues into one ordinance would dilute the effectiveness of the ordinance. It would have been better if these issues would be addressed specifically and independently. Nevertheless the ordinance is the step in the right direction.

RBI Regulations and Guidelines

(1) Acquisition of Financial Assets

(a) The Asset Acquisition Policy shall provide that the transactions take place in a transparent manner and at a true price in a well informed market, and the transactions are executed at arm's length in exercise of due diligence;

(b) The Policy so framed should provide for checks in the matter of acquiring assets from a single Bank/FI, own sponsors and any single entity upto a desirable level of ceiling so that possible departures from desirable practices are avoided;

(i) The percentage of financial assets to be acquired should be appropriately and objectively worked out keeping in view the fact that the percentage of ownership stake has a bearing on the speed with which security interest rights can be enforced in accordance with the provisions of the ordinance;

(ii) For easy and faster readability, financial assets due from a single debtor to various banks/FIs may be considered for acquisition. Similarly, financial assets having linkages to the same collateral may be considered for acquisition to ensure relatively faster and easy realisation;

(iii) Both fund and non-fund based financial assets may be included in the list of assets for acquisition. Standard Assets likely to face distress prospectively may also be acquired;

(iv) Acquisition of funded assets should not include takeover of outstanding commitments, if any, of bank/FI to lend further. Terms of acquisition of security interest — in non-fund transactions, should provide for the relative commitments to continue with bank/FI, till demand for funding arises;

(v) Loans not backed by proper documentation should be avoided;

(vi) The valuation process should be uniform for assets of same profile and a standard valuation method should be adopted to ensure that the valuation of the financial assets is done in scientific and objective manner. Valuation may be done internally and/or by engaging an independent agency, depending upon the value of the assets. Ideally, valuation may be entrusted to an asset acquisition committee, which shall carry out the task in line with an Asset Acquisition Policy laid down by the Board in this regard;

(vii) A record indicating therein the details of deviations made from the prescriptions of the Board in the matter of asset acquisition, pricing, etc. should be maintained;

(viii) To ensure functioning of Securitisation Companies/Construction Companies on healthy lines, the operations and activities of such companies may be subjected to periodic audit and checks by internal/external agencies.

(2) Engagement of Outside Agency

Securitisation Companies/Reconstruction Companies may engage the services of reputed specialised external agencies to handle the task of taking possession of secured assets in pursuance of its right to enforce security interest.

(3) Sale Committee

It is desirable that the Sale Committee authorises in case of joint/consortium financing, the secured creditor with the highest outstanding, or more preferably, the Securitisation Company/Reconstruction Company as the designated secured creditor to arrange for the sale of secured assets.

(4) Issue of Security Receipts

(a) The parties in question may finalise the price at which a receipt will be issued as per the mutually agreed terms assessment of the risks involved;

(b) In cases where security receipts are issued involving of risks to the full extent and rewards to a limited extent could be a possibility of sharing of surplus between the parties and the investors;

(c) The issuer may consider obtaining credit rating from a recognised credit rating agencies. The matters relating to 'management fee' by the Securitisation or Reconstruction Company, for managing schemes floated may be as per the mutually agreed terms.

Impact on Banks

The securitisation process is complex and involves banks playing range of roles. Banks may act as the originator of the asset transferred, as the servicing agent to the securitised assets sponsors or managers to securitisation programs that securities party assets. In addition, banks may act as a trustee for the securitisations, provide credit enhancement or liquidity facilities a swap counterparty, underwrite or place the ABS, or invest securities.

Banks that securitise assets are able to accomplish several objectives. First, in selling or otherwise transferring, rather than holding originated assets, banks are able to:

(a) Reduce their regulatory capital requirements;

(b) Obtain an additional source of funding, generally at a low;

(c) Enhance financial ratios; and

(d) Manage their portfolio risk, e.g., reduce large exposures or concentrations. As investors, banks are able to driver portfolios by acquiring different asset types from the geographic areas.

While benefits accrue to banks that engage in securitisation activities, these activities have the potential of increasing the overall risk of the bank if they are not carried out in a prudent manner. G the risk exposures that banks encounter in securitisation are to those that they face in traditional lending. These involve en concentration risk, operational risk, liquidity risk, interest risk (including prepayment risk), and reputational risk. However securitisation unbundles the traditional lending function into limited roles, such as originator, servicer, sponsor, credit enhancer, provider, swap counterparty, underwriter, trustee, and invest types of risks may be less obvious and more complex the encountered in the traditional lending process. Accordingly, supervisors should assess whether banks fully understand and adequately manage the full range of the risks involved in securitisation activities. The following are the key areas where concentration is required:

(a) True Sale (Isolation from bankruptcy of the Originator)

The central idea of a securitisation transaction is to isolate the assets of the Originator from Originator's balance sheet and seek a higher credit rating than the Originator's own rating. A key requirement for that is to achieve a "true sale" of the assets to the Special Purpose Entity.

(b) Tax neutral bankruptcy-remote SPE

The special purpose entity that buys assets from the Originator should be a bankruptcy-remote conduit for distributing the income from the assets to the investors. While banks have experimented with company revocable trust and mutual fund structures, no clear vehicle has emerged for performing securitisation. This should be addressed by the securitisation Act.

(c) Stamp Duties

Stamp Duty is a state subject in India. Stamp Duties on transfer of assets in securitisation can often make a transaction unviable. While five Indian states have recognised the special nature of securitisation transactions and have reduced the stamp duties for them, other states still operate at stamp duties as high as 10% for transfer of secured receivables. The Working Group of RBI has recommended a uniform rate of 0.1% duty on all transactions. The acceptance of these recommendations by other states can boost the securitisation activity in India especially in the MBS area.

(d) Taxation and Accounting

At present there are no special laws governing recognition of income of various entities in a securitisation transaction. Certain trust SPE structures actually can result in double taxation and make a transaction unviable. The securitisation Act, when it comes to force, should address all taxation matters relating to securitisation. Securitisation legislation should also specify requirements for off-balance-sheet treatment for securitisation and regulatory capital requirements for Originator and Investors.

(e) Eligibility

Only recently mutual funds have been allowed to invest in Pass-through certificates. The government should lay down norms governing investment eligibility for various securitisation instruments.

Debt Market

Lack of a sophisticated debt market is always a drawback for securitisation for lack of benchmark yield curve for pricing. The appetite for long ended exposures (above 10 years) is very low in the Indian debt market requiring the Originator to subscribe to the bulk of the long ended portion of the financial flows. The development of the Indian debt market would naturally increase the securitisation activity in India.

Lack of Investor Appetite

Investor awareness and understanding of securitisation is very low. RBI, key drivers of securitisation in India like ICICI and Citibank and rating agencies like CRISIL and ICRA should actively educate corporate investors about securitisation. Mandatory rating of all structured obligations would also give investors much needed assurance about transactions. Once the private placement market for securitised paper gathers momentum, public retail SECURITISATION issuances would become a possibility.

The SECURITISATION market in India, though in its infancy, holds great promise especially in the MBS area. While more complex SECURITISATION transactions and public issuance of securitised paper are still a distant dream, appropriate legislation and investor education can give the securitisation market in India a much-needed thrust.

11.8 ACCOUNTING FOR SECURITISATION IN INDIA

Securitisation started in India during the early nineties. However, it is only over the last 2-3 years that issuance have seen volume growth, in this context, it is necessary that the Institute of Chartered Accountants of India come out with a guidance note on accounting treatment for securitisation. The process of arriving at the guidance note has been iterative. The ICAI has come up with 3-4 exposure drafts for the same. It is a very positive development that the guidance note is a huge improvement on any of the exposure drafts.

Given below is an overview of the accounting conventions associated with securitisation and the various issues that are concerned with the same in India.

11.8.1. Importance of Accounting Standard

The essential question in securitisation is whether the transfer of receivables involved in the securitisation transaction is a sale, or should the asset be retained on books? If it is a sale, the asset in question will go off the books, and the transfer might result into a gain or loss in sale.

Another issue, which crops up as a consequence of true sale is consolidation of the SPV with the Originator. This has been dealt with AS 21 and AS 23. These standards prescribe the amount of holding or any other relation that a company may have with a Special Purpose Entity to be termed as subsidiary. In that case, the accounts of that entity have to be consolidated/partially consolidated with the company. It is understood that a true sale to an arms length SPV will ensure no consolidation of accounts with the originator.

The accounting concept of true sale is not greatly different from the legal equivalent. Thus, if the transferor loses control over the asset putting the assets beyond the reach of his creditors or liquidator, or he himself, it will be a sale; otherwise it will be considered a financial liability or a secured lending.

The treatment of gain on sale in securitisation has been the topic of a lot of controversy. The Guidance Note lays methodology for computation of gain on sale, which is largely at par with FAS 140 (US GAAP).

In the absence of a clear-cut guideline, a sale treatment could be accorded and thus a gain on sale recorded when actually the sale has not occurred. This guidance note will hopefully prevent such a situation.

11.8.2. Treatment for Gain on Sale

The computation of gain on sale is not as simple as in a plain said, since, in a securitisation transaction, typically, the originator would retain some interests in form of subordinated interests, servicing, call options etc.

These are most often subordinated, and hence, highly credit and prepayment-risk sensitive. Therefore, the valuation of these assets is passed on estimated residual cash flows, which in turn in based on all the factors that affect the repayment behavior of the portfolio. These 'estimates" have often turned out to be incorrect and losses has to be booked on the occurrence of such events.

11.8.3. Accounting for Securitisation vs. Tradition Accounting Practices

Securitisation accounting has the "financial components" approach versus the traditional retention of risk. Though retention of risk would form/very simple form of accounting treatment, accounting standards all over the world have veered away film it. The exposure draft that ICAI had issued before issuing this guidance note took the approach of detention of risk.

As per the components approach, if the transferor has lost control on the asset, though he has retained components of interest in the asset, the components transferred would still go off the books. The justification of the "retention of control" approach can be illustrated by the following example. Suppose there is a portfolio that has a traditional default rate of 2%. Suppose the Originator has given recourse of 8% in the same. Then, the risk retained is probably much more than the portfolio risks. By that logic, the entire risk has been retained and thus the pool should not go off the books. If that is the case, any third party guaranteeing 8% should also have the portfolio on its books. This clearly is not right. Thus, retention of risks cannot be the sole criteria for determining the character of securitisation. As a result, accounting standards hinge on the "loss of control" by the originator.

The ICAI Guidance Note has stressed on loss of control as a criteria for derecognition of assets.

Quoting the Guidance note on derecognition of assets:

"Securitised asset should be derecognised in the books of the Originator, if and only if, either by a single transaction or by a series of transactions taken as a whole, the Originator loses control of the contractual rights that comprise the securitised asset. The Originator loses such control if it surrenders the rights to benefits specified in the contract. Determining whether the Originator has lost control of the securitised asset depends both on the Originator's position and that of the SPE. Consequently, if the position of either the Originator or the SPE indicates that the Originator has retained control, the Originator should not remove the securitised asset from its balance sheet."

Some conditions that violate a transfer of Control are:

(i) The creditors of the originator are entitled to attach or otherwise deal with securitised assets.

(ii) The SPE does not have the right (to the extent it was available to the originator) to pledge, sell, transfer or exchange for its own benefits the securitised assets.

(iii) The originator has the right to reassume control of the asset, except under certain specified conditions like a call option that can be at fair values and a cleanup call.

(iv) The originator is both entitled to and obligated to buy the asset at a predetermined price. However, only an obligation to repurchase at a particular price is not a violation of "loss of control". Servicing the assets is not a violation of loss of control.

11.9 SECURITISATION IN INDIA

In India CitiBank pioneered in securitisation by executing the first securitised transaction in 1991. Since that date, CRISIL has rated over .00 transactions with the volume exceeding ₹ 8,500 crores (USD 700 million) since 1991. Over the last 2-3 years, there have been 35 issuances of securitised debt for a total of ₹ 4,200 crores (USD 860 million) distributed to a wide range of investors. As of June 30, 2001, the mustarding securitised assets in the US were over USD 5 trillion (ABS-USD 1.2 trillion, MBS-USD 3.8)[3], a staggering 25% of all debt outstanding.

For India, this figure is a paltry 1.6% with less than INR 100 billion of outstanding securitised debt. In India, very few transactions of small value have taken place so far. Several obstacles are hindering the growth of securitisation in India:

- Stamp duty on transfer of assets by originator to the SPV, as high as up to 13%.
- If PTC is issued in the form of a receipt, it is not transferable by endorsement and delivery; if PTC is issued in the form of a promissory note, it will attract stamp duty.
- Ambiguity on whether PTCs can be regarded as negotiable promissory notes.
- Unresolved tax issues — who will be taxed?
- Weak foreclosure laws failing to provide adequate comfort to investors in ABSs.
- Given the importance of securitisation in modern economy, concerted efforts are required to develop it. Hopefully, initiatives will be taken to overcome the obstacles that are hindering the growth of securitisation. While there has been a lot of discussion about the potential of securitisation in India, actual deal activity has not kept pace. While some early adopters like ICICI, TELCO and Citibank have been actively pursuing securitisation, almost all the transactions in the market so far have been privately placed with a majority of them being bilateral fully bought-out deals. Lack of appropriate legislation and legal clarity, unclear accounting treatment, high incidence of stamp duties making transactions unviable, lack of understanding of the instrument amongst investors, originators and, till recently, even rating agencies are some of the glaring reasons for the lack of activity in the area of securitisation in India.

11.10 REVIEW QUESTIONS

Short Answer Questions

1. What is meant by Securitisation?
2. Explain special purpose vehicle.
3. Define Asset-backed Security.
4. Write short notes on:
   (a) Mortgage-backed security
   (b) Asset-backed commercial paper
   (c) Conduit
   (d) Collateralised mortgage obligation
   (e) Commercial MBS
5. Why do firms want to securitise the instruments?
6. Which assets can be securitised?
7. What are the two methods used to price an instrument?

Essay Type Questions

1. Explain the securitisation process with examples.
2. Who are the main parties involved in the securitisation process?
3. What are the various terms used in the securitisation process?
4. Why do firms prefer securitisation?
5. What are the legislations used to govern the securitisation process?
6. Describe the pricing strategies in securitisation.
7. Critically examine the present status of securitisation in India.

* * *

CHAPTER 12

Credit Rating

Objectives

The student, after studying the chapter, should be able to:

- Describe the concept of "credit rating'
- Make a historical account of credit rating in the world as well as in India
- Initiate the process of credit rating
- Appreciate the services rendered by the credit rating agencies in India
- Evaluate the ratings of existing agencies in India
- Understand the various legislations controlling Credit Rating Agencies (CRAs) in India.

Structure:

12.1 Introduction
12.2 Evolution of Credit Rating
12.3 Scope for Credit Rating
12.4 Rating Process
12.5 Rating Framework
12.6 Credit Rating Agencies in India
12.7 Criticisms
12.8 Regulation of CRAs
12.9 Review Questions

12.1 INTRODUCTION

People talk about quality whenever any paid service is being received by them from any individual or from any organisation. They try to order according to the merit of these organisations in rendering services. Ordering the organisations based on their merit by using some alphabetical symbol is called rating. When someone says 'A1', he means that the service rendered by an organisation is the best or better than the services rendered by other organisations in the same field. Therefore, ratings in the field of finance are a simple and easily understood tool enabling the investor to differentiate between debt instruments on the basis of their underlying credit quality. Credit rating is, thus, a symbolic indicator of the current opinion of the relative ability of the issuer to service debt obligations in a timely fashion with specific reference to the instrument being rated. Rating is also a communicative tool. It communicates to investors the relative ranking of the different loss probability for a given fixed income investment, in comparison with other rated instruments.

A rating is specific to a debt instrument and is intended as a grade, an analysis of the credit risk associated with the particular instrument. It is based upon the relative capability and willingness of the issuer of the instrument to service the debt obligations (both principal and interest) as per the terms of the contract. Thus, a rating is neither a general purpose evaluation of the issuer, nor an overall assessment of the credit risk likely one be involved in all the debts contracted or to be contracted by such entity.

12.1.1. Scope for Using Credit Rating Facility

A word of warning should be made at this point. The credit rating is not foolproof recommendation whether to buy or sell a bond. The objective of such prediction is to help one to have opinion about a company and its debt-servicing ability.

Perhaps, it would also be useful to explain what credit rating does not connote.

First, a rating is specific to the issue or debt or instrument that is rated. A rating is neither a general purpose evaluation nor overall assessment of credit risk associated in all debts contracted by an issuer.

Second, it is not a recommendation to buy, hold or sell. It is an opinion, perhaps well-informed opinion.

Third, they are not predictors of default but opinions about the relative probability of default and loss. Thus, the difference between the highest rated instrument and another rated a rung lower is that the probability of default of interest, and principal in the case of the former is lower than that of the latter.

Fourth, ratings are not guarantees against losses. Under no conditions do they or can they predict losses due to 'shocks' or highly unexpected situations.

Fifth, credit ratings relate only to credit and thus, for example, have no relationship to risk preferences of investors or attractiveness of equity. Hence, the perceptions of different stakeholders, *viz.*, creditors, lenders, shareholders, etc. in responding to ratings could be different.

To quote:

"In determining a rating, both quantitative and qualitative analyses are employed. The judgement is qualitative in nature and the role of the quantitative analysis is to help make the best possible overall qualitative judgement because, ultimately, a rating is an opinion."

—Standard & Poors

Credit Rating is a simple and easy to understand symbolic indicator of the opinion of a credit rating agency about the risk involved in a borrowing programme of an issuer with reference to the capability of the issuer to repay the debt as per terms of issue. This is neither a general purpose evaluation of the company nor a recommendation to buy, hold or sell a debt instrument.

12.1.2. Credit Rating — Definition

"A rating is an opinion on the future ability and legal obligation of the issuer to make timely payments of principal and interest on a specific fixed income security. The rating measures the probability that the issuer will default on the security over its life, which depending on the instrument, may be a matter of days to 30 years or more. In addition, long term ratings incorporate an assessment of the expected monetary loss should a default occur."

— Moodys

"Credit ratings help investors by providing an easily recognisable, simple tool that couples a possibly unknown issuer with an informative and meaningful symbol of credit quality." **— Standard & Poors**

12.2 EVOLUTION OF CREDIT RATING

12.2.1. In the World

In 1837, there existed a financial crisis in America. Credit rating had its origin from there. Due to the crisis, financial obligation of many organisations in USA mounted up. The first mercantile credit rating agency was set up in New York in 1841. The purpose of establishing the agency was to rate the ability of the merchants to pay financial obligations. Robert Dun took over the agency later. It published its first rating guide in 1859. John Bradstreet set up the second credit rating agency in 1849. It published a rating book in 1857. In 1933, these two agencies were merged to form Dun and Bradstreet. In 1900, John Moody established Moody's Investor Service. He published in 1909 the Manual of Railroad Securities. Moody further published a rating of utility and industrial bonds in 1914 and the rating of bonds issued by American cities and other municipalities in the early 1920s.

Poor's Publishing Company brought out their rating issue for the first time in 1916. Standard Statistics Company followed the suit in 1922. These two organisations were merged in 1941 to form a Standard and Poor's which was subsequently taken over by McGraw-Hill in 1966. A number of credit rating agencies were set up in 1970s. These included the Canadian Bond Rating Services, Thompson Bankwatch, Japanese Bond Rating Institute, McCarthy Crisitani and Maffei, Dominican Bond Rating Service, IBCA Ltd., and Duff and Phelps Credit Rating Company.

12.2.2. In India

The first credit rating agency established in India was the Credit Rating and Information Services of India (CRISIL). It was set up in 1987. This was followed by the setting up of ICRA in 1994, this was formerly called as Investment Information and Credit Rating Agency of India Ltd. Credit Analysis and Research Ltd. (CARE) was set up in 1994. In 1996, Duff & Phelps Credit Rating (P) Ltd. was set up by Duff & Phelps in association with Indian non-banking finance companies (NBFCs).

12.3 SCOPE FOR CREDIT RATING

Debt instruments alone are rated in India. These debt instruments include bonds, fixed deposits, commercial paper, etc. Equity shares are not rated in India. But then equity shares are rated in UK and USA for the guidance of equity investors. Credit rating is made an obligatory one for all organisations in the world to rate instruments.

12.4 RATING PROCESS

Rating is an interactive process with a prospective approach. It involves series of steps. The main points are described as below:

(a) Mandate

Rating agencies are approached by the clients. That is the first step, the requisition of the clients is also called a mandate. This mandate consists of the terms of the rating task. Some of the terms are: binding the credit rating agency to maintain confidentiality, the right to the issuer to accept or not to accept the rating and binds the issuer to provide information needed by the credit rating agency for rating and subsequent surveillance.

(b) Team

The team usually comprises two members. The composition of the team is based on the expertise and skills required for evaluating the business of the issuer.

(c) Information

Issuers are provided a list of information requirements and the broad framework for discussions. These requirements are derived from the experience of the issuer's business and broadly conform to all the aspects which have a bearing on the rating. These factors have been discussed in detail under rating framework.

(d) Secondary Data

The credit rating agency also draws on the secondary sources of information including its own research division. The credit rating agency also has a panel of industry experts who provide guidance on specific issues to the rating team. The secondary sources generally provide data and trends including policies about the industry.

(e) Meetings and Visits

Rating involves assessment of number of qualitative factors with a view to estimate the future earnings of the issuer. This requires intensive interactions with the issuer's management specifically relating to plans, future outlook, and competitive position and funding policies. Plan visits facilitate understanding of the production process, assess the state of equipment and main facilities, evaluate the quality of technical personnel and form an opinion on the key variables that influence level, quality and cost of production. These visits also help in assessing the progress of projects under implementation.

(f) Preview/Meeting

After completing the analysis, the findings are discussed at length in the internal committee, comprising senior analysts of the credit rating agency. All the issues having a bearing on the rating are identified. At this stage, an opinion on the rating is also formed.

(g) Committee Meeting

This is the final authority for assigning ratings. A brief presentation about the issuer's business and the management is made by the rating team. All the issues identified during discussions in the internal committee are discussed. The rating committee also considers the recommendation of the internal committee for the rating. Finally, a rating is assigned and all the issues which influence the rating are clearly spelt out.

(h) Rating Communication

The assigned rating along with the key issues is communicated to the issuer's top management for acceptance. The ratings which are not accepted are either rejected or reviewed. The rejected ratings are not disclosed and complete confidentiality is maintained.

(i) Rating Reviews

If the rating is not acceptable to the issuer, he has a right to appeal or a review of the rating. These reviews are usually taken up only if the issuer provides fresh inputs on the issues that were considered for assigning the rating. Issuer's response is presented to the Rating Committee. If the inputs are convincing, the Committee can revise the initial rating decision.

(j) Surveillance

It is obligatory on the part of the credit rating agency to monitor the accepted ratings over the tenure of the rated instrument. As has been mentioned earlier, the issuer is bound by the mandate letter to provide information to the credit rating agency. The ratings are generally reviewed every year, unless the circumstances of the case warrant an early review (a surveillance review — the initial rating could be retained or revised upgraded or downgraded). The various factors that are evaluated in assigning the ratings have been explained under rating framework.

12.5 RATING FRAMEWORK

The basic objective of rating is to provide an opinion on the relative credit is (or default risk) associated with the instrument being rated. This, rating nutshell, includes estimating the cash generation capacity of the user through operations (primary cash flows) *vis-à-vis* its requirements or servicing obligations over the tenure of the instrument. Additionally, assessment is also made of the available marketable securities secondary cash flows) which can be liquidated, if required, to supplement the primary cash flows. It may be noted that secondary cash flows have greater bearing in the short-term ratings, while the long-term ratings are generally entirely based on the adequacy of primary cash flows. All the factors which have a bearing on future cash generation and claims that require servicing are considered to assign ratings. These factors can be conceptually classified into business risk and financial risk drivers (Refer to Table 12.1).

Table 12.1

Business risk drivers	Financial risk drivers
Industry characteristics	Funding policies
Market position	Financial flexibility
Operational efficiency	New projects
Management quality	

12.5.1. Operational Efficiency

In a competitive market, it is critical for any business unit to control the costs at all levels. This assumes greater importance in commodity or "me too" businesses, where low cost producers almost always have an edge. Cost of production to a large extent is influenced by:

(i) Location of the production unit(s)

(ii) Access to raw materials

(iii) Scale of operations

(iv) Quality of technology

(v) Level of integration

(vi) Experience

(vii) and last but not the least the ability of the unit to efficiently use its resources.

A comparison with the peers is done to determine the relative efficiency of the unit. Some of the indicators for measuring production efficiency are: resource productivity (both assets and manpower), material usage or input-output ratios) and energy consumption. Collection efficiency and inventory levels are important indicators of both the market position and operational efficiency.

12.5.2. New Project Risks

The scale and nature of new projects can significantly influence the risk profile of any issuer. Unrelated diversifications into new products are invariably assessed in greater detail. The main risks from the new projects are: time and cost overruns, even non-completion in an extreme case, during construction phase; financing tie-up; operational risks; and market risk. Besides clearly establishing the rationale of new projects, the protective factors that are assessed include: track record of the management in project implementation, experience and quality of the project implementation team, experience and track record of technology supplier, implementation schedule, status of the project, project cost comparisons, financing arrangements, tie-up of raw material sources, composition of operations team and market outlook and plans.

Besides on the assessment of various project risks, assumptions about completion and contribution to/from these projects are incorporated in the issuer's overall projections. It needs to be emphasised that the impact of the project risk on the rating depends on the scale of projects in relation to the size of assets and cash flows of the existing operations.

12.5.3. Management Quality

The importance of this factor cannot be overemphasised. When the business conditions are adverse, it is the strength of management that provides resilience. A detailed discussion is held with the management to understand its objectives, plans and strategies, competitive position and views about the last performance and future outlook of the business.

These discussions provide insights into the quality of the management. It also helps in establishing management's priorities. A review of the organisation structure and information system is done to assess whether it aligns with the management's plans and priorities. The interactions with key operating personnel help in determining the quality of the management. Issues like dependence on a particular individual and succession planning are also addressed.

Other important factors are labour relations, track record of meeting promises specifically relating to returns and project implementation, performance of "group" companies, transactions with the "group" companies, etc.

12.5.4. Funding Policies

This determines the level of financial risk. Management's views on its funding policies are discussed in detail. These discussions are generally focused on the following issues:

(i) Future funding requirements
(ii) Level of leveraging
(iii) Views on retaining shareholding control
(iv) Target returns for shareholders
(v) Views on interest rates
(vi) Currency exposures including policies to control the currency risk
(vii) Asset-liability tenure matching.

12.5.6. Financial Flexibility

While the primary source for servicing obligations is the cash generated from operations, an assessment is also made of the ability of the issuer to draw on other sources, both internal (secondary cash flows) and external, during periods of stress.

These sources include: availability of liquid investments, unutilised lines of credit, financial strength of group companies, market reputation, relationship with financial institutions and banks, investor's perceptions and experience of tapping funds from different sources.

Generally, financial flexibility factor facilitates determination of the relative strength within a rating category (*i.e.*, + or – prefix with the rating) and has a greater bearing on the short-term ratings.

12.5.6. Past Financial Performance

The impact of the various risk drivers is reflected in the actual performance of the issuer. The focus of rating exercise is to determine the future cash flow adequacy. This tells one the debt servicing ability of an organisation. This is possible by having a detailed review of the past financial statements of an organisation. It is critical for better understanding of the influence of all the business and financial risk factors. Evaluation of the existing financial position is also important for determining the sources of secondary cash flows and claims that may have to be serviced in future.

12.5.7. Accounting Quality

Consistent and fair accounting policies are a pre-requisite for financial evaluation and peer group comparisons. It may be mentioned that accounting quality is also an important indicator of the management quality. Rating analysts review the accounting policies, notes to the accounts and auditors' comments in detail. Where it is necessary, rating analysts adjust the financial statements to reflect the correct position. Over a period of time, the focus of financial analysis at the credit rating agency has shifted towards evaluation of cash flow statements as cash flows to a large extent offset the impact of "financial engineering".

12.5.8. Indicators of Financial Performance

Financial indicators over the last few years (typically five years) are analysed and performance of the issuer is compared with its peers. Comparison with peers is important for better understanding of the industry trends and determining the relative position of the issuer.

12.5.9. Profitability

A traditional indicator of success or failure of any business endeavour has been its ability to add value to its wealth or generate profits. A few important indicators are, trends in:

(i) Return on capital employed

(ii) Return on net worth

(iii) Gross operating margins

Higher profitability implies greater cushion to debt holders. Profitability also determines the market perception, which has a bearing on the support of shareholders and other lenders. This support can be an important factor during stress.

12.5.10. Gearing or Level of Leveraging

This is an important determinant of the financial risk. Some important indicators are:

(i) Total debt as a % of networth

(ii) Long-term debt as a % of networth

(iii) Total outside liabilities as a % of total assets

It needs to be emphasised that business risk is a prime driver, while gearing has a secondary role in determining the overall rating (especially long term). To illustrate, an issuer whose gearing level is favourable but relative business fundamentals are weak is unlikely to get a favourable long-term rating. This is so because gearing is considered to be a "controllable" factor while business factors are relatively difficult to alter significantly.

12.5.11. Coverage Ratio's

Coverage ratios are considered to be of primary importance to the debt holders. The important ratios are:

(i) Interest coverage ratio (OPBDIT/Interest)

(ii) Debt service coverage ratio

(iii) Net cash accruals as a % of total debt

The level of these ratios reflects the result of business risk drivers and the funding policies. Generally speaking, higher the level of coverage, higher is the rating. However, as mentioned earlier, business with lower level of coverage can get higher ratings if the earnings are steady (*i.e.*, business with low industry risk).

12.5.12. Liquidity Position

The indicators of liquidity position are, the levels of:

(i) Inventory

(ii) Receivables

(iii) Payables

The state of competition, issuer's market position and policies, relationship with customers and suppliers are the important factors that impact the above levels. Comparison with peers on these indicators helps to determine the relative position of the issuer in the industry. The funding profile with respect to matching of asset-liability tenures also has an important bearing on the liquidity position.

12.5.13. Cash Flow Analysis

Cash is required to service obligations. Thus, any financial evaluation would be incomplete if cash flow analysis is not carried out. Cash flows reflect the sources from which cash is generated and its deployment. It has been mentioned earlier, cash flows also to a very large extent offset the impact of diverse accounting policies and hence facilitate peer comparisons.

The coverage ratios enumerated above can be modified to factor the impact of actual cash flows only. Issuers who are not able to generate sufficient cash to service obligations do not normally get favourable ratings.

12.5.14. Future Cash Flow Adequacy

The ultimate objective of the rating is to determine the adequacy of cash generation to service obligations. Number of assumptions based on the future outlook of the business is made to draw projections of financial statements. Invariably, the financial projections are carried out for a number of scenarios incorporating a range of possibilities in the set of assumptions for the key cash flow drivers. A few important drivers are expectations of growth, selling prices, input costs, working capital requirements, value of currencies, etc.

12.6 CREDIT RATING AGENCIES IN INDIA

Ratings awarded by major credit rating agencies:

12.6.1 Credit Rating Information Services of India Limited (CRISIL)

The Credit Rating Information Services of India Ltd. (CRISIL) began operations in 1987, offering credit rating services in a market where the concept was totally new. Interest rates at that time were government determined, and CRISIL's business was therefore built entirely on guiding the market for its investment decisions. CRISIL had the challenge of building a new business in an unknown area from a zero base.

Table 12.2

AAA	Highest Safety
AA	High Safety
A	Adequate Safety
BBB	Moderate Safety
BB	Sub-moderate Safety
B	Inadequate Safety
C	Substantial Risk
D	Default

Challenges

CRISIL faced several other challenges in its effort. When CRISIL started its operations, secondary markets for debt in India were at an embryonic stage, and a source of automatic demand for ratings was therefore denied the agency. Studies undertaken by GCRAs had indicated that the market size in India would not support a rating agency. To add to this, CRISIL was starting out entirely on its own, without backing or expertise from any of the global agencies, and was therefore obliged to develop methodologies and criteria, and train its pool of analytical talent, entirely on its own.

CRISIL identified the following immediate and long-term objectives:

- To assist investors in making investment decisions
- To assist issuers in raising funds from a wider investor base

Objectives

- To provide a marketing tool to entities placing debt with clients
- To provide regulators with a market-driven system for bringing about the development of the capital markets
- To institutionalise a viable and market-driven system of credit rating in India
- To facilitate individuals in investing in financial instruments rather than in non-productive assets into play.

Strategy

The strategy that emerged was three-fold:

- Creating awareness of the concept amongst all market participants
- Wining credibility, confidence and trust of participants
- Generating ratings business that would increase in size as a system of market-driver interest rates into play

Performance and Volume of Ratings

In this very difficult market, CRISIL attained profitability in its first quarter of operations, and has remained profitable ever since. CRISIL issued 400 ratings in its first two years of operations. Around 1992, the Reserve Bank of India and the Securities and Exchange Board of India (the main regulators of India's financial markets) made ratings mandatory for various classes of debt instruments, which helped boost revenues. As of November 2002, CRISIL had rated a total of 4303 instruments, totalling INR 4.31 trillion (over US$ 85 billion).

Progress and Achievements

(a) Recognition in the Indian context: CRISIL's ratings are benchmarks universally recognised by banks fixed income market participants, investors and a host of other entities. This recognition is geographically universal, and applies across all categories and scales of issuers.

(b) Effective: CRISIL is today the largest credit rating agency in India, and among the world's five largest. CRISIL's diversified shareholding, and separation between ownership, management and the rating process, insulates it from pressure of ownership interests. Similarly, its diversified client base and activity profile protect CRISIL from client pressure on rating decisions.

(c) Systematic rating procedures: As mentioned CRISIL has explicit methodologies and criteria for different categories of instruments and issuers, all of which are in the public domain. Process integrity is always strongly maintained.

(d) Extent of contacts: CRISIL has, in its years of rating experience, built its franchise as the rating agency of choice in virtually all sectors of the economy. CRISIL's Opinions on economic issues, sectors and entities are listened to with respect, and aggregative rating actions have in the past proved good predictors of economic trends. CRISIL has rated issuances by most of India's large corporates, financial sector entities, state governments and urban local bodies.

12.6.2. Investment Information and Credit Rating Agency of India (ICRA)

ICRA Limited (formerly, Investment Information and Credit Rating Agency of India Limited) was incorporated on January 16, 1991 and launched its services on August 31, 1991. ICRA is an independent and professional company providing investment information and credit rating services. ICRA's major shareholders include Moody's Investors Service and leading Indian financial institutions and banks. As the growth and globalisation of Indian capital markets have led to an exponential surge in demand or professional credit risk analysis, ICRA has actively responded to this need by executing assignments including credit ratings, equity grading, and mandated studies spanning diverse industrial sectors. In addition to being a leading credit rating agency with expertise in virtually every sector of the Indian economy, ICRA has broad-based its services to the corporate and financial sectors, both in India and overseas, and presently its services are under three banners namely:

- Rating Services
- Information Services
- Advisory Services

Rating Services

As an early entrant in the credit rating business, ICRA is one of the most experienced credit rating agencies in India today. ICRA rates rupee denominated debt instruments such as,

- Bonds and Debentures (Long-term)
- Fixed Deposit Programmes (Medium-term)
- Commercial Paper and Certificates of Deposit (Short-Term)
- Structured obligations and sector-specific debt obligations (Issued by infrastructure companies)

The ICRA rating is a symbolic indicator of the current opinion of the relative capability of timely servicing of debts and obligations by the corporate entity with reference to the instrument rated. The rating is asked on an objective analysis of the information and clarifications obtained from the concerns as also other sources, which are considered ICRA to be reliable. The independence and professional approach of ICRA ensure reliable, consistent and unbiased ratings. Ratings facilitate wasters to factor credit risk in their investment decision. ICRA rates long-term, medium-term and short-term debt instruments. ICRA offers its rating services to a wide range of issuers including:

- Manufacturing companies
- Banks and financial institutions
- Power companies
- Service companies
- Construction companies
- Insurance companies
- Municipal and other local bodies
- Non-banking financial service companies and Telecom companies
- Companies involved in infrastructure such as ports, dams, roads, and highways.

Information Services

Leveraging on ICRA's core competence of business analysis, ICRA Information Services is focussed on addressing the unique information needs of investors and the capital markets community. The emphasis is on providing up-to-date, authentic and value-added information in a user-friendly format to supplement investment decision-making. The products of ICRA Information Services are all designed to promote efficiency in the financial markets. They reflect independent, professional and impartial opinions, which help issuers — including lesser known companies-access a broader investor base.

Table 12.3 Long-term rating scale all Bonds, NCDs and other debt instruments (excluding Public Deposits) with original maturity exceeding one year

[ICRA]AAA	Instruments with this rating are considered to have the highest degree of safety regarding timely servicing of financial obligations. Such instruments carry lowest credit risk.
[ICRA]AA	Instruments with this rating are considered to have high degree of safety regarding timely servicing of financial obligations. Such instruments carry very low credit risk.
[ICRA]A	Instruments with this rating are considered to have adequate degree of safety regarding timely servicing of financial obligations. Such instruments carry low credit risk.
[ICRA]BBB	Instruments with this rating are considered to have moderate degree of safety regarding timely servicing of financial obligations. Such instruments carry moderate credit risk.
[ICRA]BB	Instruments with this rating are considered to have moderate risk of default regarding timely servicing of financial obligations
[ICRA]B	Instruments with this rating are considered to have high risk of default regarding timely servicing of financial obligations.
[ICRA]C	Instruments with this rating are considered to have very high risk of default regarding timely servicing of financial obligations.
[ICRA]D	Instruments with this rating are in default or are expected to be in default soon.

The quality and authenticity of information is a derivative of ICRA's wide research base which includes Monetary and Fiscal, Industry and Corporate research in its ambit. The in-house capabilities in these areas are further complemented by a panel of advisors who bring expertise in Banking, Infrastructure, and Monetary and Fiscal sectors. We are committed to providing a healthier environment for the market participants and regulators by promoting wider investor awareness and interest, and increasingly bridging the information gap in the Indian financial market. It is our endeavour to constantly upgrade our existing products and introduce new ones in cognisance of the dynamic and evolving nature of the Indian business environment. This, we believe, will sustain our pre-eminence in providing quality research material that market participants, with India and overseas, will continue to need to make investment decisions in the increasingly complex and volatile markets.

ICRA Rating Symbols for Debt Funds

The ICRA Rating Symbols for Credit Risk Rating of Debt Funds and their implications are as follows:

Table 12.4

Symbol	Meaning
mfAAA	Indicates highest quality. The investment quality is of highest grade and is similar to that of fixed income obligations of highest safety.
mfAA+	Indicates high quality. The investment quality is of high grade and is similar to that of fixed income obligations of high safety.
mfAA mfAA- mfA+ mfA mfA-	Indicates adequate quality. The investment quality is of upper medium grade and is similar to that of fixed income obligations of adequate safety.
mfBBB+ mfBBB mfBBB-	Indicates moderate quality. The investment quality is of medium grade and and is similar to that of fixed income obligations of moderate safety.
mfBB+ mfBB mfBB-	Indicates inadequate quality. The investment quality is of low grade and is similar to that of fixed income obligations of inadequate safety.
mfB+ mfB mfB-	Indicates poor quality. The investment quality is of lowest grade and is similar to that of fixed income obligations that are risk prone.

The ICRA Rating Symbols for Market Risk Rating of Debt Funds and their implications are as follows:

Table 12.5

M1	Indicates very low sensitivity to changing interest rates and other market
M2	Indicates low sensitivity to changing interest rates and other market conditions.
M3	Indicates moderate sensitivity to changing interest rates and other market conditions.
M4	Indicates high sensitivity to changing interest rates and other market conditions.
M5	Indicates very high sensitivity to changing interest rates and other market conditions.

12.6.3. Credit Analysis and Research Limited (CARE)

Credit Analysis and Research Ltd. (CARE), incorporated in April 1993, is a credit rating, information and advisory services company promoted by Industrial Development Bank of India (IDBI), Canara Bank, Unit Trust of India (UTI) and other leading banks and financial services companies. In all, CARE has 15 shareholders.

CARE assigned its first rating in November 1993, and upto August 31, 2003, had completed 2339 rating assignments for an aggregate value of about ₹ 3,572 billion. CARE's ratings are recognised by the Government of India and all regulatory authorities including the Reserve Bank of India (RBI), and the Securities and Exchange Board of India (SEBI). CARE has been granted registration by SEBI under the Securities and Exchange Board of India (Credit Rating Agencies) Regulations, 1999.

The rating coverage has extended beyond industrial companies, to include public utilities, financial institutions, infrastructure projects, special purpose vehicles, state governments and municipal bodies. CARE's clients include some of the largest private sector manufacturing and financial services companies as well as financial institutions of India. CARE is well equipped to rate all types of debt instruments like Commercial Paper, Fixed Deposit, Bonds, Debentures and Structured Obligations.

CARE's Information and Advisory Services Group prepares credit reports on specific requests from banks or business partners, conducts sector studies and provides advisory services in the areas of financial restructuring, valuation and credit appraisal systems. CARE was retained by the Disinvestment Commission, Government of India, for assistance in equity valuation of a number of state owned companies and for suggesting divestment strategies for these companies.

Advisory Services

Credit Reports

CARE offers credit reports on companies based on published information and CARE's in-house database. These confidential credit reports are useful to entities considering financing options, joint ventures, acquisitions and collaborations with Indian companies.

Sector Studies

CARE from time to time conducts studies on select sectors of the Indian economy, particularly those which were largely government controlled and funded till recently, but have been thrown open for private investment. Studies on the Indian Power Sector, Fertilizer Industry and Municipal Finances have been completed. These studies examine the legal framework and the rules and regulations under which these sectors function. They also discuss the opportunities for private sector investment, the risks and returns on these investments and the financing options. CARE has also prepared reports on twelve of the larger states of the Indian Union, which account for the bulk of foreign direct investment into India. These reports have been used by investors setting up infrastructure projects in India and by domestic and international banks to determine the strength of guarantees and other credit enhancements provided by the state governments for these projects. CARE also regularly prepares reports on important segments of the Indian economy. These reports are used by industry participants, financial intermediaries and also by analysts in CARE for their rating reports.

Project Advisory Services

For financing its infrastructure, India is increasingly relying on private sector participation. CARE uses the expertise gained in evaluating the credit risk of projects in areas such as roads, ports, power and telecom to advise investors and banks about the regulatory framework, the specific project risks and the ways of risk mitigation. CARE has helped independent power producers in India understand the functioning of the principal power purchasers, the State Electricity Boards and evaluate options for mitigating purchaser risk. CARE has also worked closely with project sponsors to structure their debt securities based on estimates of cash flows.

Financial Restructuring

The business risk faced by Indian companies increased following the liberalisation of Indian economy in 1991. To compete in the changed environment, companies have had to reassess their capital structures. CARE uses its knowledge about various industry sectors to advise companies about the optimal capital structure and the financial restructuring options.

Valuation

CARE carries out enterprise valuations for company managements, prospective and existing business partners or large investors. The Disinvestment Commission, Government of India, has used CARE's services for valuing 20 state owned enterprises.

Credit Appraisal Systems

CARE helps banks and non-banking finance companies to set up or modify their credit appraisal systems.

Debt Market Review

CARE's Advisory division also publishes a monthly bulletin "debt market review" on the happenings in the debt market and general development in the economy in the previous month.

Credit Rating: Rating Services

(a) CARE's Credit Rating is an opinion on the relative ability and willingness of an issuer to make timely payments on specific debt or related obligations over the life of the instrument. CARE rates rupee denominated debt of Indian companies and Indian subsidiaries of multinational companies.

(b) CARE undertakes credit rating of all types of debt and related obligations. These include all types of medium- and long-term debt securities such as debentures, bonds and convertible bonds and all types of short-term debt and deposit obligations such as commercial paper, inter-corporate deposits, fixed deposits and certificates of deposit.

(c) CARE also rates quasi-debt obligations such as the ability of insurance companies to meet policyholder's obligations. CARE's preference share ratings measure the relative ability of a company to meet its dividend and redemption commitments.

(d) CARE has a strong structured finance team and has been instrumental in developing rating methodologies for innovative asset-backed securities in the Indian capital market. The term 'structured financing' refers to securities where the servicing of debt and related obligations is backed by some sort of financial assets

Table 12.6 Care Rating for Long-term and Medium-term Instruments

Rating	Safety Level
CARE AAA	Highest Safety
CARE AA	High Safety
CARE A	Adequate Safety
CARE BBB	Moderate Safety
CARE BB	Inadequate Safety
CARE B	High Risk
CARE C	Substantial Risk
CARE D	Default

and/or credit support from a third-party to the transaction. The securities are termed "structured' because through specific choices relating to the type and amount of assets and particular structural features, these securities may be structured to achieve a desired rating level. CARE assigns the suffix (SO) to denote that the rating has been achieved by suitably structuring the transaction to enhance the credit quality of the securities and not on the basis of the credit quality of the issuer alone.

12.7 CRITICISMS

A number of criticisms have been levelled against credit ratings or CRAs, and indeed of the whole credit rating system. It is necessary to recognise them and assess the validity of such criticisms.

(a) Since issuers are charged for ratings by CRAs, *i.e.*, the issues are paymasters, the independence of ratings becomes questionable. According to the argument, the CRAs may be tempted to assign higher ratings than warranted or hesitate to downgrade issuers from fear of spoiling business relationships. The argument adduced against this notion is that the reputational risk that CRAs face provides an overriding incentive to maintain high quality and accurate ratings.

(b) CRAs are not accountable for the ratings given by them.

(c) Ratings may lead to herding behaviour thereby increasing the volatility of capital flows. This criticism gained ground during the Asian crisis when many commentators argued that the downgrading of the crisis-hit countries during a crisis might have worsened rather than helped the situation. Rating agencies argue that ratings are not intended to predict the exact timing of default or when a crisis would occur and that change in rating would occur if the new information received so warranted. CRAs point out that most of the lending in East Asia was done by big banks with their own analytical capacity.

(d) Credit ratings change infrequently since the rating agencies are unable to constantly monitor developments. Furthermore, owing to time and cost constraints, credit ratings are unable to capture all the characteristics of an issuer and issue. Credit Rating Agencies argue that they supplement their ratings with credit watches and outlook designed to indicate the agencies' perspectives on factors that might prompt a rating review over a future period. It is often argued that rating change affects prices and quantities since it forces certain portfolio managers to sell. There is also a view that prices may not be affected since the market would have already factored the developments leading to announcement. The results of studies are not uniform. One set of studies found that positive announcements in ratings were followed by movements in bond yield in the expected direction while negative rating changes did not have significant effect on yield movements. In contrast to these results, another set of studies found that yield movements occurred only when a downgrade in rating was announced. However, an analysis by IMF has shown that the largest announcement effects are noticed in respect of emerging market sovereign spreads. In other words, impact of rating changes is far higher in respect of emerging market economies and hence of special concern to India.

As mentioned, international rating agencies faced severe criticism in the wake of the Asian crisis since they facilitated large flows; they did not anticipate the events in Asia, and later they appear to have overreacted in a panic of downgrades attenuating the falling trend in currencies. Some of them have openly admitted their mistakes. They have announced that they have since changed their rating methodology to take into consideration the dynamics of capital flows. For instance, increased emphasis is now being placed on the proportion of short-term debt, private sector external debt, soundness of banks and corporate, etc.

12.8 REGULATION OF CRAs

In the aftermath of the Asian crisis and the scathing criticism on the failure of CRAs to predict the crisis and later on its role in precipitating it through downgrades, the role of credit rating agencies has been placed under microscopic scrutiny. The merits and demerits of regulating credit rating agencies and the issue of rating the rating agencies have been discussed in many international fora.

There is no international regulatory authority overseeing rating agencies. Whether they are regulated or not depends on specific country circumstances. In general, however, countries impose a modest regulation over CRAs. In USA, Securities and Exchange Commission gives recognition to CRAs as Nationally Recognised Statistical Rating Organisations (NRSO) for specific purposes. The main form of regulation in USA is officially recognising a CRA. Thereafter, there is hardly any regulation. Similarly in UK, recognition as a rating agency is required from the Financial Services Authority (FSA). So is the case in Japan, Australia, France and Spain.

12.8.1. Regulation of CRAs in India

In India, in 1998, SEBI constituted a Committee to look into draft regulation for CRAs that were prepared internally by SEBI. The Committee held the view that in keeping with international practice, SEBI Act 1992 should be amended to bring CRAs outside the purview of SEBI for a variety of reasons. According to the Committee, a regulator will not be in a position to objectively judge the appropriateness of one rating over another. The competency and the credibility of a rating and CRA should be judged by the market, based on historical record, and not by a regulator. The Committee suggested that instead of regulation, SEBI could just recognise certain agencies for particular purposes only; such as allowing ratings by CRAs recognised by it for inclusion in the public/rights issue offer documents.

In consultation with Government, in July 1999, SEBI issued a notification bringing the CRAs under its regulatory ambit in exercise of powers conferred on it by Section 30 read with Section 11 of the SEBI Act 1992. The Act now requires all CRAs to be registered with SEBI. Since then, all the four CRAs in India have been registered with SEBI. SEBI Act now defines "credit rating agency", "rating", and "securities". Details of who could promote a CRA and their eligibility criteria are specified. The Act also mentions about agreement with clients, method of monitoring of ratings, procedures for review of ratings, disclosure of ratings and submission of details to SEBI and stock exchanges. Restrictions have now been placed on CRAs from rating securities issued by promoters or companies connected with promoters, *i.e.*, companies in which directors of CRAs are interested as directors.

12.8.2. Changing Perspectives and Issues

It is clear that the credit ratings are playing increasingly important role in financial markets. The most significant change in the recent past relates to emphasis on their accountability and more importantly, the caution in regulators' use of ratings. In India, rating is a more recent phenomenon, but the changing global perspectives on the subject do impact the financial system. In the light of the East Asian experience, it is clear that appropriate disclosure of information and accounting standards across the board are necessary to help viable rating systems. While freedom of expression and independence of CRAs would also help improve the systems, credit awareness by investors, especially on the operations of rating system needs to be encouraged. Several issues and dilemmas being faced by all stakeholders in the matter of credit rating should be self-evident from the presentation so far. However, flagging a few specific issues of policy significance to the Reserve Bank of India at the current juncture would be appropriate.

12.9 REVIEW QUESTIONS

Short Answer Questions

1. What is meant by credit rating?
2. Explain in brief the scope for using the credit rating facility.
3. Write a short note on evolution of credit rating in India.
4. What is rating reviews?
5. Which industrial characteristics should be considered at the time of rating an organisation?

6. Write a short note on "CRISIL".
7. List out the functions of CARE

Essay Type Questions

1. Explain the meaning and the basic tenets of credit rating agencies.
2. What are the various steps involved in the rating process?
3. Describe the credit rating framework prevailing in India.
4. What are the major credit rating agencies operating in India? Explain the nature of credit rating agencies of both public and private.
5. Write a note on "Legislation for Credit Rating Agencies in India".

CHAPTER 13

Consumer Finance

Objectives

The student, after studying the chapter, should be able to:

- State the target population for consumer finance in India.
- Identify the consumer finance transactions.
- State the impact of consumer finance on durable goods and evaluate various consumer finance institutions

Structure:

13.1 INTRODUCTION

Consumer Finance includes all asset-based financing options provided to investors for acquiring consumer durables. In a consumer finance transaction, an individual initially pays a fraction of the cash on purchase while promising to pay the balance with interest over a specified time period.

Consumer finance is available for a large number of durables like televisions, refrigerators, air-conditioners, washing machines, cars, two-wheelers, personal computers and four-wheelers too.

13.2 MIDDLE-INCOME CLASSES IN INDIA

- India has registered a very impressive growth of its middle class — a class which was virtually non-existent in 1947 when India became a politically sovereign nation.
- At the start of 1999, the size of the middle class was unofficially estimated at 300 million people.
- The middle class comprises of three sub-classes: the upper-middle, middle-middle and lower-middle.
- The upper-middle class has an estimated 40 million people. They have annual incomes of US$ 600,000 each in terms of Purchasing Power Parity (PPP).
- The middle-middle class has an estimated 150 million people, each with PPP incomes of US$ 20,000 per year each.
- The lower-middle class comprises an estimated 110 million people. An estimate of their annual income is not available, but they are mostly the relatively affluent people-in the rural areas of India.
- The middle classes on the whole (*i.e.*, upper-middle + middle-middle + lower-middle classes) are expected to grow by 5% to 10% annually.

13.3 CONSUMING CLASS IN INDIA

Table 13.1 **Estimated households by annual income**

Annual income (in Rupees) at 1994-95 prices	No. of households (in million)
<25,000	80.7
25,001-50,000	50.4
50,000-77,000	19.7
77,000-106,000	8.2
>106,000	5.8
Total number of households	164.9 million

Source: National Council of Applied Economic Research (NCAER).

Table 13.2 **Structure of the Indian consumer market (1995-96)**

Annual income (in Rupees) at 1994-95 prices	Classification	Number of households (in million)		
		Urban	Rural	Total
<16,000	Destitute	5.3	27.7	33.0
16,001-22,000	Aspirants	7.1	36.9	44.0
22,001-45,000	Climbers	16.8	37.3	54.1
45,001-215,000	Consumers	16.6	15.9	32.5
>215,000	The rich	0.8	0.4	1.21
Total no. of households		46.6	118.2	64.8

Source: National Council of Applied Economic Research (NCAER).

1. Data on income distribution of households is insufficient in determining market size for different consumer products in India.
   (a) This is because of the lack of homogeneity of the consuming class and the varying prices of a single product in different parts of India. In other words, purchasing power is location-specific, not income-specific.
   (b) Consumption habits of households are therefore better determinants of consumer market size than income distribution.
   (c) Other factors are also to be considered and they are detailed below.
2. While determining market size for a consumer product, the structure of the consuming class as seen in Table 13.2 above, can be both revealing as well as misleading depending on the kind of product. For example, any specific consuming class would be fit to be a market for consumer products like tea or soap, but a product such as vacuum cleaners would find market largely only in the "consumers" and "rich" segments of the market as defined in Table 13.2 above.
3. Identifying a plausible market size for a consumer product is therefore a hazardous task in a heterogeneous country like India. Yet, the marketer needs some data to come as close to the real picture as possible. For this purpose, it can be cautiously assumed that purchasing power is proportional to income despite variables such as location, taste, etc. Companies are, therefore, advised to plan their consumer product marketing strategies on an area-by-area basis, rather than on an all-India basis.
4. Income data is insufficient. Therefore, it must be supplemented by product-specific information regarding its existing stock in the marketplace (in the case of consumer durables) and existing rate of purchases.
5. It is also advisable to further refine the plausible market size by taking into account details based on social, cultural and demographic factors. Marketing a super-premium product such as a Rolex watch is relatively easy. Just go for the income class above ₹ 106,000 per annum (in 1995-96) as per Table 13.1 above. This class, Table 13.1 shows, comprises 5.8 million households. But the problem lies in the fact that the 5.8 million households are spread all over India.
6. The prime market for consumer products in India is aware of the cost-benefit or value for money aspect. Their concept of value incorporates socio-cultural benefits in addition to product utility. For example, many households in the "consumers" class and the "rich" class (as defined in Table 13.2) may have two television sets, but both the sets may not be top-of-the-line. Thus, while there may be demand for an additional TV set in many households in the two mentioned classes, it must not be mistaken as demand for the higher-priced TV models. The prime consumer market in India therefore is not a market for absolute premium products, but for something between the "high end popular brands" to the "premium brands".

7. The class described in the previous paragraph is actually the "consumers" class defined in Table 13.2. This class comprises 33.5 million households as at 1995-96 and it owned and 'consumed' most of the expensive consumer products such as refrigerators and washing machines as well as premium expendables. At 1994-95 prices, their annual household incomes ranged between ₹ 45,000 and ₹ 215,000 (to calculate the latest income statistics, use an annual inflator of 5%). In addition to this class, the "climbers" and "aspirant" classes (defined in the Table 13.2) totalling 23.9 million households in urban India, also have the socio-cultural traits of the "consumers" class and, with time, will join the consumer's class. Medium-to-long-term marketing strategy must therefore aim at the aspirants and the climbers as well. This is based on the safe assumption that, except for the destitute class as defined in Table 13.2, the other classes are on the way to the next higher class. For companies with long-term marketing plans in India, the "consumers" (urban + rural), "climbers" (urban only) and "aspirants" (urban only) classes can be clubbed together to give a market size of around 57 million households which can be said to be the "prime segment" of the Indian consumer market. This becomes even truer as consumer financing and the credit card culture picks up. Fine-tuning between the classes is of course important, as explained in the next paragraph.
8. Suppose you are marketing washing machines. Go for two broad types: fully automatic and semi-automatic. Target the fully automatic machines at the "consumers" class and the semi-automatic at the "aspirant" class; the "climbers" class will then overlap the market for both the types of washing machines.
9. All of the above may be confusing, but the marketing strategist has to live with it because that's how the Indian consumer market is in reality. There is hardly a characteristic that applies across the market. Hence, the term "Indian consumer market" is a misnomer: it would be more accurate to describe it as a collection of different consumer markets.

13.4 CHARACTERISTICS OF CONSUMER FINANCE TRANSACTIONS

(a) Parties and Structure of the transaction

A consumer finance transaction can either be bipartite or tripartite. A bipartite transaction involves the dealer-cum-financier and the borrower or customer while in a tripartite transaction, the dealer and financier are two separate entities. Transactions can either be structured in the form of hire purchase, conditional sale or credit sale, but a majority of the tripartite consumer finance transactions are of the hire purchase type.

(b) Payment for the transaction

Consumer finance schemes are divided into two categories:

(i) Down Payment Schemes

(ii) Deposit Linked Schemes

The down payment varies from 20%-25% of the value of goods and financing is available for 75%-80% or as the case may be. In a deposit-linked scheme, the down payment varies between 15% and 25% of the total value of the asset. The financier pays the full amount to the seller. Deposits are of cumulative nature and carry a prescribed interest rate. Zero Deposit schemes are also available, under which the Equated Monthly Installment (EMI) is higher than the EMI under 15%-25% deposit schemes.

(c) Rate of Interest and Repayment Period

The borrower can choose a repayment period ranging from 12-60 months. Finance companies notify the customer indicating the amount of equated monthly installments that need to be paid through post-dated cheques.

(d) Security

The credit provided is secured through first charge on the asset concerned. The borrower is prohibited from disposing, pledging or hypothecating the asset during the credit period.

(e) Eligibility Criteria for Borrowers

Individuals, partnership firms and private and public limited companies are eligible to borrow. Different companies follow different criteria for financing. A sample hire purchase may include the following conditions:

(i) Individual

1. He should have a minimum of ₹ 1,00,000 as gross annual income.
2. His net take-home monthly salary should be about three times the Equated Monthly Installment.
3. He should have had two years of employment with the current employer.
4. He must have a minimum of five years of employment until retirement.
5. He should not have changed more than two jobs during the last five years.

(ii) Partnerships and Companies

It must have a minimum net worth of ₹ 2.5 lakhs. It should exist for a minimum period of four years. It should make profits for two of the last three years. The Net Profit plus Depreciation must be at least three times the annual instalment.

(iii) The Big Small Scale Industry Problem

The problem of credit delivery is easier to handle. The Reserve Bank of India is continuously extending its settlement schemes but banks are not playing ball. They appear to be more interested in either investing in government securities or in consumer finance. This has to be immediately corrected and the government should ensure that no viable small scale units will be closed due to lack of finance. It is interesting that the finance minister has announced a large fund to be routed through SIDBI for providing cheap and long-term capital.

13.5 CHANGING CONSUMER BEHAVIOUR

The following are the changes taking place in the attitude of the consumer in India:

(a) The Indian consumer is fast changing his habits, borrowing money to buy the products he wants, not content with buying what he can afford. The resultant consumer boom is what market strategists explain as the key to the success of the Indian consumer finance market.

(b) Consumer finance today is a win-win system in which everyone stands to gain. For the Indian consumer, it is an opportunity to upgrade his standard of living right now instead of waiting for years for his savings to accumulate. For manufacturers, it stimulates demand and lowers inventory. For middlemen, it's a sales boosting device. For players of consumer finance, it's a means of profit generation.

(c) The buy-now-pay-later culture is still fairly nascent in India, evolving through various forms like consumer lending, consumer credit, consumer loans, friendly and family borrowings, kitties, daily payment schemes, etc.

(d) The basic underpinning of consumer financing is that the consumers' present spending habits tend to be geared to expectations of future income. They are losing their fear of borrowing, riding surfboards of consumer finance.

(e) Along with buying a home, consumers prefer Consumer Finance (CF) to buy home appliances and vehicles, opting for CF based on the rate of interest, administrative fee, processing fee, commitment charges, prepayment penalty, types of facilities, standard and kind of services mix and sundry terms and conditions.

(f) These are the members of a growing breed of normally conservative middle-class Indians who are shedding their inhibitions about opting for CF loans despite the high interest cost.

13.6 IMPORTANCE OF CONSUMER FINANCE IN INDIA

(a) Increasing Risk of Disintermediation in Corporate Lending

Retail finance has become the preferred business of banks on account of its higher spreads. It is due to the fact of the increasing risk of disintermediation in corporate lending. The supernormal growth in retail finance has made it the primary driver of banks' asset books. It is expected to capture 40-60% of banks' incremental lending by end of financial year 2004.

(b) Housing Loans

Housing loans have been the product of choice for state-owned banks because of their attractive profitability, low risk weight, low delinquency history, and the ease of processing loans. The priority-sector status accorded to residential mortgages for less than ₹ 1 million is another factor in their favour.

All the state-owned banks have recorded explosive growth (albeit over a small base) in their mortgages; this has vastly expanded the market.

Table 13.3 **Banks' share in incremental retail advances (%)**

	FY2003	*FY2004E*
State Bank of India	39.1	40.4
HDFC Bank	39.1	62.9
ICICI Bank	209.7	174.1
Corporation Bank	72	64.3
Andhra Bank	48.8	48.8
Union Bank of India	23.5	21.3
Punjab National Bank	0	0
ING Vysya Bank	28.1	22.8
Oriental Bank of Commerce	107	66.2
Bank of Baroda	75.3	29.4
Canara Bank	25.6	35.7

Source: Informatics.

(c) Consumer Durables

Banks have entered almost all the segments in retail finance. They are gaining share from NBFCs. Private Banks have started offering loans for low-ticket items like consumer durables and two-wheelers, besides personal loans. Some schemes of some banks are given below:

- SBI has struck a preferred-financier arrangement with carmaker Maruti, and now markets these car loans from more than 2,000 branches. The bank has also tied up with Bajaj Auto and TVS Motors to finance two-wheelers.

- SBI is offering 3-year two-wheeler loans at an interest rate of 10% across all sales outlets of these companies. These alliances are significant, because they have extended the availability of car and two-wheeler finance to second- and third-tier towns.
- Union Bank has tied up with Ford Credit as a preferred financier for Ford cars.
- Punjab National Bank has struck a similar arrangement with Hyundai.
- More such alliances are expected between car makers and state-owned banks. These arrangements will drive strong growth in car finance market over the next three years.

(d) Reduction in Interest Rates

Falling interest rates, coupled with increasing loan durations, have substantially reduced the EMIs on retail loans, thereby making them affordable to more people than ever before.

13.7 IMPACT OF CONSUMER FINANCE GROWTH ON CONSUMER DURABLES MARKET

The retail finance boom will have a direct impact on the fortunes of the consumer durables market, including two-wheelers and passenger cars. This correlation is already clear from the surge in demand in recent times. Availability of cheaper loans will drive a CAGR of 14.9% in two-wheeler volumes over our forecast period FY2003-2007E. Sales of cars would grow at an even faster 20% annualised, as the gradual decline in excise duties makes the vehicles more affordable.

(a) Passenger Cars and Two-wheelers

Sales of passenger cars increased by 26.5% in the first half of this fiscal, owing to the lowering of excise duties in the general budget. The two-wheeler industry grew by 8.9% during this period, much slower than the heady high-teens growth over the past two years, as the agricultural slowdown last year hit rural incomes. Two-wheeler sales is expected to increase at a compounded 15.6% over FY2003-FY2007E. Car sales would rise at an even faster 20% over the same period.

(b) Key Issues and Success Factors

For the consumer finance companies to flourish, there is need to develop a credit information system, which will ease the process, making it faster and easier to determine the creditworthiness of customers.

- Partnerships with leading consumer durables and automobile manufacturers.
- Ability to offer simple, convenient and innovative consumer finance products, a wide distribution network and choice of repayment tenor, documentation and loan offer.

As a result of the large number of players, market pressures, increased competition, increased awareness and wider offerings, consumer-financing activities need to become customer-oriented and user-friendly.

One of the perceived problem relating to consumer finance is the absence of credit bureaus to rate the creditworthiness of consumers. As of now, the advent of Information technology has paved way for sharing data about defaulters among private sector banks. Any loan proposal is based on this shared information before further process.

(c) Innovative Solutions

The banks are lending against collateral and have concentrated on small potential borrowers to achieve disbursal targets.

- The Vijaya Bank offers 'V stock' for loans against shares; 'V equip' loans to help professionals acquire equipment and vehicles; and V-cash' to enable clean loans against salaries after getting an employer's guarantee.

- Judges, cops and teachers can now get cheaper loans with banks spinning out new products to cash in on the great retail rush. The country's largest commercial bank, State Bank of India, will charge lower interests to these set of borrowers for buying a home, car, two-wheeler or simply opting for personal or festival loans. Concessions would be given to them on interest rate, processing fees and margins under three new schemes — 'teacher plus', 'police plus' and 'justice plus'. The move, SBI officials say, is aimed at capturing the market share in different segments. The bank aims to tie up with various organisations, to put in place a structure, where the EMI (or equal monthly installment) for servicing the loan will be debited from the salary accounts of the borrower. A tie-up would minimise default risk. On home loans, teachers, policemen and judges will be charged 0.25% lower than interest charged to other borrowers. At present, the normal SBI home loan rates are 9.25% for loans up to 5 years, 9.75% for loans between 5 and 10 years and 10.25% for 10 to 20 years. Similarly, car loans will also be charged 0.25% lower than the usual rate, currently pegged at the medium-term lending rate (MTLR) of 11.25%. For scooter and motorcycle loans, the rates will be 0.35% lower. SBI normally charges a spread of 0.85% over its MTLR, but for teachers, policemen and judges, the spread will be 0.50%. Effectively, they would be charged 11.75% as against 12.1% for other customers. In case of personal loans, the spread over MTLR will be reduced to 2% against 2.23%. Effectively, these three special categories of borrowers would be required to pay 13.25%, instead of 13.6%.
- For festival loans, SBI would be offering a spread of 2.25% over the MTLR, as against 2.5% charge to its regular customers. Thus, the festival loans would cost 13.5%, as against 13.75%.
- Again, the processing fee on personal and two-wheeler schemes will stand reduced to 0.75%, as against 1% charged to its regular customers. The absolute fee for festival loan schemes has been reduced from ₹ 100 to ₹ 75. Margins are also being relaxed. For home loans, it has been brought down from 15% to 10%, and for repair and renovation, it will be reduced from 20% to 15%. In case of car loans, the margins are pegged at 10%, against 15% for cars priced up to ₹ 4 lakhs and 20% for cars above ₹ 4 lakhs. Margin for second hand cars has been lowered by 10%. A two-year old car would attract 20% margin, while a 2-4 year old car will attract 30% margin. For scooters and motorcycles up to ₹ 50,000, the margin would be 5% as against 10% for regular customer and 10% (as against 20%) for over ₹ 50,000. The bank does not charge any margin for festival and personal loans. On home loans, SBI has waived off the processing fees till March 31, '03 for all its customers, while it doesn't charge any processing fee for car loans.

(d) Credit Constraint in Rural India for Consumer Durables

According to a new survey, 'Role of Consumer Finance in Rural India' conducted by Chennai-based Anugrah Madison and Delhi-based Marketing and Research Team (MART), the future growth for consumer durable is Rural India. The constraints involved are the reluctance of banks to provide finance and the lack of electricity in 2/3rd of the homes. "Penetration of consumer durables would be deeper in rural India if banks were ready to finance them. Banks have shown reluctance in this sector and restrict themselves to tractors and diesel pumps."

While the consumer durables market is facing a slowdown due to saturation in the urban market, rural consumers are ready to put their money on the counter if consumer finance is made available and basic infrastructure requirements such as electricity and voltage are ironed out. Currently, rural consumers purchase their durables from the nearest towns, leading to increased expenses due to transportation. Hence, purchase is necessarily only done during the harvest, festive and wedding seasons — April to June and October to November in North India and October to February in the South, believed to be months 'good for buying'. The question remains as to why the banks shy away from financing rural consumers.

(e) Consumer Preferences

Indian consumers identify ease and speed of the loan application and approval process, as well as flexibility of evaluation procedures, as the key drivers of financing satisfaction. Consumer Financing Satisfaction Performance is measured by four factors:

- Application process (44%);
- Approval and documentation (22%);
- Finance advisor (18%); and
- Loan value (16%).

Customers who obtained their loans from a nationalised bank are relatively more satisfied than those choosing a non-banking finance company (NBFC) or a foreign bank. Low interest rates and the reputation of the finance company are among the key reasons for customers who opted either for an NBFC or a foreign bank. In comparison, past experience and personalised service are the main reasons indicated by those opting for a nationalised bank. Furthermore, more than 50% of NBFC and foreign bank customers obtained their financing at an automobile dealer or through a direct selling agent of the finance provider. In contrast, more than 90% of nationalised bank customers obtained their financing directly through the bank.

The car finance market has reached a new level of maturity, so much so that the car-maker, the automobile dealer and the financier now work together to provide better features and funding options for the buyer. Depending on the manufacturer, tenure of the loan and credit history of the car buyer, interest rates, on a reducing balance basis, now hover in the 10% to 13.5% range for new cars compared to 13% to 16.5% till early last year. There is an increased preference for financing car purchases through loans.

(f) Consumer Finance by GE Countrywide

GE Countrywide is one of India's leading consumer finance companies. It was set up in 1994. The company today has a strong retail distribution network and is present in over 2,500 outlets across 42 locations. The company has a wide range of products — Car finance, Consumer durable finance, Two-wheeler finance and Personal loans. In addition, a new product line Home equity or Mortgage has been launched in 2002.

Strong operations backed by the latest information technology support the product lines. A single database housing 1.6 million customer accounts, latest technology and centralised operations ensure the best service standards in the industry. Simple, convenient documentation and innovative consumer finance programmes are on offer for individuals, corporates and institutions.

(a) Maruti Countrywide Auto Financial Services, one of India's leading Maruti car financiers, provides a wide range of simple, convenient and innovative auto finance schemes for Maruti customers. The company has also built up the used cars' finance market. Corporate leasing of cars is another area of focus for the company.

(b) GE Countrywide Auto Financial Services provides auto finance for non-Maruti cars.

(c) Consumer durable and Two-wheeler finance. Innovative schemes and fast turnaround time ensures market dominance.

(d) Personal Loans programme has been re-launched in 2002 with walk-in centres or branches in 15 large cities. In 2003, over 50 branches nationwide would service cash loan requirements of consumers.

(e) CRM programme is among the most successful customer retention programmes wherein existing customers are cross-sold cash loans. Customer retention is currently at an average of 22%.

(f) Home equity is the newly launched product from the GE Countrywide portfolio. It is designed to cater to the needs of property owners seeking cash loans.

13.8 CONSUMER PROTECTION

During the course of a lifetime, an individual comes into contact with and carries out business dealings with large corporate, associations of persons, government departments and other bodies. These are large, impersonal bodies with resources much larger than an individual's. There are instances where injustice is done to the individual due to callous and indifferent attitude of certain personnel of these bodies. Individuals often do not have recourse to costly litigation to seek justice and has to, per force, bear such injustice. Such submission to injustice emboldens the perpetrators and makes them even more brazen. Most developed countries have set up watchdog bodies to help the individuals in this unequal fight and the individual enjoys an enviable amount of protection from the avarice and indifference of large bodies. In India, however, this movement is in a fledgling stage. Nonetheless, forums exist which can help one seek justice against corrupt and avaricious practices without incurring exorbitant litigation costs.

Under the Consumer Protection Act, every district has at least one Consumer Redressal Forum, more commonly called a Consumer Court. Here, consumers can get their grievances heard. Above the district forums are the State Commissions. At the top is the National Consumer Disputes Redressal Commission in New Delhi.

A written complaint to the company is taken as proof that the company has been informed. The complaint must be backed by copies of bills, prescriptions and other relevant documents, and should set a deadline for the company to respond. Consumers can also complain through a consumer organisation.

If the company does not respond, consumer can approach the consumer court. Again, this can be done directly or through a consumer organisation. Claims of less than ₹ 5 lakhs should be filed with district forum, claims of ₹ 5-20 lakhs directly with the State commission, and claims of more than ₹ 20 lakhs with the National Commission.

The set-up of consumer forum is geared to provide relief to both parties, and discourages long litigation. In a process called 'informal adjudication', forum officials mediate between the two parties and urge compromise. If a defaulter does not appear in court despite notices and reminders, the court may decide the matter in his absence. The forum can sentence them to a maximum of three years' imprisonment and impose a fine of ₹ 10,000. Forums can issue warrants to produce defaulters in court. They can use the police and revenue departments to enforce orders.

Please note that consumer courts provide redress only in cases of products or services for personal use, defects in products used for commercial purposes are not entertained.

13.8.1. Complaint Procedure

(a) Complaint is to be filed within two years of buying the product or using the service.

(b) Complaint needs to be in writing, and should be acknowledged. Letters should be sent by registered post or should be hand delivered against acknowledgement.

(c) In the Complaint, consumer should mention clearly the name and address of the person who is complaining and against whom the complaint is being filed.

(d) Copies of relevant documents must be enclosed.

(e) The consumer must mention details of the problem and the demand on the company for redressal. This could be replacement of the product, removal of the defect, refund of money, or compensation for expenses incurred and for physical/mental torture. However, please ensure that the claims are reasonable,

(f) One should preserve all bills, receipts and proof of correspondence related to the case. Avoid using e-mail, voice mail or telephone because such communications cannot be proved.

(g) The complaint can be in any Indian language, but it is better to use English.

(h) There is no compulsion to hire a lawyer. Main cost consists of correspondence and travelling to the consumer forum for the hearing.

13.9 REVIEW QUESTIONS

Short Answer Questions

1. Explain consumer finance.
2. What are the groups classified under "middle class" category in India?
3. What is the growth rate of middle class in India at present?
4. What are the two types of consumer finance transactions?
5. Explain tripartite consumer finance transaction.
6. Name the two schemes of consumer finance and explain.
7. Write a short note on 'Deposit Linked Scheme'.
8. Explain the eligibility criteria for borrowers of consumer finance.
9. Write a note on 'EMI'.
10. List the GE countrywide consumer finance schemes.

Essay Type Questions

1. Explain the impact of the growth of middle income classes on consumer finance?
2. 'Indian Consumer Market is a misnomer.' — Critically examine the statement.
3. Discuss the basic characteristics of consumer finance transaction in India.
4. What are the changes that are taking place in the attitude of consumers in India now?
5. Explain the importance of consumer finance in India.
6. Critically examine the present status of consumer finance in India.
7. Evaluate various consumer finance schemes of banks operating in India.

CHAPTER 14

Credit Card

Objectives

The student, after studying the chapter, should be able to:

- Describe the mechanism of credit card transaction
- Evaluate the debit card and its features
- Identify various types of credit cards
- Prescribe the eligibility criteria for getting a card
- Evaluate the credit card and its features
- Critically examine the status of cards in India.

Structure:

14.1 INTRODUCTION

A credit card is a monetary instrument that enables the cardholder to obtain goods and services without actual payment at the time of purchase. It is also popularly known as plastic money. The value of purchases made by the cardholder using the card is recovered at the end of a specified period, usually a month, called the billing cycle. It can be said that a credit card is basically a "Pay Later" card that is provided to a customer.

14.1.1. Benefits of Holding Credit Card

The following are the common benefits if one has a credit card:

(a) Credit can be availed for a period of 30-45 days.

(b) A cardholder need not have the required amount in his account to the extent of the transaction made.

(c) The card carries a predetermined limit up to which the holder can spend.

(d) At the end of each billing cycle, the cardholder has to pay only 5-10% of the outstanding value and the rest can be paid in installments over the next few months/years.

(e) An outstanding balance, a nominal rate of 2-3% per month is charged as interest.

(f) Regular use of the credit card by the user earns him additional points that provide the cardholder with discounts on purchases.

14.1.2. Mechanism of a Credit Card Transaction

Every transaction made on a credit card involves three parties:

(a) The Card Issuer

(b) The Cardholder

(c) The Merchant Establishment (ME)

A credit cardholder, subsequent to making a purchase or availing a service at a designated merchant establishment (ME), presents his credit card instead of paying cash. The ME checks the number of the card against the hot list provided to him by the card issuer, to ascertain the authenticity of the cardholder. The signature of the cardholder on the voucher provided by the ME should tally with the signature on the credit card. The ME then presents the sales vouchers to the bank, which reimburses it, after charging commission. At the end of each billing cycle, the value of the transaction is included in the statement mailed to the cardholder.

MEMBER AFFILIATED: The card issuer sometimes enters into a contract with organisations that also issue cards on behalf of the issuer to the clients. The organisations that issue cards are known as member affiliates. Cards issued by member affiliated are similar to credit cards except for the name and logo of the member affiliate besides the name and logo of the issuer. This type of arrangement enlarges the scope and operations of the credit card issuer.

CLEARING AGENCIES: The card issuer generally affiliates itself with master card international or visa card international that act as clearing agencies on behalf of the issuer. This enables the cardholder of one affiliate to use his card at the merchant establishment of another affiliate. The next section is devoted to explain first the debit card.

14.2 DEBIT CARD

It is the accountholder's mobile ATM. Open an account with a bank that offers a debit card, and payments for purchases are deducted from your bank account. The retailer swipes the card over an electronic terminal at this outlet, you enter the personal identification number on a PIN pad and the money is immediately debited at the bank. Citibank and a few domestic banks like Times Bank offer this.

Debit cards have been witnessing a slow and steady growth. It has made a delayed entry into India during 1998. The growth is phenomenal today. The present debit card base in India is estimated to be more than 1.5 crore.

The issuance and usage of debit cards has been steadily increasing over the last two years. But the awareness about the benefits and technology used is very low. Creating awareness among the customers will mark the future of debit cards in India.

14.2.1 Benefits of Debit Cards

Debit cards offer wide range of benefits to the customers. Some of them are:

(a) One can plan Budget within the savings instead of going for credit.

(b) He can access his own money 24 hours a day.

(c) He saves fee and other service charges on cash withdrawals.

(d) He can carry one card to use both at ATMs and at merchant locations

Benefits based on valued services are:

(a) The card is issued free.

(b) Free personal accident insurance cover for ₹ 1,00,000.

(c) Free lost card insurance from the time of intimation received by the bank.

(d) Free cash withdrawal facility at the bank ATMs. Shortly, it will be extended to branches also.

(e) Discounts will be arranged at selected merchant establishments for using debit card to settle the bill.

(f) Cardholder can access four of his accounts in one branch through a single card in the ATMs.

14.2.2 Features of Debit Card Technology

The technology involved in making the debit cards is sophisticated and almost all the issuing banks use the same kind of technology. Some of the features of the technology involved include:

(a) Technology is more or less similar.

(b) Debit cards can be used only at Point of Sale (POS) terminals and at ATMs where the data is read from the magnetic stripe positioned on the back of the card.

(c) There will not be any individual card limit. Whatever the balance maintained by cardholder, is accessible for usage.

(d) Some debit cards are only Personal Identification Number (PIN)-based whereas many are both PIN and signature based.

14.2.3 Safety Standards of Debit Cards

To safeguard the interests of the customer, the bank ensures the following:

(a) The card and the Personal Identification Number (PIN) are sent separately.

(b) The card has an inactive status, *i.e.*, it cannot be used for transactions at ATMs or at POS. The cardholder needs to activate his card by carrying out a transaction at the ATM using his PIN number.

The bank has a department that closely monitors all high-risk transactions on debit cards. Special reports on spend patterns are generated on a daily basis to mitigate potential loss on account of misuse of cards.

Debit cards use magnetic stripe-based technology. Debit cards can only be used for online transactions whereas Credit cards can also be used for offline transactions. Debit card transactions are subject to daily limits on the card and subject to the available balance in the customer's account whereas Credit cards transactions are subject to the credit limit of the customer.

The magnetic stripe and signature have been used on plastic cards since the early 1970s but they no longer form the best form of security. Chip and PIN will make payments more secure and are expected to dramatically reduce fraud losses.

There are two elements involved in making a plastic card transaction secure. The first is to ensure that the card is genuine; the second that the person presenting the card is the true owner. Chip does the former and PIN does the latter. The chip protects against counterfeit fraud and the PIN against lost and stolen cards and those intercepted in the post.

Banks and brands like Visa and MasterCard are investing significantly in migration from magnetic stripe technology to microchip technology. The chip — a small microchip is embedded into a debit or credit card and provides both highly secure memory and complex processing capabilities. The chip not only holds the same personal data as the magnetic stripe (cardholder name, card number, expiry date etc.) but also adds a range of indicators and counter mechanism to cyber-attacks which reduce the opportunities on misuse of the card. Chip technology uses highly sophisticated processing to identify genuine cards and makes counterfeiting more complex and expensive.

The PIN is a four-digit code assigned to or chosen by cardholders to prove that they are the rightful owners of the card when paying for goods and services. It will replace signature when the card is chip-enabled and when the retailer terminal is PIN-enabled.

IDBI Bank is in the process of migrating 100% of its card base from magnetic stripe to chip-based cards, which will ensure completing of all transactions in a secured environment.

14.3 TYPES OF CARDS

(a) MasterCard: MasterCard is a product of MasterCard International and along with VISA is distributed by financial institutions around the world. Cardholders borrow money against a line of credit and pay it back with interest if the balance is carried over from month to month. Its products are issued by 23,000 financial institutions in 220 countries and territories. In 1998, it had almost 700 million cards in circulation, whose users spent $ 650 billion in more than 16.2 million locations.

(b) Visa Card: Visa Card is a product of visa USA and along with MasterCard is distributed by financial institutions around the world. A visa cardholder borrows money against a credit line and repays the money with interest if the balance is carried over from month to month in a revolving line of credit. Nearly 600 million cards carry one of the visa brands and more than 14 million locations accept visa cards.

(c) Affinity Cards: A card offered by two organisations, one a lending institution the other a non-financial group. Schools, non-profit groups, pro-wrestlers, popular singers and airlines are among those featured on affinity cards. Usually, use of the card entitles holders to special discounts or deals from the non-financial group.

(d) Standard Card: It is the most basic card offered by issuers.

(e) Classic Card: Classic card is the brand name for the standard card issued by visa.

(f) Gold Card or Executive Card: Gold card is a credit card that offers a higher line of credit than a standard card. Income eligibility is also higher. In addition, issuers provide extra perks or incentives to cardholders.

(g) Platinum Card: Platinum card is a credit card with a higher limit and additional perks than a gold card.

(h) Titanium Card: itanium card is a card with an even higher limit than platinum card.

(i) Secured Card: It is a credit card that a cardholder secures with a savings deposit to ensure payment of the outstanding balance if the cardholder defaults on payments.

(j) Charge Card: It falls between a debit and credit card. It works like the latter and a person doesn't have to be an accountholder. The cardholder has to pay up in full when the bill arrives with the mail. No outstanding are allowed, in other words, no revolving credit facility either. American Express and Diners are providers.

(k) Rebate Card: This is a card that allows the customer to accumulate cash, merchandise or services based on card usage.

(l) Co-branded Card: This is an agreement between two service providers who want a trade-off with the other's strengths. Specific facilities are made to members through these tie-ups. So, Times Bank and Citibank have a co-branded card that allows concessional rates for add-on cards or telephone banking. Stanchart and Hindustan Lever Limited have a co-branded card to sell Aviance beauty products. SBI-GE Capital has a co-branded card for retail loans.

(m) Cash Card: Cash cards, similar to prepaid phone cards, contain a set amount of value, which can be read by a special cash card reader. Participating retailers will use the reader to debit the card in installments until the value is gone. The cards are like cash. They have no built-in security, so if lost or stolen, they can be used by anyone.

(n) Travel Card: These work mostly as debit cards for the limited purpose of travel. Citibank Dollar Card, American Express, BOB Card Global and Hong Kong Bank Thomas Cook International Card are among the players in this section.

(o) Laghu Udyami Credit Card (LUCC) Scheme: Encouraged by the response given to Kisan Credit Card Scheme, the Government launched a Laghu Udyami Credit Card Scheme (LUCC) in the Budget 2002-03. The Public Sector Banks would issue Credit Cards to small businessmen, retail traders, artisans, small entrepreneurs, professionals and other self-employed persons including those in the tiny sector. The scheme aims at providing simplified and borrower-friendly credit facilities.

14.4 NEW TYPES OF CREDIT CARD

Banks and other financial institutions have started issuing new types of credit cards. These include:

1. Corporate Credit Cards
2. Smart Cards
3. Global Credit Cards

14.4.1. Corporate Credit Cards

Companies, both public and private sector, issue these cards. The companies also issue other add-on cards to directors, secretaries and other persons depending upon their requirements. The name of the company is embedded on the add-on cards issued to the cardholder. Generally, the main card has a dummy card, which is used for the purpose of billing all the charges of the add-on cards. All transactions made through add-on cardholders are billed to the main card, which are debited from the company's account.

14.4.2. Smart Cards

Smart cards mark the next natural step in the world of plastic cards. A smart card has an integrated step embedded into it, which enables it to perform different functions. It has the capacity to store up to 80 times more information than other magnetic stripe cards. Smart cards are now available with 16 Kilobytes of memory. When read by special terminals, the cards can perform a number of functions or access data stored in the chip. These cards can be used as cash cards or as credit cards with a preset credit limit, or used as ID cards with stored-in passwords. Smart cards allow companies to deliver more personalised products and service that suit the individual lifestyle of the customers.

The best example could be the PetroCard, launched by Bharat Petroleum. It is India's first retail and loyalty card for petroleum applications with smart capabilities. The scheme allows its customers to make electronic payments for fuel and other goods. It also awards loyalty points that can be redeemed at any of the Bharat Petroleum retail stations or even at its convenience stores.

Smart cards also allow the consumers to carry multiple currencies when travelling. He can make secure purchases over the internet anytime, anywhere. He can pay for public transportation and public phone calls as well as make traditional credit and debit purchases — all with significantly fewer cards. Smart cards carry the electronic proof of its holder's identity enabling its holder to make secure purchases anywhere on the globe, leading to a dramatic increase in electronic commerce.

14.4.3. Global Card

Credit cards issued in India can only be used in India and Nepal. To overcome this drawback, a new card called a "Global Card" has been introduced. The card can be used anywhere across the globe as well as in India. The card can also be used to make foreign payments through the net, to import books, etc.

14.5 ELIGIBILITY TO GET A CARD

Following are the some of the criteria used by banks to oblige a potential client:

(a) Place of Residence: One of the important criteria for getting a card is that the applicant has to own a house. If an applicant stays in a rented house, the criteria would be that he should have stayed in the rented house fairly long.

(b) Telephone: Another criterion is that the applicant must have a telephone connection. It is because that the customer can easily be tracked down in case of default.

(c) Profession: Profession is yet another criterion for granting the service.

(d) Place of Work: Card issuers will normally check the reputation of the company you work in, the number of years you have put up there and your designation.

(e) Age: The applicant has to be above 18 years of age if he or she wants to have a credit card.

Other than this broad set of factors, issuers will also like to check the number of dependents of the applicant, whether he or she is servicing a loan and whether the applicant has another credit card. If a person possesses more than one credit card, one's credit history can easily be verified and depending on the record issuers will think of giving you another card or not.

14.6 COSTS OF CREDIT CARD PAYMENT

The following costs are involved in holding credit card.

(a) Renewal: The card has to be renewed every year for which the cardholder has to pay renewal charges. Often, the card issuer or bank will slip in renewal fees and even an unsolicited upgrade of class of card (e.g., classic to premium that means higher annual fees).

(b) Interest-free period on every bill: Interest is not charged for one month on every bill. In practice, part payments in a month by a cardholder are adjusted in such a way that the second bill will not be free from interest for the period assured. Assuming a person has a bill of ₹100 in the first month and the person settles ₹ 25. His or her second bill has a fresh purchase amount of ₹ 100 and the previous outstanding of ₹ 75 plus interest. If he or she gives ₹ 50 as part payment, the money goes toward clearing the previous outstanding and the current billing is taken as further outstanding. In other words, the second bill has no interest-free period.

(c) Purchases on credit: In some shops or retail outlets, card payments means an extra payment added to the bill by an establishment that does not want to encourage plastic money.

(d) Fuel on credit: Every time a person fills the tank, the service charge that accompanies each transaction could be 2.5%. Small charge adds up to fat sum in the total.

(e) Billing period: Every cardholder gets the bill in regular monthly cycles. If a person makes a purchase close to the billing date, he or she gets shorter payback time. Suppose the first billing date is April 25, after which there is a pay-by-due-date of a fortnight later, around May 9. A purchase on May 26 will be payable approximately around June 9 but a purchase on April 23 will be payable by May 9, that is a much shorter credit time.

(f) Cash advance: There are two sets of interest that are applied the moment the cash leaves the teller machine. First, there is a flat transaction fee. Second, there is a rate of interest that is applied on a daily basis. Thus, in the bill, one ends up with a dual interest. The cash advance payment is not included, usually, in the general bill.

14.7 CHOOSING THE RIGHT CARD

(a) **Acceptability:** This determines how widely the card is accepted. It depends on the network and the affiliation. For instance, Visa and MasterCards are more widely accepted than Diners or American Express. Also, a global card scores higher on acceptability than a domestic one.

(b) **Eligibility:** All cards have basic minimum income criterion for issuing cards. This ranges from ₹ 60,000 p.a. for Cancard and Stanchart-Classic to ₹ 200,000 p.a. for Amex-Gold and BoI Gold cards.

(c) **Fees:** One of the most important factors, the fees include joining fees, annual subscription and fees for add-on cards. All these fees are billed in the first bill and are not charged upfront.

(d) **Other Charges:** It's always better to pay on time. Otherwise you pay charges for late payment. These are only in case you do not pay the minimum required amount. Late payment charges range from 2.5% of outstanding to 15% of minimum payment.

(e) **Credit Period:** That's what it's all about! Buy now, pay later. Most cards have different credit periods ranging from 30 days to 50 days. That is the length of the billing cycle. This implies that the bill comes to you every nth day where n is the credit period. Also, credit covers finance charges. Most cards carry heavy credit charges ranging from 2.5% per month to 3% p.m. which works out to 34% and 42% p.a. respectively. There is a minimum payment required by most cards — from 5% of total value of the bill to 20%.

(f) **Cash Advance:** You can also borrow money from the card, but obviously pay interest charges on that. You also have to pay cash withdrawal charges — generally 2.5% of the amount withdrawn. Interest is also charged on the amount withdrawn-again around 2.5% p.m. Every card has a limit for the amount withdrawn-some cards have an absolute limit like ₹ 10,000 p.m. while most cards have a cash withdrawal limit as a %age of total credit limit.

(g) **Insurance Cover:** Insurance cover on cards is available only in the case of an accident. The limits are higher for air accidents than for other types.

Excessive Credit Card Accounts

Lenders dislike seeing many open credit card accounts and therefore lower his credit rating if he has too many credit cards. For this reason, he should close any department store credit cards and other accounts. He is not using or does not need at least 90 days before applying for a loan. If he is using more than 1 or 2 credit cards and borrowing heavily on them, it is wise to seriously look at how he is using credit and make sure he is not headed for financial disaster. If he is concerned about how he is handling debt, there are many non-profit organisations and websites offering consumer advice and debt consolidation services to help him manage and eliminate his debt.

14.8 USES OF CREDIT CARDS

Many problems associated with credit can be avoided through the use of credit cards. In many businesses, particularly in the retail and consumer service fields, credit arrangements for customers are available through the use of these cards. Under these plans, there is little or no commitment of the business's own capital, and the costs and risks of administration and collection are almost entirely the responsibility of the credit card company or bank.

Credit card service is available from one's regular commercial bank. Receipts from bank credit card purchases can be deposited daily and are immediately credited. The bank assumes all credit risks provided that one follows instructions for approval of credit card purchases. Typically, these instructions require that one checks the validity of the card against a master list of cancelled cards and contact the credit service before accepting the customer's card for purchase above a certain limit.

Credit card services are particularly vital for businesses with a large number of relatively small accounts. They eliminate the need for credit approval, invoice preparation, record maintenance, and collections. They also minimise one's commitment of capital and virtually eliminate the risk of uncollectible accounts. From a marketing standpoint, the availability of instant credit could often encourage a customer to buy immediately, rather than postpone the decision to a later date or bypass it completely.

Credit cards are most often used for retail accounts. However, they have also been used successfully in selling to small commercial accounts. Businesses such as repair shops, supply firms, and stationery stores, which have a mixture of consumer and commercial accounts, often find it convenient and economical to extend credit card service to small commercial accounts. Benefits provided by credit cards are not limited to the credit facility alone. Credit cards, today, are offering a number of other benefits such as:

(a) **Personal Accident Insurance:** Credit card issuers have introduced a free insurance cover to the cardholder against loss of life due to accidents.

(b) **Cash Withdrawal Facility:** A predetermined credit and cash limit is provided to the cardholder at Automated Teller Machine (ATM) facilities.

(c) **Increase in Credit:** Cardholders with a good credit track record, are provided with an increased credit limit for a short period of time, whenever required.

(d) **"Add-on" Facility:** The spouse, parents and children, over eighteen, of the cardholder, are provided with add-on cards on payment of a specified fee.

(e) **Leveraged Investment Facility:** This facility enables the cardholders to subscribe to designated equity or debenture issues in the primary market and schemes floated by mutual funds.

14.9 INDIAN EXPERIENCE

The perception to own credit cards has changed and cards are being viewed as a convenient substitute to carrying cash and also availing credit for short periods.

Cards in India

India ranks at the bottom in terms of usage of credit cards when compared to China, Taiwan and Malaysia. Usage of credit card picks up only last ten years. Indians viewed the cards as a luxury. Therefore, Indian banks were not willing to venture it. Over the last ten years, things have changed drastically. The idea of owning a credit card has had its roots in the minds of millions of Indians. They started viewing the card as a convenient substitute to carrying cash. The change in mindset is clear from the growth, both in terms of absolute numbers and growth rates. The industry has grown at the rate of 30% and is on the way to gain a critical mass in coming years.

Table 14.1 **Credit Cards in India**

Year	No. of Cards (in lakhs)
2000	37.34
2001	48.35
2002	60.60
2003	84.04

Source: Chartered Financial Analyst, Jan. 2004.

According to Visa International, an average Indian cardholder uses his card 9.3 times, spending about ₹ 23,000 per year. A number of card owners do not use their cards and almost 20-30% cards are inactive. In India, two players dominate the credit cards industry, Visa and MasterCards and 15 out of 17 banks provide credit card services through Visa or MasterCards.

The importance of having a pie in the credit cards segment was not lost on any bank, and most banks started their credit card operations. Currently, there are more than 20 banks offering credit cards, but the market share of the top five exceeds 75%.

Credit card is a low-margin, high-volume business. The initial investments required by a bank are very high. The income per card is low, thereby requiring large volumes in terms of cards issued and the transactions finance to make the operations profitable.

Another reason for the inability of players to upstage the well-entrenched ones is lower patronage by the merchant and business outfits. The bigger businesses and merchants are already acquired by the existing players, so for new banks, braking into this business and convincing a merchant is increasing because the banks are shifting towards lower end merchants. Secondly, because of competition in acquiring business, new categories of merchants are coming up.

The foreign banks have a dominant share due to various reasons like having been in the field for decades, sound operational and financial strength, strong brand recognition, etc. They were catering to the upper segments and charged high annual fees. Later, with aggressive entry of SBI, ICICI Bank and HDFC Bank, the rules of the game changed. The cards were positioned in manners which gave an impression that the cards can be acquired by people from not only the upper class, but also the middle income categories. This was the strategy followed by SBI-GE as a result of which it is the third largest issuer of credit cards today. It positioned itself in a segment as to be of mass appeal and at the same time reinforced a clean and dependable image of the bank.

Table 14.2 **Major Players and Their Ranks**

	No. of Cards (in Lakhs)		
Banks	**2001**	**2002**	**2003**
Citibank	14.00	16.00	20.00
StanChart	12.50	14.00	18.00
SBI-GE	6.00	9.03	13.00
HSBC	4.73	5.88	7.40
ICICI	2.50	5.00	8.0
AMEX	2.90	3.53	7.00

Source: Chartered Financial Analyst — January, 2004.

The new private banks like ICICI and HDFC are also aggressively increasing their share. They adopted a strategy of reaching lower down the income strata by lowering down their eligibility norms. Of course, the credit limits are set at lower levels as compared to the foreign banks. As a result of this strategy, the credit cards base is widening day by day with the increase of base in B-grade cities.

14.10 REVIEW QUESTIONS

Short Answer Questions

1. What is meant by credit card?
2. List out the benefits of holding a credit card in general.
3. Describe the mechanism of credit card transactions.
4. Explain the debit card.
5. What are the uses of debit cards?
6. Explain the uniqueness of debit card technology.
7. How does one safeguard himself with debit card?
8. Write short notes on:
   (a) Mastercard
   (b) Visacard
   (c) Affinity card
   (d) Smart card
   (e) Charge card
   (f) Travel card
   (g) Laghu Udyami card
   (h) Global Credit Cards
9. What are the eligibility criteria for getting a card?

Essay Type Questions

1. What is plastic money? Explain the features of different types of cards.
2. Describe the features of debit card.
3. Discuss the importance of holding a credit card.
4. What are the formalities to be fulfilled by one to get a credit card?
5. Write about the costs involved in holding a credit card.
6. How does one choose his card?
7. List the uses of credit cards.
8. Critically examine the present status of credit cards in India.
9. Discuss the growth prospects of credit card business in India.
10. Who are the players in the credit card market? Briefly explain their roles.

❋ ❋ ❋

CHAPTER 15

Micro Finance

Objectives

The student, after studying the chapter, should be able to:

- Describe the concept of "Micro Finance".
- The role of Self Help Groups (SHGs) in Micro Credit.
- Explain the various Micro Credit Delivery Models.

Structure:

15.1 INTRODUCTION

Availability of credit is the basic requirement to any citizen, more so, to a poor person. Credit should be timely as well as easily available. Formal institutions, including nationalised banks are unable to meet the micro credit requirements of the poor people, as normally credit for income generation has been institutionalized rather than micro credit for various purposes. This has left poor persons with no option except to depend on moneylenders for credit. Moneylenders with abundant common sense offer timely — but a exploitative credit, which act as a poverty trap for the poor. Various studies have proved that in rural India, a person taking credit from moneylender for health or for a ritual like marriage forever has gone below poverty line.

Poverty as we understand is a complex phenomena and it cannot be solved only by providing income generation assets but through comprehensive personality development of poor person enabling him/her to meet various needs.

15.2 MICRO CREDIT

Micro Credit is defined as provision of thrift, credit and other financial services and products of very small amount to the poor in rural, semi-urban and urban areas for enabling them to raise their income levels and improve living standards. Micro Credit Institutions are those which provide these facilities

15.3 GRAMEEN CREDIT

Whenever I use the word "micro credit", I actually have in mind Grameen type micro credit or Grameen credit. But if the person I am talking to; understands it as some other category of micro credit my arguments will not make any sense to him. Let me list below the distinguishing features of Grameen credit. This is an exhaustive list of such features. Not every Grameen type programme has all these features present in the programme. Some programmes are strong in some of the features, while others are strong in some other features. But on the whole, they display a general convergence to some basic features on the basis of which they introduce themselves as Grameen replication programmes or Grameen type programmes.

Grameen Credit is based on the premise that the poor have skills which remain unutilised or underutilised. It is definitely not the lack of skills which make poor people poor. Grameen believes that the poverty is not created by the poor, it is created by the institutions and policies which surround them. In order to eliminate poverty all we need to do is to make appropriate changes in the institutions and policies, and/or create new ones. Grameen believes that charity is not an answer to poverty. It only helps poverty to continue. It creates dependency and takes away individual's initiative to break through the wall of poverty. Unleashing of energy and creativity in each human being is the answer to poverty. Grameen brought credit to the poor, women, the illiterate, the people who pleaded that they did not know how to invest money and earn an income. Grameen created a methodology and an institution around the financial needs of the poor, and created access to credit on reasonable term enabling the poor to build on their existing skill to earn a better income in each cycle of loans. If donors can frame categorywise micro credit policies, they may overcome some of their discomforts. General policy for micro credit in its wider sense, is bound to be devoid of focus and sharpness.

15.3.1. General Features of Grameen Credit are:

(a) It promotes credit as a human right.

(b) Its mission is to help the poor families to help themselves to overcome poverty. It is targeted to the poor, particularly poor women.

(c) Most distinctive feature of Grameen credit is that it is not based on any collateral, or legally enforceable contracts. It is based on "trust", not on legal procedures and system.

(d) It is offered for creating self-employment for income-generating activities and housing for the poor, as opposed to consumption.

(e) It was initiated as a challenge to the conventional banking which rejected the poor by classifying them to be "not creditworthy". As a result, it rejected the basic methodology of the conventional banking and created its own methodology.

(f) It provides service at the doorstep of the poor based on the principle that the people should not go to the bank, bank should go to the people.

(g) In order to obtain loans, a borrower must join a group of borrowers.

(h) Loans can be received in a continuous sequence. New loan becomes available to a borrower if her previous loan is repaid.

(i) All loans are to be paid back in installments (weekly, or bi-weekly).

(j) Simultaneously, more than one loan can be received by a borrower.

(k) It comes with both obligatory and voluntary savings programmes for the borrowers.

(l) Generally, these loans are given through non-profit organisations, or through institutions owned primarily by the borrowers. If it is done through for-profit institutions not owned by the borrowers, efforts are made to keep the interest rate at a level which is close to a level commensurate with sustainability of the programme rather than bringing attractive return for the investors. Grameen credit's thumb-rule is to keep the interest rate as close to the market rate, prevailing in the commercial banking sector, as possible, without sacrificing sustainability. In fixing the interest rate market, interest rate, is taken as the reference rate, rather than the moneylenders' rate. Reaching the poor is its non-negotiable mission. Reaching sustainability is a directional goal. It must reach sustainability as soon as possible, so that it can expand its outreach without fund constraints.

(m) Grameen credit gives high priority on building social capital. It is promoted through formation of groups and centres, developing leadership quality through annual election of group and centre leaders, electing board members when the institution is owned by the borrowers. To develop a social agenda owned by the borrowers, something similar to the "sixteen decisions", it undertakes a process of intensive discussion among the borrowers, and encourage them to take these decisions seriously and implement them. It gives special emphasis on the formation of human capital and concern for protecting environment. It monitors children's education, provides scholarships and student loans for higher education. For formation of human capital, it makes efforts to bring technology, like mobile phones, solar power, and promote mechanical power to replace manual power.

15.4 BANKING RATES AND NORMS

The reform of the interest rate regime has constituted an integral part of the financial sector reforms initiated in our country in 1991. In consonance with this reform process, interest rates applicable to loans given by banks to micro credit organizations or by the micro credit organizations to Self-help Groups/member-beneficiaries has been left to their discretion. The interest rate ceiling applicable to direct small loans given by banks to individual borrowers, however, continues to remain in force.

Banks have been given freedom to formulate their own lending norms keeping in view ground realities. They have been asked to devise appropriate loan and savings products and the related terms and conditions including size of the loan, unit cost, unit size, maturity period, grace period, margins, etc. Such credit covers not only consumption and production loans for various farm and non-farm activities of the poor but also include their other credit needs such as housing and shelter improvements.

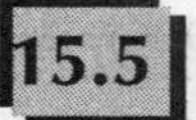

15.5 ROLE OF SELF-HELP GROUP (SHG)

A Self-Help Group (SHG) is a registered or unregistered group of micro entrepreneurs having homogenous social and economic background voluntarily, coming together to save small amounts regularly, to mutually agree to contribute to a common fund and to meet their emergency needs on mutual help basis. The group members use collective wisdom and peer pressure to ensure proper end-use of credit and timely repayment thereof. In fact, peer pressure has been recognised as an effective substitute for collaterals.

15.6 ADVANTAGES OF FINANCING THROUGH SHGs

An economically poor individual gain strength as part of a group. Besides, financing through SHGs reduces transaction costs for both lenders and borrowers. While lenders have to handle only a single SHG account instead of a large number of small-sized individual accounts, borrowers as part of a SHG cut down expenses on travel (to and from the branch and other places) for completing paperwork and on the loss of workdays in canvassing for loans.

15.7 ROLE OF NON-GOVERNMENTAL ORGANISATION (NGO) IN MICRO CREDIT

A Non-governmental Organisation (NGO) is a voluntary organisation established to undertake social intermediation like organising SHGs of micro entrepreneurs and entrusting them to banks for credit linkage or financial intermediation like borrowing bulk funds from banks for on-lending to SHGs.

15.8 MICRO FINANCE CREDIT LENDING MODELS

Micro finance institutions are using various Credit Lending Models throughout the world. Some of the models are listed below:

Associations

This is where the target community forms an 'association' through which various microfinance (and other) activities are initiated. Such activities may include savings. Associations or groups can be composed of youth, or women; they can form around political/religious/cultural issues; can create support structures for micro enterprises and other work-based issues.

In some countries, an 'association' can be a legal body that has certain advantages such as collection of fees, insurance, tax breaks and other protective measures. Distinction is made between associations, community groups, people's organisations, etc. on one hand (which are mass, community based) and NGOs, etc. which are essentially external organisations.

Bank Guarantees

As the name suggests, a bank guarantee is used to obtain a loan from a commercial bank. This guarantee may be arranged externally (through a donor/donation, government agency, etc.) or internally (using member savings). Loans obtained may be given directly to an individual, or they may be given to a self-formed group.

Bank Guarantee is a form of capital guarantee scheme. Guaranteed funds may be used for various purposes, including loan recovery and insurance claims. Several international and UN organisations have been creating international guarantee funds that banks and NGOs can subscribe to, to on-lend or start microcredit programmes.

Community Banking

The Community Banking model essentially treats the whole community as one unit, and establishes semi-formal or formal institutions through which micro finance is dispensed. Such institutions are usually formed by extensive help from NGOs and other organisations, who also train the community members in various financial activities of the community bank. These institutions may have savings components and other income-generating projects included in their structure. In many cases, community banks are also part of larger community development programmes which use finance as an inducement for action.

Cooperatives

A cooperative is an autonomous association of persons united voluntarily to meet their common economic, social, and cultural needs and aspirations through a jointly-owned and democratically-controlled enterprise. Some cooperatives include member-financing and savings activities in their mandate.

Credit Unions

A credit union is a unique member-driven, self-help financial institution. It is organised by and comprised of members of a particular group or organization, who agree to save their money together and to make loans to each other at reasonable rates of interest.

The members are people of some common bond: working for the same employer; belonging to the same church, labour union, social fraternity, etc.; or living/working in the same community. A credit union's membership is open to all who belong to the group, regardless of race, religion, colour or creed. A credit union is a democratic, not-for-profit financial cooperative. Each is owned and governed by its members, with members having a vote in the election of directors and committee representatives.

Grameen

The Grameen model emerged from the poor-focussed grassroots institution, Grameen Bank, started by Prof. Mohammed Yunus in Bangladesh. It essentially adopts the following methodology:

A bank unit is set up with a Field Manager and a number of bank workers, covering an area of about 15 to 22 villages. The manager and workers start by visiting villages to familiarise themselves with the local milieu in which they will be operating and identify prospective clientele, as well as explain the purpose, functions, and mode of operation of the bank to the local population. Groups of five prospective borrowers are formed; in the first stage, only two of them are eligible for, and receive, a loan. The group is observed for a month to see if the members are conforming to rules of the bank. Only if the first two borrowers repay the principal plus interest over a period of fifty weeks do other members of the group become eligible themselves for a loan. Because of these restrictions, there is substantial group pressure to keep individual records clear. In this sense , collective responsibility of the group serves as collateral on the loan.

Group

The Group Model's basic philosophy lies in the fact that shortcomings and weaknesses at the individual level are overcome by the collective responsibility and security afforded by the formation of a group of such individuals.

The collective coming together of individual members is used for a number of purposes: educating and awareness building, collective bargaining power, peer pressure, etc.

Individual

This is a straightforward credit lending model where micro loans are given directly to the borrower. It does not include the formation of groups, or generating peer pressures to ensure repayment. The individual model is, in many cases, a part of a larger 'credit plus' programme, where other socio-economic services such as skill development, education, and other outreach services are provided.

Intermediaries

Intermediary model of credit lending position is a 'go-between' organisation between the lenders and borrowers. The intermediary plays a critical role of generating credit awareness and education among the borrowers (including, in some cases, starting savings programmes. These activities are geared towards raising the 'creditworthiness' of the borrowers to a level sufficient enough to make them attractive to the lenders.

The links developed by the intermediaries could cover funding, programme links, training and education, and research. Such activities can take place at various levels from international and national to regional, local and individual levels. Intermediaries could be individual lenders, NGOs, micro enterprise/micro credit programmes, and commercial banks (for government financed programmes). Lenders could be government agencies, commercial banks, international donors, etc.

Non-governmental Organisations

NGOs have emerged as a key player in the field of micro credit. They have played the role of intermediary in various dimensions. NGOs have been active in starting and participating in micro credit programmes. This includes creating awareness of the importance of micro credit within the community, as well as various national and international donor agencies. They have developed resources and tools for communities and micro credit organisations to monitor progress and identify good practices. They have also created opportunities to learn about the principles and practice of micro credit. This includes publications, workshops and seminars, and training programmes.

Peer Pressure

Peer pressure uses moral and other linkages between borrowers and project participants to ensure participation and repayment in micro credit programmes. Peers could be other members in a borrowers group (where, unless the initial borrowers in a group repay, the other members do not receive loans. Hence, pressure is put on the initial members to repay); community leaders (usually identified, nurtured and trained by external NGOs); NGOs themselves and their field officers; banks, etc. The 'pressure' applied can be in the form of frequent visits to the defaulter, community meetings where they are identified and requested to comply, etc.

Rotating Savings and Credit Associations

Rotating Savings and Credit Associations (ROSCAs) are essentially a group of individuals who come together and make regular cyclical contributions to a common fund, which is then given as a lump sum to one member in each cycle. For example, a group of 12 persons may contribute ₹ 100 (US$ 33) per month for 12 months. The ₹ 1,200 collected each month is given to one member. Thus, a member will 'lend' money to other members through his regular monthly contributions. After having received the lump sum amount when it is his turn (i.e., 'borrow' from the group), he then pays back the amount in regular/further monthly contributions. Deciding who receives the lump sum is done by consensus, by lottery, by bidding or other agreed methods.

Small Business

The prevailing vision of the 'informal sector' is one of survival, low productivity and very little value added. But this has been changing, as more and more importance is placed on small and medium enterprises (SMEs) — for generating employment, for increasing income and providing services which are lacking.

Policies have generally focussed on direct interventions in the form of supporting systems such as training, technical advice, management principles, etc.; and indirect interventions in the form of an enabling policy and market environment.

A key component that is always incorporated as a sort of common denominator has been finance, specifically micro credit — in different forms and for different uses. Micro credit has been provided to SMEs directly, or as a part of a larger enterprise development programme, along with other inputs.

Village Banking

Village banks are community-based credit and savings associations. They typically consist of 25 to 50 low-income individuals who are seeking to improve their lives through self-employment activities. Initial loan capital for the village bank may come from an external source, but the members themselves run the bank: they choose their members, elect their own officers, establish their own bye-laws, distribute loans to individuals, collect payments and savings. Their loans are backed, not by goods or property, but by moral collateral: the promise that the group stands behind each individual loan.

15.9 LOAN DELIVERY MODELS

- Conventional/Branch Model
- Partnership Model

Under both the models, the loan deliver to individual member on their joint liability. Each model is almost similar except infrastructure and group size, which are described as under:

Conventional Model

In Conventional Model, Cashpor has adapted FI (Financial Intermediation) methodology, where Cashpor takes money from different banks in a pool and lend it to clients. Here, the outstanding occurs in the books of the Cashpor.

Operational Features

1. Under this model, we have 10 Branch offices associated with a District office.
2. Each branch has 8 CM (Center Manager).
3. CM reports to Branch Manager, whereas Branch Manager reports to Area Manager and Area Manager reports to District Manager.
4. A group consist 5 members and a Center consist 4 groups.
5. Center Meeting happens once in a week.

Partnership Model

In Partnership Model, Cashpor has adapted SI (Social Intermediation) methodology, where Cashpor manages the money of its partner Banks/FIs. Here, the outstanding occurs in the books of the partner (Banks/FIs). Cashpor takes service charges in lieu of its services. As a Social Intermediary, Cashpor undertakes the following functions:

1. Identification of poor clients.
2. Group formation.
3. Imparting training to the groups.
4. Grading/recognizing the groups.
5. Taking loan proposals.
6. Disbursing loans to poor clients.
7. Taking care of repayments and managing delinquency.

Operational Features

1. Under this model, we have a District office divided into 4 units, whereas units don't have its offices.
2. District office is headed by District Manager and units are headed by their Unit Managers.
3. Each unit has 20 CM.

4. CMs reports to Unit Manager, Unit Managers reports to District Manager and District Manager report Managing Director.
5. All the center managers and Unit Managers report once in week to District office.
6. Here, a group consists of 15-20 members.

15.10 RECENT STUDIES ON MICRO CREDIT

With a view to facilitating smoother and more meaningful banking with the poor, a pilot project for purveying micro credit by linking Self-help Groups (SHGs) with banks was launched by NABARD in 1991-92 with a view to facilitating smoother and more meaningful banking with the poor. RBI had then advised commercial banks to actively participate in this linkage programme. The scheme has since been extended to RRBs and cooperative banks. The number of SHGs linked to banks aggregated 4,61,478 as on March 31, 2002. This translates into an estimated 7.87 million very poor families brought within the fold of formal banking services as on March 31, 2002. More than 90% of the groups linked with banks are exclusive women groups. Cumulative disbursement of bank loans to these SHGs stood at ₹ 1,026.34 crores as on March 31, 2002 with an average loan of ₹ 22,240.00 per SHG and ₹ 1,316.00 per family. As regards model-wise linkage, while Model I, viz., directly to SHGs without intervention/facilitation of any NGO now accounts for 16%, Model II, viz., directly to SHGs with facilitation by NGOs and other formal agencies amounts to 75% and Model III, *viz.,* through NGO as facilitator and financing agency represents 09% of the total linkage. While 488 districts in all the states/UTs have been covered under this programme, 444 banks including 44 commercial banks (including 17 in the private sector), 191 RRBs and 209 co-operative banks along with 2,155 NGOs are now associated with the SHG-bank linkage programme. While the SHG-bank linkage programme has surely emerged as the dominant micro finance dispensation model in India, other models too have evolved as significant micro finance purveying channels.

The other successful models that have emerged are:

(a) An Intermediate Model that works on banking principles with focus on both savings and credit activities and where banking services are provided to the clients either directly or through SHGs;

(b) There is also a Wholesale Banking Model where the clients comprise NGOs, MFIs and SHG Federations. This Model involves a unique package of providing both loans and capacity building support to its partners; and

(c) Further, there is an Individual Banking-based Model that has its clients as individuals or joint liability groups. While programme management and client appraisal in this Model may be a challenge, it is best suited to lending to enterprises.

Keeping these validated models for delivery of credit to the poor and the unorganised sector in view, RBI is moving towards a systems perspective for providing effective policy support not only because a number of different institutions, viz., banks, MFIs, NGOs and SHGs are involved, but also because these institutions have very different institutional goals. With this in view, a series of initiatives is being planned in the coming months for putting in place a more vibrant micro finance dispensation environment in the country where complementary and competitive models of micro finance delivery would be encouraged to co-exist.

Foreign Investment and Micro Credit

Government of India vide their notification dated August 29, 2000 have included 'Micro Credit/Rural Credit' in the list of permitted non-banking financial company (NBFC) activities for being considered for Foreign Direct Investment (FDI)/Overseas Corporate Bodies (OCB)/Non-resident Indians (NRI) investment to encourage foreign participation in micro credit projects. This covers credit facility at micro level for providing finance to small producers and small micro enterprises in rural and urban areas.

Micro Finance Development Fund

There is an urgent need for micro credit providers to shift from a minimalist approach — that is offering only financial intermediation — to an integrated approach to poverty alleviation taking a more holistic view of the client including provision of enterprise development services like marketing infrastructure, introduction of technology and design development. In this context, the setting up of the Micro Finance Development Fund marks an important step. Pursuant to the announcement of Union Finance Minister in his budget speech for the year 2000-01, this ₹ 100 crore fund has been created in NABARD to support broadly the following activities: (a) giving training and exposure to self-help group (SHG) members, partner NGOs, banks and government agencies; (b) providing start-up funds to micro finance institutions and meeting their initial operational deficits; (c) meeting the cost of formation and nurturing of SHGs; (d) designing new delivery mechanisms; and (e) promoting research, action research, management information systems and dissemination of best practices in micro finance. This Fund is, thus, expected to address institutional and delivery issues like institutional growth and transformation, governance, accessing new sources of funding, building institutional capacity and increasing volumes. RBI and NABARD have contributed ₹ 40 crore each to this Fund. The balance ₹ 20 crore were contributed by 11 public sector banks.

15.11 LEGAL FRAMEWORK

The position is as under:

Categories of Providers	Legal Framework governing their activities
(a) Domestic Commercial Banks: Public Sector Banks; Private Sector Banks and Local Area Banks	(i) RBI Act 1934 (ii) BR Act 1949 (iii) SBI Act (iv) SBI Subsidiaries Act (v) Acquisition and Transfer of Undertakings Act 1970 & 1980
(b) Regional Rural Banks	(i) RRB Act 1976 (ii) RBI Act 1934 (iii) BR Act 1949
(c) Cooperative Banks (d) Cooperative Societies (e) Registered NBFCs	(i) Cooperative Societies Act (ii) BR Act 1949 (AACS) (iii) RBI Act 1934 (for scheduled banks)
(f) Unregistered NBFCs	(i) State legislation like MACS (i) RBI Act 1934 (ii) Companies Act 1956
(g) Other providers like Societies, Trusts, etc.	(i) NBFCs carrying on the business of a FI prior to the coming into force of RBI Amendment Act 1997 whose application for CoR has not yet been rejected by the Bank (ii) Sec. 25 of Companies Act (i) Societies Registration Act '60 (ii) Indian Trusts Act (iii) Chapter IIIC of RBI Act '34 (iv) State Moneylenders Act

15.12 REVIEW QUESTIONS

Short Answer Questions

1. What is Micro Credit?
2. List out the various features of Grameen credit.
3. What is an SHG?
4. List out the advantages of financing through SHGs.
5. Who is an NGO?

Essay Type Questions

1. Trace the background of Micro Finance and explain its advantages.
2. Explain the various Micro Credit Lending Models.
3. Explain the various Micro Credit Loan Delivery Models in brief.
4. What are the Legal Framework governing the micro finance activities?

❋ ❋ ❋

CHAPTER 16

Derivatives

Objectives

The student, after studying the chapter, should be able to:

- Understand the meaning and importance of derivatives
- Understand the various types of derivatives
- Familiarize the terminologies used in Options
- Understand the various models in option valuation
- Distinguish between futures and forwards
- Understand the working of Swaps.

Structure:

16.1 Importance of Derivatives
16.2 Definition of Derivative
16.3 Types of Derivatives
16.4 Options
16.5 Options Styles
16.6 Option Terminology
16.7 Factors Affecting Option Premium
16.8 Option Valuation Model
16.9 Forwards
16.10 Future Contract
16.11 Distinction between Futures and Forwards
16.12 Swaps
16.13 Review Questions

Introduction

Derivatives have made the international and financial headlines in the past for mostly with their association with spectacular losses or institutional collapses. But market players have traded derivatives successfully for centuries and the daily international turnover in derivatives trading runs into billions of dollars.

Are derivative instruments that can only be traded by experienced, specialist traders? Although it is true that complicated mathematical models are used for pricing some derivatives, the basic concepts and principles underpinning derivatives and their trading are quite easy to grasp and understand. Indeed, derivatives are used increasingly by market players ranging from governments, corporate treasurers, dealers and brokers and individual investors.

16.1 IMPORTANCE OF DERIVATIVES

Derivatives have become very important in the field finance. They are very important financial instruments for risk management as they allow risks to be separated and traded. Derivatives are used to shift risk and act as a form of insurance. This shift of risk means that each party involved in the contract should be able to identify all the risks involved before the contract is agreed. It is also important to remember that derivatives are derived from an underlying asset. This means that risks in trading derivatives may change depending on what happens to the underlying asset.

16.2 DEFINITION OF DERIVATIVE

A derivative is a product whose value is derived from the value of an underlying asset, index or reference rate. The underlying asset can be equity, forex, commodity or any other asset. For example, if the settlement price of a derivative is based on the stock price of a stock, e.g., Infosys, which frequently changes on a daily basis, then the derivative risks are also changing on a daily basis. This means that derivative risks and positions must be monitored constantly.

Stock markets by their very nature are fickle. While fortunes can be made in a jiffy, more often than not the scenario is the reverse. Investing in stocks has two sides to it: (a) Unlimited profit potential from any upside (remember Infosys, HFCL, etc.) or (b) a downside which could make you a pauper.

16.3 TYPES OF DERIVATIVES

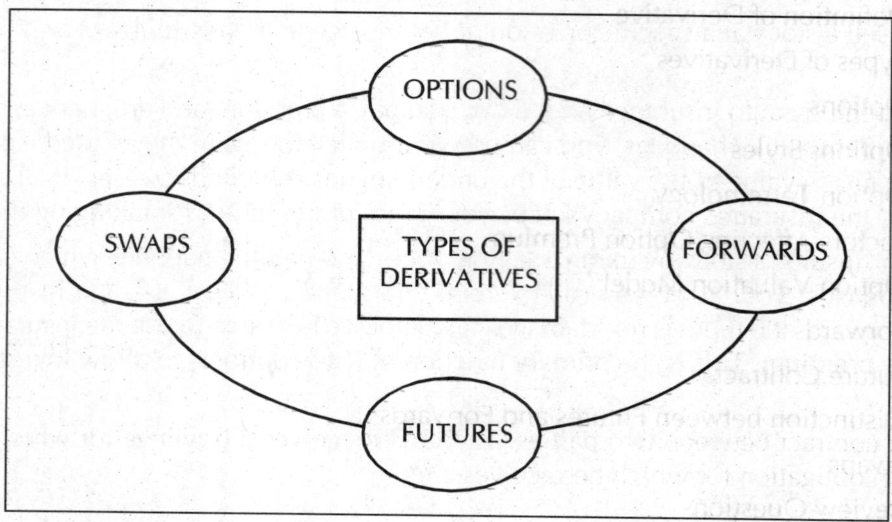

16.4 OPTIONS

Meaning

Some people remain puzzled by options. The truth is that most people have been using options for some time, because options are built into everything from mortgages to insurance.

An option is a contract, which gives the buyer the right, but not the obligation to buy or sell shares of the underlying security at a specific price on or before a specific date.

'Option', as the word suggests, is a choice given to the investor to either honour the contract; or if he chooses not to walk away from the contract.

Definition

An option is a contract between two parties giving the taker (buyer) the right, but not the obligation, to buy or sell a parcel of shares at a predetermined price possibly on, or before a predetermined date. To acquire this right, the taker pays a premium to the writer (seller) of the contract.

Option types

There are two types of options:

- Call Options
- Put Options

Call Option

A Call Option is an option to buy a stock at a specific price on or before a certain date. In this way, call options are like security deposits. If, for example, you wanted to rent a certain property, and left a security deposit for it, the money would be used to insure that you could, in fact, rent that property at the price agreed upon when you returned. If you never returned, you would give up your security deposit, but you would have no other liability. Call options usually increase in value as the value of the underlying instrument rises.

When you buy a Call option, the price you pay for it, called the option premium, secures your right to buy that certain stock at a specified price called the strike price. If you decide not to use the option to buy the stock, and you are not obligated to, your only cost is the option premium.

Put Option

Put Options are options to sell a stock at a specific price on or before a certain date. In this way, Put options are like insurance policies

If you buy a new car, and then buy auto insurance on the car, you pay a premium and are, hence, protected if the asset is damaged in an accident. If this happens, you can use your policy to regain the insured value of the car. In this way, the put option gains in value as the value of the underlying instrument decreases. If all goes well and the insurance is not needed, the insurance company keeps your premium in return for taking on the risk.

With a Put Option, you can "insure" a stock by fixing a selling price. If something happens which causes the stock price to fall, and thus, "damages" your asset, you can exercise your option and sell it at its "insured" price level. If the price of your stock goes up, and there is no "damage," then you do not need to use the insurance, and, once again, your only cost is the premium. This is the primary function of listed options, to allow investors ways to manage risk.

Technically, an option is a contract between two parties. The buyer receives a privilege for which he pays a premium. The seller accepts an obligation for which he receives a fee.

Buyer and Writer

CALL OPTION BUYER

- Pays premium
- Right to exercise and buy the shares
- Profits from rising prices
- Limited losses, potentially unlimited gain

CALL OPTION WRITER (Seller)

- Receives premium
- Obligation to sell shares if exercised
- Profits from falling prices or remaining neutral
- Potentially unlimited losses, limited gain

PUT OPTION BUYER

- Pays premium
- Right to exercise and sell shares
- Profits from falling prices
- Limited losses, potentially unlimited gain

PUT OPTION WRITER (Seller)

- Receives premium
- Obligation to buy shares if exercised
- Profits from rising prices or remaining neutral
- Potentially unlimited losses, limited gain

16.5 OPTIONS STYLES

They are put into two different styles:

- **European**
- **American**

European Style

These options give the holder the right, but not the obligation, to buy or sell the underlying instrument **only** on the expiry date. This means that the option **cannot be exercised early**. Settlement is based on a particular strike price at expiration. Currently, in India, index and stock options are European in nature.

American Style

These options give the holder the right, but not the obligation, to buy or sell the underlying instrument **on or before** the expiry date. This means that the option **can be exercised early**. Settlement is based on a particular strike price at expiration.

16.6 OPTION TERMINOLOGY

(Strike price, In-the-money, Out-of-the-Money, At-the-Money, Covered call and Covered Put)

Strike Price

The Strike Price denotes the price at which the buyer of the option has a right to purchase or sell the underlying. Five different strike prices will be available at any point of time. The strike price interval will be of 20. If the index is currently at 1,410, the strike prices available will be 1,370, 1,390, 1,410, 1,430 and 1,450. The strike price is also called **Exercise Price**. This price is fixed by the exchange for the entire duration of the option depending on the movement of the underlying stock or index in the cash market.

In-the-money

A Call Option is said to be "In-the-money" if the strike price is less than the market price of the underlying stock. A Put Option is In-the-money when the strike price is greater than the market price.

e.g., Raj purchases 1 SATCOM AUG 190 Call — Premium 10

In the above example, the option is "in-the-money", till the market price of SATCOM is ruling above the strike price of ₹ 190, which is the price at which Raj would like to buy 100 shares anytime before the end of August.

Similarly, if Raj had purchased a Put at the same strike price, the option would have been "in-the- money", if the market price of SATCOM was lower than ₹ 190 per share.

Out-of-the-money

A Call Option is said to be "Out-of-the-money" if the strike price is greater than the market price of the stock. A Put option is Out-of-money if the strike price is less than the market price.

e.g.: Sam purchases 1 INFTEC AUG 3500 Call — Premium 150

In the above example, the option is "out-of- the-money", if the market price of INFTEC is ruling below the strike price of ₹ 3,500, which is the price at which SAM would like to buy 100 shares anytime before the end of August.

Similary, if Sam had purchased a Put at the same strike price, the option would have been "out-of-the-money", if the market price of INFTEC was above ₹ 3,500 per share.

At-the-money

The option with strike price equal to that of the market price of the stock is considered as being "At-the-money" or "Near-the-money".

e.g.: Raj purchases 1 ACC AUG 150 Call or Put — Premium 10

In the above case, if the market price of ACC is ruling at ₹ 150, which is equal to the strike price, then the option is said to be "at-the-money".

If the index is currently at 1,410, the strike prices available will be 1,370, 1,390, 1,410, 1,430 and 1,450. The strike prices for a call option that are greater than the underlying (Nifty or Sensex) are said to be out-of-the-money in this case 1,430 and 1,450 considering that the underlying is at 1,410. Similarly, in-the-money strike prices will be 1,370 and 1,390, which are lower than the underlying of 1,410.

At these prices, one can take either a positive or negative view on the markets, i.e., both call and put options will be available. Therefore, for a single series 10 options (5 calls and 5 puts) will be available and considering that there are three series, a total number of 30 options will be available to take positions in.

Covered Call

Covered option helps the writer to minimise his loss. In a covered call option, the writer of the call option takes a corresponding long position in the stock in the cash market; this will cover his loss in his option position if there is a sharp increase in price of the stock. Further, he is able to bring down his average cost of acquisition in the cash market (which will be the cost of acquisition less the option premium collected).

e.g.: Raj believes that HLL has hit rock bottom at the level of ₹ 182 and it will move in a narrow range. He can take a long position in HLL shares and at the same time, write a call option with a strike price of 185 and collect a premium of ₹ 5 per share. This will bring down the effective cost of HLL shares to 177 (182-5). If the price stays below 185 till expiry, the call option will not be exercised and the writer will keep the ₹ 5 he collected as premium. If the price goes above 185 and the option is exercised, the writer can deliver the shares acquired in the cash market.

Covered Put

Similarly, a writer of a Put Option can create a covered position by selling the underlying security (if it is already owned). The effective selling price will increase by the premium amount (if the option is not exercised at maturity). Here again, the investor is not in a position to take advantage of any sharp increase in the price of the asset as the underlying asset has already been sold. If there is a sharp decline in the price of the underlying asset, the option will be exercised and the investor will be left only with the premium amount. The loss in the option exercised will be equal to the gain in the short position of the asset.

Pricing of Options

Options are used as risk management tools and the valuation or pricing of the instruments is a careful balance of market factors. Pricing of options will help the investor to decide whether to purchase the option. Pricing of the option means calculating the premium for the options. Premium of the option is decided based on the volatility of the stock and exercise price of the option. We will discuss further in depth about the pricing of Options below:

To understand the option premium, first we will understand the basic characteristics of stock valuation.

A stock is valued based on its intrinsic value. Then the question arises what is intrinsic value?

Intrinsic Value — Definition

Intrinsic value is defined as the sum of present value of all dividends and present value of the current market price of the share.

Intrinsic value decides whether the stock is undervalued or overvalued. According to fundamentalist, ***the stock prices will always move towards the intrinsic value***. Most of the investors gain money in the stock market if they accurately forecast the intrinsic value of the stocks.

The Intrinsic Value of an Option

The intrinsic value of an option is defined as the amount by which an option is in-the-money, or the immediate exercise value of the option when the underlying position is marked-to-market.

For a call option: Intrinsic Value = Spot Price – Strike Price

For a put option: Intrinsic Value = Strike Price – Spot Price

The intrinsic value of an option must be positive or zero. It cannot be negative. For a call option, the strike price must be less than the price of the underlying asset for the call to have an intrinsic value greater than 0. For a put option, the strike price must be greater than the underlying asset price for it to have intrinsic value.

16.7 FACTORS AFFECTING OPTION PREMIUM

There are four major factors affecting the Option premium:

- Price of Underlying
- Time to Expiry
- Exercise Price Time to Maturity
- Volatility of the Underlying

And two less important factors:

- Short-term Interest Rates
- Dividends

Price of Underlying

The premium is affected by the price movements in the underlying instrument. For Call options — the right to buy the underlying at a fixed strike price — as the underlying price rises so does its premium. As the underlying price falls so does the cost of the option premium. For Put options — the right to sell the underlying at a fixed strike price — as the underlying price rises, the premium falls; as the underlying price falls, the premium cost rises.

Exercise Price at the Time of Maturity

Exercise price also affects the option premium. If the price of the stock decreases at the time of maturity, the cost of option premium falls.

Time to Expiry

Generally, the longer the time remaining until an option's expiration, the higher its premium will be. This is because the longer an option's lifetime, greater is the possibility that the underlying share price might move so as to make the option in-the-money. All other factors affecting an option's price remaining the same, the time value portion of an option's premium will decrease (or decay) with the passage of time.

Volatility

Volatility is the tendency of the underlying security's market price to fluctuate either up or down. It reflects a price change's magnitude; it does not imply a bias toward price movement in one direction or the other. Thus, it is a major factor in determining an option's premium. The higher the volatility of the underlying stock, the higher the premium because there is a greater possibility that the option will move in-the-money. Generally, as the volatility of an underlying stock increases, the premiums of both calls and puts overlying that stock increase, and *vice versa*.

Higher volatility = Higher premium

Lower volatility = Lower premium

Interest Rates

In general, interest rates have the least influence on options and equate approximately to the cost of carry of a futures contract. If the size of the options contract is very large, then this factor may take on some importance. All other factors being equal as interest rates rise, premium costs fall and *vice versa*. The relationship can be thought of as an opportunity cost. In order to buy an option, the buyer must either borrow funds or use funds on deposit. Either way, the buyer incurs an interest rate cost. If interest rates are rising, then the opportunity cost of buying options increases and to compensate the buyer, premium costs fall. Why should the buyer be compensated? Because the option writer receiving the premium can place the funds on deposit and receive more interest than was previously anticipated. The situation is reversed when interest rates fall — premiums rise. This time it is the writer who needs to be compensated.

16.8 OPTION VALUATION MODEL

The Black and Scholes Model

The Black and Scholes Model was published in 1973 by Fisher Black and Myron Scholes. It is one of the most popular options pricing models. It is noted for its relative simplicity and its fast mode of calculation: unlike the binomial model, it does not rely on calculation by iteration.

The intention of this section is to introduce you to the basic premises upon which this pricing model rests. A complete coverage of this topic is material for an advanced course.

The Black-Scholes model is used to calculate a theoretical call price (ignoring dividends paid during the life of the option) using the five key determinants of an option's price: stock price, strike price, volatility, time to expiration, and short-term (risk-free) interest rate.

The original formula for calculating the theoretical option price (OP) is as follows:

$$OP = SN(d_1) - Xe^{-rt}N(d_2)$$

where

$$d_1 = \frac{\ln\left(\frac{S}{X}\right) + \left(r + \frac{v^2}{2}\right)t}{v\sqrt{t}}$$

$$d_2 = d_1 - v\sqrt{t}$$

The variables are:

S = stock price

X = strike price

t = time remaining until expiration, expressed as a per cent of a year

r = current continuously compounded risk-free interest rate

v = annual volatility of stock price (the standard deviation of the short-term returns over one year.

ln = natural logarithm

N(x) = standard normal cumulative distribution function

e = the exponential function

Lognormal distribution: The model is based on a lognormal distribution of stock prices, as opposed to a normal, or bell-shaped, distribution. The lognormal distribution allows for a stock price distribution of between zero and infinity (*i.e.*, no negative prices) and has an upward bias (representing the fact that a stock price can only drop 100% but can rise by more than 100%).

Risk-neutral valuation: The expected rate of return of the stock (i.e., the expected rate of growth of the underlying asset which equals the risk-free rate plus a risk premium) is not one of the variables in the Black-Scholes model (or any other model for option valuation). The important implication is that the price of an option is completely independent of the expected growth of the underlying asset. Thus, while any two investors may strongly disagree on the rate of return they expect on a stock they will, given agreement to the assumptions of volatility and the risk-free rate, always agree on the fair price of the option on that underlying asset.

The key concept underlying the valuation of all derivatives — the fact that price of an option is independent of the risk preferences of investors — is called risk-neutral valuation. It means that all derivatives can be valued by assuming that the return from their underlying assets is the risk-free rate.

Limitation: Dividends are ignored in the basic Black-Scholes formula, but there are a number of widely used adaptations to the original formula, which I use in my models, which enable it to handle both discrete and continuous dividends accurately.

However, despite these adaptations, the Black-Scholes model has one major limitation: it cannot be used to accurately price options with an American-style exercise as it only calculates the option price at one point in time — at expiration. It does not consider the steps along the way where there could be the possibility of early exercise of an American option.

As all exchange traded equity options have American-style exercise (i.e., they can be exercised at any time as opposed to European options which can only be exercised at expiration), this is a significant limitation.

The exception to this is an American call on a non-dividend paying asset. In this case, the call is always worth the same as its European equivalent as there is never any advantage in exercising early.

Advantage: The main advantage of the Black-Scholes model is speed — it lets you calculate a very large number of option prices in a very short time. Since high accuracy is not critical for American option pricing (e.g., when animating a chart to show the effects of time decay), using Black-Scholes is a good option. But, the option of using the binomial model is also advisable for the relatively few pricing and profitability numbers where accuracy may be important and speed is irrelevant. You can experiment with the Black-Scholes model using online options pricing calculator.

The Binomial Model

The binomial model breaks down the time to expiration into potentially a very large number of time intervals or steps. A tree of stock prices is initially produced working forward from the present to expiration. At each step, it is assumed that the stock price will move up or down by an amount calculated using volatility and time to expiration. This produces a binomial distribution, or recombining tree, of underlying stock prices. The tree represents all the possible paths that the stock price could take during the life of the option.

At the end of the tree — *i.e.*, at expiration of the option — all the terminal option prices for each of the final possible stock prices are known as they simply equal their intrinsic values.

Next, the option prices at each step of the tree are calculated working back from expiration to the present. The option prices at each step are used to derive the option prices at the next step of the tree using risk-neutral valuation based on the probabilities of the stock prices moving up or down, the risk-free rate and the time interval of each step. Any adjustments to stock prices (at an ex-dividend date) or option prices (as a result of early exercise of American options) are worked into the calculations at the required point in time. At the top of the tree, you are left with one option price.

Advantage: The big advantage the binomial model has over the Black-Scholes model is that it can be used to accurately price American options. This is because, with the binomial model, it's possible to check at every point in an option's life (i.e., at every step of the binomial tree) for the possibility of early exercise (e.g., where, due to e.g., a dividend, or a put being deeply in the money, the option price at that point is less than the its intrinsic value).

Where an early exercise point is found, it is assumed that the option holder would elect to exercise and the option price can be adjusted to equal the intrinsic value at that point. This then flows into the calculations higher up the tree and so on.

Limitation: As mentioned before, the main disadvantage of the binomial model is its relatively slow speed. It's great for half-a-dozen calculations at a time but even with today's fastest PCs it's not a practical solution for the calculation of thousands of prices in a few seconds which is what's required for the production of the animated charts in my strategy evaluation model.

16.9 FORWARDS

Meaning

A forward contract is the simplest mode of a derivative transaction. It is an agreement to buy or sell an asset (of a specified quantity) at a certain future time for a certain price. No cash is exchanged when the contract is entered into.

Definition

A forward contract is an agreement to buy/sell an asset on a specified date for a specified price. It is very useful in hedging and speculations. A very serious limitation of forward contracts is counterparty risk arising from possibility of default of any one party to the transaction.

Illustration 1:

Shyam wants to buy a TV, which costs ₹ 10,000 but he has no cash to buy it outright. He can only buy it 3 months hence. He, however, fears that prices of televisions will rise 3 months from now. So, in order to protect himself from the rise in prices. Shyam enters into a contract with the TV dealer that 3 months from now he will buy the TV for ₹ 10,000. What Shyam is doing is that he is locking the current price of a TV for a forward contract. The forward contract is settled at maturity. The dealer will deliver the asset to Shyam at the end of three months and Shyam in turn will pay cash equivalent to the TV price on delivery.

Illustration 2:

Ram is an importer who has to make a payment for his consignment in six months time. In order to meet his payment obligation, he has to buy dollars six months from today. However, he is not sure what the Re/$ rate will be then. In order to be sure of his expenditure, he will enter into a contract with a bank to buy dollars six months from now at a decided rate. As he is entering into a contract on a future date, it is a forward contract and the underlying security is the foreign currency.

16.10 FUTURE CONTRACT

A future contract is an agreement between two parties to buy/sell an asset at a certain time in future at a certain price. It may be offset prior to maturity by entering into an equal but opposite transaction. It eliminates counterparty risk and offers more liquidity.

16.11 DISTINCTION BETWEEN FUTURES AND FORWARDS

Futures	Forwards
Traded on an organised stock exchange	Over the Counter (OTC) in nature
Standardised contract terms, hence, more liquid	Customised contract terms, hence, less liquid
Requires margin payments	No margin payment
Follows daily settlement	Settlement happens at the end of the period

Index Futures

A futures contract is an agreement between two parties to buy or sell an asset at a certain time in the future at a certain price. Index futures are all futures contracts where the underlying is the stock index (Nifty or Sensex) and helps a trader to take a view on the market as a whole.

Index futures permits speculation and if a trader anticipates a major rally in the market, he can simply buy a futures contract and hope for a price rise on the futures contract when the rally occurs. We shall learn in subsequent lessons how one can leverage one's position by taking position in the futures market.

In India, we have index futures contracts based on S&P CNX Nifty and the BSE Sensex and near 3 months duration contracts are available at all times. Each contract expires on the last Thursday of the expiry month and simultaneously a new contract is introduced for trading after expiry of a contract.

16.12 SWAPS

A Swap is a simultaneous buying and selling of the same security or obligation. Perhaps, the best-known Swap occurs when two parties exchange interest payments based on an identical principal amount, called the "notional principal amount."

What are Swaps?

- A swap is an agreement between the two parties to exchange payments or income over a period of time
- The swapped payments might be in different currencies (currency swap) or at different rates of interest (interest rate swaps).
- Both liabilities and assets can be swapped.
- Asset swaps involve exchange of income on one investment for income in another.
- Liability swaps, which are more common, involve an exchange of payments on one debt (liability) for payments on another.
- A currency swap is an agreement to exchange payments in one currency for payments in another.
- Since swaps are derived from underlying transactions in the cash markets for currency borrowing, they are classed as derivative instruments.

Illustration:

Think of an interest rate swap as follows: Party A holds a 10-year $ 10,000 home equity loan that has a fixed interest rate of 7%, and Party B holds a 10-year $ 10,000 home equity loan that has an adjustable interest rate that will change over the "life" of the mortgage. If Party A and Party B were to exchange interest rate payments on their otherwise identical mortgages, they would have engaged in an interest rate swap.

Interest Rate Swaps

Interest rate swaps occur generally in three scenarios. Exchanges of a fixed rate for a floating rate, a floating rate for a fixed rate, or a floating rate for a floating rate.

- Interest rate swaps (IRS) involve periodic payments to settle interest costs on a notional principal.
- Normally, in a plain vanilla IRS, there is an exchange of fixed-rate interest rate for a floating rate interest rate.
- The entity paying fixed- rate is called a fixed rate payer (and a floating rate receiver).
- The entity paying floating rate is called a floating rate payer (and a fixed rate receiver).
- Fixed interest rates are paid or received and so also in the case of floating rate.
- Settlement for interest costs can involve either a two-way exchange of interest payment or a single settlement of the difference between the two amounts.

Currency Swap

- A plain vanilla currency swap is an agreement between two parties to exchange a quantity of one currency for another.
- There is an exchange of principal at the start of the agreement (near value date) at an agreed rate (typically spot rate).
- A re-exchange of the same quantities at the end of the agreement (far value date).
- Periodic intermediate payments to settle interest costs in each currency at an agreed interval during the term of the swap.
- The settlements for interest costs can involve either a two-way exchange of interest payments in each currency or a single settlement of the difference between the two amounts in one of the currencies to the swap.
- Currency swaps need not involve an exchange of principal at the near value date in which case there is only periodic exchange of interest payments and exchange of principal at the far value date, with currency amounts exchanged at a rate fixed in the swap agreement.

Illustration:

Exhibit 16.1: A Marched Pair of 3 × 6 FRA Transactions

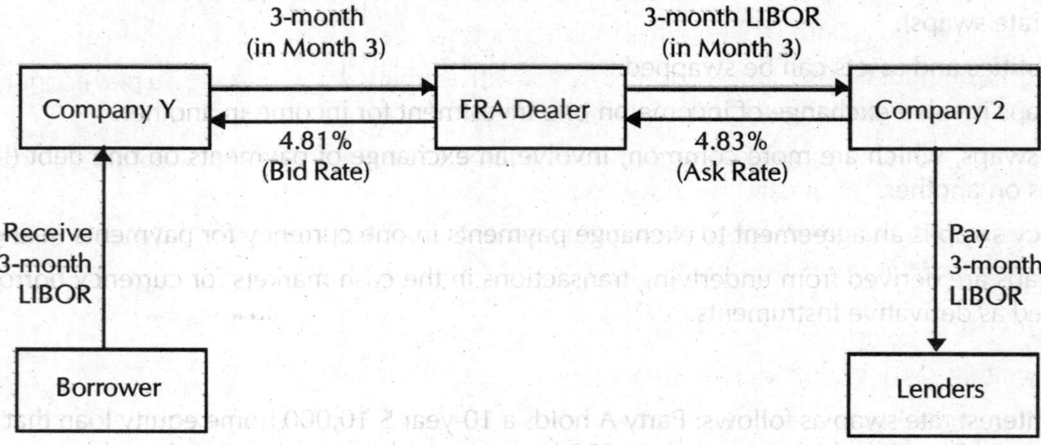

16.13 REVIEW QUESTIONS

True/False

(a) American option cannot have a value less than that of European option (keeping all other option features same).

(b) An option contract may have future contracts as underlying asset.

(c) As long as put option remains out-of-the-money or at-the-money, the option will have intrinsic value.

(d) Delta is the rate of change in option premium for a unit change in time.

(e) Exercise price is the price for which the underlying may be purchased (in case of a call) or sold (in case of put) by the option seller upon exercise of the option.

(f) Gamma is the rate of change in option premium for a unit change in price of the underlying.

(g) In exercising call option on an index, the option holder receives from the option writer cash amount equal to excess of spot price, at the time of exercise, over exercise price.

(h) At present, no individual investor can write an equity option on Exchange.

(i) Intrinsic value of an option is sum of option Premium and Time Value.

(j) Option premium is adjustable against the exercise price on settlement, if the option is exercised on maturity.

(k) Premium of an ACC call option cannot be more than the market price of ACC Stock.

(l) Time value is always lesser than Intrinsic Value.

(m) Vega is the change in delta of an option for a unit change in volatility in underlying's price.

(n) Contract multiplier, along with the price, determines the value of the futures contract.

(o) Impact cost is low when the liquidity in the system is poor. In forward contracts, the maximum amount by which the price would change (tick) and the price limits for a day's operations are specified by an authority.

(p) Backwardation is a situation, where price for later delivery stands below the price for earlier delivery.

(q) "Basis" is the difference between the futures price and cash or spot price of an asset.

(s) A long position in a futures contract can be reversed only with the same counterparty from whom the contract was initially purchased.

(t) In case of futures, the initial margin is paid only by the seller and not the buyer.

(u) Contract month is the month in which the futures contract is entered into.

(v) Hedgers are sufficient for efficient working of a derivatives market and there is no real economic need of either speculators or arbitrageurs.

(w) If a mutual fund wants to increase its exposure to equity, say from 30% to 40% without actual buying of equity in the cash market, it can buy index futures.

(x) In a futures contract, the party who is buying the futures, provides a guarantee to the clearing corporation, while the selling party offers no such guarantee.

Short Answer Questions

1. State the meaning and importance of derivatives.
2. What are the various types of derivatives?
3. What are 'Swaps'?
4. Explain with examples different types of swaps.
5. Write notes on the following:
   (a) Call Options
   (b) Put Options

Essay Type Questions

1. How does a 'future contract' differs from a 'forward contract'?
2. What is the economic rationale for the existence of futures market?
3. How can a futures contract the used for either speculation or hedging?
4. State the features of 'put' and 'call' options. Illustrate the difference between a 'European' and an 'American' call option. Which of these two is used in India?
5. State the underlying assumptions of the Black and Scholes option pricing modes. Briefly explain this model and critically evaluate it.
6. What are 'Swaps' and what purpose do these serve?
7. Discuss the factors that affect the put option price and show their impact on such price.

❋ ❋ ❋